CONSPIRACY

Plots, Lies and Cover-Ups

Richard M. Bennett

with a Foreword
by Gordon Thomas

Virgin BOOKS

First published in Great Britain in 2003 by
Virgin Books Ltd
Thames Wharf Studios
Rainville Road
London W6 9HA

A catalogue record for this book is available from the British Library.

ISBN 1 85227 093 4

Typeset by Phoenix Photosetting, Chatham, Kent

Printed and bound by CPD, Wales

For my daughter, Kate,
my late mother, Florence,
and my late father, Harry.
Who could ever have wished for better!

Paul Copperwaite, my editor, as always.

FOREWORD

Men and women learned how to create conspiracies once they moved on from grunting to using joined-up words.

The Old Testament would be all the poorer without its conspiracies; so would the Gospels. Jesus, after all, has attracted more conspiracies than any living mortal on this earth. Were the "missing years" of his childhood and youth deliberately excluded because of some "dark secret"? Was he not so much a preacher as a terrorist – an early version of Osama bin Laden, intent on overthrowing the established law and order of his day? Did he really marry Mary Magdalene? And perhaps the ultimate manna for all conspiracy seekers to explore: why did he stay silent during his trials?

There are small libraries devoted to presenting the answers. There are almost as many dealing with the assassination of President John F. Kennedy, the Roswell conspiracy, the murder of Patrice Lumumba and, of course, the death of Princess Diana.

Conspiracies are the staple diet of the secret world of intelligence. No self-respecting security service could – would – operate without its specialist staff able to create plots which are designed to frustrate the truth, and facts contrived towards some distant, unwritten goal. For them, conspiracies are designed to leave their complicity hidden and ambiguous.

Conspiracies are history through falsehood, lacking the historian's discipline. Macauley once wrote that the perfect historian should possess an imagination of such power as to make his narrative affecting and picturesque. Yet he must also control it so absolutely as to satisfy himself with the material he discovers, and to supply deficiencies by additions of his own.

With conspiracies, the deficiencies are essential to support their theories. Thus we get questions like what were the unadmitted intentions in the death of Stephen Ward on the assassination of Ghandi. In conspiracies, actions cannot always wait for certainty; motive, deception, things not seen but seeable – these are at the core of all good conspiracies.

Their purveyors have their techniques, to be sure. They create situations – experiments if you will – which are designed to draw fact out of darkness. For them, the art of informed conjecture is a substitute for truth. They do not trouble to stay in the middle possibility of probability; their writ allows them to operate in the realm of surmise.

But do not be shocked by their lack of precision, their imaginative leaps, their readiness to violate all the texts. They are comfortable in their own carapace where they can dismiss the aspiration for simple truths. The secret fears of popes and presidents, a condemned dictator's private thoughts, can all be filled in by the conspiracy peddlers.

Gordon Thomas, 2003

CONTENTS

INTRODUCTION

The history of the world is a history of conspiracies.

The choice of which conspiracies to include has of course, like many such decisions, resulted in a compromise and a combination of famous but highly relevant cases that deserved a closer look, and those equally important plots and cover-ups rarely covered, particularly in the United States. It is not a perfect list and there are indeed many others I seriously wanted to include, but short of running into several volumes, a cut-off point had to be reached. However, and somewhat reluctantly, I have still addressed a number of the hairy old 'conspiracy theory' gems so beloved of the committed enthusiast. These are here as much because I find it difficult to understand the fascination the conspiracy theorist has for such often highly unlikely scenarios, particularly when there are so many genuine, eminently important and hugely interesting conspiracies which have a direct effect on the daily lives of countless millions of people, in the past, the present and, indeed, the future. I have to admit to a distinct distaste for wild and wacky theories that appear to be based on prejudice whether racial, extreme political or religious, as well as to a growing disquiet at what appears to be a sizeable minority with a near tragic inability to distinguish between fact and science fiction. Entertaining they may be, but the plethora of populist magazines, websites, books, films and TV series such as *The X-Files*, *Dark Skies* or *Taken* do little to advance an informed approach to the subject. Without a shadow of doubt the main beneficiaries of this deterioration of the critical faculties, and of course, of making 'conspiracy theories' a non-subject amongst the serious news media, the chattering classes and both politicians and academics alike, have been those with the most to hide. The multinational corporations, local and national government, intelligence and security services, the military, health, science and service industries in general, who often make appalling blunders or have illegal projects to keep secret, or indeed where there is straightforward gross inefficiency or, worst still, corruption to cover-up. Plots and paranoia go together, and intrigue and conspiracy have always been the lifeblood of the real world of politics, intelligence and business. This book, then, intends to take the notion of conspiracy away from the highly imaginative fringe of reality and put it back where it has always belonged – in the mainstream, where it can once again be a fit and right subject for discussion by journalists, politicians, academics and the general reading public alike. Truth, it is said, is stranger than fiction and there can be little doubt that real conspiracies are of a much greater and enduring fascination than the merely fanciful and the downright odd.

Richard M. Bennett

Part One
Up to 1945

2330 BC – A ROYAL CONSPIRACY Princess Idut didn't live to reach adulthood. The limestone reliefs that line her mortuary chapel show her only as a child, and the finely modelled scenes celebrating the abundance of the Nile River Valley surround her with fish and waterfowl, a crocodile snapping at a newborn hippo, cows with their calves, gaggles of geese: all normal decoration for a royal Egyptian burial. But on closer inspection there are strange erasures: a foot and a man's kilt have been chiselled out and sanded over. In the background can just be made out the hint of a well-built and tall male figure, hovering behind the demure girl.

Princess Idut is believed to have died around 2330 BC and she was interred beneath her mortuary chapel, which stands near the pyramid tombs of her grandfather, King Unas, and her father, King Teti, at the place now known as Saqqara. The site of Egypt's first monumental stone tombs, Saqqara was one of the most revered Royal cemeteries of ancient Egypt. When Idut's tomb was discovered in the mid-1920s, little attention was paid to the altered reliefs, but in recent years closer examination revealed traces of unexpected intrigue. The hieroglyphs identified the tomb's original owner as Ihy, a vizier, or prime minister, of King Unas. Like most wealthy and influential Egyptians of his time, Ihy had spent years preparing his final resting place. The replacement of Ihy by the Princess has led to a new theory about a palace coup and the mysterious circumstances surrounding King Teti's accession. Little is known about Teti's history apart from the fact that he married a daughter of Unas and became king when his father-in-law died. To some historians it would appear that he took the throne by force and Ihy had conspired against him, unsuccessfully. As a lasting punishment, Teti gave Ihy's tomb to a daughter. This dynastic succession that once seemed so simple is one of many past events acquiring a new spin at Saqqara, where burials span the entire 3,000 years and 31 dynasties of ancient Egyptian civilisation. Focusing on periods when the rich and most powerful heavily used the site, archaeologists are discovering fresh evidence of royal conspiracies, assassinations, acts of revenge, traitorous queens, ambitious politicians, and religious extremes. Little appears to have changed over the following five thousand years.

1168 BC – THE WIVES' CONSPIRACY Rameses had a reputation as a mighty warrior, a powerful and courageous ruler who had many victories on the battlefield and reigned over a happy and prosperous country. However, the truth was very different and in fact he had suffered a series of military defeats at the hands of lesser powers in the Middle East. His people were at times starving and rebellious, and his reign was to see the first labour strike in Egyptian history. Rameses III was in reality a weak and indecisive man and had already reigned over Egypt for 31 years when he fell victim to an attempted palace coup. Unable even to officially designate a successor, he provoked a vicious war amongst his many wives, all of whom naturally wanted to be the mother of the next pharaoh. This resulted in an astonishing conspiracy organised by one of his lesser-known queens, Tyi, who wanted to replace the ageing Pharaoh with her son. Tyi is believed to have had the support of some of the other wives within the royal household and a number of the personal servants and elements of the royal guard. The conspirators tried rather unusual methods to kill the Pharaoh, first with magic and then perhaps using poison, but having failed they then resorted to a more direct attack. A large group of household servants and renegade guards attempted to assassinate the Pharaoh. They were fought off by his loyal supporters, but not before Rameses III received serious wounds, which probably led in part to his death shortly afterwards. He survived long enough, however, to identify many of the conspirators, 12 of whom were executed, while others had their ears and noses cut off before being imprisoned indefinitely.

336 BC – THE ASSASSINATION OF PHILIP Philip of Macedonia was a highly successful and astute statesman, as well as a military leader of some genius who had unified the Greek states during his reign of 23 years. However, while King Philip was attending the celebrations for his daughter's marriage, Pausanias, who was a young member of a noble family and a trusted member of the royal bodyguard, drew a short sword and stabbed Philip to death. Pausanias was captured, along with his accomplices, before they could make their escape on horses hidden nearby. The murderer and his two brothers were quickly tried, convicted and executed. Pausanias was probably fixed to a stake and starved to death; his fellow conspirators most likely died by stoning.

The motives behind the murder are open to conjecture. It was rumoured at the time that Philip's rejected wife, Olympias, encouraged Pausanias, but others believe that the conspiracy was more political. Philip was preparing his armies for a major war against the

Persian Empire and the assassination may well have been the work of agents of the Persian Emperor or even those within Greece opposed to what they saw as a dangerous adventure designed to further Philip's own ambitions. Demosthenes said in his famous *Second Oration against Philip*, 'ambition is his greatest passion, universal empire the sole object of his views; not peace, not tranquility, not any just purpose'. If, as seems most likely, it was a political conspiracy, then it failed as such, since Philip was replaced by his son, the even more ambitious warlord Alexander the Great. That is unless, as some historians have suggested, Alexander was also involved in the murder because he was known to be angry with his father over Philip's repudiation of his mother, Olympias. However, Alexander is understood to have believed that the Persians were behind the conspiracy, and indeed revenge may well have been finally taken some five years later with the killing of the Persian Emperor Darius III.

44 BC – BEWARE THE IDES OF MARCH Caesar's rise to power began after Sulla's death in 78 BC as his military campaigns abroad brought him wealth and public acclamation. Soon his only real rivals were the great military leader Pompey, honoured with the title *Pompeius Magnus* by Sulla, and General Crassus, who had ruthlessly suppressed the slave revolt led by Spartacus. To prevent civil war between the different factions, Julius Caesar formed a coalition with his two fellow officers, further strengthened by the marriage of Pompey to Caesar's daughter.

The triumvirate representing the democratic, or popular, party now succeeded the republican, or conservative, party in governing Rome. Caesar spent the best part of the next nine years in military conquest abroad, bringing much of Europe under the rule of Rome by his brilliant leadership. During his absence, however, the triumvirate broke down. Crassus was killed during the failed invasion of Mesopotamia, and Pompey's wife died while still young. Pompey was increasingly jealous of the public popularity of his father-in-law and, while Caesar was campaigning in Gaul, passed new laws in the Senate that favoured his own advancement and was eventually elected sole consul. A confrontation between the two was assured when Pompey returned his support to the aristocratic party and, having persuaded the senators that Rome was in danger from a vengeful Caesar, demanded his return as a private citizen. Caesar, however, crossed the Rubicon with his army in a show of strength. Though under Roman law this was an act of treason, it had the desired effect and Pompey withdrew to the east to raise new forces while panicked senators fled Rome. Caesar first won over Pompey's armies in Spain and only then returned to Rome to seize power. Caesar soon moved on to Greece to extend his campaign against Pompey, who he defeated in a decisive encounter at Pharsalus. Pompey fled to Alexandria, where in 48 BC he was stabbed to death by a former Roman centurion, Septimus, in a conspiracy organised by Ptolemy, King of Egypt, and Julius Caesar. Caesar arrived in Egypt to receive Pompey's head on a platter and, having stayed long enough to add Cleopatra to his list of lovers, returned to Rome to take over from his deputy Mark Antony.

As sole ruler of Rome, Julius Caesar soon fell victim to his own ambitions. He managed to alienate the Senate, his fellow generals and the people of Rome. He was an ageing, vain and increasingly unpopular epileptic demagogue.

The final conspiracy against Caesar was organised by Cassius and involved at least sixty members of the Senate and military leadership. Caesar ignored the warnings of his wife, his advisors and, ever scornful of superstition, even soothsayers to 'beware the Ides [15th] of March' and attended the Senate on that day in 44 BC. Caesar was attacked while standing near the base of Pompey's statue and apparently pulled his toga over his face as he was stabbed 23 times and bled to death on the floor of the Senate. The conspiracy to assassinate Caesar resulted in probably the most famous murder in history, but the justice of the killing is still hotly debated. Some see the arch-conspirators, Brutus and Cassius, as champions of liberty, others as history's worst traitors. However, the results are undeniable: the murder plunged Rome into civil war and ultimately brought about precisely what the killing was meant to prevent. Rome was to be saddled with a succession of increasingly unstable emperors and succumbed to many years of far greater tyranny, civil wars, corruption and cruelty than could ever have been imagined by the citizens of republican Rome.

AD 64 – NERO AND THE CHRISTIANS On 19 July a terrible fire began near Rome's Circus Maximus, and by the time the fierce conflagration had ended some nine days later, most of the great city lay in smouldering ruins. It is probable that agents of the Emperor Nero had started the fire, as many historians have maintained over the centuries, and there is little question that the Christians were blamed unjustly for the disaster. Although holding all members of the new sect responsible for the blaze would have too greatly stretched credulity even for Nero, he nonetheless found a pretext for condemning the followers of Christ to mass persecution by claiming that they were 'enemies of mankind'. Tacitus records that the Christians 'were convicted, not so much on the charge of burning the city, as of hating the human race'. Tacitus also records the incredibly cruel tortures and savage deaths to which many of these innocent scapegoats were then subjected.

Nero was, however, no newcomer to the idea of using conspiracies to further his aims. The mad Emperor Caligula had been assassinated in AD 41 at the age of only 29 by a conspiracy led by officers of the Praetorian Guard to rid a frightened Rome of his appalling excesses of cruelty. He was succeeded by Claudius, who some historians contend was murdered by his fourth wife, Agrippina, who supposedly fed him poisonous mushrooms in order to secure the succession of her son Nero to the throne. What *is* known is that Nero had Agrippina murdered later, on the grounds that she was now conspiring against him. After a failed attempt to drown Nero's mother during a sea voyage, naval officers first disabled her with blows to the head and then ran her through with their swords. According to the Roman historian Tacitus, Agrippina directed them to strike at her womb because she had given birth to an epileptic son, Britannicus, from her marriage to Claudius and whom Nero had poisoned when the boy was a mere fourteen years old. Despite being a royal prince and having official food and wine tasters, Britannicus' assassins had given him a drink that was far too hot, and in response to the expected complaint had cooled down the drink with water laced with a deadly poison. The philosopher Seneca shamelessly made a speech in the Senate justifying the murder of Agrippina and was so persuasive that the Senate actually congratulated Nero for killing his mother.

AD 96 – DEATH OF EMPEROR DOMITIAN Domitian had earned his reputation for unpopularity with a reign of near legendary cruelty and tyranny, and there were several failed plots against him before a group of conspirators broke into his bedroom and stabbed him to death. Domitian famously said that all emperors' lives were wretched, because it was only when they were actually murdered that people were convinced that the conspiracies they feared were real ones. These prescient words have come down the centuries to haunt the modern-day investigators of many successful assassinations and conspiracies around the world. Nor would Domitian be the last Roman Emperor to die at the hands of conspirators: Commodus was strangled by a professional wrestler in AD 192 at the instigation of the Praetorian Guard and other members of his household. He was replaced by Pertinax, who in turn was also soon to fall victim to the hostility of the Praetorian Guard and after just three months in power was cut down at the gates of the royal palace and his head paraded though the streets on the point of a lance. The military faction responsible for both assassinations was now totally out of control and put the leadership of the Roman Empire up for auction.

In May AD 480, the Emperor Nepos was murdered in his house in Dalmatia by two of his body-servants, almost certainly as part of a conspiracy instigated by the former Emperor Glycerius, who had been overthrown by Nepos and bought off with the Bishoprics of Salonae and later Milan. The barbarian King of Italy, Odoacer, marched on Dalmatia to supposedly avenge the assassination, but in reality to take advantage of the power vacuum in order to seize the region for himself.

The numerous murders by conspiracies of supposedly loyal bodyguards highlights a theme that has continued to run through the centuries and is still apparent in the murder of Mrs Gandhi and perhaps even the killings of John F. Kennedy and his brother Robert: despite the ever-present dangers of a deranged lone nut, the most likely and certainly the greater danger often comes from the very people entrusted to guard your life.

602 – BYZANTINE CONSPIRACIES The Byzantine Emperor Maurice was by all accounts and for those times a relatively wise ruler; yet after twenty years in power he was overthrown by a military conspiracy led by a centurion by the name of Phocas, who then assumed the throne. Maurice and his family fled Constantinople and had reached the port of Chalcedon before they were captured. His five sons were tortured and killed one by one in front of him and then he was also murdered. Their heads were placed on display in Constantinople while the rest of their bodies were thrown into the sea.

This atrocity caused Chosroes II, King of the Sassanid Kingdom of Persia, who owed his ascent to the throne to the support offered to him by the murdered Byzantine monarch, to embark on a 25-year crusade of vengeance. His Persian armies invaded Syria, Asia Minor and North Africa; he seized Jerusalem, Alexandria and the Island of Rhodes, until the expanding Persian Empire caused a Roman army under Heraclius to march against him. His overstretched forces soon suffered serious defeats and the hard-pressed Persians turned against him. His eldest son, Siroes, on learning that his father had appointed another son, a favourite, as his nominated successor, planned a well-organised conspiracy and overthrew Chosroes. He promptly massacred his brothers in his father's presence and then threw his father into a dungeon where some time later he died, probably of starvation.

882 – DEADLY PAPAL CONSPIRACIES The elderly Pope John VIII was definitely the object of a conspiracy, being poisoned and then beaten to death by trusted members of his entourage. Some fifteen years later, Pope Stephen VI was deposed, thrown into prison and later strangled by conspirators. Some historians have argued, though with little proof, that Pope Benedict IV was assassinated by a conspiracy instigated by Berengar, the King of Italy, in 903. He was succeeded by Leo V, and here there is little doubt that a palace revolution led by one of his clergy by the name of Christopher overthrew Leo, who was murdered by the conspirators while in prison in 904. Christopher named himself Pope, but he too was soon overthrown and executed.

In 929 John X is thought to have been murdered by suffocation in Castel Sant'Angelo where he had been imprisoned after being deposed by a Roman woman called Marozia. Though described as a 'lady', she was almost certainly a prostitute. She was also, more importantly, a Senatrix and head of the house of Theophylact and therefore virtually the sole ruler of Rome. She was practised at grand conspiracies and, through a succession of three royal or noble husbands and by becoming the mistress of Pope Sergius III, she had gained great power and influence. She conspired to 'appoint' temporary Popes Leo VI and Stephen VII to succeed the murdered John X, in order to place her bastard son by Pope Sergius III on the papal throne as John XI, as soon as he was old enough. The next Pope was to be Leo VII, according to some yet another of Marozia's offspring, and was appointed by Alberic, also Marozia's son. Later still, in an ongoing papal conspiracy, her grandson, Alberic's illegitimate son, became the infamous John XII. He gained his unenviable reputation for living in public adultery with the matrons of Rome, for turning the Lateral

Palace into a virtual school for prostitutes, and for his rapes of virgins and young women, which deterred most female pilgrims from visiting the tomb of St Peter.

978 – MURDER OF YOUNG KING EDWARD Edward, son of Edgar, had become King of the Anglo-Saxon Kingdom of England when he was around twelve years old. The son of Edgar's first wife, he had an even younger half-brother, Aethelred, born of his father's second wife, Aelfthryth, and this provided the grounds for a future conspiracy against him, since Aelfthryth entertained the thought that her son should occupy the throne instead. The popular young King paid a visit to his stepmother and half-brother, who were at that time in residence at the majestic Corfe Castle in Dorset in southwestern England. On arrival Edward was treated with all the respect he would have expected and was welcomed warmly by his half-brother's servants and guards; however, even before he had dismounted from his horse, he was suddenly seized and stabbed to death. Edward's body was hidden in a well, but when discovered it was taken first to Wareham and later to be buried in Shaftsbury Abbey. Edward was thought of by many of his subjects as a saint and soon became known as 'Edward the Martyr'. The conspirators having covered their tracks well, no really damning proof of complicity in the killing could be found against either his stepmother or half-brother and Aethelred therefore succeeded to the throne, though only to go down in history as 'the Unready'.

1327 – DEATH OF EDWARD II Edward's twenty-year rule has been described as a disaster for England and he was finally forced to abdicate because of a conspiracy instigated by his wife, Queen Isabella, sometimes known as the 'she-wolf of France' and her lover, Marcher Lord[1], Roger Mortimer. Though Edward was humiliated for his homosexuality and imprisoned, this was not enough for Isabella and Mortimer, who still felt that while he lived there remained the possibility of a palace counter-revolution in his favour. They arranged for him to be removed to Berkeley Castle in Gloucestershire, with his head and beard closely shaved to reduce the chance of his being recognised on the journey. Although Edward had abdicated in favour of his fourteen-year-old son, Edward III, attempts to rescue the

[1] The Marcher Lords were the major nobles in the Welsh Marches.

imprisoned former monarch sealed his fate. The conspiracy against Edward was to come to a truly gruesome end on 21 September 1327 when his gaolers, apparently lacking the patience to starve him to death and having been ordered to dispose of him without leaving a mark on his body, inserted a metal tube into his anus through which they cruelly murdered him by ramming a red-hot poker deep into his innards. His death ushered in three centuries of instability where politically active nobles risked their lives, and indeed three more kings of England would be deposed and murdered before 1485.

1483 – THE PRINCES IN THE TOWER The deaths of the two young Princes have long fascinated both the academic world and the general public.

That their deaths were due to a monstrous conspiracy can hardly be in question, but exactly who was ultimately responsible certainly is. The main suspect is King Richard III, but some historians point the finger firmly at Henry Tudor as the murderer and at a second conspiracy to blacken the name of Richard. Some time in the summer or early autumn of 1483, twelve-year-old Edward V and his ten-year-old brother, Richard of York, disappeared. Their father, King Edward IV, had died in April, and they had been lodged in the Tower of London since the end of May by their Uncle Richard. In mid-July Richard had his young nephews legally declared illegitimate, preventing their accession to the throne of England and clearing the way for him to be crowned Richard III. Two years later, in August 1485, Richard III was defeated and killed by Henry Tudor at the Battle of Bosworth Field. The victor was crowned Henry VII.

The question of whether the missing Princes had died before or after Richard's death is paramount. The traditional view is that Richard III had ordered the murders of his nephews, while revisionists maintain that Richard III's reputation has been besmirched by his successor, Henry Tudor, the first of the Tudor kings and father of Henry VIII.

The first clues emerged in July 1674 when building work began on the stairs leading up to the Chapel of St John the Evangelist in the White Tower. This part of the structure had been crumbling for a number of years, and King Charles II had ordered its demolition and replacement. The large broken stones were removed by the workmen's picks and a large pile of rubble had formed in the open area leading to the steps. The workmen had reached the floor of the basement and had been surprised to find a layer of loose stones, rather than the anticipated stone floor. After they had removed a ten-foot layer of stones they discovered a wooden chest. Clearing away the last of the debris, the lid was carefully raised to uncover the gruesome remains of two small bodies. Charles II ordered that the bones be examined by the royal surgeon, who was afterwards satisfied that they were the remains of the two Princes, Edward V and his brother. Four years later, after having lain in a safe place in the Chapel of the White Tower, the bones were placed in a small marble casket and given a place of honour in Westminster Abbey. At the service conducted by the Archbishop of London, Charles II spoke: 'It is right and meet that we commend the bones of these young Princes to a place of final rest. Their fates at the order of Richard III grieves us, and though almost two centuries have passed, the vile deeds of that villain shall ne'er be forgotten.' The King crossed himself, turned, and led the small funeral procession out of Westminster Abbey.

Two and a half centuries after the burial ceremony in Westminster Abbey, King George V, disturbed by the mounting pressure from supporters of Richard III, gave his approval in 1933 for the examination of the bones in the white marble coffin by leading scientists of the day. The examination did not totally resolve the question, as it could still be argued that it had assumed from the very beginning that the bones in the casket were indeed those of the Princes. It merely therefore confirmed this assumption and, despite the urging of Richard's supporters, the bones have not been re-examined and subjected to modern techniques of radiocarbon-dating.

The murder of the Princes in the Tower of London was part of a political conspiracy and had been prompted by the sequence of events that began with the death of Edward IV. Upon the death of her husband, Elizabeth Woodville, Edward's Queen, sought to keep her family in power by moving swiftly to establish her son, Edward V, on the throne. To accomplish this, she dispatched her brother, Lord Rivers, and her son from a previous marriage, Lord Richard Grey, as well as Grey's chamberlain, Sir Thomas Vaughan, to bring young Prince Edward from the North. The idea was to have Edward crowned as soon as possible, leaving him free to choose his own advisors, which would undoubtedly have been his mother, his Woodville uncles and half-brothers and other nobles loyal to Edward IV. Thus Richard, as protector, would have his power neutralised by Elizabeth Woodville and her relatives. Lord Hastings, a close friend and advisor of the dead King, protested against the size of the escort that the Queen intended to send and Elizabeth Woodville reluctantly reduced the size of the force to 2,000 men. In the meantime, couriers from Hastings informed Richard, still with his supporters in York, of these developments and urged him to place himself at the head of an army and join Rivers before he could get the young King safely to London. Richard left York for Northampton with an army of 600 men. Here he was hoping to join Rivers and Edward V and proceed to London with them. By the time Richard arrived, he learned that Rivers and his troops had passed through the town and were now in Stony Stratford, some twelve miles closer to London. Rivers travelled back to Northampton to extend the young King's greetings to his uncle. Richard invited Rivers to stay for supper, and proposed that the next morning they ride together to meet the King. Richard's supporter, the Duke of Buckingham, arrived during the meal. After Rivers retired for the night, Richard and Buckingham plotted. In the morning, Rivers was arrested. Richard and Buckingham then travelled the twelve miles to Stony Stratford and met with the young King. Richard gave his condolences, and told Edward V that the same men who had encouraged Edward IV's vices were conspiring to ambush the protector. The interview, according to Thomas More, ended with the twelve-year-old King in tears, and his half-brother, Richard Grey, and his chamberlain under arrest.

When the news reached the Queen, she took her remaining children and sought sanctuary in Westminster Abbey. London was in an uproar, mollified only to some degree by a letter from Richard promising an early coronation for Edward V. Richard, Buckingham and their army of supporters arrived in London and the young King was safely lodged in the Palace of St Paul. All seemed calm, until Richard learned that Lord Hastings had begun to conspire with Elizabeth Woodville, shifting his loyalty from Richard, probably because he felt that Buckingham would now have access to the spoils that Hastings felt were rightly his. Richard summoned the unsuspecting Hastings to a meeting at the Tower, where he asked Hastings what should happen to those who would conspire against the protector. Lulled into a sense of relief when Richard seemed to be accusing the Woodvilles, he started to speak, when Richard slammed his fist on the table, calling Hastings a traitor. Given that sign, armed men rushed into the room, took Hastings away and, within minutes, he was 'brought forth into the green beside the chapel within the

Tower, and his head laid down upon a log of timber and there striken off.' Richard immediately called a meeting of a number of influential citizens and declared that Hastings and others had planned his assassination and that of Buckingham, and that the traitor had to be killed immediately. The other 'conspirators' were pardoned, no doubt to quiet the fears of the nobility. One of them, Bishop Morton, was to be kept in the custody of the Duke of Buckingham and would rise again in opposition to Richard.

It is probable at this point that Richard decided that if he were to survive, he must become the monarch. Edward, the boy King, had shown some maturity, and would not be pleased to be ruled by his uncle, who had imprisoned his mother's brother, Lord Rivers, and his half-brother, Richard Grey, and who had driven his mother and younger brother into sanctuary. Worst of all, his uncle had beheaded his lord chamberlain, Hastings, within sight of the royal apartments in the Tower where young Edward was now lodged. While Richard began his programme to usurp the throne, he had Rivers, Grey and Vaughan executed at their prison in Pontefract. Most of the important opponents, including the powerful Hastings, were now out of the way. On the day of the planned assassinations, Buckingham led his men up the long staircase to the upper level of the East Tower. Pausing at the door to the chamber of the Princes, he is believed to have said to the men who were to murder the boys, 'Do it now, and do it quickly and quietly. Do not let your hearts be swayed by their pleas for mercy. Dispose of them in some secret spot where they will ne'er be found. If you fail, you will forfeit your lives. Come to me when your task is complete. I will be in the constable's apartment.' King Richard's present-day supporters suggest that the Princes were still alive at the time of Richard's death and were not murdered until more than two years after their disappearance from public view.

Richard III was killed on 21 August 1485, at the Battle of Bosworth Field, fighting valiantly against the forces of Henry Tudor. If he had not been betrayed by Lord Stanley, who had kept his forces out of the battle until he saw his chance to turn it into a decisive victory for Henry, Richard would probably have been victorious. There would have been no Tudor dynasty, no Henry VIII and no Elizabeth I. In the aftermath of the battle, Richard's naked body was treated with great indignity. It was tied on to a horse's back, his head and arms dangling on one side, legs on the other, and was taken to the church of the Grey Friars in Leicester where it was exposed for two days so that people might see that he was dead. Widely vilified as a murderer, Richard III's reputation was constantly under attack, and during the reign of Henry VII, 'official' biographers made certain that Richard's reputation would be that of a murderous tyrant. Well into the reign of Henry VIII, surviving members of the York family, including the Duke of Clarence's daughter, were to be persecuted and even executed. It was not until the middle of the seventeenth century, some 150 years after the events of Richard III's reign, that any reasoned form of defence for Richard appeared. This was the sympathetic view put forward by Sir George Buck and eventually published by his nephew, also named Sir George Buck. As even the most committed defenders of Richard will usually admit, there will never be any certainty about the exact circumstances surrounding the death of the Princes in the Tower. The writings of Sir Thomas More, the contemporary accounts by Mancini and certain other chroniclers and, of course, the discovery of the bones in the Tower all tend to support the popular view that the Princes were indeed dead by the end of 1483 and that their uncle, Richard, had conspired with others to murder them and seize the Crown of England.

1560 – MARY, QUEEN OF SCOTS Mary was born at Linlithgow Palace in Scotland in 1542, the daughter of James V of Scotland and the French Mary of Guise. She became Queen of Scotland before she was a week old because of the death of her father and spent her early childhood with her mother in Scotland. In 1548 the French King, Henry II, proposed that the young Mary would be an ideal future wife for his son, Francis, the marriage forming a perfect alliance between the two countries at a time when England was attempting to further exert its influence over its northern neighbour. Mary went to live at the French court and at the age of fifteen married Francis, heir to the French throne. Francis II reigned for only a few months with Mary as his queen and, when he died in 1560, Mary was left without an obvious role. She decided to return as Queen to Scotland, agreeing to recognise the Protestant Church as long as she could privately worship as a Catholic. The Scots regarded this with some suspicion and John Knox stirred up anti-Catholic feeling against her.

The man her future was to become so tragically involved with, Henry Stuart (Stewart), Lord Darnley, was born and brought up in England, where his father was in exile. In 1565, at the age of nineteen, he was allowed by Queen Elizabeth to follow his father to Scotland,

and within a short time he married Queen Mary. The motives of the Scottish Queen were predominantly political: Darnley was a Catholic and his right of succession to the English throne reinforced Mary's own. However, his handsome appearance and courtly manners must also have impressed Mary because at first she was quiet, obviously infatuated with him. The Protestant lords, dismayed at what appeared to be a Catholic triumph, rebelled; however, Mary defeated them easily. As time passed it became clear to Mary that her husband was, in fact, an arrogant bully with a drinking problem. Darnley had shown himself to be at times a vicious and dissipated man and Mary regretfully denied him the crown matrimonial, which would have given him political power in Scotland virtually equal to that of the Queen. Wounded in pride and suspicious of Mary's growing relationship with her advisor David Rizzio, he joined a conspiracy to rid the royal court of Rizzio, and on 9 March 1566 Darnley and a group of nobles seized Rizzio in the Queen's presence and stabbed him to death. They may also have intended to harm the Queen, but she escaped by winning over Darnley and fleeing from her captors to the safety of loyal nobles. Darnley soon found himself without a friend in either camp and, although Mary made efforts toward reconciliation after the birth of their son, Darnley remained intractable and the council demanded that the Queen rid herself of him. Possibly with Mary's knowledge, another conspiracy was instigated by the Earl of Bothwell. The Earl of Morton was later executed for his part in it, and others may well also have had a hand in the eventual murder. Recovering from an illness, Darnley arrived in Edinburgh early in 1567 and lodged in Kirk o' Field, a house just outside the city. On the night of 9 February and after a visit from Mary, the house was blown up by gunpowder. In the morning the bodies of Darnley and a page were found strangled in an adjoining garden some distance from the house, and it is supposed that he was murdered while making his escape. The remains were afterwards buried in the chapel at Holyrood just outside Edinburgh. Mary had grown close to the ruthless Earl of Bothwell and rumour soon spread that Bothwell and Mary had been responsible for the murder, particularly following their hasty marriage a few weeks later. By now, however, Scotland was tiring of Mary and she was to be imprisoned at Lochleven Castle and later forced to abdicate the Scottish throne. Her young son was crowned James VI on the 29 July 1567.

Mary did not give up her crown without further intrigue. Having already shown herself to be a poor judge of character, Mary now made the huge mistake of misjudging Elizabeth. She still hoped to win over Elizabeth to rally to her cause. Once again ignoring the pleas of her advisors, Mary managed to escape from Lochleven and, disguised as a man, fled the country believing she would receive the support of the English monarch. Elizabeth, however, had other ideas. Mary was the granddaughter of Henry VIII's elder sister, Margaret, and so had a claim to the English throne. She had married Darnley, whose lineage could be traced back to Henry VII, creating an even stronger claim. Worse still, Elizabeth had herself been declared illegitimate in a statute which had never been formally repealed and knew that many Catholics considered Mary to be the rightful Queen of England. Her presence in England could indeed spark a much-feared Catholic uprising. Mary was immediately taken to stay at Carlisle Castle by one of Elizabeth's ministers but, as days turned into weeks, she became increasingly suspicious. Eventually, sent to stay in the bleak and cheerless Tutbury Castle, Mary finally accepted that she was nothing more than a prisoner. Elizabeth remained, however, fascinated by the Scottish Queen and was to remain paralysed by indecision. She did not wish to help the woman she considered her rival, but knew that if she released Mary her own life would be in danger. Mary was said to be a great beauty who exerted a strange power over men and, whenever any minister returned from a visit to the now belligerent Mary, he was quizzed by the Queen on her looks, her clothes, her attractiveness compared to herself. Similarly Mary would ask after Elizabeth. But the two Queens were never to meet. Mary quickly became the focus of plots to overthrow Elizabeth and return England to the Catholic faith. In 1569 the Northern Uprising failed when the Catholic Earls, marching southwards, discovered that Mary had quickly been moved from Tutbury to Coventry and their plans to rescue her were thwarted. The Ridolfi Plot of 1570–71 went further by enlisting Spanish support to depose Elizabeth and place Mary on the throne.

It was clear that, as long as Mary, Queen of Scots, was alive, Elizabeth's life would be in danger. Francis Walsingham, one of Elizabeth's most loyal ministers, was acutely aware of this. He set out to convict Mary, and in 1586 this became possible. Walsingham's much-vaunted spy network discovered that she was secretly corresponding with a group of Catholic conspirators and, having intercepted her letters, Walsingham's allies forged a postscript in her hand asking for the identities of those involved. The names and details were duly supplied by those very same conspirators. At last Walsingham had proof of her guilt. Mary's trial began on 15 October 1586 at Fotheringhay Castle. Mary was not allowed legal advice and, while attempting to defend herself, was not even permitted to consult her own papers. Found guilty of treason, Mary was sentenced to death. Walsingham had, however, reckoned without Queen Elizabeth's reluctance to sign the execution warrant. To Elizabeth, Mary was a member of the royal family and to execute any queen was a precedent she did not wish to set. She also feared that Mary's relations in Europe would take revenge on England. As the weeks passed, Elizabeth procrastinated. In February 1587 the warrant was finally signed and the execution took place before the Queen could change her mind. It is believed that when Elizabeth heard the bells pealing to celebrate the death of Mary, Queen of Scots, she was horrified. It had all happened too quickly. The warrant had been taken to Fotheringhay before she was fully convinced of its necessity. Elizabeth was apparently inconsolable and locked herself in her room where she is said to have wept for days. As she had feared, Catholic Europe reacted swiftly to the news and the Pope urged Philip of Spain to invade England; undoubtedly Mary's execution was one of the factors that contributed heavily to the sailing of the Spanish Armada the following year. Her death took a heavy toll on Elizabeth, one observer noting, 'I never knew her fetch a sigh, but when the Queen of Scots was beheaded.'

1570–71 – RIDOLFI PLOT This was one of many conspiracies planned against Elizabeth I, all of which seemed to require her assassination or eventual execution, though ostensibly their prime object was simply to replace the Protestant Queen with one of a Catholic persuasion. A Florentine businessman, Roberto Ridolfi, was in league with Spain to put Mary, Queen of Scots, on the English throne. Elizabeth, probably in common with all the Tudor monarchs of England, had a more than efficient intelligence network, and the conspiracy was discovered by Walsingham and thoroughly dismantled before it became a genuine threat. The conspirators included a number of leading figures in the English court, and the biggest threat, the 4th Duke of Norfolk, was duly executed.

1605 – GUNPOWDER PLOT This most famous of conspiracies may not have been quite the plot depicted by popular history. There are a body of historians who suggest the possibility that the small group of Catholics including Robert Catesby, Guido (Guy) Fawkes, Thomas Winter, John Wright and Thomas Percy, who had apparently decided to blow up the King on the State opening of Parliament, were themselves victims of a state conspiracy to undermine the chances of there ever being another Catholic King of England.

The accepted conspiracy involves Guido (Guy) Fawkes, the explosives expert who had served with the Spanish army in the Netherlands. The group rented a cellar beneath the Houses of Parliament and stored there barrels of gunpowder supplied by Fawkes. The date for the explosion was set for 5 November. They recruited others sympathetic to their cause, including Francis Tresham, whose brother-in-law, Lord Monteagle, was a Member of Parliament. Concerned for his brother-in-law's safety, Tresham sent him a letter advising him not to attend Parliament on 5 November. Monteagle alerted the authorities and a search of the Houses of Parliament led to the discovery of Guido Fawkes standing guard over the barrels of gunpowder. He was tortured and revealed the names of the conspirators. Catesby, Percy and two others were killed resisting arrest. The others were tried for treason and executed.

However, there are many historians today who agree with the Catholics of the time that the Gunpowder Plot conspirators were themselves framed by James I's chief minister, Robert Cecil. Cecil hated the Catholics and wanted to show them to be traitors to England. It is believed that Francis Tresham, who sent the warning note to his brother-in-law, may have been working for Cecil as a spy. There is indeed some evidence to support this view: Cecil is quoted as saying, 'we cannot hope to have good government while large numbers of people [Catholics] go around obeying foreign rulers [the Pope]'; Lord Monteagle received the warning letter at night, and strangely this was the only night in 1605 that he stayed at home, perhaps in anticipation of its delivery; all available supplies of gunpowder were kept in the Tower of London and a close friend of Robert Cecil rented the cellar to the Catholic conspirators; all of the conspirators were executed except one – Francis Tresham; and there is even some suggestion that the signature on Guy Fawkes' confession did not match his normal signature.

The conspiracy against the King is thought to have been hatched when the original members met in secret, probably in early 1604, to discuss their plans in the Lambeth home of one John Wright deep in the suburbs of the City of London. King James VI of Scotland had only recently succeeded to the English throne as James I but, despite promises of a relaxation in the anti-Catholic laws, it now appeared that the new King would be even more severe in their persecution than his predecessor had been. Being no stranger to plots and intrigue, Robert Catesby, a notorious Northamptonshire Catholic, now felt the time was right to strike a blow for his religion. He had called his cousin, Thomas Wintour, to the house of his friend, Wright, in order to lay before them his plan to blow up the King and the House of Lords at the next Opening of Parliament. With the monarch, the Prince of Wales and most of his leading ministers dead, they would seize the young Prince Charles and Princess Elizabeth and raise a general revolt to return Catholicism to the land. In May 1604, Thomas Wintour enlisted the help of a Yorkshire mercenary named Guy Fawkes, who had distinguished himself on the continent serving in the Spanish army. With his vast experience of dangerous situations, Fawkes was to be the man of action in a group which was growing quickly as Catesby persuaded relatives, friends and colleagues to enter the conspiracy and help finance his plans. Robert Wintour, Christopher Wright, Thomas Percy, John Grant, Ambrose Rokewood, Robert Keyes, Sir Everard Digby, Francis Tresham and Catesby's servant, Thomas Bates, were all to join the plot. Originally Catesby rented a house near to the Palace of Westminster and the group began to dig a tunnel towards the Houses of Parliament. However, progress was far too slow for men not used to hard labour and eventually, sometime in March 1605, Thomas Percy was able to use his connections at the royal court to rent a cellar right under the House of Lords. The tunnel was quickly abandoned and, posing as Percy's servant, one 'John Johnson' Fawkes was able to fill the underground storehouse with some 36 barrels of gunpowder hidden beneath coal and wooden sticks under the pretext of their being a store of fuel for the winter. Everything was set in place: all the conspirators had to do now was wait. In the first apparent mistake by the plotters and only ten days before the Opening of Parliament, Lord Monteagle, widely believed to be a reformed Catholic, sitting down to dinner in his Hoxton home, was to receive an important letter. It read:

> My lord, out of the love I bear to some of your friends, I have a care for your preservation. Therefore I would advise you, as you tender

> your life, to devise some excuse to shift of your attendance of this Parliament, for God and man hath concurred to punish the wickedness of this time. And think not slightly of this advertisement but retire yourself into your country, where you may expect the event in safety, for though there be no appearance of any stir, yet I say they shall receive a terrible blow, the Parliament, and yet they shall not see who hurts them. This counsel is not to be contemned (*sic*), because it may do you good and can do you know (*sic*) harm, for the danger is past as soon as you have burnt the latter (*sic*): and I hope God will give you the grace to make good use of it, to whose holy protection I commend you.

Francis Tresham's authorship of the letter has never been confirmed. Monteagle immediately showed the letter to Robert Cecil, the Earl of Salisbury and Secretary of State. Surprisingly slow to act and perhaps suspiciously so in light of later accusations of a state conspiracy, the Privy Council eventually had the vaults beneath the Lords searched on 4 November, first by the Earl of Suffolk and late the same evening by Sir Thomas Knyvett. Composed to the end, Fawkes coolly let the officials into Percy's cellar. The gunpowder was quickly discovered and Guy Fawkes was overpowered. On hearing that their plans had been foiled, Robert Catesby and Thomas Wintour fled to the Midlands where they met up with the rest of their party in Warwickshire, but failed to rally any support. They managed to travel amongst the houses of friends and sympathisers for three days before finally being captured in a bloody raid on Holbeech House in Staffordshire. Catesby, Percy and the two Wright brothers were killed, while a wounded Thomas Wintour and Ambrose Rokewood were taken away to London. The others were captured a few days later, with the exception of Robert Wintour, who was to remain at large for a further two months. All the conspirators save for Tresham were executed for their crimes. Francis Tresham died while still a prisoner in the Tower of London and it has often been suggested that his death was arranged to finally cover up his complicity in both the conspiracy and being a government spy. Whether through having second thoughts or because he was a 'plant', Tresham may have warned his brother-in-law, Lord Monteagle, of the plot some time before the arrival of the now-famous letter, and together they may have agreed upon this as the best means of betraying the conspiracy while remaining free of suspicion.

The questions that this conspiracy asks include: how were these known Catholic troublemakers able to operate freely so close to the inner sanctum of English government? The mystery letter was addressed to Monteagle, but it was read out aloud by his servant. Why? Was Monteagle looking for a witness to the receipt of this letter? The government had a monopoly on gunpowder in this country and it was stored in places such as the Tower of London. How did the conspirators get hold of 36 barrels of gunpowder without drawing attention to themselves? Did they get help from the government? How was the gunpowder moved across London from the Tower of London to Westminster, a distance of some two miles, without anyone seeing it? Why were men who were known to be Catholic agitators allowed to rent a house so near to the Houses of Parliament? How did they move the 36 barrels, along with hay, straw, etc., from that house to the cellar of the Houses of Parliament without anyone noticing? Why, and apparently for the first time in history, was there a search of the Houses of Parliament's cellars that conveniently found 'John Johnson', as Guy Fawkes called himself, just before he lit the fuse? Why was the soldier who killed Catesby and Percy at Holbeech House in the Midlands given such a large pension (10p a day for life) when their arrest and torture was far more desirable in order to discover the names of any other conspirators? Was Tresham acting as a double agent? Did Robert Cecil instigate the plot in order to force a reluctant King to take tougher measures against the Catholics, or did his agents merely penetrate and take advantage of an existing conspiracy?

A further mystery surrounds Tresham's death. Once Tresham had been arrested he was promptly locked in a cell in the Tower of London on his own. He died on 23 December 1605, and it was later found that he had been poisoned. How did he get the poison? Did he knowingly take it or did someone want to silence him before he talked?

What is certain, and indeed may well be a pointer to a highly successful government conspiracy and cover-up, is that King James I's chief minister, Robert Cecil, hated Catholics and saw them as a constant source of trouble. Cecil also feared that there was a chance that James I would be lenient with the Catholics during his reign, and this he could not tolerate. That James had only expelled priests was not good enough for Cecil. He wanted to remove Catholicism from England as he saw it as a threat and the Gunpowder Plot may have been just one of the means he used to achieve this.

1720 – SOUTH SEA BUBBLE: CONSPIRACY TO DEFRAUD

'One of the most terrible social disasters that had ever fallen upon England', was how one historian described 'the Bubble'. It had been the ultimate financial conspiracy, a 'get rich quick' scheme that brought ruin and considerable misery to a vast number of people and threatened the stability of the whole country. It was the first great stock market crash to hit England.

The early 1700s had been a time of fast growth in international finance and risk-taking as never before. The South Sea Company that was to play such a leading role in this giant conspiracy had entirely respectable beginnings and had been created in 1710 by George Caswall, London merchant, financier and stockbroker, and John Blunt, London scrivener turned stockbroker. They proposed to the Tory government of Robert Harley that the £9,500,000 of outstanding short-term debts resulting from fighting wars largely against the French and not funded by a specific tax should be converted into equity in a new joint-stock company. Similar debt-equity conversions had been used previously by the Bank of England and the New East India Company. The purpose of the new company was to trade with Spanish America and to offset the financial support which the Bank of England had provided for previous Whig governments. Money would later be freely invested in company stock because the trading privileges and monopolies granted to Britain after the Treaty of Utrecht of 1713, which had concluded the so-called Marlborough Wars, were expected to prove enormously profitable. By late 1718 the South Sea directors sought to imitate the manipulation of public credit that the Scot John Law had achieved in France with the Mississippi Company, which was given a monopoly of French trade to North America; Law had connived to drive the price of its stock up, and the South Sea directors hoped to do the same. Many believed that some action was necessary to halt the diversion of English capital to France. In 1719 the South Sea directors were confident enough to make the famous proposal to assume the entire public debt of the British government when the company outbid the Bank of England for the conversion of an additional £31,000,000 of that debt. On 12 April 1720 this offer was accepted and a bill was passed enabling persons to whom the government owed portions of the national debt, which had been growing steadily larger since it had originated after the Glorious Revolution of 1688–89 (as a means of meeting government expenditures), to exchange their claims for shares in company stock. Within a relatively short time the directors of the South Sea Company had assumed three-fifths of Britain's national debt, a sum of over £9,000,000. The bill triggered an enormous burst of speculation in company stock with shares rising in value eightfold. A number of large bribes to influential Whig politicians including, it is believed, James Stanhope and Charles Spencer, Earl of Sutherland, and others including the royal mistresses Madam von Platen and the Duchess of Kendal (who had a reputation for accepting financial inducements and outright bribes), had much to do with the result of the vote and the bribes were to be paid in fictitious holdings of stock. The company immediately started to drive the price of the stock up by spreading positive misinformation involving pro-trade-with-Spain stories designed to give the impression that the stock could only go higher and encouraging new investors to become deeply involved. Not only did capital stay in England, but also many Dutch investors bought South Sea stock, further increasing the inflationary pressure. South Sea stock rose steadily from January through to the spring and, as every apparent success soon attracts its imitators, all kinds of joint-stock companies suddenly appeared, hoping to cash in on the speculation mania. Some of these companies were indeed legitimate but the bulk were bogus schemes by unprincipled speculators who took advantage of investors to obtain subscriptions for patently impossible projects designed to take advantage of the credulity of the market. Several of the bubbles, both large and small, had some overseas trade or 'New World' aspect and, in addition to the South Sea and Mississippi ventures, there was also a project for improving the Greenland fishery and another for importing walnut trees from Virginia. Raising capital sums by selling stock in these enterprises was apparently easy work, and brokers, or 'jobbers' as they were then called, had a field day. Such a free for all was considered to be damaging for the speculation business and so, largely through the pressure of the South Sea directors, the so-called 'Bubble Act' was passed on 11 June 1720 requiring all joint-stock companies to have a Royal Charter. For a short while the confidence of investors and the City of London was given an extra boost, and they responded accordingly. South Sea stock, which had been around £120 in the middle of February, was at £380 by the end of March, and around £520 by 29 May. It finally peaked at the end of June at over £1000. With credulity now stretched to the limit and rumours of ever more investors including the directors themselves selling stock, the bubble developed a slow leak. By mid-August the bankruptcy listings in the *London Gazette* reached an all-time high, an indication of how people bought on credit or margin, and when the bubble finally burst in September 1720, largely because the profits from the South Seas which had been expected to sustain the project had still not materialised, it resulted in vast numbers of investors being entirely ruined. Thousands of fortunes were lost, both large and small. The Duke of Chandos lost £300,000 and the Duke of Portland had to flee the country, though in a kindly gesture the King appointed him Governor of Jamaica. Practically every landowning family had mortgaged their homes to buy shares and was now left penniless. The poets Alexander Pope and Matthew Prior were victims, while John Gay, author of *The Beggars Opera*, failed to sell his shares in time and took to his bed in despair. Suicides were not unknown as the true nature of the disaster was realised. The directors attempted to encourage even more speculation, but when this failed it led to a dramatic collapse at the end of September when the company's stock had fallen back to only £135. Fearing major civil disruption with mobs already crowding around Westminster, Parliament was recalled and George I hastened back to London. A committee was formed to investigate the South Sea Company and by early 1721 it had uncovered widespread corruption and fraud among the directors, company officials and their friends at Westminster. Many of the leading members of this financial conspiracy, however, made good their escape with the most incriminating records in their possession and their fortunes intact. The South Sea Bubble had indeed been a financial conspiracy to defraud on a vast scale and indeed nearly brought a whole country to its knees. As a result of the political fallout from the scandal, the Whig Party was to form the government for the next forty years and, having learned a hard financial lesson, Britain went on to become one of the wealthiest countries in Europe.

1727 – COMMITTEE OF 300 (THE OLYMPIANS) The Committee of 300 is supposedly born out of the East India Company's Council of 300, founded by influential Britons in 1727. The conspiracy theorists believe that this committee made a vast fortune out of some form of involvement in the opium trade with China and that it is still somehow a controlling influence in the growth of narcotics crime in the USA. The theory continues that the Committee of 300 long ago decreed that there shall be a smaller, less well-populated and better world, and that the myriads of useless consumers, producing little except pollution and devouring scarce natural resources, were to be culled. The Committee is supposedly anti-industrial development, since progress supports population growth. Therefore the command to multiply and subdue the earth found in Genesis has to be subverted. This, according to the 'theory', calls for an attack upon Christianity itself; obviously other religions are not included.

The Committee of 300 is therefore behind the slow but sure disintegration of industrial nation states, the destruction of hundreds of millions of people, referred to by the Committee as 'surplus population', and the removal of any leader who dares to stand in the way of the Committee's global planning to reach their objectives. The Committee of 300 looks to social convulsions on a global scale, followed by depressions, as a softening-up technique for bigger things to come and its principal method of creating masses of people all over the world who will become its 'welfare' recipients of the future.

The Committee has apparently had many highly influential, not to say famous, people as members: Arthur Balfour, George H. Bush, Lord Carrington, Lloyd George, Henry Kissinger, J. P. Morgan, Cecil Rhodes, the Rothschilds, the Vanderbilts, George Schultz, Cardinal Spellman and Earl Warren. Most interestingly of all, the Committee is now said to be controlled directly by none other than Queen Elizabeth II herself.

The Committee of 300 is an interesting insight into current 'mega-conspiracy theories', though the idea that Buckingham Palace may indeed be the centre of the world's narcotics smuggling network and, according to some, the power that effectively controls the world, and that Queen Elizabeth II is an international crime boss at the head of the Colombian drugs cartels and Albanian crime syndicates, is perhaps more than a little difficult to believe.

1764 – MURDERS IN THE ROYAL HOUSE OF RUSSIA Peter II, Tsar of Russia, was strangled to death at Ropsha, four days after being forced to abdicate in favour of his wife, Catherine. The murder was carried out at Catherine's instigation by one of her many lovers, Count Orloff, and a group of army officers. Catherine III went on to become widely know as 'The Great' and developed a well-earned reputation for sexual deviance and cruelty. Soon after Peter II's murder, Catherine probably had the former Tsar Ivan VI murdered. He had spent much of his tortured life in solitary confinement since being replaced by Tsarina Elizabeth in 1741. Catherine attempted later to bypass her son Paul, whom she detested, apparently with good reason, by naming her grandson Alexander as her successor. However, soon after her death, Paul destroyed her will and took the throne himself. He was the disaster his mother had feared: he was epileptic, tyrannical and arguably insane, and within a few years a small group of conspirators headed by Count Pahlen and probably with the knowledge, if not the encouragement, of the British government formally asked him to abdicate for the sake of the Russian people. Paul was a supporter of Napoleon and was preparing to join France in a war against Britain. The conspirators brought a document effecting the abdication to Paul in his bedroom in the Mikhailovsky Palace in St Petersburg. When he not unsurprisingly refused to sign it, he was promptly strangled. Napoleon blamed the assassination of his close ally on his British enemies. Paul's son and successor may have had some prior knowledge of the conspiracy and, though still shocked by the killing, took no steps to punish his father's murderers. Conspiracy, plots, intrigue and murder became an everyday part of the life of the Russian royal family, their households and the Russian nobility for the best part of the next 150 years until the last of the Tsars was to be replaced by the first of the Commissars, but this did little to change the deplorable state of Russia or the appalling life led by the majority of its inhabitants.

1776 – THE ILLUMINATI Is there a vast Masonic conspiracy plotting to destroy the present world system and replace it with some sort of perverted New World Order? Or have they already succeeded? Many conspiracy theorists seem to think so and spend countless hours trying to prove it to a disbelieving, or should that be a 'brainwashed', public.

One the founders of this supposed secret anarchical movement was Adam Weishaupt who had been appointed a professor at the University of Ingolstadt in Germany around 1772 and was later elevated to the post of Professor of Canon Law sometime between 1773 and 1775, the first secularist to hold that position, which was previously held only by clergy. Weishaupt began planning a group to challenge the authoritarian actions of the Catholic rulers of Bavaria in 1775 and the organisation was apparently established by 1 May 1776.

This group was to later evolve into the 'Illuminati' or those claiming to have superhuman knowledge, and which according to Websters dictionary is also the plural of 'enlightened'. The group quickly established themselves as a very 'learned' society and indeed Weishaupt drew the earliest members of his new order from among his own students. The first damaging public revelations about the society came in 1785 when a bolt of lightning apparently struck a courier en route to Paris from Frankfurt-am-Main. In the tract written by Weishaupt, entitled the 'Original Shift in Days of Illuminations', which was recovered from the dead messenger, the secret society's conspiratorial plans for 'The New World Order through world revolution' were exposed.

As a result of this the Illuminati was to be quickly suppressed by a series of Bavarian government edicts and Weishaupt himself was exiled later in the year. In 1787 the Bavarian Government published the details of the purported conspiracy in 'The Original Writings of the Order and Sect of the Illuminati'. In this document the secret society reportedly claimed that 'By this plan, we shall direct all mankind in this manner. And, by the simplest means, we shall set all in motion and in flames. The occupations must be so allotted and contrived that we may, in secret, influence all political transactions.' Though banished the Illuminati has survived the centuries and the group has been quite successful in attracting new members, and had apparently already helped to establish similar groups in the United States.

On 5 December 1776, students at the William and Mary College in Williamsburg, Virginia, founded a new secret society in the image of the Illuminati, the Phi Beta Kappa. A second chapter was formed later at Yale, in 1780. The anti-Masonic movement in the United States during the 1820s held that groups such as Phi Beta Kappa were dangerous and, because of the mounting pressure from its critics, the society decided to become an open, even semi-public, university society. However, it is believed by some theorists that this was to directly cause the creation of Yale's Order of Skull and Bones in the 1830s as a more secretive alternative to the Phi Beta Kappa. The *Cyclopedia of Fraternities*, a genealogical chart of general Greek-Letter college fraternities in the United States, shows that while the Phi Beta Kappa is seen as 'the parent of all the fraternal systems in higher education' there is only one lineal descendant: the Yale chapter of 1780. The line then continues to the creation of the Skull and Bones in 1832, and on through the other senior societies, Scroll and Key and the Wolf's Head, both also only found at Yale.

The suggestion that the Illuminati also spread its beliefs to other European countries is confirmed by John Robison, a professor of natural philosophy at Edinburgh University, Scotland, and a member of a Freemason's lodge, who said that he was once asked to join the Illuminati. After careful study, he concluded that the purposes of the Illuminati were not for him and in 1798 Robison published a book called *Proofs of a Conspiracy* in which he claimed that 'An association has been formed for the express purpose of rooting out all the religious establishments and overturning all the existing governments . . . the leaders would rule the world with uncontrollable power, while all the rest would be employed as tools of the ambition of their unknown superiors.' A copy of this book was sent to President George Washington and, in his response to the sender, he said that he was indeed aware that the Illuminati were active in America. Washington felt that the Illuminati had 'diabolical tenets' and that their object was 'a separation of the people from their government'. In *Proofs of a Conspiracy*, Robison printed a description of the ceremony of the initiation of the 'Regent degree' in Illuminism. Robison said that a skeleton is pointed out to the initiate, at the feet of which are laid a crown and a sword. The initiate is asked whether that is the skeleton of a king, nobleman or a beggar. Since the initiate cannot decide, the president of the meeting tells him, 'The character of being a man is the only one that is importance (*sic*)'. Significantly this is also essentially the same as the initiation ceremonies reportedly linked to the Skull and Bones secret society founded at Yale University some thirty years later.

The Illuminati are, of course, also strongly linked to yet another secretive organisation, the Freemasons and their worldwide Masonic networks. The so-called 'enlightenment rationalist' ideas of the Illuminati were reportedly brought into the Masonic lodges where they played a role in a factional fight against the more traditional teachings of the 'occultist philosophy'.

The Freemasons themselves had begun as members of craft guilds who united into lodges in England in the early 1700s. They initially stressed religious tolerance, the equality of their male peers, and the themes of classic liberalism and the Enlightenment. The idea of a widespread Masonic conspiracy originated in the late 1700s and flourished in the US in the 1800s and to some extent is still believed by many 'theorists' in 2003. Weishaupt, his Illuminati society, the

Freemasons and other secret societies have been portrayed as bent on despotic world domination through a secret conspiracy using front groups to spread their influence. It is claimed that the conspirators had sworn hatred to both altar and throne, had sworn to crush the God of the Christians, and to utterly extirpate the Kings of the Earth. The grand plot hinges on how the leading Illuminati, known quaintly as 'adepts of revolutionary Equality and Liberty', had buried themselves deep within the lodges of Masonry where they apparently instigated the French Revolution, and then ordered rebellion against the established order to be spread far and wide. Soon, every nation was supposedly to have its own apostle of Equality, Liberty, and Sovereignty of the People.

The Scottish professor John Robison argued that the Illuminati had in fact evolved out of Freemasonry, and called the Illuminati philosophy 'Cosmo-politism'. Their first and immediate aim was apparently to possess riches, power and influence and, to accomplish this, Robison claimed that they wanted to 'abolish Christianity, and then dissolute manners and universal profligacy will procure them the adherents of all the wicked, and enable them to overturn all the civil governments of Europe; after which they will think of farther conquests, and extend their operations to the other quarters of the globe, till they have reduced mankind to the state of one indistinguishable chaotic mass.' In the aftermath of the French Revolution in 1789, the supporters of the deposed or threatened monarchies have been accused by many with Republican and Revolutionary sympathies of trying to create a counter-history in defence of the aristocracy. Winning the hearts and minds of the masses would assuage some of the pain of recent defeat and mobilise defences for the future, it was thought. The French Revolution, some monarchists argued, was not rooted in poverty and despotism. Rather than a popular rising of the masses, it was in fact the evil work of Adam Weishaupt's Illuminati, a secret society that plotted to destroy all civil and religious authority and abolish marriage, the family and private property. It was the Illuminati who schemed to turn contented peasants from compliant God-fearing Christians to blood-soaked revolutionaries.

The major immediate effect of the allegations of an Illuminati–Freemason conspiracy aimed at undermining the special status of the Catholic Church in Europe was to create a widely held belief in a network of secret societies designed to destroy respect for property and the natural social hierarchy. Orthodox Christianity was to be destroyed and replaced with universalism, deism, socialism . . . or worse still a form of Jewish-inspired Communism. Anyone with a cosmopolitan outlook, who encouraged free thinking and international co-operation, was at risk of becoming suspect as a potentially disloyal subversive or traitor out to undermine national sovereignty and to promote anarchy. In an even more disturbing trend, conspiracy theories about the Illuminati and the Freemasons were to become firmly mixed with growing anti-Semitism in Europe and later in the USA. It is a sad reflection on modern society that so many people choose to believe in highly unlikely conspiracy theories, made up of myth, magic and prejudice, as a substitute for taking a somewhat more rational approach to trying to understand an increasingly complicated and confusing world.

1816 – CATO STREET CONSPIRACY Along with the 'Angry Brigade' in the 1970s, the Cato Street Conspirators are almost unique in having formed a genuine, if limited, left-wing armed revolutionary movement in Britain. Thomas Spence, a schoolteacher from Newcastle, arrived in London in December 1792. Over the next 22 years Spence developed a reputation as an important radical figure in Britain. He wrote books, pamphlets and produced a journal, *Pig's Meat*, where he argued for the radical transformation of society, and for which he endured several periods of imprisonment. Spence did not believe in a centralised radical body and instead encouraged the formation of small groups that could meet in local public houses. At these meetings he argued forcefully, 'if all the land in Britain was shared out equally, there would be enough to give every man, woman and child seven acres each'. Spence encouraged men to walk the streets at night, chalking on walls slogans such as 'Spence's Plan and Full Bellies' and 'The Land is the People's Farm'. In 1800 and 1801 the authorities believed that Spence and his followers were responsible for bread riots in London. However, they did not have enough evidence to arrest them for this offence.

Thomas Spence died in September 1814 and was buried by 'forty disciples' who pledged that they would keep his ideas alive. They did this by forming the Society of Spencean Philanthropists. The men met in small groups all over London, usually in the back rooms of public houses like the Mulberry Tree in Moorfields, the Carlisle in Shoreditch, the Cock in Soho, the Pineapple in Lambeth, the White Lion in Camden, the Horse and Groom in Marylebone and the Nag's

Head in Carnaby Market, and there they discussed the best way of achieving an equal society. The government became so concerned about this group that they employed an undercover agent, John Castle, to join the Spenceans and report on their activities. In October 1816 Castle reported to John Stafford, supervisor of the Home Office intelligence network, that the Spenceans were involved in a conspiracy to overthrow the British government. On 2 December 1816, the Spencean group organised a mass meeting at Spa Fields, Islington. The speakers at the meeting included Henry 'Orator' Hunt and James Watson. The magistrates decided to disperse the meeting and, while Stafford and eighty police officers were doing this, one of the men, Joseph Rhodes, was stabbed. The four leaders of the Spenceans, James Watson, Arthur Thistlewood, Thomas Preston and John Hopper, were arrested and charged with high treason. James Watson was the first to be tried. However, the main prosecution witness was the government spy John Castle, and the defence council was able to show that Castle had a criminal record and that his testimony was unreliable. The jury concluded that Castle was an *agent provocateur* and therefore a person employed to encourage suspected people to some open action that will make them liable to punishment, and refused to convict Watson. As the case against Watson had failed, it was decided to release the other three men who were due to be tried for the same offence. The Spenceans continued to meet after the trial but the members now disagreed about the future strategy of the group. Arthur Thistlewood was convinced a successful violent revolution was possible. James Watson now doubted the wisdom of this strategy and, although he still attended meetings, he gradually lost control of the group to the more militant ideas of Thistlewood. The government remained concerned about the Spenceans, and in January 1817 John Stafford asked a police officer, George Ruthven, to join the group. Ruthven discovered that the Spenceans were planning an armed rising. Arthur Thistlewood claimed at one meeting that he could raise 15,000 armed men in just half an hour. As a result of this information, John Williamson, John Shegoe, James Hanley, George Edwards and Thomas Dwyer were also recruited by Stafford to spy on the Spenceans.

The Peterloo Massacre in Manchester increased the anger the Spenceans felt towards the government and reinforced their belief that the time was ripe for an armed uprising. At one meeting a spy reported that Arthur Thistlewood said, 'High Treason was committed against the people at Manchester. I resolved that the lives of the instigators of massacre should atone for the souls of murdered innocents.' On 22 February 1820, George Edwards pointed out to Arthur Thistlewood an item in the *New Times* that said several members of the British government were going to have dinner at Lord Harrowby's house at 39 Grosvenor Square the following night. Thistlewood believed that this was as good an opportunity as they were likely to get and it was decided that a group of conspirators would gain entry to the house and massacre the government ministers. The heads of Lord Castlereagh and Lord Sidmouth would be placed on poles and taken around the slums of London, since Thistlewood was convinced that this would incite an armed uprising that would finally succeed in overthrowing the government. This would be followed by the creation of a new government committed to creating a society based on the ideas of Thomas Spence. Over the next few hours Thistlewood attempted to recruit as many people as possible to take part in the plot. Many people refused and, according to the police spy, George Edwards, only 27 people finally agreed to participate. One member of the gang, John Harrison, knew of a small, two-storey building in Cato Street that was available for rent. The ground floor was a stable and above that was a hayloft and, as it was only a short distance from Grosvenor Square, it was decided to rent the building as a base for the operation. Edwards told Stafford of the plan and Richard Birnie, a magistrate at Bow Street, was put in charge of the operation. Lord Sidmouth instructed Birnie to use men from the Second Battalion Coldstream Guards as well as police officers from Bow Street to arrest the conspirators. Birnie decided to send George Ruthven, a police officer and former spy who knew most of the Spenceans, to the Horse and Groom, a public house that overlooked the stable in Cato Street. On 23 February, at two o'clock in the afternoon, Ruthven took up his position. Soon afterwards, Thistlewood's gang began arriving at the stable. By seven-thirty Richard Birnie and twelve police officers joined Ruthven at Cato Street.

The Coldstream Guards had not arrived and Birnie decided he had enough men to capture the conspirators. Birnie gave orders for Ruthven to carry out the task while Birnie waited outside. Inside the stable the police found James Ings on guard. He was quickly overcome and George Ruthven led his men up the ladder into the hayloft where the final plans for the attack were being agreed. Though taken completely by surprise, Arthur Thistlewood and William Davidson raised their swords while some of the other men attempted to load their pistols. One of the police officers, Richard Smithers, moved forward to make the arrests, but Thistlewood fatally wounded him with his sword. Some of the gang surrendered promptly, but others, like William Davidson, were only taken after a struggle, while four of the conspirators, Thistlewood, John Brunt, Robert Adams and John Harrison, actually managed to escape out of a back window. However, George Edwards had given the police a detailed list of all those involved and the men were soon tracked down and arrested. Eleven men were eventually to be charged with being involved in the Cato Street Conspiracy. After the experience of the previous trial, Lord Sidmouth was unwilling to use the evidence of his undercover agents in court. George Edwards, with a great deal of knowledge about the conspiracy, was never called. Instead the police offered to drop the most serious charges against any member of the group willing to give evidence against the rest of the conspirators. Two of these men, Robert Adams and John Monument, agreed and they provided the vital evidence needed to convict the others. On 28 April 1820, Arthur Thistlewood, William Davidson, James Ings, Richard Tidd and John Brunt were found guilty of high treason and sentenced to death. John Harrison, James Wilson, Richard Bradburn, John Strange and Charles Copper were also found guilty but their original sentence of execution was subsequently commuted to transportation for life. Thistlewood, Davidson, Ings, Tidd and Brunt were executed at Newgate Prison on 1 May 1820, bringing an end to one of the very few British groups to have mirrored, even if in a very small way, the activities of the massive revolutionary conspiracies that wreaked so much havoc in France, Ireland, Russia and elsewhere.

1833 – THE ORDER OF SKULL AND BONES This rather weird conspiracy theory encompasses three very interesting threads of American history, namely espionage, drug smuggling and secret societies, and claims that many of its initiates have or still do fill the ranks of the global elite. The theory goes on to suggest that the Order of Skull and Bones is the American branch of the Illuminati and is involved in a Masonic worldwide conspiracy manipulating national and global events as part of a so-called grand Hegelian equation, thesis and antithesis yielding a New World Order synthesis.

Elihu Yale was born near Boston, educated in London, and served with the British East India Company, eventually becoming governor of

Fort Saint George, Madras, in 1687. He amassed a great fortune from trade and returned to England in 1699. Yale became known as quite a philanthropist; upon receiving a request from the Collegiate School in Connecticut, he sent a donation and a gift of books. After subsequent bequests, Cotton Mather, a noted theologian and a Puritan minister in Boston, suggested the school be named Yale College in his honour in 1718.

Nathan Hale, along with three other Yale graduates, was a member of the 'Culper Ring', one of America's first intelligence operations. Established by George Washington, it was successful throughout the Revolutionary War. Hale, however, was discovered by the British and, after speaking his famous regrets, he was hanged in 1776. A statue of Nathan Hale stands on Old Campus at Yale University. There is a copy of that statue in front of the CIA's headquarters in Langley, Virginia. Yet another stands in front of Phillips Academy in Andover, Massachusetts, where future President George H. W. Bush went to prep school and joined a secret society at the age of only twelve, we are told. Ever since the founding of the Republic, the relationship between Yale and the 'Intelligence Community' has been virtually unique.

However, the involvement of alumni in crime has also been considerable. In 1823, Samuel Russell established Russell and Company for the purpose of acquiring opium in Turkey and smuggling it to China. Russell and Company merged with the Perkins (Boston) syndicate in 1830 and became the primary American opium smuggler. Many of the great American and European fortunes were built on the 'China' (opium) trade. Boston-based Russell and Company's chief of operations in Canton was Warren Delano, Jr, grandfather of Franklin Roosevelt. Other Russell partners included John Cleve Green, who financed Princeton University, Abiel Low, who financed the construction of Columbia University, Joseph Coolidge, whose son organised the United Fruit Company and whose grandson, Archibald C. Coolidge, was a co-founder of the Council on Foreign Relations, and the Perkins, Sturgis and Forbes families. William Huntington Russell, Samuel's cousin, studied in Germany from 1831–32 when it was a hotbed of new ideas. When Russell returned to Yale in 1832, he formed a senior society with Alphonso Taft. According to information acquired from a break-in to the Skull and Bones meeting hall, known as the 'tomb', in 1876, 'Bones is a chapter of a corps in a German University'. William H. Russell, along with fourteen others, therefore became the founding members of 'The Order of Scull and Bones', later changed to the more acceptably modern spelling of 'The Order of Skull and Bones'.

Conspiracy theorists draw considerable import from the fact that the secretive Order of Skull and Bones exists only at Yale. Fifteen juniors are 'tapped' each year by the seniors to be initiated into next year's group, and it has been suggested that each initiate is given a five-figure sum and a grandfather clock. This secretive group concentrates on the success of its members in the post-collegiate world, and certainly the family names of those involved make an impressive reading list: Lord, Whitney, Taft, Jay, Bundy, Harriman, Weyerhaeuser, Pinchot, Rockefeller, Goodyear, Sloane, Stimson, Phelps, Perkins, Pillsbury, Kellogg, Vanderbilt, Bush and Lovett, among many others. 'Bonesmen' are considered privileged and often there are complaints that great favouritism is shown to them both while still at Yale and later in business and politics. It has been claimed that 'Bonesmen' effectively control Yale and its financial affairs. When a person is initiated into Skull and Bones, they are given a new name, similar to the practice of the Illuminati, and indeed according to 'theorists' many recorded Illuminati members can be shown to have influenced many of the professors that taught 'Bonesmen' in Berlin. The links between Skull and Bones and the intelligence community since World War II has been considerable, so it is reported. One such is Eugene Stetson, a friend of George H. W. Bush, who was an assistant manager for Prescott Bush at Brown Brothers, Averill Harriman's New York office. He organised the H. Smith Richardson Foundation, which in the late 1950s participated in the MK-ULTRA, the CIA's domestic covert psychological warfare operation. The H. Smith Richardson Foundation helped to finance the testing of psychotropic drugs, including LSD, at Bridgewater Hospital in Massachusetts, the centre of some of the most brutal MK-ULTRA experiments. During the Iran-Contra operations, the H. Smith Richardson Foundation was a 'private donors steering committee', working with the National Security Council to co-ordinate the Office of Public Diplomacy. This was an effort to propagandise in favour of, and run cover for, the Iran-Contra operations, and to co-ordinate published attacks on opponents of the programme. The H. Smith Richardson Foundation also runs the Center for Creative Leadership at Langley to 'train leaders of the CIA', as well as another centre near Greensboro, North Carolina, that trains CIA and Secret Service agents. Almost everyone who achieves the military rank of general also gets this training and thus spreads the influence of the Order of Skull and Bones. The conspiracy theorists have had an absolute field day with the influence the 'Bonesmen' are supposed to wield in modern-day America in particular. However, in the absence of any hard evidence to the contrary, it would seem far more likely that this secretive university society is nothing more than a rather more effective version of the British 'old school-tie' system, based on mutual and class self-interest.

1858 – CONSPIRACY AGAINST NAPOLEON III In January 1858 an attempt was made on the lives of Emperor Napoleon III, Napoleon Bonaparte's nephew, and the Empress Eugenie as they arrived at the Paris Opera. This followed a failed attempt at assassination in 1856 when three Italians named Tibaldi, Grilli and Bartoletti had been arrested and tried for being part of a conspiracy instigated by the Italian Republican, Mazzini. The man behind the later attempt was Count Felice Orsini, an Italian patriot who had been one of Mazzini's lieutenants and firmly believed that Napoleon II had betrayed Italy after the destruction of the Roman Republic. Orsini and his co-conspirators carried out a bomb attack which succeeded in only inflicting slight injuries on the Emperor and Empress, but which killed eight others and wounded and blinded over 150. Orsini and the three other Italian revolutionaries, named as Pieri, Gomez and Rudio, were arrested and tried. Osini and Pieri were guillotined, while Gomez and Rudio were sentenced to life imprisonment. It was discovered that Orsini had travelled to France on a British passport in the name of Thomas Allsop and had used bombs made in Birmingham. France bitterly criticised Britain for harbouring terrorists and failing to prevent such conspiracies. It was to cost Britain its prime minister, when Palmerston resigned having been defeated in parliament on his attempt to amend the law in response to the criticism flooding across the Channel.

1865 – LINCOLN ASSASSINATION CONSPIRACY Despite Abraham Lincoln's assassination being undoubtedly one of the most famous events in history, researchers have never yet satisfactorily explained the exact circumstances surrounding his death nor the full ramifications of the conspiracy against him. Lincoln and his wife, Mary Todd Lincoln, attended the play *Our American Cousin* at Ford's

Theater, Washington, on 14 April 1865. They were to be accompanied by General Ulysses S. Grant and his wife, Julia Dent Grant. However, Grant and his wife changed their plans and did not attend the play. One of Lincoln's bodyguards, John Parker, arrived at Ford's Theater before Lincoln and checked out the lobby, the stairs to the dress circle, and the presidential box. The Lincoln party, consisting of the President, Mrs Lincoln, Major R. Rathbone and his fiancée, Miss Clara Harris, and Lincoln's personal aide, Charles Forbes, arrived at the theatre after the play had already begun. As soon as the presidential party had been seated, guard John Parker took up his assigned post. However, after a short while, Parker moved to an empty seat at the front of the gallery from which spot he could watch the play. Lincoln's back was now unguarded. But Parker soon grew bored with the play and he went downstairs to the lobby, then outside and indeed walked up to the presidential carriage. Parker woke the sleeping driver, Burns, and asked him if he would like to join him for a beer at the nearby Taltavul's Star Saloon. The driver accepted the invitation. Presidential aide Forbes joined Parker and Burns at the bar. As the play progressed, Parker, Forbes and Burns continued drinking in the saloon. Therefore John Wilkes Booth was able to safely walk into the theatre, climb the stairs and enter the presidential box without hindrance. Booth apparently took a quick step from the antechamber, crossed the three or four feet to the President's back and extended the pistol. Lincoln started to turn his head to the left as the sound of the derringer's firing ripped through the laughter in the theatre. Booth dropped his pistol and sprang towards the box railing. Rathbone thought he heard someone cry, 'Freedom!' Booth cried, '*Sic semper tyrannis!*' ('Thus always to tyrants!') Booth broke his leg as he jumped on to the stage, but still managed to escape, with a little help, in the confusion. Doctors in the audience examined the President's wound and pronounced it fatal: the President's eyes showed evidence of severe brain damage. The bullet had gone in the left side of the head, behind the ear near the top of the spine. There was no exit wound. Fingers were thrust into the wound, but could not reach the bullet. From the patient's slightly protruding right eye, the doctors correctly concluded that the 44-calibre ball had entered behind the left ear and lodged in the brain just behind the right eye.

While the attack on the President took place, co-conspirator Lewis Powell, sometimes known as Paine or Payne, attempted to assassinate

Secretary of State William Seward at his home, but only managed to injure him. David Herold had accompanied Powell, but fled before the attempt was finished, though five people in all had been attacked. At the same time, George Atzerodt was supposed to have killed Vice-President Andrew Johnson. However, Atzerodt did not go through with the assassination. Booth and Herold escaped the capital and travelled to Mary Surratt's Tavern in Maryland, where they picked up supplies. They then travelled to Dr Samuel Mudd's house, where Booth's leg was set. Lincoln was taken to the Petersen House across the street from Ford's Theater, where he eventually died at 7.22 a.m., 15 April 1865.

Secretary of War Edwin Stanton stayed with the Lincolns at the Petersen House and co-ordinated the efforts to capture the conspirators. On 26 April Herold and Booth were found hiding in a barn near Port Royal, Virginia. Herold surrendered but Booth refused to come out of the barn and it was set on fire. In the ensuing chaos, a soldier shot and killed Booth. Eight Lincoln conspirators were caught over the next few days and were eventually tried by a military court. They were found guilty on 30 June and were given various sentences depending upon their involvement. Lewis Powell (Paine), David Herold, George Atzerodt and Mary Surratt were charged with conspiring with Booth and hanged on 7 July 1865. Dr Samuel Mudd was charged with conspiring with Booth and sentenced to life in prison. Andrew Johnson eventually pardoned him early in 1869. Samuel Arnold and Michael O'Laughlen had conspired with Booth to kidnap President Lincoln, and were found guilty and sentenced to life. O'Laughlen died in prison but Arnold was pardoned by Johnson in 1869. Edman Spangler was found guilty of helping Booth to escape from Ford's Theater. He was also pardoned by Johnson in 1869.

John Wilkes Booth is a shadowy historical figure. While ostensibly an actor, he is known to have smuggled medicines and other contraband into the South. For example, at one time Booth 'obtained 1,000 ounces of valuable quinine, hid the contraband medicine in a trunk and sent it by blockade runner to Richmond.' While in hiding in Montreal, Booth was recruited by Confederate agents Clay and Thompson to organise the kidnapping of Abraham Lincoln. John H. Surratt, Jr, was suggested to Booth as a good man to help in his organising efforts, and when Booth finally returned to Washington a sum of $12,499.28 had been transferred from the Bank of Montreal to Booth's account at the Chaffey Company in New York. This was, to the penny, what Daniel Watson, a Tennessee cotton speculator, had deposited in the Bank of Montreal on 4 July for some then-unknown reason. Booth was to later write in his diary, 'I am to find and send North 15 men whom I trust. The messenger brings me $20,000 in gold to recruit them. I'm to start at once.' It is somewhat suspicious that the messenger who brought the gold was believed to be connected with the Union's Judge Advocate General's Office. It is widely accepted that the first goal of the conspirators had originally been to kidnap the President, but that when the Confederacy finally surrendered to the North, Booth's thoughts turned to killing the President. The judge advocates, however, feared that talk of an abduction plot might lead to an innocent verdict for some, if not all, of the conspirators. They are believed to have suppressed important evidence such as John Wilkes Booth's diary. It is still surprising that, given the number of plots exposed and direct threats made to Lincoln, the War Department did not provide Lincoln with adequate protection. Was the President's single bodyguard bribed to be absent from his post during the murder, and why was he never punished or even questioned? Why were all the escape routes out of Washington closed, except the route Booth used? And who, for hours after the murder, blacked out telegraph lines from Washington? Before details of the night of terror could be flashed from Washington to morning newspapers, the commercial telegraph went dead; indeed, within fifteen minutes of the murder, the wires were severed entirely around the city, except for the secret wires used by the government. Why was the existence of Booth's diary hidden until long after the famous 1865 Conspiracy Trial? Was it simply because of the kidnapping problem? And, when revealed, why had eighteen pages been cut out? And indeed who removed those eighteen pages, and when? The conspiracy to kidnap or kill Lincoln was almost certainly hatched within the Confederate intelligence services and Booth and a group of co-conspirators were employed to carry out the operation. However, the Union won the war before any real attempt could be mounted. Booth and his fellow conspirators had probably decided that Lincoln, the Vice President and the Secretary of State should be assassinated in revenge, and perhaps in the hope that the enormous blow this would have been to Northern morale would have encouraged further resistance from the former Confederate states. It cannot be ruled out, however, that some dissident members of the Union may have tired of Lincoln's somewhat dictatorial administration and connived in some way with the conspirators, and that the fear of this damaging exposé led to the widescale cover-up in Washington.

1872 – BOHEMIAN GROVE: A SATANIC CONSPIRACY? The ideal 'mega-conspiracy theory' with Big Brother, satanic rites and New World Order all rolled into one. In August 1982 *Newsweek* magazine reported that the world's most prestigious summer camp, the Bohemian Grove, was once again in session 75 miles north of San Francisco. The fiercely guarded, 2,700-acre retreat is the country extension of San Francisco's all-male, ultra-exclusive Bohemian Club, to which every Republican president since Herbert Hoover has belonged. With its high-powered clientele, coveted privacy and apparently cabalistic rituals, the Bohemian Grove has prompted considerable suspicion among conspiracy theorists. The most important events are considered to be the 'lakeside talks', with past orators including Alexander Hague, Henry Kissinger and Casper Weinberger. Each summer, for three weekends, nearly 2,000 Bohemians, with specially invited guests, will speed in by car, corporate jet and helicopter to the heavily guarded Grove, near the tiny hamlet of Monte Rio on the Russian River. While ruling-class cohesiveness rarely lets slip details of agreements reached or new ideas broached, some – including the 1967 agreement by Ronald Reagan, over a less than friendly drink with Richard Nixon, to stay out of the coming presidential race – have played a major part in shaping US history.

Media interest in this regular meeting of the rich and the powerful has been constant since it was formed one night in 1872 by five bored news hacks on the old *San Francisco Examiner* to promote good and 'to help elevate journalism to that place in the popular estimation to which it is entitled'. That aspiration went down the drain when membership was extended to showpeople, and since 1878 journalists have been effectively barred from reporting the annual event, at least from the inside. A prospective member now faces an interrogation that, according to one club man, 'would satisfy the old KGB'. There is supposed to be a waiting list of some 1,500 notables, all eager to pay the huge initiation fee and annual subscription. Even a partial list of those believed to be members is highly impressive: George Shultz, Stephen Bechtel, Jr, Gerald Ford, Henry Kissinger, William F. Buckley, Jr, Fred L. Hartley, Merv Griffin, Thomas Haywood, Joseph Coors, Edward Teller, Ronald Reagan, A. W. Clausen, George Bush, William

French Smith, John E. Swearingten, Casper Weinberger, Dick Cheney, Justin Dart and William E. Simon.

However, conspiracy theorists believe that the Bohemiam Grove is far more than just a posh booze-up and claim, as usual without a shred of provable evidence, that these luminaries not only indulge in drunkenness and unbounded use of drugs with vague homosexual overtones but also in much more serious activities, such as kidnapping, rape, paedophilia, sodomy and ritual murder. For decades, say the theorists, there have been vague rumors of weird happenings in the more remote parts of Bohemian Grove's 2,200 acres. Theorists' reports claim that Druidic-like rituals occur, with Druids in red hooded robes marching in procession and chanting to the Great Owl (Moloch). Indeed, in July 1993 an article in a local community newspaper, the *Santa Rosa Sun*, reported on the Cult of Canaan and the legend of Moloch at Bohemian Grove. The Moloch Pagan Cult of Sacrifice is, of course, human sacrifice. About the mid-1980s there were rumours of murders in the more remote parts of the property, though a local police investigation is said to have got nowhere. Heads of states, both domestic and foreign, congressmen, government officials, the military, media moguls, religious leaders, heads of multinational corporations, with their supporters in the highest decision- and policy-making positions, are all reported to take part in these satanic rituals, which must make the White House and Wall Street seem rather tame by comparison. Thousands of children are stolen every year and used as human sacrifices, we are told; 3,500 children are missing in Florida alone and they cannot be found anywhere and conspiracy theorists know why! So it would seem that between alien abduction and the world's political and business leaders at Bohemian Grove, no child in America is safe any longer. In the absence of concrete evidence of activities which, if proven true would undoubtedly rock the political world to its foundations, there must be little that this conspiracy theory, or its many weird offshoots that can be found all over the Internet, has to offer other than a passing interest for the rational reader.

1882 – PHOENIX PARK MURDERS The murders of Lord Frederick Cavendish, Secretary of State for Ireland, and T. H, Burke, the permanent Irish Under-Secretary, rocked the nation and led directly to attempts to destroy the reputation of the leading Irish Nationalist politician, Charles Parnell. Committed by Irish Nationalist revolutionaries calling themselves the 'Invincibles', the murders took place as the two politicians walked through Phoenix Park towards the Vice Regal Lodge in Dublin. Four men attacked them, and one of the attackers, named Brady, drove a long abattoir knife into the back of Burke, while another, Kelly, then cut Burke's throat. Lord Cavendish was stabbed to death as he tried to come to Burke's aid. Both men were then savagely mutilated with surgical knifes. Burke, a Catholic and considered a traitor by hardline Nationalists, had been the prime target for the conspirators. The British government quickly tried to implicate Parnell in the conspiracy without notable success. However, the British Prime Minister, William Gladstone, offered the enormous sum, for those days, of £10,000 as a reward for identification of the killers, and it was made widely known that any participant in the conspiracy who informed on the other members would be given immunity from prosecution. A long and careful police investigation, probably with at least some inside information, eventually led to the arrest of some 27 conspirators, three of whom also turned informers. Brady, Kelly and three others were hanged for their part in the murders, while some of the other participants were given long terms of imprisonment. The result of these murders was a hardening of resolve on both sides, setting the scene for a British-instigated conspiracy to destroy the political career of Parnell once and for all, and the eventual increase in violence that led to the Easter 1916 uprising in Dublin and the bloody Irish civil war that followed.

1887 – PARNELL CONSPIRACY Did Britain frame an Irish Nationalist hero with a 'jubilee plot' to murder Queen Victoria in the 1880s? It is a story of intrigue and conspiracy to equal anything by Tom Clancy. In one of the most remarkable examples of a black operation ever exposed, British government ministers were so concerned about the rise of 'Home Rulers' in the 1880s that it used secret service agents to infiltrate and support Irish Republican terrorist organisations in actions reminiscent of US support for Osama Bin Laden's terrorist ambitions in the 1980s. Ministers believed that the 'plot' to kill the Queen, revealed with great drama during Victoria's golden jubilee, would fatally undermine Charles Stewart Parnell, the charismatic Irish Nationalist leader, in Westminster and destroy the Republican movement. It highlights Britain's often treacherous involvement in Irish affairs that continued through the Easter Rebellion and the Colin Wallace affair to the present day.

During the 1860s and 1870s, Irish-American groups launched a series of attacks across London, most infamously killing six people in an attack in Clerkenwell. The Home Office, the House of Commons and Scotland Yard were all targeted. With the country in a state of near panic, police revealed evidence of a plot to kill the Queen a few days before a golden jubilee service of thanksgiving at Westminster Abbey in 1887. Victoria was due to attend along with most of her family and most of the Cabinet. The police said that the plot, as audacious in its target as the 1605 Gunpowder Plot, had been hatched in New York by the Fenian Brotherhood, Clan na Gael, an Irish-American secret society. It is thought by some that when the purported Irish conspiracy was revealed to an astonished and fearful public, the British Government was not only fully aware of it but had actively supported it; intelligence officials based in Dublin and London used the Fenian Brotherhood to stir up violence against British targets; and known Republican sympathisers were hired by the Foreign Office to play a leading role in the attacks. When the bombing plot was revealed, the press jumped on the story, dubbing it the Jubilee Plot. The government immediately ordered an inquiry and six months later, with the campaign seemingly neutered, two Americans were arrested and sentenced to long periods in prison for conspiracy to commit terrorist acts. The developments appeared to be a vindication of the British state's methods of handling terrorism and was highly damaging to Parnell.

However, the actual leader of the Jubilee Plot was in fact a British agent who had been hired with the sanction of the Conservative leader, Lord Salisbury, the Prime Minister and Foreign Secretary. General Francis Millen, a Fenian Brotherhood figure who had mysteriously managed to escape back to New York despite one of the biggest police operations Britain had ever seen, was well known to the British secret service. He had been recruited in Mexico City a few years earlier. In a letter from the government's consul in Mexico, Salisbury was told that 'XXX', the code for Millen, was ready to start his first operation and the Foreign Office was happy to pay his salary. *The Times* was the unwitting stooge in the affair, publishing sensational accounts accusing Parnell of condoning the crime. The 'evidence' was later exposed as a forgery and soon after Millen was offered £10,000, a huge amount in the 1880s, to return to Britain and testify to what the government really knew of the conspiracy; he was later found dead in New York. Some might be prepared to suggest that the British intelligence services were simply being careful about 'clearing up the house'; whatever the truth, the death of Millen was convenient and saved the British government much potential embarrassment. Parnell was perhaps the most remarkable political leader to come out of Ireland, but he was to see his career virtually destroyed by a divorce scandal that erupted in 1890, and he died the following year a saddened and disillusioned man and, according to his many followers, of a 'broken heart'. It was certainly a heart that had bled for his beloved Ireland.

1888 – JACK THE RIPPER Conspiracies abound: was there a government cover-up to hide the involvement of a member of the royal family? Was there a security cover-up to hide an anti-Jewish element? Or merely to hide a botched police investigation? Despite the lack of hard facts there are one or two theories that appear to hold the biggest chance of being true. The known facts about the 'Ripper' reported at the time and gathered from 'eye witnesses' (that most unreliable source of evidence), police investigations and forensic examination, suggest that he was a white male of average or below average height, between twenty and forty years of age in 1888. He did not appear to dress as a labourer or indigent poor and apparently had lodgings in the East End. He seems to have had some medical expertise, though this has been doubted by some historians. He may have been a foreigner, was right-handed and was presumed to have a regular job since the murders all occurred at the weekends. And he was probably single so that he could roam the streets at all hours without questioning from a suspicious wife.

The most important detective in the hunt for the 'Ripper' was Chief Inspector Frederick George Abberline. In 1903 he said, 'You can state most emphatically that Scotland Yard is really no wiser on the subject than it was fifteen years ago.' However, Chief Inspector Abberline did eventually have a favourite suspect of his own, one *George Chapman*, who was hanged in 1903 for poisoning his wife. Many other names have entered the frame at one time or another, including *Walter Sickert*, a very highly regarded British painter, who become a semi-celebrity when American crime novelist Patricia Cornwell made him the subject of her book *Portrait of a Killer: Jack the Ripper – Case Closed*. *Montague John Druitt*, said to be a doctor and of good family, who disappeared at the time of the Miller's Court murder and whose body was later found in the Thames on 31 December roughly seven weeks after that murder, was sexually insane and there appears to be little doubt that his own family believed him to have been the murderer. *Aaron Kosminski,* a Polish Jew and resident in Whitechapel, became insane owing to, we are told, many years of happy indulgence in solitary vices. He had a great hatred of women, especially of the prostitute class, and we are told he had strong homicidal tendencies; he was removed to a lunatic asylum about March 1889. There were many circumstances connected with this man which made him a strong 'suspect' to some historians of the 'Ripper' murders. *Michael Ostrog*, a Russian doctor and a convict who was subsequently detained in a lunatic asylum as a homicidal maniac, reportedly had antecedents of the worst possible type, though unfortunately not specified in any detail, and his whereabouts at the time of the murders could never be ascertained. *Prince Albert Victor Christian Edward*, the Duke of Clarence, was known as Eddy. He was the grandson of Queen Victoria and was born in 1864. He fell short of any royal ambitions for him and was not distinguished by any important positive traits. However, lazy, aimless and spoiled though he might have been, he was not an evil or violent man. He died from influenza in the epidemic of 1892.

The subject that appears to provide a likely and believable candidate for the 'Ripper' is one *Francis Tumblety.* He was born either in Canada or Ireland in 1833. His family found its way to Rochester, NY, by 1849. First reports of Francis are not promising: in 1848 he was described by neighbours as 'a dirty, awkward, ignorant, uncared-for, good-for-nothing boy . . . utterly devoid of education.' In 1850 he moved to Detroit, and set up a practice as a physician sometime later. There is no indication that he ever finished school or even attended any form of medical school. Despite that detail, he became quite a prosperous doctor. He moved across North America setting up various medical practices and living in flamboyant splendour. Occasionally he would run into problems with the law and would set up practice somewhere else. He went to Liverpool in 1874 and is reported to have had a homosexual affair with Sir Henry Hall Caine. When he returned to New York, he became known for his 'mania for the company of young men and grown-up youths'. He was also known to despise women, particularly 'fallen women'. Tumblety returned to England in June of 1888 and was arrested for homosexual activities. He was then charged on suspicion of involvement in the Whitechapel murders. He jumped bail on 24 November, fled to France and then onwards to New York. Police in New York were on the lookout for him and, although they finally found him, he was not arrested because there was no proof that he was implicated in the 'Ripper' murders. Eventually, he moved back to Rochester and lived with his sister. He died in 1903 in St Louis, after earning considerable wealth as a medical quack. While there were numerous newspaper articles on Tumblety in New York papers, English papers seemed silent on the subject. It was only in 1993 that a letter belonging to Chief Inspector John Littlechild was discovered:

> amongst the suspects, and to my mind a very likely one, was a Dr T. He was an American quack named Tumblety and was at one time a frequent visitor to London and on these occasions constantly brought under the notice of police, there being a large dossier concerning him at Scotland Yard. Although a *Psychopathia Sexualis* subject he was not known as a 'Sadist', which the murderer unquestionably was, but his feelings toward women were remarkable and bitter in the extreme, a fact on record.

Tumblety must rank high on the list of suspects, but still without sufficient evidence. Like all the best mysteries, that of the 'Ripper' is likely to remain unsolved, perhaps until the day that damning proof is discovered somewhere in the attic of an old house long after the death of a relative of the real killer. One can always hope.

1889 – THE GHOSTS OF MAYERLING Since 30 January 1889 one name has symbolised the mystery of a scandalous and tragic double death: Mayerling. The death of the Archduke Rudolf of Habsburg, Crown Prince of Austria-Hungary, which immediately caused a dynastic crisis, and that of his mistress Baroness Marie Vetsera, occurred at the Crown Prince's hunting lodge, Mayerling. Both were officially the tragic victims of a double suicide by shooting. The death of his only son devastated Emperor Franz-Joseph I, since he had no other male heirs and the Austro-Hungarian crown would therefore pass to the Emperor's brother, Karl-Ludwig, and Karl-Ludwig's descendants. Karl-Ludwig had three sons: Franz-Ferdinand, of a sickly complexion; Otto, of a wild and debauched nature; and Ferdinand-Karl, who was only too ready to give up his imperial rights and become a commoner under the name Ferdinand Burg. Franz-Ferdinand contracted a morganatic marriage in 1900 with Countess Sophie Chotek: his children could not inherit the throne. Otto married Princess Maria-Jose of Saxony to satisfy the dynasty's pressing need for heirs. The marriage was loveless and, even though two children were born of it, Emperor Karl I and Archduke Ferdinand, Otto never stopped womanising and enjoying all the pleasures that Vienna offered to a handsome member of the Habsburg dynasty. After Franz-Joseph's death in 1916, it was Archduke Otto's son Karl who finally inherited the crown. Archduke Karl was in fact the sixth heir-presumptive to Franz-Joseph's throne. Mayerling will forever represent the sign of tragedy and despair that later engulfed the Habsburg family.

Crown Prince Rudolf was the only son of Emperor Franz-Joseph I and Empress Elisabeth, one of Europe's most beautiful princesses. Rudolf was born on 21 August 1858. He married Princess Stephanie of Belgium in 1881. Their marriage, as happened frequently in the house of Habsburg, was arranged, and involved little love between the young couple. Rudolf needed a wife with a more interesting personality than that of his child-bride. Stephanie was not even seventeen years of age at the time of her wedding, and she failed to keep her husband from wandering the streets of Vienna in search of licentious enjoyments. The couple had only one daughter, Archduchess Elisabeth, born in 1883. Since that fateful winter day in 1889 much has been said, speculated and written about the deaths at Mayerling. There has been considerable speculation about political intrigues, unspeakable love affairs and international conspiracies. The last Austrian Empress, Zita, who died in 1989, said that she firmly believed that Rudolf had been the victim of an international political conspiracy engineered by Georges Clemenceau, the French Prime Minister. Zita did not believe that, with such a promising life ahead of him, Crown Prince Rudolf would have chosen suicide under any circumstances. Zita alleged that Clemenceau was conspiring to overthrow Franz-Joseph and place Germanophobe Rudolf on the throne. This would allow Austria to break away from her allegiance to Germany and sign an alliance with France. Rudolf, Zita believed, refused to partake in the conspiracy and was killed to secure his silence.

Many historians argue that the Austrian police cover-up of the deaths of Rudolf and Marie Vetsera, his young and foolish lover, shrouded Mayerling in unnecessary mystery. Half a century later, in 1946, the tomb of Marie Vetsera was desecrated by the occupying Soviet forces. Possibly looking for jewels, Soviet troops had disturbed Marie Vetsera's remains. This was not discovered until 1955 when the Red Army abandoned Austria. In 1959 specialists in funereal preservation, accompanied by a doctor and a member of the Vetsera family, examined the remains. They were all shocked to discover that the body of the young woman in the vault did not present any traces of death by firearm. What they did observe was a large trauma on the crown of the head. This fact supported another version of the story which alleged that the mistress of the Austrian Crown Prince had not been killed by Rudolf, but had fallen foul of Rudolf's assassins. It is strange that this macabre discovery was curiously ignored by all concerned in 1955. If in fact this was indeed Vetsera's body, then the official version of a double suicide at Mayerling had been a hoax all along. Zita's version of the Mayerling tragedy seemed to perhaps be more believable. The old Empress Zita's observations on Mayerling had been founded on several disturbing facts and these were also an echo of the many speculations freely roaming around Viennese court circles soon after the death of Rudolf. On 9 February 1889 the German ambassador in Vienna sent a message to Berlin in which he reported a conversation with the Papal Nuncio, Monsignor Luigi Galimberti, and the Habsburg Court Chaplain, Monsignor Lorenz Mayer. During this conversation, the ambassador reported that the two well-informed prelates expressed their serious doubts concerning the official version of the events at Mayerling. The German note, as well as the forensic evidence found in Vetsera's body, are just some of the contradictory evidence that continues to challenge the official version of Rudolf and Marie's death. Some historians have alleged that Rudolf's body showed definite signs of a violent confrontation before death. Lacerations were discovered in several parts of the body and his hands showed signs of a struggle, which might be taken to suggest that the Crown Prince had indeed tried desperately to fight off his assassins. It also seems that the revolver used to kill both Rudolf and Vetsera was not the one owned by the Crown Prince, and that all six bullets were fired. In this case, Marie Vetsera was not just part of a tragic love affair but the unwilling victim of one of two daring political assassinations.

Rudolf's death brought ruin to his parents' marriage, uncertainty over the Austro-Hungarian imperial succession, and ultimately the end of the ancient house of Habsburg. If he had not met with an untimely demise, Europe's history could have been very different indeed. Mayerling not only meant the death of two love-struck people, but it also robbed the Habsburgs of the one person who seemed most capable of keeping the tattered multinational monarchy from its eventual disintegration and collapse. The tragic events at Mayerling continue to trouble many people who desperately want the mystery revealed. For example, just days before Christmas 1992 it was discovered that the mortal remains of Marie Vetsera had been mysteriously removed from the cemetery at Heiligenkreuz where they had lain for more than a century. After initial consternation, the local police were able to track down the coffin and recover Vetsera's remains. To verify that the remains were those of young Marie, the police asked the Viennese Medical Institute to examine the remains and identify if indeed they were those of the Mayerling victim. Upon inspection of the human remains recovered by the police, medical examiners discovered that the head of the young woman lacked any traces of a perforating bullet. The cranial cavity was not destroyed by a bullet that the Crown Prince Rudolf had supposedly fired into his lover's head. On the contrary, the cranial cavity showed signs of trauma. These lacerations could have been caused by a heavy object or some gardening equipment, but not by a bullet, confirming the discovery of 1955. What little fresh evidence that has appeared over the years all seems to point towards a conspiracy to hide a political murder, perhaps by a foreign power. But actual proof remains missing.

1894 – THE DREYFUS AFFAIR The Dreyfus case underscored and intensified the bitter divisions within French politics and society. The conspiracy to frame Dreyfus and the lengths that certain officers and officials were prepared to go to cover up their actions involved all the critical institutions and issues, including monarchists and Republicans, the political parties, the Catholic Church, the army and a strong anti-Semitic sentiment. Alfred Dreyfus, an obscure captain in the French army, came from a Jewish family that had left their native Alsace for Paris when Germany annexed that province in 1871. The French counter-espionage network, also called the Section of Statistics, was responsible for national security in France at that time. It had received word of espionage operations being conducted from the German embassy. Documents were being leaked to Germany about France's military preparations and capabilities. The Statistical Section under the command of Colonel Sandherr managed to place agents throughout the embassy and in 1894 one of the agents discovered an unsigned document in a wastebasket of the office of the German military attaché, Maximillian von Schwartzkoppen. The document became known as the *bordereau*, or schedule. It was a draft letter addressed to the Bureau of Information in Germany by the military attaché, speaking of dealings to be initiated with a French officer who had spoken of having worked in the Bureau of Intelligence; it made it appear that a French military officer was providing secret information to the German government. Dreyfus came under suspicion, probably because he was a Jew and also because he had access to the type of information that had been supplied to the German agent. Dreyfus was not the easiest officer to like or to deal with. His intellectual arrogance and aloofness earned him the mistrust of many of his colleagues and indeed many of the officers of the General Staff were openly anti-Semitic and the only reason Dreyfus made it into his position was because of his intelligence and high grades in the *École de Guerre*. The army authorities declared that Dreyfus's handwriting was similar to that on the papers and, despite his protestations of innocence, he was found guilty of treason in a secret military court martial, during which he was denied the right to examine the evidence against him. The army stripped him of his rank in a humiliating ceremony and shipped him off to life imprisonment on Devil's Island, a penal colony located off the coast of South America. The political right, whose strength was steadily increasing, cited Dreyfus's alleged espionage as further evidence of the failures of the Republic. Édouard Drumont's right-wing newspaper, *La Libre Parole*, intensified its attacks on the Jews, portraying this incident as further evidence of Jewish treachery.

The case against Dreyfus during the affair was deliberately mishandled through a conspiracy that led to tampering with the evidence and by corruption in the military. General Mercier was able to open official proceedings because of pressure from the media and the gravity of the affair. The people were looking for someone to blame for writing the *bordereau* and Dreyfus was the perfect candidate. Right from the beginning of the case, handwriting experts were hand-picked by Mercier to falsely make a correlation between the writing of the *bordereau* and that of Dreyfus even though none should have been found. He was determined to obtain Dreyfus's conviction at any price. Dreyfus seemed destined to die in disgrace as he had few defenders, and anti-Semitism was becoming rampant in the French army. An unlikely defender came to his rescue, motivated not by sympathy for Dreyfus but by the evidence that he had been 'railroaded' and that the officer who had actually committed espionage remained in a position to do further damage. Lieutenant Colonel Georges Picquart, an unapologetic anti-Semite, was appointed chief of army intelligence two years after Dreyfus was convicted. Picquart, after examining the evidence and investigating the affair in greater detail, concluded that the guilty officer was a major named Walsin Esterhazy. Picquart soon discovered, however, that the army was more concerned with preserving its image than rectifying its error, and when he persisted in attempting to reopen the case the army transferred him to Tunisia. A military court then acquitted Esterhazy, ignoring the convincing evidence of his guilt. 'The Affair' might have ended then but for the determined intervention of the novelist Émile Zola, who published his denunciation ('J'accuse!') of the army cover-up in a daily newspaper. Zola was found guilty of libelling the army and was sentenced to imprisonment. He fled to England, where he remained until being granted amnesty. At this point public passion became more aroused than ever, as the political right and the leadership of the Catholic Church – both of which were openly hostile to the Republic – declared the Dreyfus case to be a conspiracy of Jews and Freemasons designed to damage the prestige of the army and thereby destroy France.

Sometime later, another military officer discovered that additional documents had been added to the Dreyfus file. He determined that a lieutenant colonel, Hubert Henry, had forged the documents which seemed to strengthen the case against Dreyfus, in anticipation that Dreyfus would be given a new trial. Immediately after an interrogation the lieutenant colonel committed suicide. In 1899 the army did in fact conduct a new court martial, which again found Dreyfus guilty, although it observed that there were 'extenuating circumstances'; and the army sent Dreyfus back to Devil's Island. Later in 1899 the President of France pardoned Dreyfus, thereby making it possible for him to return to Paris, but he had to wait until 1906, some twelve years after the case had begun, to be finally exonerated of the charges and restored to his former military rank. 'The Affair' had inspired moderate republicans, radicals and socialists to work together, and the ultimate exoneration of Dreyfus strengthened the Republic, in no small part because of the conduct of its enemies, most notably the army and the Catholic hierarchy. In 1905 the Radical party, emphasising the role of the Catholic leadership in the Dreyfus case, succeeded in passing legislation separating church and state. The conspiracy against Dreyfus exposed the hypocrisy of French officialdom and the latent anti-Semitism that lurked close beneath the surface of an otherwise urbane and civilised nation.

1912 – *TITANIC* CONSPIRACY The very thought that the famous ship that struck an iceberg in 1912, taking some 1,500 passengers and crew to their deaths in the icy wastes of the North Atlantic and spawning a veritable industry of books and films on the subject, wasn't even the original *Titanic*, may indeed raise more than just the odd eyebrow. However, a number of seemingly well-informed conspiracy theorists have quite seriously advanced this as more than just a possibility. The 45,000-ton *Olympic* and her sister ship, the *Titanic*, were built by Harland and Wolff in Belfast for the White Star Line. Although both ships were very similar to the untrained eye, one difference was that the *Olympic* had sixteen portholes on the forward deck while the *Titanic* had fourteen. On 14 June 1911 *Olympic* was first to make her maiden voyage under Captain Edward J. Smith. Within a month there was an accident off the coast of California and three months later she collided with a British warship *HMS Hawk*. The damage was substantial below and above the waterline, with steel frames buckled, plates dislodged over four decks and damage to the starboard propeller and crankshaft. Worst of all, the keel was bent, giving the ship a slight list to port. *Olympic* was blamed by the Board of Trade for the accident and there was no insurance payout for White Star Line. On 12 February 1912 the *Olympic* had another accident, again while captained by Edward J. Smith, which resulted in a broken propeller. She limped back to Belfast where the propeller blade was replaced with one from the *Titanic*. Close inspection showed that the *Olympic's* accidents had seriously damaged the ship and repairs would cost a fortune, possibly even seriously jeopardising the company's future. Without the White Star Line, Harland and Wolff and thousands of employees' futures would also be put in jeopardy.

The Belfast shipbuilder's chairman was Lord Pierrie and he was also a shareholder in the White Star Line, now owned by America's Mercantile Marine, ran by financier J. P. Morgan. White Star Line's chairman was J. Bruce Ismay. The conspiracy that has been proposed suggests that these two men planned a gigantic fraud: the *Olympic* and the recently launched *Titanic* would be switched, swapping name-plates, lifeboats, lifebelts and menus, among other items. The plan was then to send the *Olympic* out under the *Titanic's* name, arrange an accident, scuttle the damaged ship and claim the insurance premiums. The White Star Line increased their insurance of the *Titanic* from $7 million to $12.5 million a week before sailing. Chairman J. Bruce Ismay was reported to have had certain effects removed from the ship, and J. P. Morgan cancelled his berth along with fifty other first-class passengers. The damaged ship, under the name of *Titanic*, set sail across the Atlantic in April 1912, half full and with a fire believed to be smouldering in coalbunker number 10.

The conspiracy is now extended to include the strange behaviour of another ship. During the spring of 1912, though there was a coal strike, this didn't stop the *California*, under Captain Stanley Lord, leaving with no cargo or passengers, five days before the *Titanic*. The conspiracy theorists believe that it was planned to rendezvous with the *Titanic* in order to transfer the passengers and crew to safety. The plan very obviously went tragically wrong. On 14 April the *California* stopped mid-Atlantic, for no apparent reason; it then sent three messages to the *Titanic* that night. Captains Smith and Lord were reported to have slept fully clothed, ready perhaps for the planned accident. The *Titanic* hit the iceberg, despite visibility being reported at between two and five miles on a moonlit night, and the so-called unsinkable ship with her sixteen watertight compartments soon began to sink. It took an incredible 35 minutes to raise the alarm, 45 minutes before the pumps were started and 1 hour 35 minutes before lifeboats were launched; the first lifeboat left the ship only half full. The *California* should have come to the rescue, but it was lying some twenty miles away, twelve miles from its planned location. The *California* misread the *Titanic's* flares for illumination flares being fired by an illegal seal-hunting ship, which lay somewhere between the *California* and the distant *Titanic*. In the event it was the Cunard liner *Carpathia* that came to the rescue, but far too late for most of the passengers and crew.

It has also been suggested that Prime Minister Asquith was compliant with the conspiracy. Thousands of jobs were at stake in the Belfast shipbuilding industry and this was an additional Irish problem Asquith could do without. He was further compromised when he heard that when American financier J. P. Morgan purchased the White Star Line, the previous government brokered the deal over the building of *Olympic* and *Titanic* in Belfast by guaranteeing that Royal Navy vessels were built in the yards as security. Unlike many seemingly far-fetched conspiracies where it is ultimately extremely difficult to build a reasonable case in the absence of any concrete evidence, it is indisputable that the White Star Line, which was said at the time to have only collected $7 million from the *Titanic* sinking, actually received far more, having revised the insurance prior to the maiden voyage. The *Olympic* was opened to the public in Liverpool before sailing; the *Titanic* wasn't. There was a fire in bunker number 10 prior to sailing, added to which was the absence of binoculars for the lookouts, of crewmen jumping ship, the missing ship's log, the *Titanic* being off course for no apparent reason and the change of officers at the last moment, all of which can, according to the supporters of this conspiracy theory, be verified by published sources. No one seems to have noticed the verifiable fact that the *California* sailed during a coal shortage with neither passengers nor cargo, or asked why the *California* was stationary mid-Atlantic, or why she sent out three ice warnings by radio, other than to pass on her position to the *Titanic*. Interestingly, there was another ship that struck an iceberg that same day, the *Niagra*, and apparently she sustained similar damage to the *Titanic* but made it safely to port. However, her third-class doors were not left open as on the *Titanic* permitting or perhaps even encouraging the fatal flooding.

There appears to be some circumstantial evidence to support the theory that the *Titanic* and *Olympic* were indeed swapped in the Belfast shipyard. How was the switch made? It all revolved around the change of shift of the tug and berthing crews when the *Titanic* and *Olympic* were moored next to each other in the Belfast dockyard. One shift takes a vessel named *Titanic* from dry dock and the next relief returns a vessel named *Olympic* into the dry dock. The ships' names were engraved into the hulls and to change them the old lettering was removed, the spaces filled in with white lead and the new names re-engraved. Preparations for this were made at Christmas 1911. The name of the man who made the new lettering patterns is known, along with his reward for doing the job. This is supported by video footage of the wreck, which shows the letters M and P behind the fading name of *Titanic*. During the weekend a group of men removed the names from the bows of both ships. This group went home and the next group came on board and replaced the names. The dockyard workforce at that time was around 15,000 men and it is highly unlikely that members of the two shifts would have conversed or even given the job a second thought.

Furthermore, you cannot add 1,000 gross registered tons to a 46,000-gross-registered-ton ship and still end up with a 46,000-ton ship. It is claimed that the side screens on the *Titanic* were fitted as a last-minute instruction from Bruce Ismay to improve passenger comfort, but why was it carried out at the last minute? The fitting of the screens had little or nothing to do with passenger comfort; it was simply to raise the GRT (gross registered tonnage) of the *Olympic* to match the Certificate of Registration of the *Titanic*. The *Olympic* had a gross tonnage of 45,324 without side screens; the *Titanic* had 46,359 without side screens. Had the screens been added to the heavier vessel she would have gone up to approximately 47,359 GRT. This cannot have been so because the two GRTs of the ships ended up equal! Put simply, the *Titanic* was already the larger of the two ships, so if screens had been added to her she would have been even larger. The ship which was supposedly the *Olympic* was cut up at Inverkeithing in 1937. Her GRT was 46,359 tons and therefore a thousand tons heavier than the *Olympic* should have been and exactly the tonnage of the *Titanic*. That is an indisputable fact. Why were these figures never discovered before? Perhaps because no one was bothering to look for them. It is also impossible to have a brand-new ship with furnaces that have seen many months of hard work. The firemen who signed on at Belfast believed they were going to serve on a brand-new ship and from the quayside the ship did appear immaculate, in fact resplendent, with her new side screens, but below decks the story was somewhat different. Upon entering the stoke hold, the firemen realised that the hold was not that of a new ship. It was that of a ship which had spent many months at sea. It is, of course, totally impossible to disguise furnaces that have been fired up. The Board of Trade surveyor was kept well away from the furnaces before sailing, for he would have undoubtedly reported the findings immediately. The men who fired up the cold stoke hold were then signed off before the voyage proper began and replaced at Southampton.

The conspiracy that hid the switching of *Olympic* for *Titanic* could have been carried out quite simply and without suspicion in a time when a man's priority was to keep his job and ask no questions. The workers in the Belfast shipyard of 1912 were unlikely to question the ethics of a management offering them a little illegal overtime pay, especially at a time when their trade union had actually banned overtime. The two shifts that weekend would have no idea that they were changing the course of history, and even if any of them had heard certain rumours of what was happening they would have been unlikely to spread further than the nearest public house for fear of losing the men's precious livelihood. That said, it is a complicated and barely believable conspiracy, but one that somehow leaves an uneasy feeling that perhaps, just perhaps, the most famous and tragic sinking in maritime history might also have been the biggest fraud of all time as well.

1914 – ASSASSINATION IN SARAJEVO This was undoubtedly a conspiracy that was to change the world for ever, a conspiracy that succeeded beyond the wildest dreams of the conspirators, but one whose tragic consequences were to haunt the Balkans for next ninety or so years. The two bullets fired on a Sarajevo street on a sunny June morning in 1914 set in motion a series of events that led directly to the Great War, World War II, the Cold War, the ethnic cleansing of the 1990s and the Kosovo campaign of 1998–99. The victims, Archduke Franz Ferdinand, heir to the throne of the Austro-Hungarian Empire, and his wife Sophie, were in the Bosnian city in conjunction with Austrian military exercises nearby, and the couple were returning from an official visit to City Hall. The main assassin, nineteen-year-old Gavrilo Princip, a fanatic Slav nationalist, was part of a conspiracy aimed at freeing the peoples of the Balkans from the control of the Emperor in Vienna. Serbia figured prominently in the plot. Independent Serbia provided the guns, ammunition and training that made the assassination possible. The Balkan region of Europe entered the twentieth century much as she left it: a cauldron of seething political intrigue needing only the slightest increase in heat to boil over into open conflict. Seven conspirators joined the crowd lining the Archduke's route to City Hall. Each took a different position, ready to attack the royal car if the opportunity presented itself. Borijove Jevtic, one of the conspirators, recounted that when Franz Ferdinand and his retinue drove from the station they were allowed to pass the first two conspirators. The six motorcars were driving too fast to make an attempt feasible and the crowds contained large numbers of Serbians: throwing a grenade would have killed many of the wrong ethnic group. However, when they approached one conspirator, Gabrinovic (or Cabrinovic), he threw his bomb only to see it bounce off the Archduke's car and explode near the following car. Unhurt, the Archduke and his wife sped to the reception at City Hall.

After the reception in the Town Hall General Potiorek, the Austrian Commander, pleaded with Francis Ferdinand to leave the city, as it was seething with rebellion. The Archduke was persuaded to drive the shortest way out of the city and to go quickly. The road to the manoeuvres was shaped like the letter V, making a sharp turn at the bridge over the River Nilgacka. Franz Ferdinand's car could go fast enough until it reached this spot, but then it was forced to slow down for the turn, and it was here that Princip had taken his position. As the car came abreast he stepped forward from the kerb, drew his automatic pistol from his coat and fired two shots. The first struck the wife of the Archduke, the Archduchess Sophie, in the abdomen. She was an expectant mother and died instantly. The second bullet struck the Archduke close to the heart. He died almost instantly. Austrian officers quickly seized Princip, as much to save him from the crowds as to arrest him. The investigation of the assassination by the Austro-Hungarian authorities soon yielded the facts to prove that the conspiracy against the life of the Archduke and successor to the throne was prepared and abetted in Belgrade with the co-operation of Serbian officials, and executed with arms from the Serbian state arsenal. Within three months Europe was at war. These were truly shots that echoed around the whole world.

1916 – RASPUTIN Grigori Efinovich ('Rasputin' meant quite appropriately 'debauched') was the son of Siberian shamans and earned his new nickname while conducting orgies at his Khlist seminary where his already growing group of followers apparently worshipped his not inconsiderable phallus and levels of sexual energy. After moving to St Petersburg his reputation as something akin to a wizard won him the attention of the rather dim-witted Tsar and particularly the Tsarina. His success in using hypnosis or auto-suggestion on Alexis, the heir to the Russian throne, to reduce the crippling effects of haemophilia, ensured his position in the Russian royal family's household, despite being filthy and smelly, drinking to excess and being without doubt grossly immoral. The Tsarina believed that he was a saintly miracle worker who had the ability to channel the power of prayer. Rasputin came to exert an evil influence at the Tsarist court, interfering in domestic, political and even military matters. At times he was known as the Tsar of Tsars, the Mad Monk or the Holy Devil. He adopted a very familiar manner with the Empress Alexandra, and indeed rumours circulated that they had an unnatural sexual relationship and that this might have included some of the young princesses as well. He is understood to have raped numerous women, including at least one nun who refused his advances. His acceptance at the Tsarist court was widely considered a national scandal.

Finally a conspiracy was instigated by a group of young officers and nobles led by Prince Felix Yussoupov who saw it as their duty to rid the court and imperial Russia of this uncouth monk. An attempt to bribe Rasputin failed and it was decided that he should be killed. The conspiracy planning took place during December 1916 in the cellars of Yussoupov's family home at the Moika Palace and included Grand Duke Dmitry Pavlovich, the politician V. Purishkevich, Lieutenant Sukhotin and an army medical officer, Stanislas Lazovert. Rasputin was to be poisoned with cakes and Madeira wine laced with cyanide. Yussoupov spent some time cultivating the monk's friendship, though there have been suggestions that this relationship may not have been quite so straightforward, as it was believed that the young Yussoupov was a homosexual and that Rasputin had rebuffed his sexual advances at an earlier time. Using Princess Irina, a well-known beauty who Rasputin had not yet met, as bait, Rasputin fell for the trap and visited Yussoupov's home. There he ate two poisoned cakes and drank two glasses of the wine without noticeable effect. After two hours the panicking conspirators fired a revolver at point-blank range into Rasputin. The doctor proclaimed him dead, but within a short while Rasputin jumped to his feet and tried to strangle Yussoupov. Freeing himself, Yussoupov called for help and Rasputin was shot two or three more times as he attempted to escape. Yussoupov may at this stage have raped the seriously wounded Rasputin before the conspirators beat his head to a bloody pulp and, it is believed, castrated him, giving his thirteen-inch phallus to a former lover who many years later in Paris described it as looking like an overripe banana about a foot long. Having wrapped Rasputin's body in a curtain, they pushed his body though a hole in the ice of the River Neva. Three days later the corpse was recovered from beneath the ice by divers and, to the horror of the conspirators, it was discovered that Rasputin, despite being given enough poison to kill a dozen men, shot at least three times, beaten and pushed beneath the ice of a frozen river, had still managed to free his arms from the ropes that bound them before he finally drowned. Rasputin was buried in the presence of the royal family, and the conspirators' wish to keep the deed secret had utterly failed; however, no one was punished for their part in killing the Tsarina's favourite. The October Revolution was soon to sweep away imperial Russia, the royal family and the very reasons for the conspiracy.

1917 – ZIMMERMAN TELEGRAM A conspiracy by the British Intelligence Service and the Foreign Office to provide the US

President with the proof he needed to take a reluctant American people into war with Germany, the Zimmerman telegram has long been seen as a near-classic use of intelligence to gain larger political aims. From 1914, when the Great War broke out, until the spring of 1917, the USA had remained neutral. The British government had felt for some time that the Americans should have joined them as allies, since there were common bonds of both history and language. However, much of the American public felt that the conflict was a European affair. In fact, in 1916 Woodrow Wilson had been elected President for a second term with the campaign slogan 'He kept us out of war'. International events, however, would soon change the USA's isolationist status. Indeed, the USA was in some senses already involved in the war, since American businesses were selling weapons and war material to the Allies. In addition, the US government was lending the Allies money, and by 1917 the war loans had reached a total of some $2 billion. However, with the young men of Europe having died in their millions, what was urgently needed were new armies of fresh troops to alter the balance of power on the European battlefields, and only the entry of America into the war could possibly provide the huge numbers of new recruits required.

Germany unwittingly played a major role in bringing America into the war. The German navy violated its pledge to limit submarine warfare, the sinking of military and commercial ships with their U-boats. The Germans had already sunk the *Lusitania* in 1915, and by 1917 the Germans were engaging in unrestricted submarine warfare, a desperate bid to starve Britain and France of imported supplies. Eight American ships were sunk in the space of two months. In response to this breaking of the Sussex pledge, which had stipulated limits on submarine naval warfare, the USA severed diplomatic relations with Germany. But the critical event that finally brought the USA into the war was the Zimmerman telegram. On 26 February 1917 President Woodrow Wilson received from Acting Secretary of State Frank Polk the text of a secret telegram that had been sent by the German Foreign Minister Arthur Zimmermann to the German ambassador in Mexico, von Eckhardt. The message was then intended to be passed on for final delivery to the Mexican President. The telegram proposed a possible German military alliance with Mexico and Japan against the USA. In the telegram, Zimmerman outlined a plan whereby the Mexican government, if they agreed to enter the war on the side of Germany, could regain the territories of New Mexico,

Arizona and California. The Zimmerman note to the German minister to Mexico read,

> Berlin, January 19, 1917
> On the first of February we intend to begin submarine warfare unrestricted. In spite of this, it is our intention to endeavor to keep neutral the United States of America. If this attempt is not successful, we propose an alliance on the following basis with Mexico: That we shall make war together and together make peace. We shall give general financial support, and it is understood that Mexico is to reconquer the lost territory in New Mexico, Texas, and Arizona. The details are left to you for settlement . . . You are instructed to inform the President of Mexico of the above in the greatest confidence as soon as it is certain that there will be an outbreak of war with the United States and suggest that the President of Mexico, on his own initiative, should communicate with Japan suggesting adherence at once to this plan; at the same time, offer to mediate between Germany and Japan. Please call to the attention of the President of Mexico that the employment of ruthless submarine warfare now promises to compel England to make peace in a few months.

The British had earlier sabotaged Germany's undersea communication cables when on the first day of war in 1914 the Admiralty had ordered the cable-laying ship *Telconia* to drag up the German undersea cables off Emden, on the Dutch/German border, cut them and deprive the Kaiser of his key communication links; thus the Germans were compelled to send the telegram by way of Sweden and, to assure transmission, through the more direct route of an American-owned cable. Both of these cable routes passed through England. It was this fact which allowed British interception of the Zimmerman telegram. On 17 January 1917 one of thousands of coded messages arrived at Room 40 along the old pneumatic message tubes. It was picked up by the talented cryptographers Nigel de Gray and the Reverend William Montgomery. They were to begin the process that changed the course of the war, and history. Nigel de Grey quietly rolled out the message. It was a string of number groups from the German codebook. The Germans used printed codebooks, and then used another book to encrypt the message again, for additional security. Room 40 had managed to obtain copies of the codebooks, often from sinking ships, a fact that remained unknown to the Germans. This message particularly interested de Grey for it was very long for a normal cable. It was also coded only once, and not enciphered again to make it more secure. To this day no one knows why it did not have the second layer of protection. The incomplete message was immediately given to Admiral Hall, Director of Naval Intelligence. The message announced the feared unrestricted submarine warfare. Hall also quickly realised the threat posed by the Zimmermann telegram. America would be so preoccupied with Mexico and Japan that it might fatally ignore the pleas for help from Britain and France. Hall knew the Germans believed their codes were unbreakable. So the problem was to get the decrypt into the hands of President Wilson without alerting the Germans, or Americans, as to the real source. It was decided to wait and see whether President Wilson would choose to respond vigorously to the onset of unrestricted submarine warfare. Admiral Hall knew, however, that the verbose Germans would recirculate the important telegram and, using contacts in Mexico, managed to intercept the next stage, a telegram from the German embassy in Washington, forwarding the contents of the Zimmerman telegram. On 10 February 1917 Hall used a smoke screen to cover the activities of Room 40. On 19 February Room 40 had the full document decoded, five weeks after receiving the telegram. The campaign was now underway to influence President Wilson who Theodore Roosevelt told everyone was 'yellow all through'. The contents of the Mexican version of the cable were given to Edward Bell of the US embassy in London. Bell's immediate reaction was 'Forgery' and disbelief that Germany would dare interfere in America, least of all offer to give Arizona and New Mexico away as booty of war. An elaborate charade was thus created to present the Mexican version to President Wilson, with the Foreign Secretary, not the intelligence services, leaking the contents. This would allow the Americans to find the original Zimmermann cable to Washington in the Western Union files and then give them time to decode it using captured codebooks brought over to the US embassy in London, from Room 40. They could then claim that it was discovered and decoded by Americans, on American soil. On Friday 23 February 1917 the contents of the Zimmermann telegram were officially presented to the American ambassador. The ambassador then spent the next twelve hours drafting the right words, to tell Wilson enough, but not too much. The resulting cable from the US embassy in London to the pacifist President Wilson in Washington is a masterpiece of diplomatic language and, while stretching the facts a little, secured final US entry into the European war. The ambassador announced that the British government had lost no time in transmitting the contents of the diplomatic cable obtained in Mexico, 'in view of the threatened invasion of United States territory'. He told friends that even threat of invasion might not budge Wilson into action. President Wilson was under attack on the home front and, since the declaration of unrestricted submarine warfare by Germany, the US ports were clogged with ships not daring to put to sea. US factories were suffering, and Roosevelt was rallying public opinion against 'the general paralysis of Wilsonism'. To gain allies in Congress first, at 4 p.m. on 28 February President Wilson leaked the contents of the cable to Senator Hitchcock of Nebraska, the leading pro-German pacifist. He was disgusted and appalled. Next it was leaked to the press on 1 March. The telegram had such an impact on American opinion that, according to David Kahn, author of *The Codebreakers*, 'No other single cryptanalysis has had such enormous consequences.' It is his opinion that 'never before or since has so much turned upon the solution of a secret message.' In an unbelievable and totally unexplained development, on 2 March Arthur Zimmermann, Foreign Minister of Germany, admitted that he had written and sent the telegram. In what must be one of the greatest blunders in political history, Zimmermann opened the door to the involvement of the USA and the final defeat of Germany. Desperate cables were sent to Berlin suggesting that Zimmermann deny the accusations. All that Zimmermann would say was, 'How can I? It is true.' Zimmermann believed that the USA must have obtained a hard copy of the telegram from one of the German diplomatic missions. He never thought for a moment that it could have been intercepted, en route, and decoded by the British. On 6 April 1917 the US Congress formally declared war on Germany and its allies. The Zimmermann telegram is therefore probably one of the most important, and far-reaching, intercepted message of all time. It certainly changed the direction of modern history.

1919 – THE GREATEST CONSPIRACY OF ALL The Comintern was probably the biggest political conspiracy of all time, with the stakes being domination of the world. Ultimately it was to prove a failure, but not before it had disrupted countless countries and caused the deaths of several million victims. Founded in March 1919, the

Communist International, or Comintern, was officially the Third International, held in Moscow at a time when Vladimir Ilyich Lenin still feared a resurgence of the Second, or Socialist, International under non-Communist leadership. The Comintern was established to claim Communist leadership of the world socialist movement. The delegates to the first congress were mainly Russians, with some members of left-wing socialist splinter groups who happened to be in the Soviet Union and one German who abstained on the crucial vote of establishing the organisation. Gregory Zinoviev was elected the first president of the Comintern and its leading members included Communists from Europe, Asia and elsewhere, who acted under the direction of Moscow as 'the General Staff of the Revolution'. It seemed in 1919 as if the whole of Europe was about to erupt into one vast revolutionary conflagration. Soviet Russia was fighting for its life in a hostile world, but its severe isolation was being broken by proclamations from groups of revolutionaries from far and near pledging their loyalty to the new republic and expressing their determination to follow its example. From 1914 on, Lenin had been speaking of the need for the formation of a new Third International, one that would not betray the workers' interests, as had the Second, which lay in shambles with the onset of the Great War.

The October Revolution of 1917 forced on the whole of the working-class movement the sharp choice of whether to stand with it or against it, and the further choice of whether to work to extend it in their own countries or to seek a less radical accommodation within the existing structures of power. In 1918 Communist parties were formed in Germany, Poland, Hungary, Austria, Holland, Finland, Latvia and Greece, and soon after in many other countries, as the movement decisively split between communists and Social Democrats.

In January 1919 the Russian Communist Party issued a manifesto calling for the creation of a new International and in March of that year the first delegates assembled in Moscow. Despite the difficulties in communication and transportation, and despite the absence of real unanimity, the Communist International was inaugurated. The congress, which declared itself the founding congress of the Communist International, set out a manifesto 'To the proletarians of the whole world' in the hope of rallying workers everywhere to side with the cause of revolution and to break with the false promise of bourgeois democracy. Events were now moving very fast. Throughout Europe, workers inspired by the October Revolution were rising up against their governments and 'Soviets' sprang up from the Dombrowa coal basin in Poland to Limerick and Tipperary in the faraway west of Ireland. In March, a Soviet Republic was proclaimed in Hungary, with Béla Kun at its head. Kun had been converted to Bolshevism while a prisoner of war in Russia and, upon his return to Hungary in November 1918, had founded the Hungarian Communist Party amid the fluid political situation caused by the dissolution of the Austro-Hungarian Empire. The new government, a coalition of communists and socialists, quickly nationalised everything from industry and land to children's sweets. However, it did not last. By August it was over. The fragile republic, weakened by internal dissent, was overcome by Czech and Romanian armies and Admiral Horthy's 'white terror' prevailed. Those Communists who survived went into exile.

Another episode that ended in tragedy took place in Bavaria. There too a 'Soviet republic' was declared that spring, though it had from the beginning something of a farcical quality about it. In the confusion following the assassination of Kurt Eisner, head of government, the Munich Workers and Soldiers Council took power in April, against the opposition of the Communists. However, when the government, now dominated by anarchist-inclined intellectuals, came under attack, the communists came to its defence and subsequently took control. On 1 May Munich was encircled by the German army and the 'Soviet republic' collapsed. A brutal massacre followed and the leaders, including anarchist Gustav Landauer and the communist Eugene Levine, were killed. Hungarian émigrés in Vienna, engaging in a postmortem on the defeat of the commune, embarked on a bitter factional dispute that was to continue through the 1920s. Most serious, however, were clashes within the German Communist Party (KPD) that resulted in a formal split at their second congress in Heidelberg in October 1919. After the murder of so many of its leaders within the first few months of its foundation – Rosa Luxemburg, Karl Liebknecht, Leo Jogiches – Paul Levi emerged as party leader.

During its first chaotic and unsettled year of existence, the Comintern elicited clandestine support from the most varied quarters. Adherents of the most diverse revolutionary tendencies pledged their clandestine support, from such syndicalist and quasi-syndicalist groups as the American 'wobblies' or Industrial Workers of the World, to the sophisticated Marxists who formed the Communist parties in

Poland and Germany. However, by the time the second world congress took place in July 1920, it had been decided to put the house in somewhat better order. The second world congress adopted a list of 21 conditions to determine the admission of parties to the Comintern, including the requirement of each party to carry out systematic propaganda within the army and in the countryside in favour of proletarian revolution, to remove reformists and centrists from all positions in the working-class movement and to replace them by Communists, and to combine legal and illegal methods of work. The congress marked a sharp breach not only between Communists and Social Democrats, but between Communists and those who were still seeking a basis for compromise, such as the Austro-Marxists, who still wished to find a third way between 'terrorist Moscow' and 'impotent Bern'.

The seat of the Communist International was to be in Moscow. It seemed only natural that it should be located in the one socialist country that existed. Indeed, the structure of the Comintern was modelled on that of the Russian party, not because of any sinister design to ensure Russian domination but simply because the Russian party was the only one to have carried out a successful proletarian revolution. From the beginning, there had been uneasiness about this situation, particularly among the KPD leadership, and Rosa Luxemburg had earlier warned against the potential subjection of the international movement to the 'Russian model'. However, it seemed possible that this danger would be circumvented. The Russians at this time fully expected that their pre-eminence would be superseded as soon as a proletarian revolution triumphed in an advanced industrialised society. Indeed, Bolshevik leaders were inclined to state the matter quite sharply, pointing to their own backwardness and to the necessity of a more advanced country taking the lead. However, it was only when the revolution obstinately stood still at the Russian frontier and the bright hopes of the summer of 1920 faded that the gap in authority between those who had succeeded in making their revolution and those who had failed widened, leaving the Comintern shaped in a Russian mould and ensuring Russian dominance.

The congress was followed by bitter debates within the parties on acceptance of the 21 conditions and the period between the second and third congresses saw a series of splits and amalgamations based on the new policies. The increasing unity on the right in Europe at the time was in sharp contrast to the growing disunity of the left, split not only between communists and socialists, but also between rival factions within both the Communist and socialist camps. Such developments had their effect in the change of mood reflected at the third world congress of the Comintern in June and July 1921 in Moscow. The prevailing atmosphere, which contrasted sharply with the heady optimism and militancy of the year before, was one of moderation and restraint. The congress signalled a tactical retreat on various fronts. The parties allied to the Comintern were soon to be torn apart by factional struggles, centred for the most part on political debates regarding strategies to be employed in achieving power. These coincided with, and were exacerbated by, the intense factional struggle going on within the Russian Party, which was then in the process of moving against Trotsky. On top of this, various parties were in open conflict with the leadership of the Comintern, and directives condemning the 'right-wing' leadership of the Polish party, the 'right deviations' of the British party and the 'ultra-leftism' of the Italian party constantly emanated from Moscow. In 1935 the Comintern abandoned the membership policies established under the '21 Conditions' and began to form coalitions, or popular fronts, with bourgeois parties. In 1936 Germany and Japan concluded the so-called Anti-Comintern Pact, ostensibly to protect the world from the Third International. The pact was renewed in 1941 with eleven other countries as signatories. A total of seven congresses and eight plenums were held until Stalin finally ordered the Comintern's dissolution in 1943 in order to allay the misgivings of its British and American allies in World War II. From 1947 to 1956 the Cominform acted as its successor. As with all such underground organisations, the Comintern soon became shrouded by rumour, conjecture and myth. What is absolutely certain, however, is that the Comintern represents the only conspiracy that can be proved to have been formed to bring about world domination by a political ideal. The encouraging lesson to be learned from this vast conspiracy is that it thankfully failed totally and absolutely in its final aims.

1923 – THE DEATH OF PRESIDENT HARDING Was President Harding yet another victim of a politically motivated killing? Some conspiracy theorists certainly believe this to be so and highlight the decidedly odd circumstances surrounding the end of his life. Warren Harding was elected President in 1920, replacing Woodrow Wilson, on the basis of a promise of strong support for Prohibition, but an equal promise not to enforce it, especially in the White House. He kept his promise, so far as it applied to the White House, but not otherwise, and an enforcement system went into effect, staffed by federal agents. Gaston Means was an agent and investigator for the Justice Department's Bureau of Investigation (the forerunner of the FBI). Means made $83 a week at his government job, but he made far more as a member of a 'political gang', the members of which are sometimes called 'conspirators' by some theorists. The gang was led by Harry M. Daugherty, the Attorney General. They installed Means in a palatial house, situated at 903 16th Street, NW, in Washington, DC. Means moved in, with his wife and children, and he spent most of his time there. He had at his constant disposal a $5,000 Cadillac and chauffeur. In the back yard, he constructed an underground safe for keeping large sums of money, derived from a number of scams including, but certainly not limited to, his involvement in Prohibition-related crime, sales of federal judgeships, dismissals of civil and criminal actions against industrial plants, sales of pardons and paroles, sales of government lands, and numerous other activities.

Alcohol prohibition was a great source of profit to the conspirators who formed the gang. For a price, government officials could provide papers which allowed people to withdraw quantities of whiskey and gin from bonded warehouses. Also, for a price, bootleggers could purchase protection from federal agents who might otherwise interfere with their business affairs. Means, himself, frequently travelled to New York to handle these transactions. There, he would rent two adjoining rooms in a first-class hotel, e.g. the Vanderbilt. Each bootlegger seeking protection for his business activities, whether they be in Brooklyn, Manhattan, the Bronx, or wherever, would be instructed to come to one of the rooms at an odd time, e.g. 11.42 a.m., 2.26 p.m., and to bring with him the required sum of money. In the room there would be a large glass jar, with a large sum of cash, e.g. $10,000 or $50,000, already deposited therein (so as to reassure the client that he was not alone and that others were also purchasing protective services). Each bootlegger would then deposit the required sum of money in bills, while Means watched through a peephole in the adjacent room to make sure that the money already in the bowl was not removed, and that the required payment was made. Not once was he short-changed, such was the honesty of his clients. In this manner, and over time, Means brought in $7,000,000 from the New York operations, and similar large sums from Detroit, Chicago, etc.

According to theorists other members of the gang of conspirators included: the Secretary of the Interior Fall; Jess Smith, Harry Daugherty's 'Man Friday', who lived with Daugherty in Washington and spent much time at 903 16th Street; Gen. Sawyer, the President's physician; C. F. Cramer, the attorney for the Veteran's Bureau; John T. King, a lobbyist and politician; Col. T. B. Felder, an attorney who served as 'advisor to the clique'; and many others.

Publicly, at least, Warren Harding was an amiable, kindly man. He was incredibly handsome and attractive to the opposite sex, and it was generally known that he had numerous affairs with a variety of different women. Florence Harding, Warren's wife, was older than him. Unlike the President, who was not an ideologue, Florence was a fervent suffragette and crusader for women's rights. She was also aggressive and argumentative, and made her husband's life miserable with her constant nagging. Early in the Harding Administration, Florence Harding summoned Gaston Means to meet with her. She had heard, she explained, that a vile rumour was circulating in Washington that her husband had sired an illegitimate son by a woman named Nan Britton, who lived in Chicago. She asked Means to investigate the rumour and prove that the story wasn't true. Means, who fancied himself as a great investigator, accepted the assignment. She promised to pay him. Through trickery, Means managed to gain admittance to the apartment in Chicago where Britton was staying and to actually steal letters which Harding had written to Britton, confirming his affair with her. Means also found numerous gifts which Harding had made to Britton's son, including a ring and a baby carriage. The investigation, of course, simply proved the rumours to be true. It also led to the suspicion, in Means's mind at least, that the conspirators were using the affair to blackmail the President into signing executive orders transferring certain government oil leases from the Navy Department to the Secretary of Interior, where as a part of the conspiracy they were able to ensure that their private financial interests benefitted through 'kickbacks', bribes and contracts granted to business colleagues. Eventually, when Means reported what he had found to Mrs Harding, she demanded that he go back to Chicago and steal all of the gifts which had been given to the baby. Means did exactly that, returning with all of them except the baby carriage.

Conspiracy theorists now add Jess Smith to the gang and its criminal activities. He was a former haberdasher who had come to Washington with Harding and Daugherty from Ohio and was a frequent visitor to the residence on 16th Street. Here, on the occasion of one of his visits, he revealed that he believed his life was in danger and that he thought that he might be singled out by the conspirators for 'knowing too much'. He had heard that there was a 'little white powder' which was sometimes slipped into the food or drink of suspected 'traitors' to kill and silence them, and this worried him. He disclosed, however, that as some form of protection he had kept detailed records of all of the relevant transactions carried out by the gang, including the Prohibition payments. When word of this reached the conspirators they apparently decided that Smith was a dangerous liability; they had all agreed not to talk, but nobody could now be sure that Smith wouldn't finally do so. On 30 May 1923 at 4.00 a.m. Means received a telephone call from one of his superiors, telling him to come to the Wardman Park hotel. When he arrived at the hotel, he was confronted by one of his superiors at the Bureau of Investigation who advised him that Jess Smith had shot himself. It was believed that Smith was carrying the papers which could have incriminated the other gang members. Means was told to search the body and retrieve the papers. Entering the apartment, Means saw Smith's body lying on the floor with arm extended, a revolver on the ground just three or four inches beyond the outstretched hand. This surprised Means, because he knew that Smith had an extreme aversion to guns and had never fired one in his life. Furthermore, nobody in the hotel had heard a gunshot. Means became concerned that a 'little white powder' might have killed Smith, who could then have been shot and moved to the hotel. Whatever the case, Means searched the body and found a shoulder harness, holding a large cache of paper; this he removed and later handed to his superiors.

While these events unfurled, Florence and Warren Harding had been preoccupied with winning a second term, but Mrs Harding now began to become even more concerned with Nan Britton. Ms Britton had come to Washington to be closer to the President and she began seeing him in both the White House and friends' homes. Mrs Harding became aware of these visits and became increasingly agitated. At a meeting at the White House, Florence Harding confronted Means. She too had heard about the lethal use of a 'little white powder', which could be slipped into a person's food or drink. She demanded that Means get hold of some of this obviously useful product but, according to his own account, he refused. In July 1923 the Hardings departed on a vacation trip to Alaska. Coming back, in Vancouver, the

President was taken ill with what appeared to be food poisoning, although no one else in the party became ill despite having eaten the same food. The party continued from Vancouver to California by train. When they got to San Francisco, the President and the First Lady checked into a hotel and General Sawyer, his physician, tended to Harding. There, the President suddenly died. Returning to Washington for the funeral, Florence Harding summoned Means to a meeting at the home of a friend. Means later related the following conversation:

> She continued: 'And one day, he [the President] was writing a letter. I casually asked him to whom he was writing. He replied that he was writing to his old father, in Marion. He lied. That letter was to Nan Britton. I intercepted it . . . No, I have no regrets' . . . I was alone with the President . . . and only for about ten minutes. It was time for his medicine . . . I gave it to him . . . he drank it. He lay back on the pillows for a moment. His eyes were closed . . . He was resting . . . Then, suddenly, he opened his eyes wide . . . and moved his head and looked straight into my face. I was standing by his bedside . . .' As she paused, I could not refrain the question: 'You think he knew?' 'Yes, I think he knew. Then, he sighed and turned his head away. After a few minutes, I called for help. The papers told the rest.'

After the funeral, Mrs Harding went to live for a time with the family of General Sawyer in Ohio. While she was there, General Sawyer died suddenly, in a manner very similar to President Harding. Some months later, Florence Harding also died.

The Harding Administration and its aftermath seemed to be littered with the corpses of people who might have revealed damaging secrets but were silenced one way or another. The theorists point at a surprisingly long list of those claimed to have died in suspicious circumstances: G. F. Cramer, attorney for the Veteran's Bureau, allegedly committed suicide; Lawyer Thurston, an independent Boston attorney who collected Alien Property graft, died suddenly in Boston; Col. T. B. Felder, who served as advisor to the Harding clique and as Means's personal attorney, died suddenly in Savannah, GA; John King, a politician and lobbyist indicted with Daugherty in the Alien Property scandal, died suddenly in New York; C. F. Hateley, an agent of the Justice Department who was close to Daugherty, died suddenly at the Burlington Hotel in Washington.

In October 1923, Means was indicted for graft and corruption. The conspirators devised a scheme requiring Means to plead guilty and admit that he was solely responsible for the acts charged in the indictment. He would not talk to the prosecutors or to the press, and in return it would be arranged that he receive a large monetary fine but escape a term in jail. At the last moment, and for reasons Means has never made entirely clear, he changed his mind and testified against the conspirators in the Senate hearings. Means entered a guilty plea and was sentenced to three years imprisonment in the Atlanta Penitentiary. He served all three years and was released on 19 July 1928. Unlike many of the conspirators, Means at least lived to tell his version of the story. It would seem that there is a plausible case for believing that Warren Harding either died at the vengeful hands of his own wife or was murdered on her behalf by other members of the criminal conspiracy that seemed to play such a defining role in his presidency.

1924 – THE ZINOVIEV LETTER This is certainly one of the most famous and obvious examples of a conspiracy designed to plant disinformation by the intelligence services on behalf of a political ideal or party. The Zinoviev letter, which was leaked to the *Daily Mail* and published virtually on the eve of the 1924 General Election, is believed by a number of historians to have played a significant part in the fall of the first Labour government of Ramsay MacDonald. Purported to have been written by Grigori Zinoviev, president of the Soviet Union's Comintern, the international Communist organisation, it called on British Communists to mobilise 'sympathetic forces' in the Labour Party. However, it is now believed that the MI6 officer Stewart Menzies, a future head of MI6, the Secret Intelligence Service, whose allegiances 'lay firmly in the Conservative camp', later admitted to sending a copy of the Zinoviev letter to the *Daily Mail*. The letter was almost certainly forged and perhaps not surprisingly MI6 apparently destroyed documents relating to the letter and one of the great political scandals of the twentieth century, some years later. A note to the Foreign Office dated April 1952 says there is 'no harm whatsoever [that] some papers should be registered and some destroyed'. The covering note is signed by the chief of MI6, who at the time just happened to be Major-General Sir Stewart Menzies. This has been interpreted as 'house clearing' prior to his retirement later in the year. A further document also released discloses that a Foreign Office official had noted later: 'Perhaps some letters and papers have been destroyed in the past which ought to be preserved under the Public Records Act.'

The conspiracy appeared to include anti-Communist Russian émigrés; members of MI5, the internal Security Service, including Joseph Ball, who in 1927 went to work for the Conservative Central Office where he pioneered the idea of spin-doctoring; members of MI6, the Secret Intelligence Service, including Stewart Menzies and Desmond Morton, later to become Churchill's 'private intelligence service' in the 1930s; senior members of the opposition Conservative Party and perhaps certain leading members of the news media. The letter seems to have been widely circulated even to senior military officers, in order to inflict the maximum damage on the Labour government. The British security and intelligence community at the time consisted of a 'very, very incestuous circle, an elite network' who went to school together, joined the same clubs and broadly supported the same political party.

The letter was probably first sent to MI6 from one of its agents in the Latvian capital of Riga and is believed to have been forged by a Lt. Ivan Dmitrevich Pokrovsky as a result of a conspiracy orchestrated by White Russians who had good contacts in London. A report said there was no hard evidence that MI6 agents in Riga were directly responsible, though of course they had close contacts with White Russians. It seems that MI6 may have deliberately deceived the Foreign Office by asserting that it did know the source of the letter, a deception it used to claim the Zinoviev letter was genuine. As part of the background to the Zinoviev letter it is interesting to note that on 8 August 1924 Ramsay MacDonald, the British Prime Minister and the leader of the Labour Party, had signed a General and Commercial Treaty with the Soviet Union. This decision was attacked by leaders of the Conservative Party and became a major political issue in the country.

In October 1924 MI5 claimed to have intercepted a letter written by Gregory Zinoviev, chairman of the Comintern, to Christian Rakovsky, a member of the Communist Party in the Soviet Union. In the letter Zinoviev urged British Communists to promote revolution through acts of sedition. Vernon Kell, head of MI5, and Sir Basil Thomson, head of Special Branch, were both convinced that the letter was genuine. Vernon Kell showed the letter to Prime Minister Ramsay MacDonald and, as the country was in the midst of the 1924 General Election campaign, MacDonald told MI5 to keep the letter a secret. Soon afterwards Stewart Menzies of MI6 apparently leaked news of the letter to *The Times* and the *Daily Mail*. On 25 October 1924, four days before the election, the *Daily Mail* splashed the following headlines across its front page: CIVIL WAR PLOT BY SOCIALISTS' MASTERS: MOSCOW ORDERS TO OUR REDS; GREAT PLOT DISCLOSED. The Labour Party lost the election, and though it is unlikely that the letter was the principle reason, it still did considerable damage to their chances of re-election and to the party's reputation. The new Conservative government refused to submit the Anglo–Russian treaties to the House of Commons for ratification. On 15 December 1924 a government minister, Austin Chamberlain, told Parliament that MI5 had verified that the Zinoviev letter was genuine. As an early example of disinformation, political spin and intelligence agency interference with the democratic process, the use by MI6, MI5 and the Conservative Party of a letter forged by anti-Bolshevic Russians to undermine the electoral chances of a British Labour government in 1924 casts an interesting light on the constant denials that something very similar occurred some fifty years later – when many firmly believe that a conspiracy of MI5, MI6 and right-wing or Conservative politicians plotted to bring down the 1974 Labour government of Harold Wilson.

1932 – LINDBERGH CONSPIRACY Charles Lindbergh finally touched down at Paris Le Bourget Airport on 21 May 1927 after the first solo flight across the Atlantic Ocean. It had taken him 27 hours in his Ryan NYP monoplane, the *Spirit of St Louis*, to complete the 3,600-mile trip from Roosevelt Field in Long Island. The reportedly shy Midwesterner was now richer by $25,000 in prize money and had a place in the history books. Lindbergh quickly became the All American Hero, the darling of the chattering classes, and was idolised by a generation of aircraft-crazy youngsters. However, some years later events were to cast an unwelcome shadow over Lindbergh and ultimately his reputation. The kidnapping and murder of the Lindbergh baby was described by the more lurid elements of the American press as the 'Crime of the Century' at the time, but what has essentially changed since the execution in 1936 of the man accused of murdering Charles A. Lindbergh, Jr, is the certainty that Bruno Richard Hauptmann was indeed guilty as charged, for by the end of his trial and his guilty verdict only his wife, his defence attorney, the Governor of the State of New Jersey and a few others still doubted that he killed the 'Eaglet'.

The Lindberghs' son Charles was twenty months old when on a chill, damp weekend in March 1932 they planned to travel that Sunday to the home of Mrs Lindbergh's parents in the elegant suburb of Englewood, NJ, some fifty miles away, accompanied by the child's nurse, Betty Gow, and a housekeeper couple. Young Charles developed a cold and they decided to delay their visit for another day or two. Except for the five adults and the grandparents, it is presumed that no one else would have known that the Lindberghs would still be at home that night, instead of visiting the in-laws. Yet sometime between 8 and 10 p.m. on the evening of Tuesday 1 March, the child was taken from his second-floor nursery by a kidnapper who left no fingerprints but did leave a note demanding $50,000 in ransom, a small fortune at the time. As soon as he discovered that the baby was gone, Lindbergh first searched the grounds and then called the state police. The township of East Amwell, where the Lindbergh house was located, had no local police force of its own. The press descended on the scene in their droves, trampling what might have been left of a kidnapper's footprints in the mud, made worse by a light fall of snow and severely hindering the investigation launched by the police. In addition to the ransom note, the police found a discarded homemade ladder and a chisel near the house.

In the days and nights that followed, a desperate Lindbergh sought help from numerous negotiators who claimed to be go-betweens with the kidnapper. Thousands of letters poured into the estate, some expressing sympathy, some with ransom demands or death threats and many with psychic predictions. The newspapers initially speculated that gangsters had taken the child – who else would have the gall to snatch the son of the Lone Eagle? they argued. Al Capone, the most notorious of them all, was so appalled at the thought that he apparently offered a $10,000 reward for information that would lead to the recovery of the child unharmed and also that, if he were released from his Chicago jail cell, he and his 'henchmen' would track down the kidnappers for the Lindberghs. A national debate ensued on whether or not to free Capone for the task. Speculation ended when the man who put Capone behind bars, Internal Revenue Service agent Elmer Irey, convinced Lindbergh that, if released, Capone would immediately flee the country.

One of many would-be go-betweens was Dr John (Jafsie) Condon, a retired teacher who claimed to be in contact with the kidnapper. One night at a cemetery in the Bronx, accompanied by Lindbergh, Jafsie paid the ransom in gold certificates whose numbers had been recorded. The kidnapper gave Condon a note saying the child was on a boat off the Massachusetts coast. Lindbergh spent days flying over the area to no avail. By that time, however, Charles, Jr had already been killed and his body dumped in the leaves off the Hopewell–Princeton road, a few miles from the Lindberghs' home. On 12 May 1932 a truck driver who had entered the woods to relieve himself discovered the remains. When found the body was face downwards, covered with leaves and infested with insects. It was little more than a skeleton, the outline of a form in a dark heap of rotting vegetation. The left leg was missing from the knee down, as were the left hand and right arm. Most of its organs were gone, scavenged by the local animal life in the wooded area. It had decomposed so completely that it was not possible at first to determine whether it was a boy or a girl. The cause of death was a massive fracture of the skull and the body had been left to the elements for two and a half months. Less than 24 hours later and only an hour after it had been positively identified as Charles A. Lindbergh, Jr, by the child's nurse and father, the remains were cremated and an agonising 73 days of waiting had come to an end.

It took more than two years of following the trail of passed ransom bills to track down the man accused of the murder, a German-born Bronx carpenter, Bruno Richard Hauptmann. When he was arrested, Hauptmann had over $14,000 worth of the ransom cash hidden in his garage. It was later discovered that a board cut from his attic floor was used in the ladder found near the Lindberghs' house. Dr Condon eventually identified Hauptmann as the man to whom he paid the ransom. Within hours of his arrest, press and police were clamouring for the death penalty for Hauptmann. From what was written in the newspapers and broadcast on the radio, few were prepared to doubt his guilt: Hauptmann was an illegal German immigrant with a past criminal record, and Lindbergh claimed that on the night in the cemetery he heard a voice with a German accent. Hauptmann insisted the money was left to him by one Isidor Fisch, a fur dealer he knew who had fled to Germany and died there, a story he could not prove. Hauptmann's wife, Anna, protested that on the night of the kidnapping she had been home with Hauptmann in the Bronx, but she was not believed. Hauptmann was extradited to New Jersey where in the century-old Hunterdon County courthouse in the little borough of Flemington on 2 January 1935 he was to face charges of kidnapping and murder.

There is no question that some of the principals who were most important to the prosecution in that trial, including the good doctor, Condon, somehow metamorphosed into unattractive personalities, according to certain journalists and writers. While not perfect human beings by any means, they seemed to change into persecutors or self-promoters, or worse. Even Lindbergh himself and, to a lesser extent, Anne Morrow Lindbergh and her aristocratic family helped change perceptions and indeed public opinion about Hauptmann's guilt. Despite some evidence to suggest Hauptmann's involvement, to many conspiracy theorists it appears that he was railroaded. The baby son of a national hero had been kidnapped and cruelly murdered:, someone had to pay the price and a working-class German immigrant fitted the bill nicely. Some theorists have argued that what evidence did exist was simply planted after the event to ensure Hauptmann's conviction, which duly occurred, followed by his execution in 1936.

The sensitive, publicity-shy Lindbergh, after sitting in the Flemington courtroom every day of the six-week trial, took his wife and new infant son to England, fleeing from the intense public scrutiny. While at first this seemed like an exile not of their own doing, the Lindberghs quickly became regarded as 'foreign', part of European society. Indeed by 1938, Lindbergh had become a well-known admirer of the German Luftwaffe, was awarded a medal by Hermann Göring and considered to be a dupe of the Nazi propaganda effort to exaggerate the strength of German air power. Lindbergh wrote a much-publicised letter to Ambassador Joseph Kennedy, another noted appeaser, suggesting that the rest of Europe had no defence against the mighty and admirable Germans. Later, after the war had begun, Lindbergh became an important voice for 'America First', the isolationist movement that persisted until the attack on Pearl Harbor.

After the war, Lindbergh slowly redeemed himself, but for younger generations he was no longer the hero of solo flight but a middle-aged conservative tainted with fascism. Claims of Hauptmann's innocence were sustained by the lifelong dedication and remarkable persistence of Anna Hauptmann, who died in 1994, at the age of 95. For sixty years, she maintained her husband's innocence. On the face of it, this certainly appears to be a simple open-and-shut criminal case; however, a dedicated group of theorists maintain that there was a police conspiracy to find and convict a suitable guilty party for the crime. They hint darkly of right-wing involvements, particularly as the accused claimed that the money had been left by someone apparently of Jewish origin who had then fled the country, while others suggest that the reason for framing Hauptmann was to cover up the real source of the crime and perhaps one much closer to home.

1933 – REICHSTAG FIRE CONSPIRACY In the early 1930s, right-wing elements throughout Europe were whipping up a fear of the Bolshevik 'Red' menace and nowhere was this more marked than in Germany where the Nazis were competing with the Communists for the vital support of the working classes. Germany was plagued by unemployment and labour unrest, and its currency had become nearly worthless only a few years earlier. In 1933, through a series of conspiracies involving major business and banking interests and, of course, political intrigue, Adolf Hitler became the chancellor of a bankrupt, chaotic and divided Germany on the verge of civil war.

Hitler convinced German President Hindenburg to hold new elections on 5 March of that year, and Hitler certainly believed the Nazi Party could gain control of the legislature. The Nazis controlled the courts and had the backing of much of the manufacturing industry that believed Hitler would be 'good for business'. They blanketed the nation with pro-Nazi propaganda from all media outlets. Then, on 27 February, shortly before the elections, the German Parliament building, the Reichstag, was set ablaze by an arsonist, the blame quickly falling on a 24-year-old Dutch Communist named Marianus van der Lubbe. 'This is a God-given signal! If this fire, as I believe, turns out to be the handiwork of Communists then there is nothing that shall stop us now crushing out this murder pest with an iron fist.' Adolf Hitler, fascist Chancellor of Germany, made this dramatic declaration in the hall of the burning Reichstag building.

The fire broke out at 9.45 p.m. in the Assembly Hall of the Reichstag. It had been laid in five different places and there is no doubt that incendiary bombs had been used. A cordon had been flung round the building and no one was allowed to pass it. After about twenty minutes the famous black motorcar of Adolf Hitler arrived, followed by another car containing his personal bodyguard. Göring, his right-hand man, who at the time was effectively the Minister of the Interior and responsible for all police affairs, said, 'This is undoubtedly the work of Communists, Herr Chancellor,' adding, 'A number of Communist deputies were present here in the Reichstag twenty minutes before the fire broke out. We have succeeded in arresting one of the incendiaries.'

The Nazis vowed to prove the fire was part of a vast Communist plot to take over Germany. Their propaganda emphasised that only they could control the threat to the nation. Despite this effort, they won only 40 per cent of the legislature. Hitler faced increasingly vocal concern from within his own party, and the opposition party controlling the legislature, about his measures. His tactic was to get an enabling act passed, giving him essentially dictatorial powers and rendering the legislature irrelevant. Hitler's solution was to eliminate the Communist party and its 100 deputies, which would give his Nazis a majority in the remaining Parliament. By ensuring that van der Lubbe succeeded in destroying the Reichstag, he could pronounce the fire a Communist conspiracy. On 23 March the newly elected Reichstag met in the Kroll Opera House in Berlin to consider passing Hitler's Enabling Act. It was officially called the 'Law for Removing the Distress of the People and the Reich'. If passed, it would in effect vote democracy out of existence in Germany and establish the legal dictatorship of Adolf Hitler. By the next morning he had secured the signature of the ageing President, von Hindenburg, on legislation that changed Germany from a democracy to a tyranny. The 100 Communist deputies were arrested, civil rights were abrogated, and the country embraced Hitler as its leader. The public was assured that the sweeping new emergency powers would never be used unjustly against its own citizens. In a speech before the deciding vote, Hitler told the lawmakers, 'The government will make use of these powers only insofar as they are essential for carrying out vitally necessary measures . . . The number of cases in which an internal necessity exists for having recourse to such a law is in itself a limited one.' Hitler pledged to end the chronic unemployment facing his country, and to promote peace, not war, with Germany's enemies: Great Britain, France and the Soviet Union. The death sentence was expanded to cover a number of crimes. As a remedy for the supposed 'crisis' facing Germany, Hitler proposed a programme of *Gleichschaltung* (co-ordination) through which the central government would absorb the power and political functions of the German states. The vote was taken, and the Reichstag, succumbing to the Nazis' conspiratorial manoeuvres, passed the Enabling Act, which made the central government responsible for all law enforcement and conferred exclusive legislative powers on Hitler's cabinet for four years. The Nazis could now control the German political process and declare war at any time, against any foe, without the legislature.

This one act provided the legal basis for the transformation of Hitler from chancellor to dictator. It did not take long to prove how empty and disingenuous were Hitler's promises that 'the government will make use of these powers only insofar as they are essential for carrying out vitally necessary measures.' Far from being aghast at the government's new powers, much of the German public would support Hitler and the Nazis through to 1945, by which time Germany would be reduced to rubble.

After being tortured by the Gestapo, van der Lubbe confessed to starting the Reichstag fire. However, he denied that he was part of a Communist conspiracy. Hermann Göring refused to believe him and had ordered the arrest of several leaders of the German Communist Party (KPD). As well as Marinus van der Lubbe, the German police had therefore charged four Communists with setting fire to the Reichstag. These included Ernst Torgler, the chairman of the KPD, and Georgi Dimitrov of the Soviet Comintern. Marinus van der Lubbe was found guilty of the Reichstag fire and was executed on 10 January 1934. Adolf Hitler was furious when the rest of the defendants were acquitted, and he decided that in future all treason cases were to be removed from the jurisdiction of the Supreme Court and given to a new People's Court, where prisoners would be judged by members of the National Socialist German Worker's Party (NSDAP).

After the war, evidence led historians to conclude that the Reichstag fire had been a Nazi conspiracy to successfully gain political power. Indeed, following close on the heels of the Reichstag fire came the 'Night of the Long Knives' of 30 June 1934, an assassination blitzkrieg in which Hitler wiped out his old friend Ernst Röhm and the top leadership of the Brownshirts or SA (*Sturmabteilung*). Röhm and his stormtroopers had become troublesome competitors and had to be eliminated, but a plausible pretext for the purge was needed. A coup 'plot' by Röhm was fabricated, which served the additional purpose of providing further justification for legalised government terror. Hitler's one-paragraph law read: 'The measures taken on 30 June and 1 and 2 July to strike down the treasonous attacks are justifiable acts of self-defence by the state.' Many more equally fraudulent 'justifiable acts of self-defence' would follow. The Nazis became past masters at making the conspiracy a highly effective part of their political system.

1934 – KILLING OF KIROV AND THE GREAT TERROR Stalin, who had closely studied Hitler's purge of Röhm and his stormtroopers, devised his own 'Night of the Long Knives' but with an added twist. His one-time friend and trusted aide Sergei Kirov had become a potential rival for Communist Party leadership and had to be eliminated. Stalin, the ultimate 'conspirator from above' arranged for Kirov's assassination and ensured that the murder would be blamed on the Zinoviev faction. Under Stalin's direction, and following the assassination, the floodgates of official adulation for Kirov were opened wide. He was declared the 'Soviet people's favourite' and 'our Kirov'. The instant Kirov cult was blended seamlessly into the Stalin cult, which therefore took on added lustre from the matyr's death. Kirov became 'Comrade Stalin's best comrade-in-arms and friend'. Stalin was shown in the honour guard with Kirov in old photos and as the first mourner at the Red Square funeral.

The conspiracy to murder Kirov in December 1934 had, however, served a design much larger than the mere elimination of a single competitor. For Stalin, the prime purpose of Kirov's murder was to make possible an official finding that Soviet Russia was beset by a Trotskyist conspiracy that had done away with Kirov as part of a larger plan of terrorist action against the regime. At least a month before the murder of Kirov, Stalin had already arranged for the issue of a statute empowering the newly created Special Board, headed by Stalin, to pass administrative sentence on 'persons deemed socially dangerous'. No definition of 'socially dangerous' was given, allowing for the widest possible 'discretion' in the exercise of this formidable new power.

Born Sergei Kostrikov in 1886, Kirov became a journalist and revolutionary and changed his name in 1912. He was no stranger to the pre-1917 prison camps and loyal to the people's cause. Kirov's eventual murder on 1 December 1934 by an NKVD assassin, Leonid Nikolaev, set off a chain of events that culminated in a drastic purge, the Great Terror, which ultimately would claim as many as 10 million victims. Stalin carried out his Great Terror with a passion. By 1939, 98 of the 139 central committee members had been executed and roughly 1,100 of the 1,966 17th Congress delegation were in prison. Millions more died in the Gulags or at the hands of Stalin's secret police force. Stalin emerged as a demigod with absolute power and ability.

Kirov had been a full member of the ruling Politburo, leader of the Leningrad Party apparatus and an influential member of the ruling elite. His concern for the welfare of the workers in Leningrad and his skill as an orator had earned him considerable popularity. Some party members had even approached him secretly with the proposal that he take over as general secretary. Kirov was one of the original leaders of the Bolshevik Revolution, and while Kirov did disagree with some of Stalin's practices, he really did not pose a threat to Stalin's power. Stalin had, however, begun to doubt the loyalty of members of the Leningrad apparatus. In need of a pretext for launching a broad purge, Stalin evidently decided that murdering Kirov would be expedient. Stalin then used the murder as an excuse for introducing draconian laws against political crime and for conducting a witch-hunt for alleged conspirators against Kirov. Over the next four and a half years, millions of innocent party members and others were arrested, many of them for complicity in the vast plot that supposedly lay behind the killing of Kirov. From the Soviet point of view, his murder was probably the crime of the century because it paved the way for the Great Terror. Stalin never visited Leningrad again, probably through fear of assassination, and indeed directed one of his most vicious post-war purges against the city, often considered Russia's historic window to the West.

Stalin, a conspirator by nature and intent, created conspiracies to defeat non-existent plots, and killed because it fitted into a bigger plan or simply because it was expedient to do so. He was responsible for more deaths than probably any other dictator, including that blood-soaked little corporal in Germany, and ran a regime that survived on terror. Yet in the post-Communist, democratic Russia of today there have been no trials of the millions of those who served in the KGB, ran the Gulag slave labour camps or tortured prisoners to death in the cellars of the Lubyanka. Perhaps the commitment to freedom is still too shallow to risk facing up to the truth about seventy years of Soviet dictatorship, or perhaps, as some conspiracy theorists suggest, nothing has really changed apart from the window dressing.

1937 – *HINDENBURG* DISASTER In one of the most memorable radio broadcasts, Herb Morrison, employed by a Chicago radio station, was covering the arrival of the giant German airship, the *Hindenburg*, at the Lakehurst air base in New Jersey. At 4 p.m. on the afternoon of 6 May 1937 and some ten hours behind schedule, the immense silver cylinder, some 830 feet long, glided towards the mooring tower. A thunderstorm had rumbled around Lakehurst all day and, as the *Hindenburg* made its final approach, a gust of wind swung the ship sharply to the left. At first there appeared to be no other problems, but then Herb Morrison's voice changed key and in rising panic he broadcast, 'It's bursting into flames and falling on the mooring mast.' Crying as he spoke, he managed to get out his immortal commentary, 'This is terrible! This is one of the worst catastrophes in the world. Oh, the humanity and all the passengers! I told you, it's a mass of smoking wreckage. Honest, I can hardly breathe. I'm going to have to stop for a moment because I've lost my voice. This is the worst thing I've ever witnessed.' In just over 30 seconds fire had destroyed the largest lighter-than-air aircraft the world had ever seen and 35 of the 97 passengers and crew on board were dead or dying. One moment the *Hindenburg* was floating elegantly in the sky and the next it had fallen in flames, nose down to the ground. The most extraordinary aspect of the whole disaster was that there were as many as 62 survivors from a burning hell created by 7 million cubic feet of incandescent hydrogen.

Many theorists are still prepared to argue that the disaster was caused by an anti-Nazi conspiracy that planted something like a termite bomb in the rigging of the giant airship and timed to destroy the *Hindenburg* for maximum embarrassment to Hitler. There was indeed talk of sabotage at the time, and since then many theories and different conspiracy ideas have been suggested. This was certainly to be expected, particularly when it involved an incident of this magnitude. Hitler, for once, did not choose to blame it on a conspiracy, not even involving the Jews or, for that matter, his arch-enemies, the Communists. He apparently believed it to be an act of God. The first theory about the cause of the disaster was that the number two hydrogen tank exploded. The majority of the investigators at the time seemed to believe that there must have been a leak, and that static electricity caused a spark which may have ignited the hydrogen, thus causing an explosion. A joint US–German investigation took place shortly afterwards in order to confirm it, and although the findings were unsure, the newspapers certainly reported hydrogen to be the cause. However, there was never any real evidence to support this theory. The reason for this is that both Germany and the US wanted to forget the whole incident, as tension between the United States and Germany was at an all-time high. Hydrogen was therefore in the frame and it was highly convenient for it to be blamed for the deaths of 35 people.

A NASA scientist at Cape Caneveral believes that he has finally discovered the real cause and has suggested that neither the hydrogen in the hull nor a bomb caused the disaster. The blame lies firmly with a special fabric used for the outer skin that, when ignited, burns fiercely. Suspicions about the Zeppelin's fabric covering were raised when he learned that a cellulose nitrate or gunpowder doped with powdered aluminum might have been used on the Hindenburg. He was able to obtain a sixty-year-old piece of the fabric used to test his hypothesis. Furthermore, a hydrogen flame is almost invisible in daylight: it burns with a light-blue flame. Many eyewitness accounts, as well as actual photographs, show that the flames were red and orange, which strongly supports the theory that hydrogen was not the source of the flames. With the theory being turned into fact, the plaque in the Kennedy Space Center was changed to give a far more accurate portrayal of the history of the *Hindenburg*. Scientists now increasingly agree that the outer covering was ignited by static electricity. It would appear that the Germans had come to roughly the same conclusion at the time, since electrical engineer Otto Beyersdorff, on 28 June 1937, wrote, 'The actual cause of the fire was the extreme easy flammability of the covering material brought about by discharges of an electrostatic nature.' Just to prove the point, a helium or non-combustible gas-filled airship went up in flames in California in 1935. Considerable changes were made to the outer skin coatings once German engineers were sure of the real causes. Production was halted and immediate modifications were made in a subsequent airship plan, which also included the addition of a fire retardant. The story was indeed covered up, but more out of embarrassment at the cause of such a disaster rather than because of a bomb plot or political conspiracy.

1941 – RIGHT-WING CONSPIRACY IN BRITAIN Was there really substantial right-wing support for a deal with Nazi Germany? Was the British government seriously concerned about a Nazi fifth column, particularly amongst the wealthy, influential landowners, major industrialists, politicians, the aristocracy and even certain members of the royal family? Was there a plot to remove George VI and replace him with a compliant Duke of Windsor? The answer to that is a very definite 'yes', it seems. A major conspiracy of silence has been continued by every British government since WW2 about the level of potential support there was not just for the appeasement of Hitler, but also for a full blown anti-Communist pact with Germany.

Later still there were those at the highest levels of British life who were potential or actual traitors, and would have been quislings in the event of a successful German invasion. Others conspired to undermine Churchill's authority and even to force him out of office.

The flight to Britain in 1941 of the Deputy Leader of Germany, Rudolf Hess, was an event of such magnitude that it simply beggars understanding even in 2003. The Deputy Leader, Hitler's confidant, flies to Britain in the middle of the War, and very little propaganda of any value is made out of it. Surely you would have expected the capture of such a senior enemy leader to have resulted in a huge publicity campaign of gloating: greater use made of suggestions that he may have actually changed sides or bolted from a soon-to-be defeated Germany; leaflets pointing out the defection of one of the Nazi hierarchy dropped over German towns; the parading of him in front of the film cameras for the benefit of the world; take him to the United States, the list is simply endless. But what actually happened, the theorists ask. It is all hushed up as soon as possible and Hess is hidden away in a prison hospital and nobody really talks about the fact that Nazi Germany's second most important leader is a prisoner of the British. Who had he come to see in Britain? What group of obviously influential people could be so important as to cause Hess to fly to Britain and risk imprisonment or even death? Or was it part of an enormous intelligence conspiracy where MI6 and MI5 had so successfully penetrated the right-wing groups in Britain that they were able to comprehensively trick the Germans into believing that Britain was ripe for defeat and that one big gesture, such as the arrival of the Deputy Führer, would tip the balance? Churchill would be out and a new, more amenable, British government would sue for peace and allow a triumphant Germany to concentrate on destroying Communist Russia. Or indeed was it designed to smoke out Britain's treacherous right wing with the thought that they were about to win and Hess was arriving to share their final triumph? Some of these conspiracies may well have more than a grain of truth in them, but just how close Britain actually was to some form of right-wing coup will perhaps never be known.

MI5 had a massive number of files on Britain's fascists, from the highly sensitive, which remain deeply buried, to those that openly confirmed their belief that Diana Mosley, the wife of the British Blackshirt leader, was probably as dangerous to security as Sir Oswald Mosley himself. It concluded that she was 'the principal channel of communication' between Mosley and Hitler before war broke out and helped get secret funds from Germany. 'Mosley herself has admitted that she had frequent interviews with the Führer. We also know that she acted as a go-between in negotiations between Mosley and the Germans.' The couple were definitely seen by the British government as potential allies of Hitler. The memo, written in June 1940, quotes an extract from a report circulated to MI5 by the deputy director of military intelligence at the then war office. It says: 'Diana Mosley, wife of Sir Oswald Mosley, is reported on the best authority – that of her family and intimate circle – to be a public danger at the present time. [She] is said to be far cleverer and more dangerous than her husband, and will stick at nothing to achieve her ambitions; she is wildly ambitious.' MI5's mention of her family is a reference to the role of Lady Mosley's sister, the author Nancy Mitford, in urging that Diana should be interned as a public danger. Sir Oswald, who died in 1980, persistently denied sharing Hitler's anti-Semitism. But on 15 March 1940, an intelligence informant, possibly from Scotland Yard special branch, sent MI5 a report on a private meeting addressed by the fascist leader in southwest London. The report stated: 'The significant feature was his expressed determination to defeat "the enemy" [the Jew] if not by the ballot box then by "other and more drastic means" – a sentiment cheered to the echo. He went on to say that we should only think and speak from day to day – and that if we had ideas, which we no doubt all had, about the ultimate future, it did not do to tell our enemies about the more unpleasant things which were liable to happen to them.' The informant went on, 'Implicit in this, and a lot more, was the suggestion of armed revolution and pogroms.' Another informant listed only as M/R reported, 'I feel he [Mosley] is relying on calling up British Union members to provide eventually an armed force which will effect revolution.'

Among the many conspiracy theories relating to the right-wing in Britain is the firm belief that Edward VIII, later the Duke of Windsor, and Mrs Wallis Simpson were more than just a pair of star-crossed lovers and were in fact the tip of a very unpleasant iceberg. That both were probably dyed-in-the-wool fascists seems likely, and it was only out of a misplaced deference to the royal family and Mrs Simpson's American background that prevented both of them from joining Hess behind bars for the duration. It would also seem likely that Edward's abdication was more of a political anti-fascist coup by Prime Minister Stanley Baldwin than an affair of the heart. But that made a more than useful smoke screen at the time. Wallis Simpson was probably a fascist sympathiser long before she met Edward, and indeed her connections were impressive and very personal. Joachim von Ribbentrop, later the Nazis' Foreign Minister, had been Wallis Simpson's lover when he was ambassador to Britain in 1936 and had sent the then Mrs Simpson seventeen carnations supposedly representing the number of times they had slept together. As an addition to the theory that there was indeed a political conspiracy to encourage Edward VIII's abdication, information that only became available in 2003 confirms that Mrs Simpson had taken another lover before Edward had finally made up his mind about his fateful decision to quit the throne. The British Security Service, MI5, were well aware of the 'who' and the 'where', but were constrained from informing Edward. It was considered more important for the political health of the nation to rid the country of a weak and probably disloyal monarch than to inform him of his future wife's love affairs.

Conspiracy theorists have of course long had considerable interest in the fate of Rudolf Hess, Prisoner No. 7. Did Hess die in Spandau Prison in 1987 as a victim of murder, or did he commit suicide or, most interestingly, was he Rudolph Hess at all? The official record holds that Hess, his importance in the Nazi hierarchy diminished by 1941, took off from Augsburg, bound for Scotland, in an abortive attempt to make peace between Germany and Britain. Running low on fuel, he baled out of his Messerschmitt 110D about twelve miles short of his destination, in the estate of the Duke of Hamilton at Dungavel. The then *Glasgow Herald* had a role to play in the affair at this stage. Detectives from Renfrewshire CID asked the paper for photographs of Hess to check his identity. On Wednesday 14 May the paper told its readers, 'Biographical records from the files of the *Glasgow Herald* assisted detectives to identify Hess.' Hess, the official historical record holds, had been under the delusion that the Duke and other prominent members of the British establishment would be amenable to discussing peace terms. The proposals were never taken seriously. After being interrogated at Maryhill barracks in Glasgow, Buchanan Castle, near Drymen, the Tower of London and Mytchett Place, near Aldershot, he spent the rest of the war at Maindiff Court Hospital near Abergavenny. He was later sentenced to life imprisonment at Nuremberg for war crimes. Inconsistencies in this official version helped prompt the conspiracy theories. Central to all of these is that the Hess sentenced at Nuremberg was not the real one, and that

Prisoner No. 7 at Spandau was a double. It is also claimed that he was murdered, and one particular theory suggests that the Hess mission was the final stage in a conspiracy for peace that had the support of royalty, prominent members of the aristocracy and, indeed, renegade elements of MI6. It appears to have failed because of interference from the Special Operations Executive and Winston Churchill, the Prime Minister. This latter view holds that there is evidence that Hess may have been spirited away from Maindiff Hospital and a double substituted. By 1987, it looked likely that the 93-year-old prisoner would soon be released. Because of fears that details of the 1941 right-wing conspiracy for peace might still come to light (albeit a perverted and dangerous sort of peace), Hess was therefore murdered according to a number of commentators, not least his own son Wolf Rüdiger Hess in a document presented in 1992 and printed in the *Journal of Historical Review*.

1941 – PEARL HARBOR: A CONSPIRACY OF NECESSITY Was Pearl Harbor part of a great conspiracy to drag the USA into WW2, in other words, a more violent version of the Zimmerman telegram of 1917? Did Roosevelt coolly sacrifice much of the Pacific fleet for a very important political victory? Or did America's greatest ally, Winston Churchill, deliberately withhold vital intelligence intercepts in order to bring the USA into the war, as an alternative theory would have us believe? All these have appeared in one conspiracy theory or other, and indeed many seem to hold some truth even after reasonably close examination. The real stumbling block is that all politicians are very careful about avoiding obviously dangerous policies; bravery, it must be remembered, has never been high on the list of a politician's known virtues. Politicians are also very aware of their long-term reputation, the more so once they have reached a position of some importance as a statesman, such as the Prime Minister of Great Britain or the President of the USA. The likelihood that a leak might have occurred in any conspiracy by Britain to trap the USA into war by allowing the Japanese to launch a surprise attack would have been more than enough to prevent its implementation: it simply would not have been possible to guarantee the level of secrecy needed to make the plan work. The risks that someone in British or Australian Signals Intelligence might have talked would have been far too great. This also applies to Roosevelt: the public response to such actions had they been discovered even a year or so later would have been enough to cause a political earthquake in Washington with incalculable long-term effects on America's continuing involvement in the war and the post-war future of Europe. Both leaders, and perhaps Churchill in particular, were very conscious of their place in history, and neither would have risked being damned for eternity as traitors who let a nation's young men be slaughtered like sitting ducks, deliberately and for political reasons, however historically important they may later become.

The bare facts of the Japanese attack around which these conspiracy theories swirl are bleak enough. Aircraft from Japan's imperial navy attacked the unprepared US naval base and other Hawaiian military facilities at Pearl Harbor, Hawaii, on the early morning of Sunday 7 December 1941. For 2 hours and 20 minutes the Japanese planes executed well-planned and well-rehearsed strikes against the ships of the Pacific fleet. By the time the attack had ended, 2,403 Americans had been killed, 1,178 wounded and 640 never accounted for; 188 military aircraft were destroyed, and 18 ships, including 8 battleships, 3 light cruisers, 3 destroyers and 4 miscellaneous ships, had been sunk. By contrast, the Japanese casualties were minimal, with only 29 aircraft and 5 midget submarines lost.

One of the biggest proponents of a Roosevelt conspiracy has claimed that the US Congress has implied that there was indeed intelligence of an impending attack by the Japanese that either went unheeded or unheard in its official investigation, the Report of the Joint Committee on the Investigation of the Pearl Harbor Attack, dated 16 July 1946, stating, 'The disaster of Pearl Harbor was the failure, with attendant increase in personnel and maritime losses, of the army and navy [to] institute measures designed to detect an approaching hostile force . . . Specifically, the Hawaiian commands failed . . . to appreciate the significance of intelligence and other information available to them.'

The conspiracy theories surrounding the attack can reasonably be summarised as follows: President Roosevelt wanted to enter the war in Europe, especially after the fall of France in June 1940. After meeting Roosevelt at the Atlantic Conference in August 1941, British Prime Minister Winston Churchill noted the 'astonishing depth of Roosevelt's intense desire for war'. Regardless of how Roosevelt felt, however, the President knew he couldn't enter the war without the overwhelming support of the American people and Congress. It's been said that, since Roosevelt realised that he couldn't change the country's collective mind directly, he resorted to deception. Some theorists believe that Roosevelt systematically and deliberately goaded the Japanese into attacking the USA. They suggest that, although his real intention was to enter the European theatre and to win the war against Hitler, Roosevelt expected, if Japan attacked and the US was forced to retaliate, the German dictator to abide by the Tripartite Pact and declare war on America. They go on to suggest that Roosevelt further expected Hitler's decision to be facilitated by a display of the USA's apparent vulnerability. Thus, even though Roosevelt was well aware of the impending attack on Pearl Harbor, he did nothing to prevent it happening even though suspicion has been expressed that he ensured that its success would still be limited by keeping the vital carriers well away from danger. Reportedly, word of the attack came a full ten hours before it took place, when the USA decoded a Japanese message which was delayed before being sent out to, and received by, all areas of the Pacific except Pearl, where the receiver was allegedly 'not working'. Roosevelt had ordered the Pacific fleet to relocate from the West Coast to Hawaii in the summer of 1940, and on 7 October 1940 US Navy Admiral McCollum wrote an eight-point memo for Roosevelt on how to force Japan into war with the USA, which included an American oil embargo against Japan. Each and every one of the steps enumerated was eventually carried out. On 18 October 1940 Roosevelt's Secretary of the Interior, Harold Ickes, noted in his diary, 'For a long time I have believed that our best entrance into the war would be by way of Japan.' On 14 September 1941 Washington allegedly deciphered an encoded message sent from Tokyo's Naval Intelligence headquarters to Japan's consul-general in Honolulu, requesting a grid of exact locations of US navy ships in the harbour. On 15 November, General George Marshall, who was then the Army's Chief of Staff, called in the Washington bureau chiefs of the country's major newspapers and magazines, including The *New York Times*, *New York Herald Tribune*, *Newsweek* and *Time* magazines. After pledging them to secrecy, he told them that the USA had broken Japanese codes and expected war to start the first week of December 1941, while on 25 November the then Secretary of War, Henry L. Stimson, wrote in his diary that Roosevelt said an attack was likely within days. 'We realised that in order to have the full support of the American people it was desirable to make sure that the Japanese be the ones to (attack) so that there should remain no doubt in anyone's mind as to who were the aggressors,' he wrote. Also on 25 November, Roosevelt received a 'positive war warning' from Churchill that the Japanese would strike against America at the end of the first week in December. On 26 November orders came from Washington to move both US aircraft carriers, the *Enterprise* and the *Lexington*, out of Pearl Harbor 'as soon as possible'. On 1 December, the Office of Naval Intelligence in San Francisco found a reported 'missing' Japanese fleet by correlating reports from four wireless news services and several shipping companies that they were getting signals west of Hawaii. On 5 December, Roosevelt wrote to the Australian Prime Minister, 'There is always the Japanese to consider. Perhaps the next four or five days will decide the matter.' Churchill later wrote in his book *Grand Alliance* that Roosevelt and his top advisors 'knew the full and immediate purpose of their enemy . . . A Japanese attack upon the US was a vast simplification of their problems and their duty. How can we wonder that they regarded the actual form of the attack, or even its scale, as incomparably less important than the fact that the whole American nation would be united?' The accusation is that the President deliberately denied the commanders in Hawaii the intelligence they would have needed to prepare the defences of the naval and air bases before the Japanese attack, deliberately misleading the commanders into thinking negotiations with Japan were continuing and having false information sent to Hawaii about the location of the Japanese carrier fleet.

There had been plenty of pointers to Japanese intentions, tactics and ability; there were suitable precedents both from Japanese and British naval actions involving a surprise attack on a fleet in harbour. In fact the conspiracy theories cite evidence from as far back as 1904, when the Japanese destroyed the imperial Russian navy in a surprise attack. In The Grand Joint Army Navy Exercises of 1932 the attacker, Admiral Yarnell, attacked with 152 planes a half-hour before dawn, forty miles northeast of Kahuku Point, and caught the defenders of Pearl Harbor completely by surprise. In 1938 Admiral Ernst King led a carrier-born air strike from the *USS Saratoga* successfully against Pearl Harbor in another exercise. In 1940 Roosevelt ordered the fleet to transfer from the West Coast to its exposed position in Hawaii and ordered the fleet to remain stationed at Pearl Harbor over complaints by its commander Admiral Richardson that there was inadequate protection from air attack and no protection from torpedo attack. Richardson felt so strongly that he twice disobeyed orders to berth his fleet there and he raised the issue personally with Roosevelt in October and was replaced soon after. His successor, Admiral Kimmel, also brought up the same issues with the President in June 1941. On 11 November 1940, just 21 elderly British Swordfish torpedo bombers destroyed much of the Italian fleet, including three battleships, at their home port in the harbour of Taranto in southern Italy by using technically innovative shallow-draft torpedoes. On 11 February 1941 Roosevelt proposed sacrificing six cruisers and two carriers at Manila to get into war. Navy Chief Stark strongly and successfully objected. On 10 August 1941 the top British agent, code-named 'Tricycle' (Dusko Popov), told the FBI of the planned attack on Pearl Harbor and that it would be soon. The FBI told him that his information was 'too precise, too complete to be believed'. In October further confirmation arrived from the Soviet spy Richard Sorge, who informed the Kremlin that Pearl Harbor would be attacked within sixty days. Moscow informed him that this was being passed to the US. Interestingly, all references to Pearl Harbor in the War Department's copy of Sorge's 32,000-word confession to the Japanese were deleted. On 14 November the Japanese Merchant Marine was alerted that wartime recognition signals would be in effect from 1 December. On 25 November the British Government Code and Cipher School decrypted the 'Winds' setup message sent on 19 November. The USA decoded it on 28 November. It was a J-19 code message that there would be an attack and that the signal would come over Radio Tokyo as a weather report, 'rain' meaning 'war', 'east' (Higashi) meaning 'US'. On 25 November Secretary of War Stimson noted in his diary, 'FDR stated that we were likely to be attacked perhaps as soon as next Monday'. On the same day the Navy Department ordered all US trans-Pacific shipping to take the southern route. PHH (Pearl Harbour Hearings) Document number 12:317. Admiral Richmond K. Turner testified, 'We sent the traffic down to the Torres Straight, so that the track of the Japanese task force would be clear of any traffic.' PHH 4:1942. Also on 25 November, the commander of the Combined Imperial Fleet Yamamoto gave this order in JN-25:

> (a) The task force, keeping its movements strictly secret and maintaining close guard against submarines and aircraft, shall advance into Hawaiian waters and upon the very opening of hostilities, shall attack the main force of the United States Fleet in Hawaii and deal it a mortal blow. The raid is planned for dawn on X-day – exact date to be given by later order. (b) Should the negotiations with the US

> prove successful, the task force shall hold itself in readiness forthwith to return and reassemble. (c) The task force will move out of Hitokappu Wan on the morning of 26 November and advance to the standing-by position on the afternoon of 4 December and speedily complete refueling.

This was decoded by the British on 25 November and the Dutch on 27 November. When it was decoded by the USA is still a national secret; however, on 26 November Naval Intelligence reported a concentration of units of the Japanese fleet at an unknown port, ready for offensive action. Also on 26 November, Secretary of State Cordell Hull's ultimatum that Japan must withdraw from Indochina and all China, the so-called 'most fateful document', was sent. The United States ambassador to Japan called this 'The document that touched the button that started the war'. On 29 November the USA made a telephone intercept of an uncoded plain-text Japanese conversation in which Kurusu, an embassy functionary, said, 'Tell me what zero hour is. Otherwise, I won't be able to carry on diplomacy.' K. Yamamoto, a senior Foreign Office official in Tokyo replied, 'Well then, I will tell you. Zero hour is 8 December [Tokyo time, i.e. 7 December US time] at Pearl Harbor.' On 30 November US time (or 1 December Tokyo time), the Japanese fleet was radioed the following imperial naval order (JN-25): 'JAPAN, UNDER THE NECESSITY OF HER SELF-PRESERVATION AND SELF-DEFENSE, HAS REACHED A POSITION TO DECLARE WAR ON THE UNITED STATES OF AMERICA.' On 1 December the Office of Naval Intelligence, (ONI), Twelfth Naval District in San Francisco, found the missing Japanese fleet by correlating reports from the four wireless news services and several shipping companies that they were getting signals of vessels west of Hawaii. The Soviet Union also knew the exact location of the Japanese fleet because they asked the Japanese in advance to let one of their ships pass. This informaton was most probably given to them by the USA because Sorge's spy ring was rolled up by 14 November. All long-range PBY (flying boat) patrols from the Aleutians were ordered to stop on 6 December to prevent contact. On 1 December the tanker *Shiriya*, which had been added to the striking force in an order intercepted on 14 November, radioed, 'proceeding to a position 30.00 N, 154.20 E. Expect to arrive at that point on 3 December.' To many conspiracy theorists the most extraordinary event in the whole scenario is that, in reply to that report, MacArthur's command sent out a series of three messages on 26 and 29 November and 2 December to Hawaii, blatantly lying about the location of the Japanese carrier fleet, claiming that it was in fact in the South China Sea. This false information was certainly one of the main reasons that Pearl Harbor and the US forces were caught totally unprepared. There were a large number of other messages that gave the location of the striking force by alluding to the Aleutians, the North Pacific and various weather systems near Hawaii. Also on 1 December Roosevelt cut short his scheduled ten-day holiday after just one day to meet with Hull and Stark. The result of this meeting was reported on 2 December by the *Washington Post*: 'President Roosevelt yesterday assumed direct command of diplomatic and military moves relating to Japan.' This politically damaging move was necessary to prevent the mutiny of conspirators.

On 2 December, Yamamoto radioed the attack fleet in Japanese, 'Climb Niitakayama 12.08' (8 December Japanese time; 7 December US time). Thus the US knew exactly when the war would start. Even Hawaii knew. Mount Niitaka was the highest mountain in the Japanese empire at 13,113 feet. On 2 December, General Hein Ter Poorten, the commander of the Netherlands East Indies army, gave the Winds setup message to the US War Department. The Dutch intercept station was Kamer 14 on Java. Throughout 1941 the Dutch, British and Americans all had liaison officers at each other's Far Eastern coding centres and secret radio contact with each other, particularly the British FECB at Singapore and the US at Station Cast in the Philippines. The Australians also had a centre in Melbourne and the Chinese are believed to have broken the JN-25. A Dutch sub had visually tracked the attack fleet to the Kurile Islands in early November and this information was passed to DC, but DC did not give it to HI. The intercepts the Dutch gave the US are still classified in RG 38, Box 792. On 2 December, the Japanese order No. 902 specified that old JN-25 additive tables version 7 would continue to be used alongside version 8 when the latter was introduced on 4 December. This means the US read all messages to the striking force through the attack. On 4 December, in the early hours, the navy's East Coast Intercept station received the 'East Winds, Rain' message, the Winds Execute, which meant war. It was put on the TWX circuit immediately. This message was deleted from the files. One of the main cover-ups of Pearl Harbor was to make this message simply disappear. On 4 December, Kilsoo Haan called Maxwell Hamilton at the State Department and told him that the Korean underground had information that the Japanese would attack Pearl Harbor the coming weekend. The same day, the Dutch invoked the ADB joint defence agreement as the Japanese crossed the magic line of 100 East and 10 North. The USA was at war with Japan three days before they were at war with us; US General Thorpe at Java sent four messages warning of the Pearl Habor attack. DC ordered him to stop sending warnings. On 5 December all Japanese international shipping had returned to the home port. That morning Roosevelt dictated a letter to Wendell Wilkie for delivery to the Australian Prime Minister. Roosevelt wrote, 'There is always the Japanese to consider. The situation is definitely serious and there might be an armed clash at any moment . . . Perhaps the next four or five days will decide the matters.' At a Cabinet meeting on the same day, Secretary of the Navy, Frank Knox said, 'Well, you know, Mr President, we know where the Japanese fleet is?' 'Yes, I know,' said Roosevelt. 'I think we ought to tell everybody just how ticklish the situation is. We have information as Knox just mentioned . . . Well, you tell them what it is, Frank.' Knox became very excited and said, 'Well, we have very secret information that the Japanese fleet is out at sea. Our information is . . .' and then a scowling Roosevelt cut him off. That same day, Station Cast in the Philippines received an urgent request from Washington to listen for a short message from Tokyo which ended with the English word 'stop'. The message arrived at 11.30 p.m. Hawaiian time on 6 December. This is the Hidden Word Code set up in a message of 27 November (e.g. in code, Roosevelt = Miss Kimiko). The message was: 'Relations between Japan and the following countries are on the brink of catastrophe: Britain and the United States.' On 6 December, the highly detailed J19 message of 18 November was finally translated by the army, as follows: '1. The warships at anchor in the Harbor on the 15th were as I told you in my No. 219 on that day.' This information was not passed to HI. At 9.30 p.m. on 6 December, Roosevelt read the first thirteen parts of the decoded Japanese diplomatic declaration of war and said, 'This means war.' When he returned to his 34 dinner guests, he said, 'The war starts tomorrow.' The War Cabinet (FDR, top advisor Hopkins, Stimson, Marshall, Secretary of the Navy Knox, with aides John McCrea and Frank Beatty) 'deliberately sat through the night of 6th December 1941 waiting for the Japanese to strike'. On 7 December the following message was sent from the Japanese Consul in Budapest to Tokyo: 'On the 6th, the American Minister presented to the Government of this country a British Government communiqué to the effect that a state of war would break out on the 7th.' The communiqué was the 5 December war alert from the British Admiralty. It has disappeared. This triple priority alert was delivered to Roosevelt personally. The Mid-East British Air Marshall told Col. Bonner Fellers on Saturday that he had received a secret signal that America was coming into the war in 24 hours. On 7 December 1941, very early Washington time, two marines, an emergency special detail, were stationed outside the Japanese Naval Attaché's door. At 9.30 a.m. Aides begged Stark to send a warning to Hawaii. He did not do so. At 10 a.m. Roosevelt read the fourteenth part; at 11 a.m. Roosevelt read the fifteenth part which set the time for the declaration of war to be delivered to the State Department at 1 p.m., about dawn Pearl Harbor time, and still did nothing. Navy Secretary Knox was given the fifteenth part at 11.15 a.m. with this note from the Office of Naval IQ: 'This means a sunrise attack on Pearl Harbor today.' Naval IQ also transmitted this prediction to Hull and about eight others, including the White House (PHH 36:532). At 10.30 a.m. Bratton informed Marshall that he had a most important message (the fifteenth part) and would bring it to Marshall's quarters, but Marshall said he would take it at his office. At 11.25 Marshall reached his office, according to Bratton. Marshall testified that he had been riding horses that morning but he was contradicted by Harrison, McCollum and Deane. Marshall, who had read the first thirteen parts by 10 p.m. the prior night, perjured himself by denying that he had even received them. Marshall, in the face of his aides' urgent requests that he warn Hawaii, delayed, reading and re-reading all of the ten-minute-long fourteenth part several times, which took an hour, refused to use the scrambler phone on his desk, refused to send a warning by the fast, more secure navy system and sent for Bratton three times to inquire how long it would take to send his watered-down warning. When informed it would take thirty or forty minutes by army radio, he appeared satisfied; it also meant that he had delayed long enough so that the warning wouldn't reach Pearl Harbor until after the 1 p.m. Washington time deadline. The warning was in fact sent commercial without priority identification and arrived six hours late. This message reached all other addressees, such as the Philippines and Canal Zone, in a timely manner.

On 7 December, 7.55 a.m. Hawaii time, the Japanese launched their air attack. At 1.50 p.m. Washington time, Harry Hopkins, who was the only person with Roosevelt when he received the news of the attack by telephone from Knox, wrote that the President was unsurprised and expressed 'great relief'. Eleanor Roosevelt wrote about 7 December in *This I Remember*, stating that her husband became 'in a way more serene'. In the *New York Times Magazine* of 8 October 1944 she wrote, 'December 7th was . . . far from the shock it proved to the country in general. We had expected something of the sort for a long time.' The theorists also point out events on 7 December some nine hours later, when MacArthur's entire air force was caught by surprise and wiped out in the Philippines. MacArthur's reaction to the news of Pearl Harbor was quite unusual: he apparently locked himself in his room all morning, refused to meet with his air commander, General Brereton, and refused to attack Japanese forces on Formosa even under orders from the War Department. MacArthur gave three conflicting orders that ensured the planes were on the ground most of the morning, using radar tracking of the Japanese planes to time his final order and ensure his planes were on the ground. Strategically, the destruction of half of all the available US heavy bombers was even more important than the naval damage in Pearl Harbor. Either MacArthur had made an enormous blunder or, so we are told by conspiracy theorists, he was under strict orders to allow his forces to be destroyed. If it was a blunder, then it is remarkable how he escaped any reprimand, kept his command and got his fourth star and Congressional Medal of Honor shortly after.

On 8 December, when in a conversation with Rosenman, his speechwriter, Roosevelt emphasised that Hitler was still the first target, but that he feared that a great many Americans would insist that Britain make the war in the Pacific at least equally important with the war against Hitler. Roosevelt reminisced with Stalin at Tehran on 30 November 1943, saying, 'if the Japanese had not attacked the US he doubted very much if it would have been possible to send any American forces to Europe.' Compare this statement with what Roosevelt said at the Atlantic Conference four months before Pearl: 'Everything was to be done to force an "incident" to justify hostilities.' Given that a Japanese attack was the only possible incident, then Roosevelt had said publicly here that he would do it. The issue of whether the President and Washington were ultimately responsible for the Pearl Harbor disaster was decided in two courts of law in 1944. Both the Navy Court and the Army Board found Washington guilty. Most of the conspirators were military men, all men of Roosevelt's own choice, men who only followed orders, since Roosevelt never delegated authority. Stark, in answer to charges that he denied intelligence to Hawaii, said publicly in August 1945 that everything he did pre-7 December 1941 was on the President's orders. The handful of military men in Washington responsible for the disaster at Pearl Harbor were directly under the control of Roosevelt and were later promoted and protected from investigation, promoted with Roosevelt's full knowledge that they were responsible for not warning Hawaii. On the record, Intelligence tried to warn Hawaii scores of times but was prevented by the President's closest advisors. In November Roosevelt had ordered the Red Cross Disaster Relief director to secretly prepare for massive casualties at Pearl Harbor because he was going to let it be attacked. When the director protested to the President, President Roosevelt told him that the American people would never agree to enter the war in Europe unless they were attacked within their own borders. It is possible that there were many warnings but that these warnings were not readily distinguishable from the thousands of other intelligence reports being received at the same time. However, the large number of instances when important information appears to have been overlooked, misunderstood or deliberately ignored can undoubtedly be made into a compelling case for some form of conspiracy and this has continued to fuel interest in this subject. This said, and taking all the conspiracy theories claiming Roosevelt knew in advance about Pearl Harbor on board, it probably remains the case that the most likely explanation for the missed warnings in 1941 was the inability of the intelligence services, and in particular their political masters, to detect the significant information from the noise; equally, the sort of blanket dismissal of the case for President Franklin D. Roosevelt's advanced knowledge of the Pearl Harbor attack that has been trotted out regularly over the last sixty years is also no longer tenable.

1942 – CONSPIRACY OF EMBARRASSMENT British government officials and members of the Special Operations Executive (SOE) hastily conspired to cover up a potentially embarrassing, but seemingly straightforward, sexual scandal at the height of WW2. However, it became clear that, like the much more famous and apparently more serious Ward affair of 1963, there were serious matters of security to be considered. When Lord Selbourne, chief of the Special Operations Executive, first made the acquaintance of Mathilde Carré at a cocktail party at Claridge's in 1942, he felt the power of her spell that had bewitched members of the Gestapo and the French Resistance alike. Carré was determined to become his mistress, and Selbourne appeared ensnared, asking her to dinner, promising to commend her to Winston Churchill and assuring the Parisienne with a taste for luxury that she would have everything she needed in London. His ardour caused deep consternation among many of Britain's senior Intelligence officers, not only among his colleagues in SOE but also among those at the rival Secret Intelligence Service, or MI6, and the counter-espionage security service, MI5. It was feared that he was about to 'make a fool of himself' with one of the most dangerous female spies of the war. Declassified Security Service documents reveal a level of serious concern that Selbourne was embarking on an affair with an 'extremely dangerous' woman who had the potential to betray Britain's entire overseas spy network to the Germans.

Carré had been second-in-command in the French Resistance organisation Interallié, where she helped provide the Allies with virtually the complete shape of the German military in France, winning over Gestapo officers with her jet-black hair, voluptuous figure and long, shapely legs. Interallié was, however, exposed by German agents in November 1941, and Carré began working for the Nazis after being given a meal in one of Paris's best restaurants and offered a hotel suite and a 60,000-franc monthly salary. She enthusiastically began betraying former comrades, became the lover of the German agent who had won her over, and continued sending messages to London as if Interallié was still functioning. Carré, then 34, travelled to England in February 1942 with her main lover, the French Resistance leader Pierre de Vomecourt, under instruction to expose the workings of the SOE. After arriving in London she admitted working for the Germans but agreed to change sides again and help the Allies by sending false information about SOE's activities to her Nazi contacts in France. MI5 and the SOE remained deeply suspicious, however, and were alarmed when Carré, whom they codenamed Victoire, charmed the spymaster Lord Selbourne, who had just taken over as head of SOE, at Claridge's. An SOE informer, known only as Mrs Barker, who was living with Carré, said Selbourne had asked Carré out to dinner, had offered to mention her to Churchill and to get her 'everything she needed'. The message, which is contained in the papers released by the Public Record Office, said, 'Victoire seems to be dreaming of becoming Lord Selbourne's mistress.

According to her, he has all the attributes she admires in a man except that he cannot dance. Lord Selbourne may be merely playing up to her but even if only half of what she has told me is true it seems that he is behaving exceedingly foolishly and is not doing himself any good nor, for that matter, us.' The next day Captain Christopher Harmer, from the SOE, said it was unlikely that Selbourne would know Carré's full history and suggested sending an agent to ask him 'what the position was' between them. He went on, 'From the point of view of running the case I don't much mind whether she goes on seeing Selbourne or not but whether we owe a duty to him to prevent him making a fool of himself is a matter which I must leave for someone else to decide.' As concern grew, Mrs Barker warned Captain Harmer that Carré was an 'utterly egotistical woman who cares for nothing and nobody but herself' and would 'burst into fury at any opposition.' Given a chance, she would sell any information she has to the other side. Added to all this, there is, of course, her interest in men. She feels she is irresistible to men anyhow and to sleep with a man seems a necessity to her. Once she gets hold of a man it is up to her to drop him and be unfaithful to him and God help the man or for that matter the service he is in, if he dares to drop her. I think she is an exceedingly dangerous woman . . . war is merely a means to an end for her, *viz* her amusement . . . and a life of luxury.' The papers do not record if Carré was successful in seducing Selbourne, but historians believe he would have been warned off quickly because the risk of associating with her was so great.

Mathilde Carré could probably be ranked alongside the best operatives in many ways. She was a significant traitor and a number of SOE agents encountered her at their cost. Many were arrested and interrogated in a brutal way by the Gestapo, and the prospect of Selbourne having an affair with her would have caused substantial panic in high quarters in the security service. Some experts believe that Carré would have had little success with Selbourne, who may have been polite to her because she was at that stage being handled with kid gloves in order that some use could be made of her. It was not yet clear whether her allegiance was more to the Germans than the Allies. Selbourne knew how a gentleman should behave, it is said, and he was also too busy running the SOE and the Ministry of Economic Warfare to have time for a mistress. Carré was arrested in July of that year when British investigations discovered the extent of her betrayal of Interallié. She was interned at Aylesbury prison in

Buckinghamshire until 1945 when she was returned to France. She was tried for 'giving intelligence to the enemy' and sentenced to death. The sentence was commuted twice and she was released in 1954. She is thought to have died in 1971. It would seem that Selbourne either behaved extremely well in the end or was warned off Carré by security officials; however, as at least one theorist has pointed out, the real conspiracy was the German attempt to position 'the Cat' as a hugely dangerous triple-agent in the SOE in order that she could build a close relationship with at least one senior officer. Carré must indeed have thought her luck was in when she nearly ensnared one of the most important and influential spymasters in Britain.

1942 – WANNSEE CONSPIRACY This most nightmarish of conspiracies was hatched in the elegant surroundings of a pleasant country retreat and followed a superb meal with a goodly supply of fine wines and cigars. There, a group of seemingly well-educated and sophisticated German officers and civilian technocrats calmly discussed the finer points of the extermination of millions of men, women and children simply because they were Jewish – the 'Final Solution'. That was the Wannsee conspiracy.

No single document has ever been found in which Hitler himself explicitly ordered the annihilation of European Jewry. Most historians agree, however, that at some point in 1941, after the launch of the Russian campaign or Operation Barbarossa, 'evacuation' became more widely understood in the Nazi hierarchy as a code word for systematic, industrial-scale murder, orchestrated by Heinrich Himmler, head of the SS and, until his assassination in the late spring of 1942, his second, Reinhard Heydrich. By that spring, the gas chambers were no longer experimental; they were operating to their full ghastly capacity.

Two crucial surviving documents frame the period in which the ultimate meaning of the Final Solution went from theory to practice. First is a letter of 31 July 1941 (drafted by Adolf Eichmann at Heydrich's bequest) in which Reichsmarshall Hermann Göring authorises Heydrich 'to carry out preparations as regards organisational, financial, and material matters for a total solution [*Gesamtlösung*] of the Jewish question in all the territories of Europe under German occupation. I charge you further to submit to me as soon as possible a general plan of the administrative material and financial measures necessary for carrying out the desired final solution [*Endlösung*] of the Jewish question.' The second document is what has come to be known as the Wannsee Protocol, the minutes of the infamous meeting of 20 January 1942 at Wannsee Haus, an elegant private home then being used as an SS guesthouse in a beautiful lakeside district of Berlin. SS Obergruppenfuhrer Reinhard Heydrich, Chief of Security Police, called together fifteen officials from the SS, the Nazi Party and state ministries to Wannsee Haus in order to discuss the Final Solution to Europe's 'Jewish problem'. Originally scheduled for 9 December 1941, the meeting was postponed due to the bombing of Pearl Harbor on 7 December and America's entry into the war. Two agendas were behind Heydrich's matter-of-fact invitation. Between the July order from Göring and Wannsee, the machinery for mass murder, the gas chambers, had been developed and tested. The major extermination camps were under construction. During the ninety-minute meeting at Wannsee, Heydrich mobilised the administrative apparatus of the Third Reich to implement the escalation of Hitler's genocidal 'Final Solution'. Heydrich also made it clear that the SS, not the Nazi Party nor any of the government ministries represented at the meeting, would be controlling activities.

What helped to make this meeting extraordinary is that the minutes survived: Eichmann sent out thirty copies that were to have been destroyed after reading, but one copy was found in the files of the German Foreign Office in 1947. Even more extraordinary is how the minutes record in the most ordinary way a dispassionate discussion of the potential slaughter of what Eichmann estimated to be 11 million Jews throughout Europe, including England and other not-yet-conquered territories.

When Hitler took power, there were perhaps only half a million Jews in Germany. Beginning with the Nuremberg Laws in 1935, German Jews had been stripped of their rights and their property. With his conquering of additional territory, first Austria, then Poland, Czechoslovakia and parts of the Soviet Union, his 'Jewish problem' escalated. Suddenly, he had millions of Jews literally at his disposal. Hitler and his henchmen had experimented with lethal treatments at euthanasia centers for the mentally ill, the disabled, and political dissenters – including Jews. The Nazis had built internment and labour camps in which hard labour and dire conditions took their natural toll. Polish (and resettled German) Jews were crowded into ghettos of Warsaw, Cracow, Lublin and Radom, where disease was rampant due to overcrowding, unsanitary conditions and food shortages. The Nazis discussed plans to force all European Jews to resettle in a 'super ghetto' in, of all places, Madagascar. They had discussed massive resettlement in part of eastern Poland. By the time of the Wannsee Conference, they had encouraged the brutal slaughter of thousands and thousands of Jews in the eastern Occupied Territories (eastern Poland, the Baltics, White Russia and Ukraine) by the Einsatzgruppen, SS paramilitary forces supported by local police. Indeed, by January 1942 Estonia was '*judenfrei*' or free of Jews. But Himmler and Heydrich and, presumably their superiors, realised that you could not shoot the entire Jewish population of Eastern Europe. Besides, Himmler had said, shooting all those victims was bad for the morale of the SS and German soldiers. By the fall of 1941, they saw Zyklon-B gas as the cheaper, 'cleaner' and more efficient way of handling their so-called 'storage problem' of the Jews. Evacuation could become elimination; relocation could, and would, become wholesale murder.

The Wannsee Protocol, which Eichmann described at his trial as highly expurgated to hide its true meanings and the freewheeling, sometimes vulgar, discussion that took place; Eichmann's trial testimony, which is, of course, suspect; and interviews with five participants in 1947 by US prosecutor Robert M. W. Kempner. At these interviews, four of the Nazis denied having been at Wannsee until confronted with the Protocol, which listed their attendance. The fifth, Dr Friedrich Kritzinger of the Reich's Chancellery, expressed shame and regret for what happened at Wannsee. (Indeed, Kritzinger tried to resign from his post not long after Wannsee, but his superior asked him to remain because it would be 'even worse' without him.) The discussion, as often grounded in legalistic language as in racist vitriol, was largely on two topics: plans for the 'evacuation' of up to 11 million Jews from European life, 'provided that the Führer gives the appropriate approval in advance' (the Wannsee Protocol notes cryptically, 'practical experience is already being collected which is of the greatest importance in relation to the future final solution of the Jewish question'); and solution to the 'problem of mixed marriages and persons of mixed blood', the so-called *Mischlinge*. It is assumed that the 'practical experience' – experiments underway with gas vans and construction of gas chambers – was indeed discussed by the participants. If any of the participants were not previously aware of these experiments or the mass executions underway in the eastern Occupied Territories, they were made aware at the conference. As for the *Mischlinge*, a complex, highly legalistic construction of racial purity had been laid out earlier in the Nuremberg Laws, co-written by Dr Wilhelm Stuckart (the State Secretary of the Interior Ministry, and an attendee at Wannsee). Heydrich was attempting to get rid of 'exemptions' for certain categories of part Jews; Stuckart surprised his colleagues by calling for cross-the-board sterilisations. The question was not resolved at Wannsee or at two subsequent conferences, and most *Mischlinge* in the Third Reich survived the war. The discussion at Wannsee, however, exemplifies how law, practicality and hatred overlapped in conversation frighteningly devoid of moral conscience. The German SS, military and civilian personnel present at this meeting included: Lt Colonel Adolf Eichmann, SS Gestapo Office of Jewish Affairs; General Reinhard Heydrich, SS Chief of Reich Security; Dr Wilhelm Stuckart, Interior Ministry; SS Major Rudolph Lange, Deputy Director SS Forces, Latvia; Dr Joseph Buhler, State Secretary; Dr Friedrich Kritzinger, Reich Chancellery; Dr Erich Neumann, Director Office of the 4 Year Plan; SS General Heinrich Muller, SS Gestapo Chief; Dr Gerhard Klopfer, Representative of Martin Boorman; Dr Roland Freisler, Ministry of Justice; Lt General Otto Hoffmann, Office of Race & Settlement; Dr Georg Leibbrandt; Martin Luther, Under Secretary of Foreign Ministry; Dr Alfred Meyer and SS Colonel Karl Schongarth.

The fifteen Nazi officials who met at the Wannsee mansion near Berlin were led by Reinhard Heydrich, head of the Reich Security Service (SD) controlled by Heinrich Himmler's Schutzstaffel (SS). This was not a true decision-making conference, more a seminar on how best to carry out the policy of genocide. Hitler had already made the decision for the Final Solution. This then was the true purpose of the 1942 meeting, to implement these decisions with a specific plan for removing Jews 'to the East' and their systematic extermination co-ordinated by several German agencies under the authority of the SS Special Units (*Einsatzgruppen*).

The SS had been killing Jews in Russia since June 1941 and Hermann Göring, in a July 31 memo drafted by Adolf Eichmann, had authorised the 'General Solution of the Jewish Question'. Auschwitz had been opened on 30 April 1940, and Zyklon-B gas was first used in 1941 – previously the Germans had either shot or used carbon monoxide on their hapless captives. On 29 and 30 September 1941, 33,771 Jews from Kiev were slaughtered at BabiYar. Men, women and children were simply lined up and shot. Perhaps almost as shocking as the events that followed the Wannsee conspiracy are the other conspiracies that followed the end of the war, those that the victorious Allies instigated to protect many of the Nazi technocrats, scientists, engineers, intelligence and military officers from justice.

1944 – US WARTIME DISASTER: AN ALLIED COVER-UP?

Accusations that Exercise Tiger, a dress rehearsal by the US VII Army Corps stationed in the west of England for the D-day landings, that took place along the sleepy Devon coastline of the South Hams, turned into an avoidable catastrophe have long been made by writers on both sides of the Atlantic. Comments such as: 'It was a disaster which lay hidden from the world for 40 years . . . an official American Army cover-up,' and, 'That a massive cover-up took place is beyond doubt. And that General Dwight D. Eisenhower authorized it is equally clear,' were not uncommon. But allegations became even more serious when it was suggested by the American media, and in particular in a three-part documentary report from WJLA-TV, the ABC affiliate in Washington DC in 1987–88, that 'Generals Omar N. Bradley and Eisenhower were determined that details of their own mistakes would be buried with their men,' and that it was 'a story the government kept quiet . . . hushed up for decades . . . a dirty little secret of World War II.' That there was a military disaster in which hundreds of young Americans died is a fact. How this occurred and whether there was a high-level military conspiracy to cover up blunders by the supreme commanders is still open to question.

The main details appear to be large agreed. On 28 April 1944 assault units of the US 101st Airborne Division had gone ashore on Slapton Sands, a stretch of seashore that closely resembled a beach on the French coast of Normandy, code-named Utah, where a few weeks later US troops were to land as part of the liberation of Europe. At around 2 a.m. on a moonless night with clear visibility and a calm sea off the Devon coast a flotilla of eight Tank Landing Ships (LSTs) were heading to reinforce the landings at Slapton, having sailed from Plymouth at 9.45 a.m. on 27 April. Commander B. J. Skahill was in charge of the LST group of convey 'T-4' in LST 515 followed by 496, 531 and 58, and off the coast near Brixham they would join up with three others: LSTs 499, 289 and 507, loaded with US troops stationed in the Torbay area. They would proceed at a speed of about four knots, at a distance between ships of about four hundred metres. This force was transporting follow-up units from the 4th Division of engineers and chemical and quartermaster troops not scheduled for participation in the initial assault but to be unloaded in orderly fashion along with trucks, amphibious trucks, jeeps and heavy engineering equipment.

Suddenly, at 1.30 a.m., out of the darkness roared nine German E-boats (S or Schnell-Boats) from Korvettenkapitän Bernd Klug's 5th Flotilla consisting of S-100, S-136, S-138, S-143, S-140, and S-142 and Kapitänleutnant Götz Freiherr von Mirbach's 9th Flotilla consisting of S-130, S-145 and S-150 under the command of Lieutenant Günther Rabe, which had broken through the British patrols and now had the American troop ships at its mercy. On what was apparently a routine patrol out of the occupied French port of Cherbourg, the commander had been informed by German naval intelligence of the interception of heavy radio traffic. The E-boats were fast and immensely manoeuvrable vessels, capable of a top speed of over forty knots and able to outrun any destroyer or corvette sent to intercept them. Each carried up to four torpedoes, as well as one 40mm and three 20mm guns. To his astonishment Rabe found his flotilla in visual contact with the American LSTs, which were strung out in an inviting way and without adequate protection. It was an opportunity of a lifetime for Rabe and his men. Closing in quickly on the totally unprepared US convoy the E-boats, in the space of a few minutes, hit the LSTs 507, 289 and 531 with torpedoes. S-136 and S-138 had identified targets and fired torpedoes at them. Immediately, LST 507 exploded. The stores of gasoline on board and in the tanks of its army vehicles ignited, turning the big ship into an inferno. The flaming ship could be seen for miles, but the escort took no action and shortly after 2 a.m. it was the turn of LST 531 to suffer the same fate. It too caught fire after being torpedoed and soon turned over and sank within some six minutes.

With little time to launch lifeboats, and with many of the soldiers trapped below decks, hundreds of US servicemen simply went down with the ships. Others leaped into the sea, but again many soon drowned as they were fatally weighed down by waterlogged uniforms, heavy overcoats and backpacks. Tragically some were to die because life belts incorrectly worn around their waists pitched them forwards to drown, while still more died from the cold before they could be rescued. When the final tally of those bodies recovered was made it came to 748: 198 US navy and 551 US army casualties. However, other sources still claim that over 300 further US servicemen were lost, still trapped within the sunken vessels. Lyme Bay was filled with the light of the burning vessels, streaks of US and German 20mm and 40mm tracers and the flash of star shells thrown up by the E-boats to illuminate their targets, but apparently the sole escort vessel, *HMS Azalea*, was not firing at all. So fast were the German vessels that no precise sighting could be made and LST 496 strafed the decks of LST 511 by mistake, probably killing and certainly wounding some of the men aboard. At 2.25 a.m., one of the LSTs sent a distress signal to the British naval base at Portland indicating an enemy attack was in progress. This message was not acknowledged because it was never received again due to the communications mix-up. By 3 a.m. the Germans broke off the engagement and returned to base leaving the waters of Lyme Bay dotted with floating corpses, wreckages and lifeboats.

The LSTs had seemed to be entirely on their own. Where was their single escort, *HMS Azalea*? During this confused phase in the fighting the LSTs received no message from *HMS Azalea* at all, and the commanders did not know whether to stay together or scatter and try to make their way back to port. *HMS Azalea* had turned the wrong side of the convoy and was unable to engage the German E-boats until it was too late, according to her commander. LST 499 radioed a distress message to the effect that the convoy had been attacked by submarines, and although the message was received at headquarters and acted upon, there was little chance that help could have reached the LSTs in time. When the German attack took place the convoy was some fifteen miles to the west of Portland Bill and afterwards *HMS Azalea* confined her activity to escorting the six undamaged LSTs towards the shore, before returning to escort the damaged LST 289 along the coast to Dartmouth. By this time there was nothing that she could have done to help LSTs 507 and 531 as both had now gone down.

With morning, the major rescue effort moved into full swing with some US and British units engaged in gathering up the remaining survivors. Corpses and fragments of the dead were left in the water by the British to be scooped up by American ships. A number of bodies washed up on shore and boats brought in many others during the course of the day. The survivors and the wounded were taken to various military hospitals where they were warned by British and US intelligence officers about speaking to anyone about the disaster. Direct threats were made that anyone revealing the nature of the disaster would be subject to the harshest penalties.

A tragic loss of life in what was an exercise intended to save lives later on D-day. Allied commanders were not only concerned about the loss of life and two LSTs, which left not a single LST as a reserve for D-day, but also about the frightening possibility that the E-boats had managed to pick up a number of US personnel from the water and take them back for interrogation. Most worryingly of all for the planners at Supreme Headquarters Allied Expeditionary Force (SHAEF), there had been around twenty US officers, code-named BIGOTs, who were privy to the most detailed information about the timing of D-day and the beaches chosen for the landings. This information would have proved so useful to the Germans that SHAEF seriously considered postponing Operation Overlord or choosing new sites for the invasion. However, SHAEF's fears were unnecessary because, by a quirk of fate, all of the bodies of the BIGOT officers were found and the Germans appear never to have seriously considered taking prisoners from the many men bobbing about in the water.

The blame was officially placed upon two main factors: a lack of escort vessels and an error in radio frequencies. Only two Royal Naval vessels, a corvette *HMS Azalea* and a 1914–18 destroyer *HMS Scimitar*, were assigned for convoy protection, and even this was depleted when the destroyer, having been very slightly damaged in a collision with a US LST, was not replaced in time by an additional warship. This was to turn out to be a costly and unnecessary blunder that undoubtedly played a major part in the disaster that would overcome the convoy. In addition, because of an administrative error, the US LSTs were operating on a different radio frequency from that being used by the British warships and RN headquarters ashore. When the German E-boats were finally spotted soon after midnight the warning reached the *HMS Azalea* but not the LSTs and, assuming the US vessels had received the report, the commander of the RN corvette made no further effort to raise them. This was an incredible oversight on his part and was to contribute in no small way to the disaster that was to follow. US historian Charles B. MacDonald argued in 1988 that these two failures probably did not greatly affect the outcome, suggesting that the tragedy off Slapton Sands was simply one of those cruel happenstances of war. However, others, like the former British policeman Kenneth Small, who having moved into the area many years later became fascinated with the tragedy through his research for a book on the subject, *The Lost Army*, became convinced that there had been a major blunder at some point and a cover-up. Indeed, in

1944 urgent orders had been issued imposing the strictest secrecy on all who knew or might learn of the tragedy, including doctors and nurses who treated the survivors. It was considered vital that the Germans should not be given any more advanced warning of the impending invasion. The order for secrecy remained in place as D-day came and passed. The units subjected to the order were to be eventually scattered throughout Europe and with the end of the war were returned to the USA and often demobilised.

A press release from SHAEF, was issued in July 1944 covering the basic details of the tragedy. Notice of it was printed, among others places, in the *Stars & Stripes*. Strangely, in 1954, some ten years after D-day, the US army authorities unveiled a monument at Slapton Sands honouring the farmers and villagers of Blackawton, Chillington, East Allington, Slapton, Stokenham, Strete and Torcross in South Devon 'who generously left their homes and their lands to provide a battle practice area for the successful assault in Normandy in June 1944'. Though General Alfred M. Guenther, the US commander of the North Atlantic Treaty Organisation, retold the story of the tragedy that befell Exercise Tiger during the ceremony, conspiracy theorists like Kenneth Small many years later questioned why there was no memorial to those many young Americans who had died. To Mr Small, and others holding the same view, this looked like further evidence of an official cover-up. Such a monument was eventually scheduled to be unveiled on 15 November 1987 and this was to finally set off international interest in the 'mystery'.

There were accusations not only of a cover-up, but also of much heavier casualties actually being suffered by the US forces including panicked firing by the US soldiers hitting other ships in the convoy. There were also claims that hundreds of additional bodies were buried in unmarked mass grave and that their deaths were hushed up by listing them later among those killed in the Normandy invasion. Even more fanciful rumours recounted long lines of US army trucks bringing the dead to be buried in further unmarked sites at what later became the Polish refugee resettlement camp at Stover, near the Devon market town of Newton Abbot. Despite considerable efforts by journalists and local historians, none of these claims has ever been substantiated. What is known, however, is that in the first few days of May 1944, and soon after the tragedy, hundreds of the dead were interred temporarily in the immediate area. Following the war, those bodies were either moved to a new US military cemetery in

Cambridge or shipped back to the United States at the request of next of kin. The Cambridge cemetery contains an impressive official memorial erected by the American Battle Monuments Commission to all those US servicemen and women who died during World War II while stationed in the British Isles. It includes among those names the 749 who 'officially' died in the tragedy off the South Devon coast, though the possibility exists that a further 300 or so are not therefore remembered.

That said there still remain a number of unanswered questions. Why was the simple procedure of checking that both the US and British vessels were operating on the same radio frequency before the start of the exercise ignored? Indeed, such radio frequencies as had been given to the Americans were suddenly changed with no notice given to anyone involved, making the failure to confirm that communications were working even more reprehensible; the US troops on the LSTs appeared to have no knowledge of how to abandon ship and had never been informed what to do in the case of an emergency at sea. The ensuing panic resulted in many preventable deaths and indeed the readiness of the US troops involved had already been questioned when one of General Dwight D. Eisenhower's aides, Harry C. Butcher, had noted that the units stationed in the area around Torbay in South Devon included many very inexperienced soldiers. During training exercises at Slapton he had concluded, 'I am concerned over the absence of toughness and alertness of young American officers whom I saw on this trip. They seem to regard the war as one grand maneuver in that they are having a happy time. Many seem as green as growing corn. How will they act in battle and how will they look in three months' time?' He added, 'A good many of the full colonels also give me a pain. They are fat, grey and oldish. Most of them wear the Rainbow Ribbon of the last war and are still fighting it.'

British radar stations in southern England had picked up the movement of the E-boats (S-boats) in the Channel about midnight, but this information was not passed to Plymouth Command; *HMS Azalea* had known of the E-boat activity around midnight, but had failed to check whether the rest of the convoy had received this warning; on 27 April, British Signals Intelligence had intercepted a German message at 10 p.m. that E-boats were to depart Cherbourg for action in the western Channel. This information was not passed to anyone else until the evening of 28 April, nearly 24 hours after the disaster. Why was such a vulnerable convoy given such a pathetic escort? What is also inexplicable is how the operation was allowed to take place in the full and admitted knowledge that there was a potent E-boat threat in the area and that the Germans were actually at sea on the night of the 27 April. Why was communications security so bad that German naval intelligence was able to hear the 'heavy radio traffic' that fatally gave away the position of the US LSTs to the German E-boats? Newton Abbot Town Councillor Julian Perkins, a former Royal Navy officer and actually serving on one of the RN convoy escorts at the time, believed that the tragedy was avoidable and was caused by bungling inefficiency. He confirmed the rumours that additional screening warships, including the modern destroyers *HMS Onslow* and *HMS Saladin*, were probably diverted at the crucial time to hunt for a reported German U-boat and that indeed fire control and discipline was less than ideal amongst some of the vessels in the convoy. The same confusion in communications and command was evident during the rescue attempts. Others have suggested that risks were taken by Eisenhower and the supreme commanders because of the mounting pressure to get sufficient units trained for D-day a few short months away. For all the sightings by shore-based observers and radar indicating that E-boats were operating in the east of Lyme Bay, convoy T-4 was still allowed to sail straight into the path of the German warships and to sail in such a way that it was strung out across the sea like a series of sitting ducks with just one small escort vessel a mile ahead of them. Had there been an escort vessel on both seaward bow and beam the E-boats would have found their task much harder.

Eventually the British Admiralty accepted responsibility for the inadequate escort cover and admitted that a second naval vessel might have averted the disaster altogether. Whatever the truth of the matter, the accusations of a cover-up to hide the serious blunders of senior commanders and to avoid the risk of bitter recriminations between the US and British officers involved damaging Allied relations just before the invasion of Normandy have not been entirely dismissed. The fact that it took 43 years before an official monument to the tragic loss of so many young US servicemen was erected near the scene of the disaster merely fuelled those suspicions.

1945 – THE ODESSA CONSPIRACY One of the most enduring conspiracy theories of all, and indeed one very much based on hard facts, has been the organised escape of hundreds or perhaps even thousands of Nazi war criminals to safe havens in South America or to Britain and the United States under new identities. The shadowy secret organisation usually credited for this is known as Odessa. By 1944 it was clear that the fortunes of war had turned against Nazi Germany. The Allies were paying a very high price to ensure that the world would most definitely not spin on a Berlin–Rome–Tokyo axis and that the Thousand-Year Reich would be limited to little more than a horrific decade. To some, this was not the future which had been anticipated. Nor was it a future to be faced without adequate preparation. On 10 August 1944 at the Maison Rouge hotel in Strasbourg, the first of a series of secret meetings was convened. It involved top German industrialists and bankers and the agenda was simple: to plan for the future, specifically a secure future for the Nazis, following the defeat of Germany at the hands of the Allies. Leading Nazi officials feared retribution from the Allies and in particular from the Red Army. Rather than face the coming punishment, these Nazis would seek out safety well away from their homeland in friendly countries with little chance of discovery or extradition. It was clear that Nazi Germany's assets would fall into the hands of the victors unless action was taken promptly. Though most of these assets were stolen from invaded countries and ravaged cultures, it was considered vitally important that they should be saved because raising a new Reich from the ashes of the soon to be defeated one would need substantial financing. The outcome of the meeting in Strasbourg was the genesis of an organisation, one well financed by private and business donors and well organised with the express purpose of helping fellow fleeing Nazis escape justice. This organisation was named very pragmatically 'The organisation of former SS members', better known as Odessa. In short order, Odessa built a large and reliable network geared to achieve its ends. Routes were mapped, contacts were established and influential Nazis started to vanish as they were secretly ushered out of Germany and off to foreign countries where they were to start a new life under false names.

At the end of the war, only 24 high-ranking Nazi officials stood trial, along with many of the less important. The Nuremberg Trials saw those accused tried on four counts: conspiracy, war crimes, crimes against peace and war against humanity. Eleven of the top Nazi officials, and hundreds of those from the lower ranks, were judged guilty and were hanged. Hermann Göring escaped justice by committing suicide while in custody. But many of the Nazi perpetrators were never tried. Instead, they escaped with the help of Odessa. Some war criminals remained in Germany and took on new identities, managing to get themselves smuggled out of Germany and to freedom during the chaos at the end of hostilities. An underground network called 'Die Spiner' (the Spider) supplied false papers and passports, safe houses and contacts that could smuggle war criminals across the unpatrolled Swiss borders. Once into Switzerland, they were quickly moved on to Italy, using what some called 'The Monastery Route'. Once in Italy, the threat was essentially over, and many then dispersed around the world. New homes were open to the fleeing Nazis. Third World countries eagerly welcomed the experience and expertise of these Nazi war criminals. Fascist countries, like Spain under Franco, as well as those in South America, particularly Peron's Argentina, became safe havens. And, with the establishment of the state of Israel in 1947, new opportunities opened in the surrounding Middle Eastern countries and in particular Egypt and Syria, as they welcomed Nazis who could and would be used to train armies intended to destroy the newly formed Jewish state.

Third World countries were not alone in providing a new home to fleeing Nazis. Both the USA and the Soviet Union made use of them. The CIA was interested in counter-intelligence to be applied in a new war, the Cold War, and it used known Nazi war criminals in its covert activities against the Soviet Union. After WW2, in an operation called 'Paperclip', the US government allowed select former Nazis into the United States. Many were scientists that would go on to help America land on the moon, so defeating the Soviet Union in that race. The Space Race was, from the very start, more than just a reach for the strategic 'high ground': it was used as part of the propaganda war being played out in the Cold War. But Odessa was not a tale comprised only of success stories. Adolf Eichmann, the 'Architect of Genocide', escaped Germany thanks to Odessa, but he was later captured in South America by Israeli intelligence agents and brought back to Israel to stand trial for his crimes against the Jewish people. On 21 May 1962 he was found guilty of the crimes as charged and was sentenced to hang.

Some have wondered, however, whether the real success of Odessa was the connections that were quickly and effectively made with Swiss intelligence to the American OSS and the Roman Catholic Church. Odessa may have existed more as a smoke screen to hide the fact that, often travelling on passports provided by the Vatican, these Nazi rocket designers, weapons experts and intelligence officers were escaping justice and finding success and wealth as important players in the USA's vast Cold War military build-up, its missile, biological and chemical warfare programmes and, above all, the Space Race.

Does Odessa still exist? What happened to the ill-gotten Nazi wealth? Where are the vanished works of art? Who has the stolen gold? Who controls the confiscated foreign currencies? Swiss bankers have never denied holding accounts belonging to Jews killed in the Holocaust. It is believed that they also hold the wealth of the Nazis, the wealth stolen from conquered countries during the Nazi reign of terror. It is believed that the Swiss banks continue to service the accounts of Nazi war criminals, and that the assets are used to fund neo-Nazi activities and white supremacy groups around the world today.

While former Nazi spymaster Reinhard Gehlen, Hitler's wartime chief of intelligence on the Eastern Front, catered to his American sponsors' anti-Communist cravings, his organisation became the life raft for legions of Hitler's SS and RSHA (Reich Main Security Office) to escape their war crimes and resettle safely in the post-war world, much indeed as the Nazi Odessa scheme had envisioned. Gehlen's main task from 1946 to 1956 when his 'Organisation' was effectively part of US intelligence seems to have been to protect Odessa Nazis by cutting out the direct involvement of the Americans. Gehlen's gambit in retrospect was an exceptionally well-orchestrated diversion. Being on the US payroll also did not guarantee abiding loyalty. Ironically, some of the Nazis recruited and supported by Gehlen would later play major roles in neo-fascist organisations in Europe and elsewhere, some of which even operated against the USA. But there was another downside. CIA officials eventually discovered that the Nazi old-boy network inside the Gehlen Organisation was riddled with Soviet spies. Gehlen's employment of ex-Nazis, many of whom despised democratic America, had enabled the Soviet Union to penetrate West Germany's secret service, later the BND. In effect, the CIA hired Gehlen to keep the Soviets out, but he ended up letting them in. Even CIA officials recognised they had invested too much trust in Gehlen and 'his spooky Nazi outfit', as one US official referred to it. 'One of the biggest mistakes the United States ever made in intelligence was taking on Gehlen,' an American espionage specialist later admitted. It is a price rarely acknowledged amid Washington's post-Cold-War triumphalism. But widespread CIA recruitment of fascists gave these anti-democratic forces a crucial respite. After fifty years, the resurgence of fascism in Europe and elsewhere underscores the need for the United States to confront and understand the threat posed by a resurgence of right-wing extremism. Odessa, the Vatican, Project Paperclip, the OSS, the CIA and the Gehlen Organisation all eventually seem to have a common cause, that of saving the skills and knowledge of the Nazi war criminals for their new paymasters in the West. When asked what he thought of working with a Nazi like Gehlen, wartime OSS officer based in Switzerland and future CIA chief Allen Dulles happily commented, 'He's on our side, and that's all that matters'.

Part Two

1946–79

1946 – THE GEHLEN CONNECTION For many interested in that fascinating period following the collapse of the Third Reich in 1945, the name of Reinhard Gehlen has become synonymous with conspiracies. Indeed his own survival, his creation of a new intelligence organisation out of the rubble of defeat, and the awe in which he appeared to be held by many US intelligence officers all involve successful intrigues of one sort or another. The ease with which Gehlen achieved a position of great importance seems distinctly strange even today. However, he was a masterspy, he had the contacts and nobody knew as much as he did about the America's new enemy, Stalin's Russia. The USA badly needed Gehlen, his expertise and his organisation, and were prepared to draw a veil over recent events and ignore the large numbers of unrepentant Nazis who escaped the justice of the Nuremberg Trials by serving in the new intelligence service in the front line of the Cold War.

For US policy-makers, the anniversary of the founding of the CIA on 8 September 2003 will provide more opportunities for self-congratulatory pronouncements about winning the Cold War and the defeat of Communism. But serious conspiracy theorists will be once again arguing that the American public would be far better served if US officials were to finally mark the occasion by owning up to one of the CIA's 'original sins'. By this they mean the widespread covert use of a Nazi spy network brimming with war criminals. US intelligence chiefs protected a veritable cast of killers so that they could ostensibly help to counter the growing Soviet threat. But for the next five decades, this decision, often described as the ultimate practice of situational ethics, markedly increased Washington's tolerance for human rights abuses and a variety of other crimes as long as they could be categorised as being in the name of anti-Communism. To some extent Washington's policy-makers are still living with the consequences to this day. Perhaps it would not be stretching the point to suggest that the resurgent neo-fascist movements in Europe can trace their ideological lineage back to Adolf Hitler's Third Reich, through many of the men who served the CIA, and supposedly operated on behalf of Western interests during the Cold War.

The key player on the German side of this unholy alliance was of course General Reinhard Gehlen, a thin, bespectacled espionage prodigy who had been Hitler's top anti-Soviet spy. Gehlen was effectively in control of all of Germany's military-intelligence capabilities throughout Eastern Europe and the Soviet Union. As the war drew to a close, Gehlen surmised that the grand anti-fascist coalition being led by the United States, Great Britain and the Soviet Union would not long survive the coming of peace. Gehlen also recognised that US intelligence operations, largely an anti-Nazi improvisation in the form of the OSS would be ill-prepared to wage a sustained clandestine war against the Soviet Union. As the war in Europe drew to a close Gehlen opted to surrender himself to an American Counter-Intelligence-Corps Team on 28 May 1945. He offered to turn over his vast and well-hidden espionage archive on the Soviets that he had accumulated for Hitler. Just months prior to his surrender, Gehlen and some of his most trusted deputies had transferred all of their documents onto microfilm and buried the cache in metal drums in the Austrian Alps. Gehlen demanded an audience with American officials, and got it, arriving at Washington National Airport on 24 August 1945. Gehlen quickly came to an agreement with his erstwhile captors: all his files, documents and staff would be at the service of the Americans, and in addition he was able to offer the priceless opportunity for the Americans of being able to reactivate an underground army of battle-hardened anti-Communists still in hiding through Communist-dominated Eastern Europe for future use in the coming confrontation with Stalin. This must have been music to the ears of harassed American intelligence officers trying to make sense of the new threats posed by its former ally. In return, Gehlen, who lived until 1979, would not be prosecuted for war crimes.

Although the ink had barely dried on the Yalta agreements, which required the USA to give the Soviets any captured German officers who had been involved in 'eastern area activities', Gehlen was soon transferred to Fort Hunt, Virginia. There he worked closely with US officials, whose appetite for Cold War intelligence was growing voraciously. General Gehlen played on their fears and their lack of knowledge with his seductive anti-Soviet pitch, which left competing elements of the growing US intelligence community positively vying for his services. During his ten months at Fort Hunt, Gehlen presented a professional image: the pure technician who liked nothing better than to immerse himself in maps, flow charts and statistics. The persona he projected was, in espionage parlance, a 'legend' or one concocted to exaggerate his wartime influence and success and importantly to promote Gehlen's false claim that he had never been a committed Nazi. He, just like his new American colleagues, was dedicated to fighting Communism. This was the basis for the Gehlen conspiracy that the USA was to promote for so many years – no, they were not using Nazis to spy on Russia; they were all vetted and found to be clean-cut anti-Communists from America's new ally, Germany. Among those who took the bait willingly, and helped create both the conspiracy and the new Gehlen organisation, was future CIA director Allen Dulles, who became one of Gehlen's biggest post-war supporters. With a mandate to continue gathering information in the East just as he had been doing for Hitler, Gehlen re-established his spy organisation, initially under US army supervision. Setting up shop back in central Germany in the Spessert Mountains, and supported by the newly formed CIA, the Gehlen Organisation began pouring often poor quality or deliberately falsified anti-Soviet intelligence back to US intelligence agencies until becoming incorporated openly into the Bonn Government as the official intelligence organisation (*Bundesnachrichtendiest*) when West Germany gained its sovereignty in 1955. The Gehlen 'Org', as it was called, enlisted thousands of Gestapo, RSHA, army and SS veterans, despite Gehlen's promise to US officials that he would not employ hardcore Nazis. Yet even the most guilty, including senior bureaucrats who administered the Holocaust, were welcomed into the Org. It is reported that Alois Brunner, Adolf Eichmann's right-hand man and personal favourite, also found gainful employment courtesy of Gehlen and the CIA. In fact it seemed that in the Gehlen headquarters one SS man simply paved the way for the next and Himmler's elite were having happy reunion ceremonies. US officials knew that many of the people they were subsidising had committed terrible crimes against humanity, but atrocities were overlooked as the anti-Communist crusade gained momentum. Through the Gehlen organisation the CIA gained access to former leaders of virtually every Nazi-puppet government from the Baltic to the Black Sea, as well as to a veritably rogues' gallery of former Waffen SS fanatics and killers. Operating alongside the CIA in the late 1940s, Gehlen's reborn Nazi intelligence apparatus functioned as Washington's secret eyes and ears in Central and Eastern Europe.

First under CIA auspices, and later as head of the West German intelligence service or BND, Gehlen was able to deeply influence the development of US policy towards the Soviet Union and the future Warsaw Pact states. The Org played a major role within NATO, too, supplying two-thirds of raw intelligence on Warsaw Pact countries. The CIA in particular came to rely heavily on Gehlen, to the point where some former intelligence officers believe that Gehlen was able to exploit the USA for his political aims. James Critchfield, a CIA operative who worked with Gehlen on a daily basis for eight years, said, 'What we had, essentially, was an agreement to exploit each other, each in his own national interest,' adding, 'The Agency loved Gehlen because he fed us what we wanted to hear'; another former CIA officer admitted, 'We used his stuff constantly, and we fed it to everybody else, the Pentagon, the White House, the newspapers. They loved it, too. But it was hyped up Russian bogeyman junk, and it did a lot of damage to this country.'

Washington's growing dependence on Gehlen made US officials sitting ducks for disinformation. Much of what the Gehlen organisation supplied exaggerated the Soviet threat and whipped up fears about Russian military intentions. The Nazi spymaster fostered a growing paranoia in the West about a worldwide Communist conspiracy. Gehlen's strategy was based on a rudimentary equation: the colder the Cold War got, the more political space for Hitler's heirs. The CIA thought that they could at least be certain of the Gehlen organisation's anti-Communist credentials, yet even in this they were to be proved wrong. Gehlen's own paranoia about the Communists led him to accept seemingly dedicated right-wing officers for highly sensitive appointments within first the Org and later the BND who it turned out were in fact East German or Soviet double-agents. Some of the most damaging espionage operations conducted against Western interests were those by spies who had totally fooled Gehlen. In consequence they had been fully accepted by the CIA. Many chastened former CIA officers will probably admit in private that the Gehlen conspiracy at times turned into one enormous 'blowback' intelligence disaster. Hitler, for one, would no doubt have been vastly amused at the ability of his trusted spymaster to bring death and political turmoil to much of Eastern Europe long after Germany's defeat in 1945.

1947 – ROSWELL CONSPIRACY According to theorists, ever since 1946 it must have been clear to defence intelligence chiefs studying the so-called Ghost Aircraft wave, as UFO sightings were known at the time, in Scandinavia and elsewhere that intelligently controlled objects of unknown origin and purpose were operating in our atmosphere. Even as early as 1942, when mysterious objects appeared over Los Angeles, General George Marshall, as Army Chief of Staff, was unable to account for the sightings in conventional terms. So, by July 1947, when sightings proliferated throughout the United

States and a UFO reportedly crashed at Roswell, New Mexico, it must have become obvious to some that the so-called flying saucers were of extraterrestrial origin. Apart from the likely fact that an admission of this nature, even if true, would generate public alarm, the military needed to learn as much as possible about the construction and propulsion of the craft, in the event that another nation such as the Soviet Union might acquire this knowledge first, thus providing an additional reason for having total secrecy attached to the investigations.

A granddaddy of UFO conspiracies, but what did actually crash near Roswell, New Mexico, in 1947? Something large and silvery wobbled through the air and ploughed into the desert with a tremendous bang, according to Ufologists. That much, generally speaking, seems to go without too much dispute. The date was 2 July 1947 and it is undisputed that the government took an immediate interest in the event and that the air force quickly dispatched a team to collect the wreckage. One metallic chunk in particular was reported to be about four feet long and this, with other recovered material, was flown back to the huge Wright-Patterson air force base in Dayton, Ohio, for further investigation. General Roger Ramey, the officer in charge, ordered his men not to talk to the press. However, before Ramey could clamp a lid on the affair, the air base public information officer issued a press release announcing that the authorities had acquired a 'flying disc'. An Albuquerque radio station picked up a leak of the story and as it broadcast the report, a wire message came through from the FBI: 'Attention Albequerque: cease transmission. Repeat. Cease transmission. National security item. Do not transmit. Stand by . . .' A day later, the air force held a press conference and announced that what crashed at Roswell was actually a balloon.

In fact, the UFO controversy had begun a few days earlier when businessman and aviator Kenneth Arnold reportedly chased a group of some nine 'bobbing and weaving' objects as he flew in his private plane. He described the objects as 'saucer shaped'. A witty reporter at an Associated Press bureau dropped the phrase 'flying saucers' into a wire dispatch and it entered into the English language. The air force said later that Arnold had pursued 'a mirage' and left it at that. However, the 'mystery' surrounding the Roswell incident has merely deepened with the passing years and the veritable flood of newspaper and magazine articles, TV investigations and popular films.

There have also been vast numbers of UFO reports since 1947.

Some have been captured on film, still and moving, invariably of poor quality, and indeed it is strange that UFOs rarely make an appearance when a professional photographer with a long lens or a TV news team are about. They appear all over the world and even reportedly in outer space. NASA astronauts have reported seeing weird objects, and conspiracy theorists draw further proof of a cover-up by claiming that photographs taken of the so-called 'dark side' of the moon remain classified for some unexplained reason. The myth that UFOs only reveal themselves to peasant farmers or those who probably live in caravans or trailer parks is, however, easily dismissed. There are indeed a disturbing number of reports from expert witnesses – airline pilots and flight crew, for instance. There have been numerous incidents in which unidentified flying objects have been pursued by fighter pilots from various nations, though no national air force has ever been prepared to release gun-camera footage, assuming of course that the fighter got that close, while further disturbing evidence has come from unexplained, fast moving and often highly manoeuvrable 'blips' on radar screens.

Theorists point to a number of what they would undoubtedly describe as genuine close encounters with UFOs. One of these encounters includes the mystery of what actually happened on 23 November 1953 to an F-89 interceptor which was chasing a UFO over Lake Superior when, according to radar operators, the two blips on the screen seemed to merge into one and then blinked off the screen. The jet and its pilot, Lt Felix Moncla, had apparently disappeared without a trace. The air force file on the vanished fighter, for some reason, contains just two pages. One of them is a page from a book debunking UFO theories.

Roswell, however, remains the most important landmark in the UFO cover-up because, apparently, something has actually been covered up. There is no mention of the crash in the air force's 'Project Blue Book' files, which were supposed to have recorded all UFO reports that crossed the air force's desk along with their various 'scientific' explanations. The Warren Report into the UFO phenomenon, generally considered by Ufologists to be a cover-up posing as an investigation, actually seems to give Roswell increased prominence by the omission of Project Blue Book. Some might write the whole incident off as unlikely, noting that a spacecraft capable of navigating the universe and engineered to endure the rigours of interstellar travel is unlikely to crash like an ordinary aircraft, but perhaps accidents happen even to the products of an extraterrestrial super race.

The UFO cover-up conspiracy really kicks in, however, when it comes to the subject of Majestic-12. In the seemingly endless search for the single central conspiracy in charge of absolutely everything, MJ-12 crops up often as the most likely candidate. A committee of twelve eminent military, intelligence and academic personages was allegedly chartered to manage and conceal the most important event in world history, the first contact with alien life forms, even if they were probably dead. According to the story the MJ-12 'eyes only' briefing paper prepared for Dwight Eisenhower when he was still President-elect stated that four 'Extraterrestrial Biological Entities' or 'EBEs' had been discovered two miles from the Roswell crash site. According to some versions of the story, two of the aliens were still alive at the time and one even put up a struggle. The preserved bodies of the EBEs are now allegedly kept on ice in Los Alamos, New Mexico. Of course, one of the major problems with the whole Majestic saga is the lack of proof that any such organisation has ever existed outside the imagination of the Ufologist. The suggestion is that the Majestic-12 document, which is the only hard evidence that MJ-12 ever held a meeting, may well be a hoax. No one in a position to do so has ever authenticated it, and given how very 'leaky' government servants tend to be, it is surprising that there has not been any further corroboration of Majestic's actual existence in some fifty years, not even in a ghosted biography by a retired, but financially challenged, former official. But some might say no one is talking because they are scared. There is only one mention of MJ-12 in any other official paper, and that is a November 1980 air force analysis of a UFO film outlining in minute detail how the government is 'still interested' in UFO sightings, which it investigates through 'covert cover'. This highly dubious document, like the original MJ-12 paper, somehow seems far too good to be true. It would be on a par with a researcher combing through the JFK files and suddenly producing a CIA document detailing how the CIA were going to assassinate the President in Dallas: just too convenient to easily accept without further evidence.

The MJ-12 controversy has, however, happily spawned many more legends and much speculation, primarily that it still exists and is still administering the UFO cover-up, coping with each alien abduction and saucer crash as it comes up. In fact, in some versions of the story, MJ-12 is in charge of co-operation and negotiation with an alien race now among us. Some Ufologists have put forward the claim that, through MJ-12, the US government has become aware of a veritable United Nations of EBEs. These range from three or more variations of insecto-humanoid 'Grays', who can be tall or short, skinny or pot-bellied and positively eggheaded, but are definitely enemies of all mankind, to the friendly 'Blonds', who look more like humans but who, despite their general good intentions, steadfastly refuse to break the galactic commitment to respect sovereignty or 'universal law of non-interference' to save the earth from whatever the evil Grays have in store for us. The list also includes the 'Hairy Dwarves' and the 'Very Tall Race' and not forgetting the mysterious 'Men in Black'.

Unlike MJ-12, the existence of the Robertson Panel is not in doubt. Convened in January 1953 by the CIA, this board of scientists issued a report that was not fully declassified until 1975. Simply denying the existence of unexplainable or extraterrestrial UFOs, as the Roberston Panel certainly did, cannot be genuinely considered a cover-up. However, the panel did move considerably beyond simple denial. It recommended that the US government take positive action to effectively rubbish UFO reports to the point of pursuing a vigorous anti-UFO 'education' campaign through the mass media using television, films and magazines. The Panel went on to suggest using 'psychologists familiar with mass psychology' to help assemble the programme and even wondered if Walt Disney Studios might be interested in producing anti-UFO cartoons. The report recommended that UFO-enthusiast groups should be placed under surveillance due to 'the possible use of such groups for subversive purposes'. None of the rather patronising or, depending on your personal view, disturbing recommendations were apparently ever acted upon and the existence of this CIA panel still falls far short of proving that a 'flying saucer' was recovered at Roswell, that the US military are using ultra-modern weapon systems based on reverse-engineered alien technology, or that Washington is about to appoint its first secret ambassador to an extra-terrestrial government. However, it does once again highlight the paranoia of the times when the CIA preferred to see an interest in UFOs as a potential Communist or subversive threat to the nation – although no doubt the dedicated theorist will simply argue that all this simply proves how effective the UFO cover-up conspiracy has been all these years.

Although there have been at least forty accounts of UFOs alleged to have been recovered throughout the US and elsewhere, the evidence suggests that it took a long time, possibly several decades, before scientists and engineers could even begin to comprehend the alien technology. No government is happy to admit that alien vehicles invading the airspace can come and go as they please, and that our defences against them are inadequate. That some UFOs have been responsible for the destruction or disappearance of aircraft is not something that could be admitted openly. In 1964 Ray Stanford discovered metal fragments at a site in Socorro, New Mexico, the same site where Sergeant Lonnie Zamora apparently encountered a landed UFO and its occupants that year. Stanford and colleagues took the samples to NASA's Goddard Space Flight Center where preliminary analysis determined that the metal shavings were highly unusual: so unusual, in fact, that they were promptly confiscated. Public reaction to an admission by one of the superpowers that some UFOs are extra-terrestrial would hinge on how much the public was told, and this would present world leaders with a major dilemma. Such an admission would lead to an avalanche of questions, some of which simply can't be answered without disclosing vital defence interests. Or as the conspiracy theorists would undoubtedly agree, just as the *X-Files* says, 'The Truth is Out There'.

1947 – THE PAPERCLIP CONSPIRACY It would be fair to say that the Paperclip conspiracy was the US version of Odessa, and indeed there is considerable suspicion that Paperclip, Odessa and the Gehlen organisation's operations to rescue Nazis from prosecution for war crimes committed throughout Europe in WW2 were in reality one and the same thing or, at the very least, worked in unison. US officials after WW2 rewrote the records of German scientists and smoothed the way for many of them to enter the US. This was even true for ardent Nazis. The rationale of the CIA and US government was that the German mind and technology was needed to battle the Communist threat. The Germans were all too willing to comply as they were ideological enemies of Communism, and many war criminals were able to escape punishment this way. Nazi scientists, professors and doctors were given new identities and, along with their families, were secretly brought into the US where they were to play an important role in US scientific, military and industrial developments. This is especially important regarding the field of psychiatry, because psychiatry played a large part in the 'scientific' justification for eradicating 'useless eaters', the 'mentally retarded' and anyone considered inferior by the Third Reich. Today the conspiracy theorists will argue that similar ideas of eugenics and psychiatric abuse have again taken hold in this and other countries under the guise of 'modern science', and often the source of these ideas are the same Nazis who were brought over after WW2.

After WW2 ended in 1945, victorious Soviet and US intelligence teams began a treasure hunt throughout occupied Germany for military and scientific booty. They were looking for things such as new rocket and aircraft designs, medicines and electronics. But they were also hunting down the most precious 'spoils' of all: the scientists whose work had nearly won the war for Germany. The US military rounded up Nazi scientists by the dozen and brought them to America where it had originally been intended to merely debrief them and send them back to Germany. But when it realised the magnitude of the scientist's knowledge and expertise, the War Department decided it would be a considerable waste to send the scientists home. There was only one major problem: it was illegal, since US law explicitly prohibited convicted, or those strongly suspected of being, Nazi officials from emigrating to America, and as many as three-quarters of the scientists in question had been committed Nazis. Convinced that German scientists could help America's post-war efforts, President Harry Truman agreed in September 1946 to authorise 'Project Paperclip', a programme to bring selected German scientists to work on America's behalf during the Cold War. However, Truman expressly excluded anyone found 'to have been a member of the Nazi Party and more than a nominal participant in its activities, or an active supporter of Nazism or militarism.'

The War Department's Joint Intelligence Objectives Agency (JIOA) conducted background investigations of the scientists. In February 1947, JIOA director Bosquet Wev submitted the first set of scientists' dossiers to the State and Justice Departments for review. The dossiers were damning. Samauel Klaus, the State Department's representative on the JIOA board, claimed that all the scientists in this first batch were 'ardent Nazis'. Their visa requests were denied. Wev was furious. He wrote a memo, warning, 'the best interests of the United States have been subjugated to the efforts expended in "beating a dead Nazi horse".' He also declared that the return of these scientists to Germany, where the USA's enemies could exploit them, presented a 'far greater security threat to this country than any former Nazi affiliations which they may have had or even any Nazi sympathies that they may still have.' Military Intelligence 'cleansed' the files of Nazi references, and by 1955 more than 760 German scientists had been granted citizenship in the United States and given prominent positions in the American scientific community. Many had been long-term members of the Nazi Party and the Gestapo, had conducted experiments on humans at concentration camps, had used slave labour and had committed other war crimes. In a 1985 exposé in the *Bulletin of the Atomic Scientists*, Linda Hunt wrote that she had examined more than 130 reports on Project Paperclip subjects and every one 'had been changed to eliminate the security threat classification.' President Truman, who had explicitly ordered no committed Nazis to be admitted under Project Paperclip, was evidently never aware that his directive had been violated. State Department archives and the memoirs of officials from that era confirm this. In fact, according to Clare Lasby's book on Project Paperclip, project officials 'covered their designs with such secrecy that it bedeviled their own President; at Potsdam he denied their activities and undoubtedly enhanced Russian suspicion and distrust,' quite possibly fuelling the Cold War even further.

A good example of how these dossiers were changed is the case of Wernher von Braun. A report on the German rocket scientist on 18 September 1947 stated, 'Subject is regarded as a potential security threat by the Military Governor.' The following February, a new security evaluation of von Braun said, 'No derogatory information is available on the subject . . . It is the opinion of the Military Governor that he may not constitute a security threat to the United States.' Project Paperclip was finally stopped in 1957, when the West German government formally protested to the United States that these efforts had stripped West Germany of its leading 'scientific skills'. There was no comment about supporting Nazis.

Paperclip may have ended in 1957, but its effects have continued ever since and not just in the United States. The Nazis became employed CIA agents, engaging in clandestine and often subversive operations. Another umbrella project that was spawned from Paperclip was MK-ULTRA. MK-ULTRA was carried out in a secret laboratory, established and funded by CIA director Allen Dulles in Montreal, Canada, at McGill University in the Allen Memorial Institute, headed by psychiatrist Dr Ewen Cameron. For the next several years Dr Ewen Cameron waged his private war in Canada. It is ironic that Dr Cameron served as a member of the Nuremberg tribunal who heard the cases against the Nazi doctors. Established at the height of the drug-experimentation period, MK-ULTRA was the brainchild of Richard Helms, who later became a CIA director, and it was designed to defeat enemies using brainwashing techniques. MK-ULTRA had another arm involved in chemical and biological warfare (CBW), known as MK-DELTA. The 'doctors' who carried out these experiments used some of the same techniques as the Nazi 'doctors', and those used by Dr Cameron and former Nazi scientists included electroshock, sleep deprivation, memory implantation, memory erasure, sensory modification, psychoactive drug experiments and many more potentially illegal practices.

The conspiracy theory surrounding Project Paperclip has been detailed above, but it must be pointed out that much of it is not mere theory: these are events that really happened and the people involved developed new and dangerous drugs, new interrogation techniques, were involved in assassinations and much else. Project Paperclip not only brought the US many of the scientists involved in MK-ULTRA, but also ultimately the key players involved in the assassination of Pope John Paul I, October Surprise, the sabotage of Carter's peace talks with Iran, and a great many other things still classified to this day. Paperclip, like the United States' involvement with the Gehlen organisation, proved ultimately to be a mixed blessing, and though both 'projects' undoubtedly provided considerable help to the United States during the height of the Cold War, the morality of conspiring to 'rescue' war criminals from justice, and the long-term damage to America's standing in the world, are an entirely different matter.

1948 – MURDER OF GANDHI 'If I am to die by the bullet of a mad man, I must do so smiling. There must be no anger within me. God must be in my heart and on my lips.' So said Mahatma Gandhi on 28 January 1948, just two days before his assassination. Contrary to popular belief there had been many failed attempts on the life of Mohandâs Karamchand Gandhi, the Mahatma. On 30 June 1946 speaking at a prayer meeting at Pune, soon after an unsuccessful assassination attempt, the Mahatma said, 'By the grace of God I have been saved from the proverbial jaws of death seven times. I have not ever hurt anybody. I consider no one to be an enemy, so I fail to understand why there have been so many attempts on my life. The attempt on my life yesterday failed. I am not ready to die just yet. I am going to live till I reach 125 years.' Five of these attempts are well documented and involve the Pune branch of the Hindu Mahasabha; three of these five also point to the involvement of two of the conspirators involved in Gandhi's assassination, Narayan Apte and Nathuram Godse. Hindu Mahasabha and the offshoot Rasthtriya Swayamsevak Sangh (RSS) have always claimed that the Mahatma was murdered by a Hindu conspiracy because he was seen as being far too partial to the Muslims at a time of great ethnic rivalry and violence. Gandhi was also held responsible by the more militant Hindu elements for the plans to partition the old India and for trying to force the government of India to give 550 million rupees, which was to be used to help establish the independent Muslim nation.

Born on 2 October 1869 in Porbandar, Mahatma Gandhi influenced an entire period of history from the end of the nineteenth to the middle of the twentieth century. He was the fourth child of Karamchand and Putliba. Educated in Rajkot, Gandhi was married to Kasturba, the daughter of Gokuladas Makharji of Porbunder, at the age of thirteen. After he had finished school Gandhi went to England to study law. On his return he was offered a job in South Africa. Suffering injustices and insults by the racial white colonialists, Gandhi launched a movement for equal rights in South Africa. It was one of the world's first mass civil disobedience movements. Gandhi established the Tolstoy Farm and the Phoenix Ashram in South Africa as the nerve centres of his equal rights movements; he published and edited the *Indian Opinion* from Phoenix Ashram. After succeeding in his fight with the colonialists in South Africa, he returned to India.

Gandhi launched his first movement for India's independence by creating the non-co-operation movement. After a few incidents of violence in Chauri Chaura, Gandhi suspended the non-co-operation movement and was jailed. Gandhi was tried for sedition and was sentenced to imprisonment. After many successful movements Gandhi finally gave an ultimatum to the British on 9 August 1942, to quit India. Gandhi and the entire top leadership of his Congress Movement were arrested but the people of India picked up the cue to protest and fought till they achieved freedom. Finally the British were forced to grant freedom in 1947, but not before tragically dividing India by exploiting the animosity of the Congress and Muslim League leadership. A dejected Gandhi refused to accept the vivisection of his beloved motherland and was devastated by the massacres of innocents in the post-partition race hate riots.

He acted as a one-man peace force in Bengal and Bihar and restored some form of order by offering his own life. Gandhi returned to a maddened Delhi and tried to pacify the frenzied mobs. On 13 January 1948, as many Hindu, Muslim and Sikh refugees dragged each other out of trains and killed one another, Gandhi began an indefinite fast, the last fast of his life. By 15 January Gandhi's health had deteriorated. He had no strength to walk or even sit unsupported. The doctors came to the conclusion that Gandhi could not survive on his fast for more than 72 hours. His weight was just 107 pounds. By the night of 17 January Gandhi's condition was very serious. His pulse was weak and irregular. He was asleep when one of his followers, Pyarelal Nayar, came in, shook Gandhi's shoulders and showed him the charter the Peace Committee had signed. Gandhi was still not satisfied as it lacked signatures of two leaders of the Hindu Mahasabha and the RSS, and said that he would not break the fast till everyone signed it. It was not until 12.45 p.m. on 18 January, when another follower, Rajendra Prasad, showed Gandhi the charter signed by all the leaders to confirm that they were fully prepared to carry out his commandments, that Gandhi accepted his first nourishment. At the age of 78, he had existed for 121 hours and 30 minutes on lukewarm water and bicarbonate of soda. Maulana Azad, a Muslim, took the glass of orange juice with glucose in his hands and raised it to Gandhi's lips. On 20 January Madanlal Pahwa exploded a bomb at a prayer meeting in Pune as a diversion so that Nathuram Godse and his gang of murderers could kill the Mahatma. The conspiracy failed on this occasion and Pahwa was arrested, though the others managed to escape. On 30 January 1948 at 5.12 p.m. just as Mahatma Gandhi walked towards the prayer meeting, the crowd parted to reveal Nathuram Godse. On the pretext of seeking Gandhi's blessings Godse came near him and, bending down, pulled out a gun and shot Gandhi three times from point-blank range. A Hindu conspiracy which had tried to kill the peace-loving figurehead of an independent India on numerous occasions had finally succeeded, and in doing so robbed India of one of its greatest citizens.

1953 – US GERM WARFARE CONSPIRACY There have been a number of accusations that the USA has been involved in the use of certain chemical, and perhaps even biological, warfare weapons over the last fifty years. The use of Agent Orange with its horrific, if unintended, side effects in Vietnam is well known, as are the development and use of various incapacitating gases such as CS and CN, and the experimentation on convicted prisoners or serving US military personnel with chemical agents. However, what has remained unverified is the reported use of deadly agents during the Korean War. The accusations suggests that the US government is hiding a biological warfare programme from the rest of the world, and actually employed such weapons in 1952 as part of Operation Artichoke. The conspiracy is extended to cover the death of the biochemist Dr Frank Olson on 28 November 1953 after a mysterious fall from the thirteenth floor of the Hotel Pennsylvania in New York City. At the time of his death, Olson had been given the highest clearance for access to classified information. He was one of the leading scientists in the field of biological weapons and had been working for ten years in the biological warfare facilities at Maryland's Camp Detrick, later renamed Fort Detrick, near Washington DC. He also occupied a leading position in Operation Artichoke, a CIA programme that co-ordinated all similar projects of the army, navy and CIA involving psychedelic drugs, fatal poisons and similar substances. Those involved in this project are reported to have included German doctors who had experimented with human beings in the Nazi concentration camps. Artichoke is also reported to have involved the use of torture and drugs to interrogate people. The effects of substances such as LSD, heroin and marijuana were studied, using unsuspecting individuals as human guinea pigs. The CIA was eager to identify military uses for substances that altered the psyche. The agency was at that time obsessed with the idea that the Soviets or the Chinese might employ methods of brainwashing to recruit double-agents or to manipulate the population of entire nations. Artichoke also included the development of poisons that take effect immediately. These substances were later used in attempts on the lives of a number of foreign leaders, including Abdul Karim Kassem of Iraq, Patrice Lumumba of the Congo and Fidel Castro.

Before Frank Olson plunged to his death he had exhibited distinct symptoms of behavioural disturbance. Friends, family members and colleagues are believed to feel that he had seen things that he felt went too far and intended to quit his work with the CIA. The possibility may have occurred to the authorities that Olson was in a mood to blow the whistle on Operation Artichoke. Prior to his death he had seen a psychiatrist on several occasions, always in the company of a CIA watchdog. He died one day before he was scheduled to be committed to a psychiatric hospital. Olson's death was officially described as suicide due to depression. Only in the mid-1970s, when the CIA's secret activities were scrutinised in the wake of the Watergate scandal, did the government admit to a certain degree of responsibility. Ten days before his death, the CIA had administered LSD to Olson without his knowledge. President Gerald Ford subsequently apologised to the family, and the CIA paid compensation to his widow.

Conspiracy theorists believe that this was part of a massive cover-up. The theorists claim that there is evidence suggesting that the death of the biochemical expert was not suicide, but murder. Frank Olson's son, Eric, is convinced that his father was assassinated. He has been trying for decades to clear up the circumstances of his father's death, and has gathered numerous pieces of evidence supporting the thesis of murder. In 1994 Eric Olson had his father's body exhumed and examined by a renowned forensic scientist, who concluded that in all probability someone had knocked Frank Olson unconscious in the hotel room and thrown him out of the window. After the report on the postmortem had been published, the public prosecutor's office in Manhattan initiated proceedings against an unknown person. However, the prosecutor lost interest as soon as the CIA stopped the questioning of the main witness, the CIA agent Robert Lashbrook, who had accompanied Olson continuously prior to his death and had been in the hotel room when Olson fell out of the window. A memorandum dated 11 July 1975 strongly indicates that the CIA has something to hide. Addressed to the White House chief of staff, the memo urgently recommended an official apology by the President so as to forestall any trial or official hearing on the Olson case; otherwise, the memo said, 'it might be necessary to disclose highly classified national security information.' Ten days later President Ford met with the Olson family in the White House. The addressee and the author of this memo are still active and hold prominent positions in the US government of George W. Bush. The former is Secretary of Defense Donald Rumsfeld, who was then White House chief of staff, and the latter is Vice President Dick Cheney, who was then Rumsfeld's deputy.

The following year, after delays in the payment of the promised compensation to the family, another well-known political figure intervened: then CIA director George Bush, who himself went on to become US President and whose son is now in the White House.

Why has there been such an obvious cover-up? In the mid-1970s, Cheney, Rumsfeld and Bush, Sr appeared to collaborate to prevent a thorough investigation into Olson's death because they feared that it might 'disclose highly classified national security information'. The question is what information was so important twenty-odd years on? The theorists maintain that it all links back to the bad old days of Project Paperclip, Gehlen and the Nazi scientists. German physicians who had worked in Nazi concentration camps were rapidly rehabilitated after the war through the US denazification programme and put to work on US research projects on biological and chemical warfare. Olson and his colleagues apparently carried out large-scale field experiments with biological weapons. In one case they spread a certain bacillus, which they regarded as harmless, across San Francisco Bay, as a dress rehearsal for a major biological attack on a large city. Both genuine and alleged enemy agents were reportedly subjected to horrifying interrogations, some of which Olson may have witnessed personally. Significantly it is claimed that in some cases these interrogations led to the perhaps accidental death of the accused. The most convincing proof of this is a telegram from 1954, in which the CIA director inquires about 'bodies available for terminal experiments'. In addition, thousands of people were used, without their knowledge or consent, for experiments with LSD, mescaline, morphine, seconal, atropine and other drugs. The CIA even ran its own brothels in order to lure its victims. As the inspector general of the US army later stated in a report to a Senate committee, '[I]n universities, hospitals and research institutions [an] unknown number of chemical tests and experiments . . . were carried out with healthy adults, with mentally ill and with prison inmates.' Most of these activities were exposed in the 1970s, when two commissions appointed by Congress, the Rockefeller Institute and the Church, investigated the secret activities of the CIA.

In 1969 the USA officially cancelled all research programmes on biological weapons. Fort Detrick was supposedly closed down; however, the site is now used by the US Army Medical Research Institute for Infectious Diseases (USAMRIID), which, according to the official line, strictly limits itself to the analysis of biological weapons for defence purposes. In 1974 the US signed the international convention against biological warfare. Theorists argue with some conviction that the real reasons for the Olson cover-up run even more deeply into the secret use of biological warfare. One possible reason is linked to Korea and indeed to the anthrax attacks against leading politicians of the Democratic Party and others that cost the lives of five people in

2001. During the Korean War, both Pyongyang and Beijing repeatedly accused the US of employing bacteriological weapons. These accusations were, it is claimed, fully supported by eyewitness reports, photos, laboratory analyses and the remains of biological bombs. In 1952 two international commissions which examined the war area with Soviet and Chinese help concluded that the US army had indeed used such weapons. This again, it is claimed, was confirmed in written statements by US pilots who were held prisoner by North Korea. Some of them appeared before the international press and repeated their confessions. The US categorically denied these accusations, describing the evidence presented as forged, characterising the international commissions as instruments of Communist propaganda, and claiming that the soldiers' confessions were the result of 'brainwashing'. Allen Dulles, the CIA director, even gave a speech devoted to brainwashing, in which he accused North Korea of 'having turned around a whole number of our boys'. When the prisoners of war who had made these confessions returned from Korea in the summer of 1953, they were interrogated by the Artichoke team, which had announced its eagerness to do so weeks in advance. In a memorandum to the top leadership of the CIA, the team said it wanted to use those 'who have been exposed to and accepted in varying degrees Communist indoctrination . . . as unique research material in the Artichoke work.' Among other things, hypnosis, anaesthetics and LSD were to be used on the former POWs. In this way, Artichoke hoped to gain insight into the enemy's interrogation methods and to make sure that the returned soldiers did not work for the other side. It could be argued, however, that Artichoke's main concerns were the confessions of the air force pilots.

Frank Olson probably witnessed some interrogations of soldiers and airmen returning from Korea. As the leading expert on the release of biological weapons, he must have known about the use of such devices if and when they were actually employed. Was his first-hand knowledge the ultimate reason for his death and did the CIA silence him when it became clear he was seeking to distance himself from the agency? A close friend, Norman Cournoyer, had worked alongside Olson in the early years of Camp Detrick and remained his best friend until the end. He knew about Olson's intention to leave the CIA. In April 2001 Cournoyer, who had read an article about the case in the *New York Times Magazine*, contacted Eric Olson and said he would tell him the truth about his father's death. 'Korea is the key,' he is quoted as saying, going on to apparently confirm that the US air force had indeed tested biological weapons during the Korean War. Frank Olson had learned about this and began to despair about what he was doing. Cournoyer is reported to have said, 'Was this the reason for the CIA to kill your father? Probably.'

Is there is a direct connection between the cover-up of the Olson case and the sluggish investigations into the anthrax attack of October 2001? The attempts on the lives of two high-ranking representatives of the American state have not been cleared up to this day. Despite the fact that all evidence points to Fort Detrick and one possible perpetrator is, it is claimed, known by name, the investigation has plodded along without any suspects being identified by the government. A serious probe into either Olson's death or the recent anthrax attacks could bring to light things that would severely damage the credibility of the United States. Does the anthrax attacker's knowledge of certain facts make it impossible for the FBI to arrest him, perhaps for fear of what he might reveal in a court of law?

The theorists go so far as to claim that there are very believable indications that the Pentagon does not give a damn about international agreements on biological warfare. They cite several such indications, including the production of a genetically improved version of the anthrax bacterium, which was reported by the *New York Times* on 11 September 2001, the plans by military institutes to develop new microbes that are able to dissolve certain materials, and the consistent refusal of the Bush Administration to sign a supplementary protocol to the international convention on biological weapons that would give teams of United Nations experts access to military laboratories in the USA. In the course of the negotiations in Geneva, according to the theorists, it became known that Secretary of Defense Donald Rumsfeld wanted at all costs to prevent any inspections of American facilities. The conspiracy takes an unusual twist if one considers whether the United Nations arms inspectors might just have found illegal weapons of mass destruction hidden at some of these US facilities rather more quickly than in Iraq.

1953 – KREMLIN DOCTORS' PLOT Shortly before he died on 5 March 1953, the Soviet dictator Josef Stalin accused nine doctors, six of them Jews, of plotting to poison and kill the Soviet leadership. The innocent men were arrested and, at Stalin's personal instruction, tortured in order to obtain confessions. 'Beat, beat, and again beat,'

Stalin commanded the interrogators. The unfortunate physicians can be described as lucky only in comparison with Stalin's 18 million or more other victims. The dictator died days before their trial was to begin, and a month later *Pravda* announced that the doctors were innocent and had been released from prison. It later became known that after a pro forma trial and conviction, Stalin intended to organise pogroms around the country, after which prominent members of the Jewish community would publicly beg him to protect the Jews by sending them all to Siberia. Indeed, when Stalin died, the supposedly spontaneous appeal by leading Jews had already been written and signed, the signatories having been 'persuaded' to sign.

In accusing the Jewish doctors of being poisoners, Stalin was, of course, reviving an accusation that was common among medieval anti-Semites. The most notorious example of the 'Jews as poisoners' charge occurred in the fourteenth century, when Jews were accused of having caused the devastating Black Plague by poisoning the wells of Europe. In addition to all the Jews who died from the plague, thousands more were murdered in pogroms prompted by these accusations. In 1610, the University of Vienna's medical faculty certified as its official position that Jewish law required doctors to kill one out of ten of their Christian patients.

The last years of Stalin's life showed themselves above all in xenophobia. There was a huge campaign against all things foreign. Many prominent Soviet writers, who supposedly had in one way or another failed to show the proper anti-Western stance towards the free world, were accused of cow-towing to all things foreign. On 12 August 1952 five prominent Yiddish writers and poets were among a group of thirteen Jews executed by Stalin's regime for alleged crimes against the Soviet Union. The murders loom so large in the Jewish consciousness that in some communities the event is commemorated each year as the Night of the Murdered Poets.

To return to the Kremlin Doctors plot: it announced in the Soviet press on 13 January 1953 that a group of mainly Jewish Kremlin doctors were accused of having acted with the help of a foreign Jewish organisation called the Joint Distribution Committee, which had been active during the war at the behest of the Anglo–American Intelligence Services to shorten the lives of Soviet leaders. The doctors were accused of having shortened the lives of prominent military leaders and two prominent Soviet leaders: one named Shcherbakov, who had died in 1945, and the other Andre Zhadanov, a member of

Stalin's Politburo, who had died apparently of heart failure in 1948. The plot was announced as having taken place and been foiled by the arrest of these doctors, who obviously were being prepared for some kind of show trial, confessing to their guilt and naming other conspirators. Stalin wanted to show that the guilt involved the British and American governments, so that what started off as an anti-Jewish pogrom could later be translated into a new political and military purge of supposed pro-Western elements, including those factions supporting senior Politburo members Georgi M. Malenkov, Vyacheslav M. Molotov, and secret police chief Lavrenty Beria, that would perhaps rival those of the Great Terror. In the early 1950s Stalin, now an old man, apparently permitted his subordinates in the Politburo, enlarged and called the Presidium by the Nineteenth Party Congress in October 1952, greater powers of action within their spheres. Indicative of the Soviet leader's waning strength, Secretary Georgi M. Malenkov delivered the political report to the Nineteenth Party Congress in place of Stalin. In January 1953, the party newspaper announced that a group of predominantly Jewish doctors had murdered high Soviet officials, including Zhdanov.

Stalin died on 5 March 1953, under circumstances that are still unclear. It appears more than possible that, fearing another brutal pogrom against the Jews with the resulting damage to relations with the West, internal destabilisation that could allow the Secret Police chief Beria to succeed to ultimate power and a very real threat to their own lives, a conspiracy was quickly formed within the Politburo: a decision was made by its leading members to 'hasten' the old dictator's end and save the Soviet Union from another blood bath. Beria was to be killed by Stalin's successors soon afterwards. During his quarter-century of dictatorial control, Stalin had overseen impressive development in the Soviet Union and taken it from a comparatively backwards agricultural society to that of a powerful industrial state. But in the course of that transformation, millions of people had been killed and Stalin's use of repressive controls had become an integral function of his regime. How Stalin's system would be maintained or altered after his death would be a question of vital concern to Soviet leaders for years to come. The Doctors' conspiracy was Stalin's invention, but in the end it backfired on him. The real conspiracy was likely to have been by the Politburo who may have 'assisted' Stalin's death and saved not only the Jews, but also the rest of Russia from another massive upheaval.

1953 – RESTORING THE PEACOCK THRONE The conspiracy by the CIA, Britain's MI6 and pro-Shah elements within Iran is a highly effective example of the use of clandestine interference to shape the future political structure of a sovereign state. It was certainly a remarkable chapter in the modern history of Iran, which saw the removal of the popular and nationalist government of the day.

The background to the coup began when Razmara had become the Prime Minister in June 1950 and had largely succeeded in improving the economy. However, he strongly opposed nationalisation of the oil industry. On 7 March 1951, he was assassinated and within a week, the Majlis passed a bill nationalising the oil industry. However, the new Prime Minister, Hossein Ala, did nothing to take over the property of the Anglo–Iranian Oil Company. As a result his government fell on 27 April. He was succeeded by Dr Muhammad Mossadegh, leader of a coalition of nationalist groups, otherwise known as the National Front, and a supporter of oil nationalisation. On 29 April the Majlis approved a law evicting the company. Attempts to settle the ensuing crisis in British–Iranian relations through direct negotiation between the two countries ended in failure. The efforts of the USA to mediate the dispute were also to no avail. On 3 October 1951 the UK, deciding against the use of force, acceded to an Iranian ultimatum and withdrew the company's technical staff from Abadan refinery. Later in the month, when the UK brought the dispute before the UN Security Council, Mossadegh flew to New York to present the case for Iran. The council agreed to postpone debate until the International Court of Justice decided on its own competence to deal with the dispute.

On 26 December Iran rejected a proposal made by the International Bank for Reconstruction and Development, or World Bank, that the oil industry be administered by the bank or by some other international authority pending final settlement. In May 1952 Mossadegh appeared before the International Court of Justice at The Hague and argued that it had no jurisdiction in the case. Parliamentary elections had been completed meanwhile, and early in July Mossadegh, having resigned in accordance with constitutional procedure, was requested by the Shah to resume his office. His acceptance was based on various conditions, notably that he be given control of the army and the right to rule by decree for six months. The Shah, the constitutional head of the army, rejected the former condition, and on 16 July Mossadegh resigned. Former Prime Minister Ahmad Qavam agreed the next day to form a new government. The public responded with riots, demonstrations and a general strike on 21 July, which forced Qavam's resignation. On 22 July Mossadegh was designated Prime Minister; the same day the Court of Justice ruled that it had no jurisdiction in the Anglo–Iranian dispute. The lower house, supported by a popular referendum, granted Mossadegh unlimited power for six months. On 30 August 1952 Iran turned down a joint Anglo-American proposal designed to break the oil deadlock. Under the proposal, the UK for the first time accepted the Iranian nationalisation law as valid, but still insisted that compensation be based on potential revenue losses as well as on the physical assets of the Anglo–Iranian Oil Company. Iran broke off diplomatic relations with the United Kingdom on 22 October.

Early in 1953, Parliament extended Mossadegh's emergency powers for another year. The Prime Minister demanded that the Shah's powers be reduced to those of a constitutional monarch. The dissension between pro- and anti-Mossadegh forces reached a climax during the summer of 1953. The Prime Minister dissolved the lower house of the Majlis on the basis of a plebiscite in which he suspended the secret ballot. The Shah, who opposed many of Mossadegh's policies, including his uncompromising stand on the oil question, dismissed the Prime Minister on 13 August. Mossadegh refused to yield his office while his followers rioted against the royalists, and on 16 August the Shah fled to Rome. The decision to intervene in Iran had been taken in principle by the US and Britain many months before, but it was now decided to rush forwards its implementation. The CIA and MI6 conspired with elements in the Iranian military, police and security services to stage a coup and return the Shah to the throne. After three days of riots, the Royalists, supported by the army and police, won control of the capital. Mossadegh and several aides were placed under arrest and on 22 August the Shah returned in triumph. The next day General Fazullah Zahedi, who had been previously designated Prime Minister by the Shah, formed a government, and on 5 September the US government granted a much-impoverished Iran an emergency loan of $45 million US. Two months later Iran resumed diplomatic relations with the UK. Mossadegh was sentenced in December 1953 to three years' solitary confinement for leading a revolt against the Shah. Western access to Iran's giant oil reserves were once again secure, or at least until the Shah was overthrown, and this time permanently, by a virulently anti-American Islamic revolutionary movement in 1979.

1954 – THE BILDERBERG GROUP Since the group's first meeting in 1954, its security network has been specifically used to prevent reporters from sneaking into the forum. With the exception of special guest reporters, journalists have been traditionally barred from Bilderberg meetings. The security services of the US and several European nations co-ordinate with local police to enforce a strict no-go area around Bilderberg venues, such as the Turnberry Hotel in Scotland. Critics have suggested that the media have been slow to investigate and report on the Bilderberg because many corporate news executives and journalists are members of the group and, like all other Bilderberg attendees, these individuals have agreed to remain silent about the meetings, in spite of their responsibilities as high-ranking members of the national and international media. 'Guests of the Bilderberg Society are bound by the same rules as members of the Bilderberg Society, not to write about the proceedings,' conservative columnist William F. Buckley wrote six months after attending the Bilderberg's 1975 meeting. The rock-hard wall of secrecy which encloses Bilderberg gatherings is more than an impediment to public knowledge: it is symbolic of the group's aloof elitism towards the great unwashed. The latter are simply not meant to be privy to the group's discussions, and those who do manage to cross the threshold get their knuckles sharply rapped. Like the group's secrecy policies, the harassment and arrest of reporters who attempt to cover Bilderberg meetings raises justified suspicions about the organisation's hidden discussions. The Bilderberg Group is a conspiracy of some sort and it is certainly conducted in such a way as to create that impression. This seems to be the view held by many conspiracy theorists and even some rather more hardened journalists who simply do not trust a non-governmental organisation that seems to have the same privileges, security protection and influence as a major diplomatic event.

Journalists who have indeed been brave enough to challenge this ring of secrecy placed around a highly privileged few have been roughed up by the local police force, as in the case of freelance journalist Campbell Thomas. He saw the ugly side of Bilderberg secrecy when he attempted to cover the 1998 conference for the *Daily Mail*. Thomas is a reporter with considerable experience and determination and like other journalists at the conference he was forced to remain outside the police security ring surrounding the Turnberry Hotel in Scotland. Hoping to get neighbours' reactions to the conference, Thomas entered a block of flats through an open door about 500 yards away. At the first door he knocked on, the young woman who answered informed Thomas that he was in the hotel's staff quarters, and that he should not be there. He left immediately but, a short while later, two Strathclyde police officers approached Thomas and told him that he was being detained. Even though Thomas showed the policemen proof of identity he was handcuffed and kept in custody for eight hours. 'I was treated in an appallingly heavy-handed way, like a common criminal,' Thomas told the *UK Press Gazette*. 'The holding cell I was put in was in a disgusting state, with excrement on every wall, and I was in that cell for the best part of five hours.' Thomas was then questioned and charged with a breach of the peace for putting the young woman he spoke to in a 'state of fear and alarm'. 'I wasn't allowed to speak to my wife,' Thomas said. 'They took my shoes, my belt, my glasses, even the wedding ring off my finger. The whole thing was ridiculous.' Although Scottish prosecutors declined to proceed with the charge against Thomas, the event left him shaken and angry.

Other intrepid reporters who have tried to gain access to the Bilderberg Group have also been treated badly – but by their employers: at least one British journalist was dismissed by a high profile national newspaper, with the suspicion that his editor, apparently involved with the Bilderberg Group, had been pressurised into taking such action. This alone suggests that the Bilderberg Group is far more than just a chance for politicians, industrialists and the power brokers of the international world merely to get together in a relaxed atmosphere. These are meetings where deals can be done quietly and without fuss, well away from the prying eyes of the press and, of course, the voters and customers whose lives may be directly affected by the decisions being made. The Bilderberg conferences have been hugely influential in developing the free market policies that were so successful in undermining the Communist bloc and shaping the post-Cold-War world. It is inconceivable that busy national leaders or directors of multinational corporations would so willingly take the time to attend these conferences merely for a relaxing weekend. It's not a publicity buzz, as they are barred quite effectively from discussing the meetings, so apart from the 'in the know' prestige, these meetings must have real business clout and political benefits for those involved. Meaningful discussions take place and important decisions are at least sanctioned, but in secret and in a way not accountable to the press or the public. Of course, the Bilderberg Group are free to dispel all such thoughts of conspiracy and intrigue by opening the meetings up to at least some press and TV coverage and perhaps an explanation of their aims and achievements.

1954 – GUATEMALAN CIA COUP This must be one of the least contested conspiracies around. In fact when the CIA declassified some 1,400 pages of reports on the 1954 coup it engineered in Guatemala to remove President Jacobo Arbenz from office, it effectively boasted about the agency's ability to remove troublesome governments. Arbenz was inaugurated in March of 1951, and just a year and a half later, towards the end of 1952, the agency set in motion PBFORTUNE, a sizeable but quickly aborted plot against Arbenz who had become a target of US distrust and anger for threatening to carry out modest land reforms against the interests of the giant United Fruit Company, among other things. In 1952 President Harry Truman gave secret approval to begin shipping guns and money to opposition forces and training mercenaries, but at the eleventh hour, Secretary of State Dean Acheson persuaded Truman to abort it. The plan was to help an exiled right-wing military officer, Carlos Castillo Armas, invade from neighbouring countries with a few hundred supporters and seize power. A month after it was authorised, the State Department became concerned that word of the operation was getting out and it was mothballed. Another year of troublesome relations between the United States and Guatemala followed and the CIA continued to support Castillo Armas.

Then, in August 1953, the new President, Dwight D. Eisenhower gave the go-ahead for PBSUCCESS, and the CIA launched a full-fledged covert action programme, including an intensive series of 'black operations' that badgered and intimidated Arbenz's allies until the Guatemalan leader was forced to forfeit the presidency on 27 June 1954.

What did Arbenz do to deserve the Eisenhower Administration's anger? He was a leftist military officer with a handful of Communist friends who helped him implement land and labour reforms, but Arbenz quickly ran foul of US investors in Guatemala, especially the powerful, Boston-based United Fruit Company. The company, which ran banana plantations and other large enterprises in the country, had enjoyed preferential treatment under previous Guatemalan leaders and it reacted violently to Arbenz's steps to bring it into compliance with local laws. So in the summer of 1954, acting under the orders of President Eisenhower, the CIA strangled Guatemala's fledgling democracy by staging the long-planned invasion and coup against Arbenz. PBSUCCESS was a uniquely successful clandestine venture, given its size and impact. The US replaced a foreign leader and maintained a manageable degree of plausible deniability about the agency's role. The coup and cover-up were largely accomplished through psychological warfare. The agency's psywar assault on the Guatemalan regime included clandestine publishing projects, high-powered radio broadcasts, aircraft-dropped leaflets and a multifaceted scare campaign targeting the President and his top aides. In the month preceding the CIA's invasion, the group mailed mourning cards and death notices to targets selected by the agency. 'Cards were to mourn the purge or execution of various Communists in the world and to hint forthcoming doom to recipients,' explained a CIA summary of the operation. The daily death threats were backed up with late-night telephone calls in which CIA covert-action ESSENCE teams reiterated the ominous warnings. The CIA judged the tactic to be especially effective in rattling Arbenz's cronies. The Guatemalans had reason to be worried – the death threats were credible ones, according to a report by Gerald K. Haines, the current head of the CIA's historical office. 'Proposals for assassination pervaded both PBFORTUNE and PBSUCCESS,' Haines concluded after a careful review of all available CIA Guatemala files. 'Even before official approval of PBFORTUNE, CIA officers compiled elimination lists and discussed the concept of assassination with Guatemalan opposition leaders. Until the day that Arbenz resigned in June 1954 the option of assassination was still being considered.' Arbenz's assassination proved unnecessary and his government succumbed to the CIA's covert operation. On 17 June 1954 Castillo Armas's force of about 300 heavily armed troops moved slowly across the border from neighbouring Honduras, and CIA contract pilots began buzzing Guatemala City in light aircraft, disgorging propaganda leaflets, with messages appealing to the army to usurp Arbenz, as well as the occasional grenade or small bomb. The invasion culminated months of combined pressures by the CIA, the Pentagon and the State Department, and it was the beginning of the end for Arbenz. In the final shot of the nerve war, the CIA jammed the broadcasts of the state radio station.

Headquarters for the operation were established in Opa Locka, Florida, on the outskirts of Miami. The Nicaraguan dictator Anastasio Somoza allowed his country to be used as a site for an airstrip and for hundreds of men, including Guatemalan exiles and US and Central

American mercenaries, to receive training in the use of weapons and radio broadcasting, as well as in the fine arts of sabotage and demolition. Thirty aircraft were assigned for use in the 'Liberation', stationed in Nicaragua, Honduras and the Canal Zone, to be flown by American pilots. The Canal Zone was set aside as a weapons depot from which arms were gradually distributed to the rebels who were to assemble in Honduras under the command of Colonel Carlos Castillo Armas before crossing into Guatemala. Soviet-marked weapons were also gathered for the purpose of planting them inside Guatemala before the invasion to reinforce US charges of Russian intervention. And, as important as arms, it turned out, hidden radio transmitters were placed in and around the perimeter of Guatemala, including one in the US Embassy.

An attempt was made to blow up trains carrying the Czech weapons from portside to Guatemala City; however, a torrential downpour rendered the detonators useless, whereupon the CIA paramilitary squad opened fire on one train, killing a Guatemalan soldier and wounding three others; but the convoy of trains made it safely to its destination. After the Czech ship had arrived in Guatemala, Eisenhower ordered the stopping of 'suspicious foreign-flag vessels on the high seas off Guatemala to examine cargo'. The State Department's legal advisor wrote a brief, which concluded in no uncertain terms, 'Such action would constitute a violation of international law.' No matter. At least two foreign vessels were stopped and searched, one French and one Dutch. The Guatemalan military came in for special attention. The USA ostentatiously signed mutual security treaties with Honduras and Nicaragua, both countries hostile to Arbenz, and dispatched large shipments of arms to them in the hope that this would signal a clear enough threat to the Guatemalan military to persuade it to withdraw its support of Arbenz. Additionally, the US navy dispatched two submarines from Key West, saying only that they were going 'south'. Several days later, the air force, amid considerable fanfare, sent three B-36 bombers on a 'courtesy call' to Nicaragua. The CIA also made a close study of the records of members of the Guatemalan officer corps and offered bribes to some of them. One of the agency's clandestine radio stations broadcast appeals aimed at military men, as well as others, to join the liberation movement. The station reported that Arbenz was secretly planning to disband or disarm the armed forces and replace it with a people's militia. CIA planes dropped leaflets over Guatemala carrying the same message. Eventually, at Ambassador Peurifoy's urging, a group of high-ranking officers called on Arbenz to ask that he dismiss all Communists who held posts in his administration. The President assured them that the Communists did not represent a danger, that they did not run the government, and that it would be undemocratic to dismiss them. At a second meeting, the officers also demanded that Arbenz reject the 'people's militia'.

During this same period, the CIA put into practice a plan to create an 'incident'. Agency planes were dispatched to drop several harmless bombs on Honduran territory. The Honduran government then complained to the UN and the Organisation of American States, claiming that the country had been attacked by Guatemalan planes. Arbenz finally received an ultimatum from certain army officers: resign or they would come to an agreement with the invaders. The CIA and Ambassador Peurifoy had been offering payments to officers to defect, and one army commander reportedly accepted $60,000 to surrender his troops. With his back to the wall, Arbenz made an attempt to arm civilian supporters to fight for the government, but army officers blocked the hand-out of weapons. The Guatemalan President knew that the end was near. The Guatemalan military command, interpreting Castillo Armas's meagre force as a precursor to large-scale US military intervention, told their President it was time to surrender. On 27 June Arbenz, his supporters marginalised and stripped away by the nerve war, stepped down and the US ambassador to Guatemala, John Peurifoy, helped CIA officers tinker with a series of short-lived military juntas and finally install the agency's hand-picked President, Carlos Castillo Armas.

Guatemala then plunged into decades of military rule and civil war, providing critics of the CIA with ample evidence that this agency 'success' had a terrible toll. The catastrophic human rights situation in Guatemala did not prevent the CIA from attempting similar operations, however. PBSUCCESS served as a general model for several subsequent covert actions, most notably the secret wars against Cuba in the 1960s, Chile in the 1970s and Nicaragua in the 1980s. In all of those cases, the CIA used forgeries, disinformation and terror tactics to undermine governments, political groups and individual leaders, employing tactics that saw their first full-fledged use in the Guatemala operation. The programme of dirty tricks against Arbenz entered agency lore as an exampler of what could be done from behind the scenes to topple America's enemies.

In a radio speech to the nation announcing his resignation, Arbenz named his attackers. 'The United Fruit Company, in collaboration with the governing circles of the United States, is responsible for what is happening to us,' he charged.

Castillo Armas celebrated the liberation of Guatemala in various ways. In July alone, thousands were arrested on suspicion of Communist activity. Many were tortured or killed. In August a law was passed and a committee set up which could declare anyone a Communist, with no right of appeal. Those so declared could be arbitrarily arrested for up to six months, could not own a radio or hold public office. Within four months the committee had registered 72,000 names. A committee official said it was aiming for 200,000. The new regime also disenfranchised three-quarters of Guatemala's voters by barring illiterates from the electoral rolls and outlawing all political parties, labour confederations and peasant organisations. To this was added the closing down of opposition newspapers, which Arbenz had not done, and the burning of 'subversive' books, including Victor Hugo's *Les Miserables*, novels by Dostoyevsky, and the works of Guatemala's Nobel Prize-winning author Miguel Angel Asturias, a biting critic of United Fruit.

The CIA has demonstrated considerable capabilities for subversion and destabilisation. Overthrowing foreign governments became regular practice during the Cold War, and along the way the intelligence agency prepared detailed studies on the art of the coup. The declassified paper trail shows that the CIA's tradecraft for coup operations included special methods for applying maximum psychological pressure against key enemies. One covert operation, an early milestone in the history of the CIA, demonstrated how 'black operations' or 'nerve war' as these tactics were called in secret documents, could put a targeted government off balance before the agency's operatives moved in to finally topple it. A highly successful conspiracy would probably be the view from Langley and a benchmark for its future operations around the world.

1960 – OPERATION NORTHWOODS Could the US government conceive of carrying out attacks against the American people under the pretext that the attacks came from a foreign enemy? Rather an emotive question at the time just nineteen years after Pearl Harbor, but in the context of the rumour mill that has surrounded the events of 9-11 it is a potential bombshell. However, the answer to that question at least for this entry appears to be a very definite 'yes'. The plan was called Operation Northwoods and it called for engaging in such unsavoury activities as assassination, hijacking aircraft, blowing up ships and orchestrating violent terrorism. Nothing new for the CIA in countries targeted for Washington's wrath, but this time the targets were to be American citizens in the major cities of the USA.

The plan contained a comprehensive conspiracy to bomb buildings, sink ships, shoot down aircraft and terrorise cities, all to find an excuse to launch a second invasion of Cuba to rid the western hemisphere of its only Communist government. America's top military brass also contemplated causing US military casualties in a scenario chillingly similar to the conspiracy theories surrounding Pearl Harbor. The plan had the written approval of the joint chiefs of staff and was presented to President Kennedy's defense secretary, Robert McNamara, in March 1962. However, they were apparently rejected by the civilian leadership and have gone undisclosed for nearly forty years.

The joint chiefs also proposed using the potential death of astronaut John Glenn during the first attempt to put an American into orbit as a false pretext for war with Cuba, and documents show that it was seriously considered. On 20 February 1962 Glenn was to lift off from Cape Canaveral, Florida, on his historic journey. The flight was to carry the banner of America's virtues of truth, freedom and democracy into orbit high over the planet. But Lyman Lemnitzer and his chiefs had a different idea. They proposed to Lansdale that, should the rocket explode and kill Glenn, 'the objective is to provide irrevocable proof that . . . the fault lies with the Communists et al Cuba [*sic*].' This would be accomplished, Lemnitzer continued, 'by manufacturing various pieces of evidence which would prove electronic interference on the part of the Cubans.' Glenn lifted into history without mishap, leaving Lemnitzer and the chiefs to begin devising new plots, which they suggested be carried out 'within the time frame of the next few months.'

The plans were motivated by an intense desire among senior military leaders to depose Castro, who seized power in 1959 and only ninety miles from US shores. The CIA-backed Bay of Pigs invasion of Cuba by Cuban exiles had been a disastrous failure, in which the military was not allowed to provide firepower for the Cuban exiles. Among the actions recommended was 'a series of well-coordinated incidents to take place in and around' the US navy base at Guantanamo Bay, Cuba. This included dressing 'friendly' Cubans in

Cuban military uniforms and then have them 'start riots near the main gate of the base. Others would pretend to be saboteurs inside the base. Ammunition would be blown up, fires started, aircraft sabotaged, mortars fired at the base with damage to installations.'

The suggested operations grew progressively more outrageous. Another called for an action similar to the infamous incident in February 1898 when an explosion aboard the battleship *Maine* in Havana harbour killed 266 US sailors. Although the exact cause of the explosion remained undetermined, it sparked the Spanish-American War with Cuba. Incited by the deadly blast, more than 1 million men volunteered for duty. Lemnitzer and his generals came up with a similar plan. 'We could blow up a US ship in Guantanamo Bay and blame Cuba,' they proposed; 'casualty lists in US newspapers would cause a helpful wave of national indignation.' There seemed no limit to their fanaticism: 'We could develop a Communist Cuban terror campaign in the Miami area, in other Florida cities and even in Washington,' they wrote. 'The terror campaign could be pointed at Cuban refugees seeking haven in the United States. We could sink a boatload of Cubans en route to Florida' – presumably with a US vessel to be on hand fortuitously to pick up the refugees in the water. 'We could foster attempts on lives of Cuban refugees in the United States even to the extent of wounding in instances to be widely publicized.' Bombings were proposed, false arrests, hijackings. 'Exploding a few plastic bombs in carefully chosen spots, the arrest of Cuban agents and the release of prepared documents substantiating Cuban involvement also would be helpful in projecting the idea of an irresponsible government.' A plan to shoot down a commercial airliner filled with US college students involved switching an actual planeload of students with an 'unmanned' drone, supposedly shot down by Cuba. The US plan called for establishing prolonged military, not democratic, control over the island nation after the invasion, and is apparently very similar to US plans for a post-invasion Iraq in 2003. Finally, there was a plan to 'make it appear that Communist Cuban MiGs have destroyed a USAF aircraft over international waters in an unprovoked attack.' It was a particularly believable operation, given the decade of shoot-downs that had just taken place. In the final sentence of his letter to Secretary McNamara recommending the operations, Lemnitzer made a grab for even more power asking that the joint chiefs be placed in charge of carrying out Operation Northwoods and the invasion. 'It is recommended,' he wrote, 'that this responsibility for both overt and covert military operations be assigned to the Joint Chiefs of Staff.' Whether the Joint Chiefs' plan's were rejected by McNamara in the meeting is not clear but, three days later, President Kennedy told Lemnitzer directly there was virtually no possibility of ever using overt force to take Cuba. Within months, Lemnitzer would be denied another term as chairman and transferred to another job.

The secret plans came at a time when there was distrust in the military leadership about their civilian leadership, with leaders in the Kennedy Administration viewed as too liberal, insufficiently experienced and soft on Communism. At the same time, however, there were real concerns in American society about their military overstepping its bounds. The American public of today appear more than willing to accept the veracity of its military and political leaders' statements, and although it is doubtful whether the Pentagon would need such a dangerous conspiracy in 2003 in order to persuade the White House to go to war, perhaps some conspiracy theorists would beg to differ.

1960 – A RIGHT ROYAL CONSPIRACY A delicate conspiracy theory if ever there was one, but still of importance and abiding interest, particularly as the behaviour of the royal family has traditionally been seen as setting a high standard to be followed by the rest of British society. So when rumours, unsubstantiated of course, continue to surface around the world about the true antecedents of not one but two royal princes several decades apart, then it is hardly surprising that the conspiracy theorists work overtime to prove that there has been a cover-up.

In *Queen Elizabeth II: A Woman Who Is Not Amused* Nicholas Davies writes on page 186 about how Queen Elizabeth became romantically involved with another man, Henry George Reginald Molyneux Herbert, Earl of Carnarvon, also known as Lord Porchester. Throughout the 1950s and 1960s Porchester and the Queen, who had married Prince Philip in November 1947, spent many, many hours together discussing racing. However, Davies adds that Elizabeth began to spend even more time with Lord Porchester than strictly necessary for racing matters and that they would frequently meet at Broadlands in Hampshire where Earl Mountbatten would be their host. They would ride together, walk for hours with the dogs and sit and chat long into the night. Mountbatten was concerned that Elizabeth was infatuated with the handsome Harry Porchester, perhaps even emotionally involved. After much thought Mountbatten took the unprecedented step of writing her a letter of warning which contained the damning sentence, 'I urge you to be more discreet in your relationship with Porchy.' According to a close confidant, Mountbatten knew what was going on and was very worried in case things got out of hand. He saw the way they were to each other, how close they had become to 'acting towards each other as though lovers'. He apparently expressed this view openly, and he used to shake his head about it, not knowing how he should tackle the situation. 'Elizabeth was so animated when Porchy was around and they got on so well together.' Elizabeth, however, appeared to take little notice of 'Uncle Dickie's' warning for she continued to see Harry Porchester regularly, but the couple certainly spent fewer weekends at Broadlands. Later they would travel abroad together on racing business and spend weekends together.

Since 1975 Elizabeth and Porchy have often visited Kentucky together during the spring yearling sales. In *The Royals*, the American author Kitty Kelley claimed that Prince Philip had agreed in 1993 to be profiled by journalist Fiammenta Rocco in the *Independent on Sunday*. The reporter referred to the allegation that Prince Andrew is not really Prince Philip's son, that he is the son of Lord Porchester, the Queen's racing manager. Philip did not flinch and he said nothing. He sat as impassive as stone. 'Like a child with porridge in his mouth,' the reporter later told a colleague. She had addressed the issue of his son's paternity because it had been raised weeks before by Nigel Dempster in the *New York Times Magazine*. 'Get hold of a picture of Prince Andrew and then one of Lord Porchester at the same age,' Dempster was quoted as telling the writer Christopher Hitchens. 'You'll see that Prince Philip could never have been Andy's father.' The Palace did not challenge the published statement.

In *The Royal Marriages* Lady Colin Campbell claimed that baby Andrew was kept under wraps as no other royal baby has been before or since. The world received little more than a glimpse of him, not even when he was christened, for there were no official photographers present to record what is normally a happy semi-official occasion shared by the royal family and the public alike. In public relations terms, such secrecy was considered a disaster which could have long-term repercussions. 'I had no idea how widespread the rumours about Andrew's paternity were until I visited Ireland for the launch of *Diana in Private*.' Campbell had always assumed that what he had heard was confined to the narrow circle surrounding the Queen, her court and her cousins but, to his consternation, Terry Keane of the *Independent on Sunday* asked him if he could confirm whether it was true that Prince Andrew was Lord Porchester's, and not Prince Philip's, son. Conspiracy theorists point to the strange matter of the Cabinet papers relating to the Macmillan Government for the year 1959, the year that Prince Andrew was conceived. The papers, released on 1 January 1990, confirm that the royal family was discussed by the Cabinet on three occasions that year but that the subject matter was sufficiently sensitive for the government to order that it be kept secret for a much longer period than normal. One of the items was apparently stamped with a 50-year embargo, as opposed to the normal 30 years, and two items were reportedly locked away for 100 years, not to be revealed until 2059. What was serious enough to warrant this kind of secrecy? It was believed to be virtually without precedent in times of peace and apart from these only the Cabinet documents relating to the abdication still seem to remain thus precluded. In 1959 there were apparently no other known scandals, political upsets or constitutional crises with a royal involvement.

Despite an additional reference to the rumours about the paternity of Andrew in *Elizabeth* by Sarah Bradford, there has been a continuing, and largely successful, Palace–press–government conspiracy to reduce the level of speculation and, where possible, to prevent publication of these rumours inside Britain. To some extent an accusation, unfounded or otherwise, that the Queen, in keeping with her errant former daughter-in-law Princess Diana, had an extra-marital affair which produced a son, and that in both cases they were to be accepted by husbands who had similar reputations for keeping at least one mistress, would still come as something of a shock to many in Great Britain – even in these supposedly more enlightened times.

1960 – KILLING CASTRO THE CIA WAY The various conspiracies about the CIA's, the Mafia's and the Cuban exiles' attempts to kill Fidel Castro often appear to have more of a natural home in the latest James Bond movie. Q would indeed have approved of some of the schemes, including exploding cigars. Cigars played an important part in Castro's life and if the CIA had got its way, in his death as well.

One of the more serious cigar schemes was recorded in a notation by Dr Edward Gunn, Operations Division, Office of Medical Services, on 16 August 1960. He had 'received a box of Cuban cigars to be treated with a lethal material. He understood them to be Fidel's favourite brand.' A member of the Technical Services Department recalled contaminating 'a full box of fifty cigars with botulinum toxin, a virulent poison that produces a fatal illness some hours after it is ingested.' The TSD worker can distinctly remember 'the flaps-and-seals job he had to do on the box and on each of the wrapped cigars, both to get at the cigars and to erase evidence of tampering.' At the time of the CIA Inspector General's report in 1967 into the Agency's attempts on Castro's life, one of the cigars was still in existence and, when tested, the toxin was found to have retained 94 per cent of its original effectiveness. 'The cigars were so heavily contaminated that merely putting one in the mouth would do the job; the intended victim would not actually have to smoke it.'

In addition to the lethal cigars, other poisons and delivery methods were at one time or another seriously considered. Cornelius Roosevelt, a chief of TSD, recalled three other approaches being considered: 'something highly toxic, such as shellfish poison, to be administered with a pin . . . bacterial material in liquid form; and a handkerchief treated with bacteria.' The decision, to the best of his recollection, was that bacteria in liquid form was the best means, since it was particularly well suited for slipping into Castro's tea, coffee or soup.

Slipping Castro a dose of botulin wasn't what the CIA originally had in mind when they started plotting with the Mafia to kill Castro. The CIA at first had envisioned 'a typical, gangland-style killing in which Castro would be gunned down.' But the Mafia boss Sam Giancana 'flatly opposed' a drive-by because it would be too hard to recruit assassins when their chances of survival and escape would be dim at best. Instead, Giancana recommended a lethal pill which one of Joe Trafficante's Cuban contacts could slip into Castro's drink. The poison was to be 'stable, soluble, safe to handle, undetectable, not immediately acting, and with a firmly predictable end result.' Again, the ever-useful botulin met all the requirements. However, when Edward Gunn tested the pills in a glass of water, they 'did not even disintegrate, let alone dissolve.' Director of Security, Sheffield Edwards, instructed Gunn to make sure the pills were truly lethal and gave him enough money to run down to the nearest pet store and buy some guinea pigs. The little animals also survived the tests, though a member of the TSD stated that the tests on guinea pigs were not valid because they had a high resistance to the toxin. To prove his point he personally tested the toxin on some unfortunate monkeys and found it to be quite effective. The botulin pills were concealed inside a pencil and delivered to Mafia capo Johnny Roselli, who in turn passed the pills to Mafia don Joe Trafficante, who delivered them to Juan Orta in Cuba, who was supposed to use them to poison Castro. However, Orta was fired from his position in the Cuban Prime Minister's office and ended up fleeing to Florida. The CIA and the Mafia gangsters found a replacement for Orta, who made several more failed attempts to finish the job.

After the Bay of Pigs invasion, the CIA had its hands full and unbelievably put all the Castro assassination plots in cold storage for a year or so. Some plans were discussed, but according to the inspector general's report, nothing was seriously put into motion until 1962–63. That was when the contaminated skin-diving-suit plan went into action, a scheme that could have come out of Hollywood, involving a brazen attempt to sabotage the secret negotiations between Kennedy and Castro via New York attorney James Donovan. In 1962 Donovan and John Nolan, from attorney general Robert Kennedy's office, had negotiated the return of the Bay of Pigs prisoners. In April 1963 Donovan and Nolan returned to Cuba for more negotiations, cracking open the door to normalisation of relations between the United States and Cuba. Needless to say, the CIA wasn't over-thrilled by the idea of normalising relations, especially after being burned over the Bay of Pigs disaster. Former CIA counter-intelligence chief James Angleton, for example, blamed Kennedy for the utter failure of the invasion. 'The Bay of Pigs fiasco, which he tried to hang on the CIA and which led to the resignation of CIA director Allen Dulles, was his own doing,' according to Angleton. 'I think the decision to withdraw air support of the invasion coloured Kennedy's entire career and impacted on everything that followed.' Ominous words from a senior member of an organisation often thought to be deeply involved in 'everything that followed'.

In light of this resentment, it is very interesting to note the lengths to which the CIA was willing to go with their skin-diving-suit operation. The CIA knew Castro was a skin-diving enthusiast, so they prepared a very special suit for him, dusting the inside with 'a fungus that would produce a disabling and chronic skin disease otherwise known as Madura foot' and 'contaminating the breathing apparatus with tubercle bacilli.' The plan was to have Donovan present the skin-diving suit as a gift to Castro. The CIA bought and prepared Castro's deadly present, but the plan was abandoned when it was 'overtaken by events: Donovan had already given Castro a skin-diving suit on his own initiative.' Strangely enough this tends to suggest that the CIA were going out of their way to appear to be doing government business, but at the same time had their own hidden agenda: if at any time the CIA engages in criminal activity, its charter dictates that it must do so under the condition of plausible deniability. In other words it is all right to assassinate irritating foreigners as long as the CIA's complicity cannot be proven beyond a shadow of a doubt in a court of law. The poisoned skin-diving suit obviously violated one of the CIA's prime directives, since it would take the Cuban Intelligence Service, the DGI, only a very short while to figure out what happened to Castro. If the poisoned suit were a gift from Donovan, Kennedy's middleman involved in discussions of normalisation of relations between Cuba and America, then it stands to reason that negotiations would have broken down pretty quickly after that. Exactly what would have suited the CIA, as they believed that Kennedy had gone soft on Cuba and certainly didn't wish for negotiations to succeed? Conspiracies within a conspiracy.

At some time in 1963, CIA special affairs staff chief Desmond FitzGerald came up with the idea of killing Castro with an explosives-rigged seashell. 'The idea was to take an unusually spectacular seashell that would be certain to catch Castro's eye, load it with an explosive triggered to blow when the shell was lifted, and submerge it in an area where Castro often went skin diving.' FitzGerald ran down to the book store and bought two books on Caribbean Mollusca, and was disheartened not only to find that none of the shells indigenous to the Caribbean were spectacular enough to snare Castro's attention, but also that none were large enough to hold a sufficient amount of explosive material. Furthermore, the midget submarine that would be needed to place the shell had too short an operating range for the operation.

Covert sparring between the CIA and the Kennedy Administration didn't end with the skin-diving-suit scheme. On 5 September 1963, thanks in part to the Donovan–Nolan negotiations, Cuban United Nations ambassador Carlos Lechuga agreed to meet William Atwood, special advisor to the US delegation to the UN. Atwood was ordered to report directly to McGeorge Bundy at the White House; the CIA was not invited to participate. Therefore it might be more than a coincidence that the CIA resumed contact with Rolando Cubela on 7 September to put another Castro assassination plot into motion. Cubela was a member of Castro's staff who the CIA had been in contact with since 1961. The plot that Cubela ended up participating in involved a team of three snipers at the University of Havana. The scheme was foiled when Castro's security detail caught them red-handed.

Attorney general Robert Kennedy and almost certainly President Kennedy himself were aware of earlier assassination plots and hadn't done anything to stop the CIA from 'sanctioning' Castro. But by October 1963 any assassination operations that the CIA was planning were being conducted without the knowledge, and certainly without the approval, of the Kennedy Administration. This made the actions of Desmond FitzGerald especially inappropriate. On 11 October headquarters got word that Cubela 'was insistent upon meeting with a senior US official, preferably Robert F. Kennedy' for assurance that the US would support Cubela's activities against Castro. Knowing there wasn't a snowball's chance in hell of that happening, FitzGerald himself met with Cubela on 29 October 1963, claiming to be a US senator representing attorney general Robert Kennedy, and later provided Cubela with assassination equipment. Five days earlier, President Kennedy had sent a personal message to Fidel Castro, and brother Robert had approved the Attwood initiative. So at the same time that Kennedy was quietly conducting negotiations to normalise relations with Cuba, which the CIA had been deliberately left out of, the CIA was continuing its own plans for Castro's death. On 18 November Attwood reported to Bundy that Lechuga would soon receive the agenda for a meeting with Attwood in Havana. Four days later, Kennedy was assassinated in Dallas. At that very moment, a CIA representative was meeting with Cubela in Paris. Upon hearing the news of the President's death, Cubela asked, 'Why do such things happen to good people?' Perhaps Cubela was asking the question of an organisation that actually knew the answer.

1961 – THE MURDER OF PATRICE LUMUMBA There were so many conspiracies aimed at Patrice Lumumba that for a long time it wasn't really certain whether the CIA, or the CIA and the Belgians, or the CIA, the Belgians and MI6, or the Katangans and the CIA were ultimately responsible for his death. However, it would now seem likely that all of these elements were involved, in conjunction with traitors within Lumumba's own administration, in the assassination of the young Congolese Prime Minister. The Belgian government later made official apologies for the role it played in his murder.

Lumumba was murdered on 17 January 1961 in Katanga, several hours after his extradition to the new authorities of Congo with Belgium's support. The Belgian authorities apparently did not give a damn for Lumumba's fate and were only really apprehensive about the fact that the Congo would be independent of Belgium and might prefer a more socialist future.

The fundamental reasons for the murder of Lumumba are complex and go back to late 1959 by which time Britain and the USA had concluded that, far from representing a threat, Pan-Africanism offered the best chance of preventing revolution in Africa. Pan-Africanists of much longer standing than Lumumba, such as Nkrumah, Kenyatta, Nyerere, Obote and Azikiwe, had also come to power around this time. However, when Lumumba showed that he could not be relied upon to control the Congolese working class, his fate was sealed. According to the conspiracy theorists, the West decided to make an example of him to the masses and to other African leaders, to show what would happen if they opposed imperialist dictates.

Mobutu, who had impressed the CIA on his brief visits to Brussels as Lumumba's military advisor, was chosen as the better candidate to safeguard Western interests. Through a mixture of brutality and political guile, Mobutu succeeded for decades in ensuring that the Congo (renamed Zaire) did not become the flashpoint for an African socialist revolution. He was helped in no small way by Moise Tshombe's attempts to create a breakaway republic in the Katanga province of the former Belgium Congo, which effectively undermined Lumumba's position as the Congolese leader.

Belgium has always claimed that it only sent troops into Katanga to protect Belgian lives and property. However, it seems certain that Belgium entered into a conspiracy with the CIA to dismember the Congo and to remove Lumumba. Belgian military chiefs made nightly visits to Mobutu, then head of the army, and President Kasavubu, to plot Lumumba's downfall. Colonel Louis Maliere spoke of the millions of francs he brought over for this purpose. The plot to kill Lumumba was called 'Operation Barracuda' and was run by the Belgian minister for African affairs, Count d'Aspremont. The Belgium government ordered Kasavubu to sack Lumumba, who turned to the new parliament and won two votes of confidence. Mobutu then staged a coup d'état and Lumumba was placed under house arrest, from which he escaped only to be captured by troops loyal to Mobutu. Contemporary film shows UN troops standing by while Lumumba is first beaten in front of Mobutu, then paraded through the streets of Leopoldville (now Kinshasa) and finally beaten again. When taken to Thysville prison, he almost provoked a mutiny among the guards in his favour. Count d'Aspremont ordered him to be taken to Katanga province and certain death. On the flight there, he and two supporters, Maurice Mpolo and Joseph Okite were beaten so badly the pilot complained the plane was in danger of crashing. At the scene of the assassination, a Belgian police officer took Patrice Lumumba by the arm and led him to a large tree. The Prime Minister walked wearily: he had apparently been tortured for hours, even days. A four-man execution squad armed with Belgian FAL and Vigneron sub-machine guns stood by, while about twenty men, including soldiers, policemen, Belgian officers, Moise Tshombe and other Katangese ministers, watched silently. A Belgian captain gave the order to fire and a rain of bullets mowed down Lumumba and two of his former ministers.

Belgium's role in this conspiracy was more than matched by that of the USA. Classified US government documents, including a chronology of covert actions approved by the National Security Council (NSC) subgroup, reveal significant US involvement with Belgium in the death of Lumumba, who was mistakenly seen by the Eisenhower Administration as an African Fidel Castro. The documents show that the key Congolese leaders who brought about Lumumba's downfall were players in 'Project Wizard', a CIA covert action programme. Hundreds of thousands of dollars and military equipment were channelled to these officials, who informed their CIA paymasters three days in advance of their plan to send Lumumba into the clutches of his worst enemies. The US authorised payments to then-President Joseph Kasavubu four days before he ousted Lumumba, furnished army strongman Mobutu with money and arms to fight pro-Lumumba forces, helped select and finance an anti-Lumumba government and, barely three weeks after his death, authorised new funds for the people who arranged Lumumba's murder. Moreover, these documents show that the plans and payments were approved by the highest levels of the Eisenhower Administration – either the NSC or its 'Special Group', consisting of the national security advisor, the CIA director, the under-secretary of state for political affairs, and the deputy defense secretary.

Among the American agents on the ground in the Congo was a young CIA man working under diplomatic cover, Frank Carlucci, who tried to work his way into Lumumba's confidence in the months before the murder. Carlucci went on to become national security advisor and defense secretary in the Reagan Administration and later the chairman of the Carlyle Group, the influential merchant bank that includes George Bush, Sr among its directors. Minutes of an August 1960 National Security Council meeting confirm that Eisenhower told CIA chief Allen Dulles to 'eliminate' Lumumba, whom Dulles himself referred to as a 'mad dog'. The official note-taker, Robert H. Johnson, had told the Senate Intelligence Committee this in 1975, but no documentary evidence was previously available to back up his statement. As part of the assassination policy Larry Devlin, the CIA's man in the Congo at the time, had been told to meet 'Joe from Paris', who turned out to be the CIA's chief technical officer, Dr Sidney Gottlieb. 'I recognised him as he walked towards my car,' recalled Devlin, 'but when he told me what they wanted done, I was totally, totally taken aback.' Gottlieb gave him a tube of poisoned toothpaste, which Devlin was to smuggle into Lumumba's bathroom. According to Larry Devlin, then the CIA station chief in Leopoldville (Kinshasa), the agency's chief technical officer arrived in the African nation shortly after the 'elimination' order from Eisenhower. The improbable plot was dropped, however, in favour of a more direct method. Lumumba was delivered into the hands of his bitterest political enemy, Moises Tshombe, the secessionist leader of Katanga. The assassination took place less than seven months after the Congo had declared its independence, with Lumumba as its first Prime Minister.

Eisenhower was not alone in coming to the conclusion that Lumumba must die. A British Foreign Office document from September 1960 notes the opinion of a top-ranking official, who later became the head of MI5: 'I see only two possible solutions to the [Lumumba] problem. The first is the simple one of ensuring [his] removal from the scene by killing him.'

Lumumba was among the most courageous and principled figures in a generation of young nationalist leaders. He was removed from power and finally murdered in cold blood by a massive conspiracy that eventually included the former colonial power of Belgium, the CIA, the Katangan rebels and members of his own government and armed forces. Even the British stood on the periphery and encouraged his removal. Lumumba never stood a chance against such powerful opposition.

1961 – THE TRUJILLO CONSPIRACY Even the most cynical critics of conspiracy theories about secret agents overthrowing governments and assassinating dictators would be hard put to deny the existence of the CIA conspiracy to do just that in the Dominican Republic. There can be no doubt that, just as in Guatemala, Iran and, later, Chile, the CIA played a direct role in the assassination of the Dominican Republic's leader, Rafael L. Trujillo on 30 May 1961. Arms for the killing of the 69-year-old dictator were smuggled into the country at the request of the assassins by the CIA. This was in part due to the close scrutiny imposed by Trujillo on the removal of guns from military bases. These controls had kept the conspirators from obtaining their own weapons, despite the involvement in the plot of the Secretary of State for the Armed Forces, Gen. Jose Rene Roman Fernandez, and other leading military officers. They were also looking for deniability if the plot failed and the weapons were captured and examined by Trujillo's security forces.

On 14 June 1959 the Dominican Republic's southern coast had been invaded by Cuba-based Dominican exiles. Those that were not killed in combat were captured and later executed, but not before Trujillo had uncovered a plot to kill him some 24 hours before it was to be carried out on 21 January 1960. Mass purges, arrests and some killings followed. Tensions within the regime mounted rapidly, as did its Byzantine-style ruler's greed. Assuming the presidency of the Dominican Central Bank, the dictator forced exporters, as part of an 'austerity' programme, to deposit half of their dollar earnings with the bank, which soon found their way into Trujillo's accounts abroad. During this time, Trujillo was completing an intensive drive, begun in the mid-1950s with the purchase of the Haina complex of sugar mills and lands in the southern part of the Republic, to expand sugar production and appropriate more and more of it for himself. He went so far as to deprive thousands of peasant families of their squatters' settlements, forcing them to sell their cattle and work as sugar peons. It had been hoped, of course, that the Dominican Republic would get a generous share of the US sugar quota previously allotted to Cuba. An intensive Washington lobbying campaign was carried out to this end, largely through the Dominican Consul-General in Washington, Marco A. Pena.

In the late summer of 1960, the US Congress did raise the Dominican allotment from 27,000 to 250,000 tons, but President Eisenhower slapped a punitive excise tax on it in September sometime after the OAS ministerial conference voted for economic sanctions against the Trujillo regime and a break in diplomatic relations. The economy of the Dominican Republic was in deep decline and the country was also in disgrace internationally as a result of Trujillo's backing of a plot against the life of Venezuelan President Romulo Betancourt. In June, a car full of explosives blew up alongside Betancourt's automobile during a Caracas Armed Forces Day procession, wounding the President and killing two others. A Venezuelan naval officer later admitted that the elaborate bomb was prepared in the Dominican Republic, presumably as an act of retaliation against Venezuela for having asked the OAS in February 1960 to censure Trujillo for 'flagrant violations of human rights'. In August that same year, the Organization of American States did censure the Dominican Republic, and the USA and several Latin American nations immediately suspended diplomatic relations with the Trujillo regime, though Washington kept a consulate in Ciudad Trujillo to protect its commercial interests.

As Trujillo's political and financial problems deepened, talks continued between US Consul Henry Dearborn, Chief Political Officer Barfield and leaders of the anti-Trujillo conspiracy. Towards the end of 1960, contact was established between Luis Amiama Tio and a CIA agent who, according to Arturo R. Espaillat, former head of Trujillo's Military Intelligence Service, was named Plato Cox. Espaillat made this statement in a press conference in Ottawa in 1962. While this cannot be taken as concrete proof alone, what is certain is that the smuggling of firearms into the Republic by the CIA for the assassination plot began in late 1960, following a series of talks between Dearborn, Barfield and Luis Amiama Tio, who had extensive banana and cattle holdings and had been mayor of Santo Domingo. Also involved in the plot was Antonio Imbert, who had been Governor of Puerto Plata province. Amiama and Imbert were tough and ambitious and both were to be made four-star generals by the provisional council that took over after Trujillo's death.

The key link between the assassins and the CIA in the arms shipments was a long-time American civilian resident of Ciudad Trujillo, Lorenzo Perry, otherwise known as 'Wimpy', who ran a supermarket in a fashionable neighbourhood close to where Trujillo also lived.

Wimpy was put under brief arrest after the killing but was later allowed to leave the country. The weapons were imported in small parts hidden among the routine grocery shipments for the supermarket arriving regularly in the capital's port. The gun-parts entered the Republic in specially marked food cans, which were turned over to the conspirators to be assembled later.

Plans for the intended assassination were worked out during the same period in which the abortive assault on Cuba was being prepared. However, when the CIA-organised 17 April 1961 invasion at the Bay of Pigs failed and world attention was focused on Washington's complicity in that operation, a postponement of the attempt on Trujillo's life was ordered because of the embarrassment another such failure might cause the USA. But the order to delay the operation came too late: the weapons were already in the hands of the conspirators, who promptly refused appeals by their US contacts Dearborn and Barfield to delay the assassination. They insisted on moving at the first opportunity, and this came on 30 May when Trujillo and his chauffeur drove out into the country in an unescorted 1959 Chevrolet for a rendezvous at a San Cristobal estate, La Fundacion, with Trujillo's 20-year-old mistress, Mona Sanchez. It was Trujillo's custom to call on his 94-year-old mother, Julia Molina, before going on to La Fundacion. His departure for San Cristobal from his mother's home was signalled to the conspirators by Sen. Modesto Diaz, a neighbour of Julia Molina and brother of General Juan Tomas Diaz, one of the principal gunmen in the assassination plot. The general had apparently become involved in the conspiracy, as he believed that he had been forced into a premature retirement from the army in 1960 on the dictator's orders. The plan was to kill Trujillo, seize control of the capital and form a provisional government to be immediately recognised by the US, and then perhaps hold the elections, which Trujillo had promised for May 1962. The assassins intended to be the main, if not the only, candidates.

It is at this point that the conspiracy began to seriously unravel. It had been planned that General Roman Fernandez was to have summoned the entire Trujillo clan to La Fortaleza de Ozama in the capital, inform them of Trujillo's death and have them killed on the spot. However, he had been ordered to the San Isidro air force base that afternoon by Trujillo and told to stay there until some administrative irregularities were corrected. Since he was thus kept ten miles outside Ciudad Trujillo until the next morning, Roman was not able to carry out the assignment he had been given. Around 10.30 p.m. on 30 May two carloads of gunmen fired 27 shots into the dictator's body after stopping his vehicle on the main highway between the capital and the Agricultural Fair Grounds, where Trujillo annually received tributes for his prize cattle. Having dumped the riddled corpse into the trunk of one of the attackers' cars, the assassins went to the house of Roman, only to learn that he was not in the capital. They then scattered and in the succeeding days all the known assassins, including Roman, were rounded up and executed either at once or shortly before the mass departure of the Trujillo family in November 1961. The two surviving exceptions were Imbert and Amiama.

It seems very likely that close associates of President Trujillo got to know of the US role in the assassination and attempted coup within a few days. Almost immediately upon his 31 May return from Paris to assume command of the Dominican armed forces, Lt. General Rafael (Ramfis) Trujillo, Jr was fully briefed. However, Ramfis and other supporters of the dead dictator were warned not to launch reprisals against the Americans involved in the plot. The new leader also felt constrained by the arrival of so many foreign newsmen in Ciudad Trujillo within 48 hours of the assassination, and indeed the reported readiness of US naval and marine forces, waiting in offshore waters, to intervene in the Dominican Republic should there be any loss of American life or property. An important OAS fact-finding commission arrived in early June, and that may have significantly helped to prevent a bloodbath. Ramfis only retained power for a further six months; however, this did allow him time to liquidate what moveable family wealth he could, while US diplomats told him that if he behaved himself he could leave the country a rich man. Dearborn and Barfield among others had meanwhile been rushed out of the Dominican Republic by US officials. Although the conspiracy was only a partial success – the dictator was dead, but the coup failed – within the year the United States had finally eased the dictator's family out of power and into a long foreign retirement in some considerable luxury.

1962 – DEATH OF AN ICON Do the weeks and months just before Marilyn Monroe was found dead cast any light on the tragedy? Was she just another suicide statistic, or was something darker involved? Was she becoming an embarrassment, perhaps even a threat to certain powerful politicians? Was she brutally silenced?

Marilyn Monroe had started shooting the film comedy *Something's Got to Give* for Twentieth Century Fox in April 1962, and some seventeen months after that had starred in *The Misfits* with Clark Gable and Montgomery Clift. Her death came just fifteen months after her divorce to playwrite and *The Misfits* screenwriter Arthur Miller, and fourteen months after she had been treated for addiction to barbiturates and alcohol. Also, the actress's respiratory infections and chronic stage fright delayed shooting of her last movie from the start. On 19 May Monroe travelled to New York City with a high fever after receiving threats from Fox that she could be fired if there were any more absences. There she was to famously sing 'Happy Birthday' at a Democratic fundraising tribute to President John F. Kennedy. Monroe stood in the darkness at the very edge of the Madison Square Garden stage while in the centre was President Kennedy's brother-in-law, the Hollywood actor Peter Lawford, teasing the political crowd with an in-joke about a secret many of them knew: that Monroe was the President's lover. Just before she stepped into the lights, Monroe appeared to sigh and then straightened her shoulders. A roar of appreciation greeted the star as she entered into the circles of stage light. She coyly clasped an ermine wrap about her, covering her $12,000 Jean Louis beaded gown, paused until the frenzy quieted, then let the fur fall backwards into Lawford's hands. As she began singing, Marilyn seemed energised, perhaps from the Dexedrine pills prescribed by studio doctors combined with megavitamins and antibiotics. 'It was like mass seduction,' the event's producer, composer Richard Adler, later recalled. 'With Marilyn whispering "Happy Birthday" and the crowd yelling, and screaming.'

Monroe had first met Kennedy in 1954 and had been having an intense affair with him since December 1961. The First Lady was not alongside her husband at Madison Square Garden. 'Jackie knew about the affair by then,' said LA Mayor Sam Yorty, a national figure in Democratic politics at the time. 'That's why she stayed away.' After the seven-minute performance, a feverish and apparently rather dizzy Monroe collapsed in her dressing room. She was carefully snipped out of the designer dress and bathed with cool hand towels in an attempt to lower her temperature. Two hours later, Monroe made her entrance at a party given by theatre magnate Arthur Krim. After an hour, President Kennedy pulled the actress away from the other guests and into a corner, where they were soon joined by Robert Kennedy. The three stood talking for approximately fifteen minutes. Later the Attorney General appeared uneasy as White House journalist Merriman Smith chatted with Monroe while writing in a small notebook. When Bobby was informed by a Secret Service agent that a candid photo had been taken of Monroe and the Kennedy brothers, he appeared to become distinctly angry. Shortly after 1 a.m. Secret Service agents escorted the President and Marilyn to the basement of Krim's apartment house and through a series of tunnels that led to the Carlyle Hotel, where JFK maintained a penthouse. 'I learned from an FBI agent that they remained in the suite for several hours,' said columnist Earl Wilson in an interview. 'It was the last prolonged encounter between them.' What kept them locked inside the bedroom wasn't just sex. Monroe complained to at least two friends that Kennedy was perfunctory in bed. 'She insisted that he made love like an adolescent,' recalled Monroe's long-time friend and former lover Robert Slatzer. Monroe and the President would gossip for hours – on the phone, at Lawford's Santa Monica mansion and in the Carlyle.

At 2.30 a.m. Merriman Smith was awakened by banging on his apartment door and was confronted by two Secret Service agents, who grilled him for an hour about his appearance at the private affair. 'They wanted to make sure I didn't write about Marilyn and Bobby,' he told Richard Adler. Her masseur, Ralph Roberts, was waiting and, as they chatted about the birthday party, Monroe had enthusiastic praise for Robert Kennedy. She had never mentioned the Attorney General until that night and he had apparently startled her by discussing politics, an acknowledgment that there was more to Monroe than just her Hollywood image. However, she told Roberts there was no chance of an affair with RFK, saying, 'He's not my type.'

Monroe returned to filming at the Fox Studios two days later with a severe sinus infection masked by amphetamines and painkillers. The following weekend, she learned that the President was about to end their affair at the urging of his political advisors who believed his public flirtation with the actress could harm his political future. Word of the brush-off left the actress shattered and filming was delayed yet again. Shortly afterward, Monroe was bedridden with a bronchial infection and missed two more days on the set. When Monroe was working, director George Cukor would often punish his fragile star by insisting on dozens of unnecessary retakes, further undermining her confidence. Finally on 8 June executives at the financially troubled film company fired Monroe and, to justify the studio's actions, Fox press agents launched a negative publicity blitz labelling Monroe as nothing more or less than mentally ill.

Shortly after Monroe was dismissed, Robert Kennedy arrived at her Brentwood home for a visit that was believed to be both personal and political. The President had changed the private Oval Office phone number he had given Monroe and she had begun calling the main White House switchboard, angrily giving her name when operators would not put her through. It is reported that at sometime during their walk around the swimming pool, the Attorney General sternly told Monroe to 'stop calling the White House'. To compensate for the loss of the President's secret line, Bobby gave her his own private number at the Justice Department. 'He was a wonderful person to tell your troubles to,' remembered his press aide, Ed Guthman, 'and Marilyn called him a lot during the summer of 1962. But then so did Judy Garland and the other ladies in trouble.'

When it came to keeping the Kennedy family name clean, Robert Kennedy must have seemed almost invincible that summer: by seeing to it that scores of documents and phone logs were given top-secret classifications, the Attorney General had also successfully hidden all traces of the President's affair with alleged Mafia party girl Judith Campbell Exner. Bobby even functioned as a marriage counsellor to control the fights and hide the infidelities within the Kennedy family; in fact columnist Walter Winchell privately described him as the family's 'sexual policeman'. When Robert Kennedy heard from the Secret Service that JFK had asked for an introduction to a young German socialite in Washington, he authorised an FBI investigation which discovered that she had been in a previous affair with a Soviet attaché. Robert ensured that she was summarily deported.

However, it was at this point that some believe the Attorney General became careless: he embarked on a blazing love affair with the most famous actress in the world. Robert Kennedy and Monroe's ninety-minute meeting in the garden of her house two months before her death led to a long-distance relationship so intense and passionate that Monroe's maid Hazel Washington described it as 'making love over the phone. And I do mean making love.' Within a few days, Monroe was able to reach the Attorney General anywhere and at any time. They saw one another often during the next few weeks because of RFK's frequent visits to LA to oversee filming of *The Enemy Within*, adapted from his bestseller about his crusade against organised crime.

Neighbours claim to have seen the couple strolling along the beach in front of the fourteen-bedroom ocean-front compound of the Kennedy's brother-in-law Peter Lawford. The mansion, according to some, offered Monroe privacy for her meetings with both Kennedy brothers. 'There were many, many rendezvous in June and July,' claimed Lynn Sherman, a friend of Pat Kennedy Lawford's, who lived nearby. 'The official car drove up, and you knew Bobby Kennedy was in town.' Robert appeared to enjoy talking long into the night with the actress and is rumoured to have been more than a little indiscreet on matters ranging from organised crime, US policy on Cuba and the Cold War. Monroe started borrowing books on current events and took notes about their political conversations. Evelyn Moriarty, the star's stand-in, recalled the 'stacks of notebooks' that appeared at Monroe's house and in her dressing room. As her phone calls to Washington proliferated, so did the notebooks, and they became a potentially powerful record of her suspected affairs with the President and his brother.

Then in mid-July Monroe found that Robert had suddenly disconnected himself from her life and, once again frantic for his advice about returning to the set of *Something's Got to Give*, Marilyn dialled her private line and later told several friends that it had been disconnected. A receptionist in Robert Kennedy's Washington office told her that Robert was in conference all afternoon. According to some observers, Robert Kennedy ended his romance with Monroe like a rich college boy dumping a girlfriend from the wrong side of the tracks. Hidden behind political functionaries, the Kennedy family quietly locked Monroe out. The reasons for Kennedy's sudden turnabout aren't too mysterious: with brother Edward's senatorial primary looming in September and FBI Director J. Edgar Hoover's loose-lipped references to colleagues concerning an 'especially hot' file on RFK and the actress, Monroe was a definite liability to Robert's political aspirations. According to some sources, Robert had been told by his mother and other family members to drop her as quickly as possible. However, Monroe would not accept that the affair was over. 'Bobby's rejection reawakened her father's complete abandonment of her,' said Lucy Freeman, a writer who interviewed Monroe's psychiatrist several times. 'Because of her father's early desertion, she created the sex goddess, the one that no man could possibly abandon.'

Contrary to the rumours of her madness and hysteria during the period of her alleged affairs with the Kennedys, Monroe's real ailment during the summer of 1962 was insomnia. Adding to her growing list of health and personal problems were disturbing signs of anorexia that had begun with a crash diet to prepare for *Something's Got to Give*. Ralph Greenson, Monroe's psychiatrist, and her other physicians ordered her to eat and gave her vitamin shots. In the months before *Something's Got to Give* started filming, Greenson had weaned Monroe down to a couple of chloral hydrates – mild sedatives – a night and a bit of champagne. According to associates on the movie set, methamphetamine shots were provided by the studio doctors, but these injections effectively destroyed Greenson's regimen, replacing it with Monroe's old uppers-and-downers habits of the 1950s which, when combined with alcohol, had damaged the star's health and led to her hospitalisation in 1960 during the filming of *The Misfits*. Most of Monroe's so-called suicide attempts were actually mild overdoses, according to close friends, who insist she had an expert's knowledge of pharmacology and knew precisely how many pills it took to get to sleep. Because her speech became slurred and she seemed confused, friends often overreacted and summoned doctors. 'Marilyn liked to be rescued. She would take a high dose of say, Nembutal, then call somebody. But even if she weren't rescued, there was no real danger,' said publicist Rupert Allan.

After three days away from home, Monroe returned on 22 July looking wan and exhausted. A number of her confidants claimed that she had actually checked into the Cedars of Lebanon Hospital under an assumed name and aborted President Kennedy's baby. Still others insisted it was Robert Kennedy's child, and as days passed and Robert remained elusive, Monroe spread bitter tales about her pregnancy. She told hairdresser Agnes Flanagan, Laguna Beach realtor Arthur James and her publicist, Rupert Allan, about it, though Allan and James believed that she had a miscarriage.

By the end of July, the Monroe question had become a powder keg for the Kennedys and a rumoured bugging operation, believed to have been ordered by Jimmy Hoffa and the Mafia, at Monroe's home threatened to confirm her stormy relationships with both the President *and* his brother. The Attorney General apparently decided to let his long-time brother-in-law handle this latest emergency. Just as Jack had dispatched Robert to sever the President's ties with the actress, now Lawford was ordered to cut his long-time friend off from all contact with the First Family. Monroe was already heartbroken by her treatment at the hands of the Kennedys. Those close to her have said she never understood why the President, and later the Attorney General, hadn't the courage or the gallantry to tell her goodbye themselves.

According to several friends, it was at this time that Monroe began threatening to hold a press conference to talk about her relationship with the Kennedy brothers. She wasn't going to be shoved aside just because she had become inconvenient. The conspiracy theories really kick in at this point and the question is asked whether Marilyn Monroe was now seen as a loose cannon, a genuine danger to the Kennedy Administration. Did the Hollywood star know enough secrets shared in unguarded moments in the bedroom by both brothers to be a potential national security threat? Did her attitude of defiance towards the rich and powerful Kennedys lead to her death? On the morning of 4 August Monroe had been up for hours when her housekeeper, Eunice Murray, and her personal publicist, Pat Newcomb, who had spent the night at Monroe's home, stirred at 9 a.m. Leaning against the kitchen wall in a terry cloth robe, Monroe became cross with Newcomb. 'I had been able to sleep and Marilyn hadn't,' said Newcomb. 'When I came out looking refreshed, it made her furious . . . Marilyn had calls that morning, and by the time I saw her she was in a rage,' Newcomb said. Some believe the phone calls were from Peter Lawford and Robert Kennedy, in that order. Monroe told Pat Newcomb that several other disturbing calls had come intermittently during the night, in which a female voice screamed, 'Leave Bobby alone!'

According to some theorists, Robert Kennedy arrived at Monroe's home on the afternoon of 4 August. Hollywood detective Fred Otash claims that 'Marilyn and Bobby had a violent argument and she told him that she felt used and passed around. At the end of the argument Marilyn ordered Bobby out of her house.' After the visit Monroe was so distraught that she summoned her psychiatrist Dr Greenson, for an extra ninety-minute session, and it is believed that she was given an injection of barbiturates similar to one given to her by her internist, Dr Engleberg, the previous afternoon. By 5.30 p.m. her analyst had left and afterwards she talked to her stepson Joe DiMaggio, Jr and her friend Jeanne Carmen, among others. None of these contacts are believed to think that she was depressed or on drugs.

Informed sources believe Monroe died before midnight on 4 August. Housekeeper Eunice Murray found the body and called Ralph Greeson. When publicist Arthur Jacobs, Pat Newcomb's boss, received word around 10.30 p.m. he rushed to Monroe's house. The first call from Monroe's house to the outside world came six hours after Arthur Jacobs had been notified. Police sergeant Jack Clemmons was on watch at the West LA substation, less than three miles from Monroe's home when at 4.25 a.m. the telephone rang. At first the caller, Dr Ralph Greenson, was so agitated that Clemmons couldn't understand him. 'Marilyn Monroe is dead,' the psychiatrist said, 'she just committed suicide.' When Clemmons arrived at the scene, Eunice Murray led him to the bedroom and gestured toward Monroe's bed. 'Marilyn was lying face down in what I call the soldier's position,' said Clemmons. 'Her hands were by her side and her legs were stretched out perfectly straight. It was the most obviously staged death scene I have ever seen. The pill bottles on her bedside table had been arranged in neat order and the body deliberately positioned. It all looked too tidy.' Indeed, as the water was off in the house due to repairs and Monroe apparently hated taking tablets without a drink, why was there no obvious sign of water or any other form of drink near to her? It is highly unlikely that Monroe could have swallowed fifty or so pills without liquid help. Far too neat and tidy for someone bent on taking their own life, claim the theorists, and probably with some justification as Monroe was not known for her obsessive tidiness at the best of times.

However, if she didn't kill herself then who did and why? Could the mob have done it because they were mad at the Kennedys? Interestingly the main source for this theory is Chuck Giancana, younger brother of a mob boss, as put forth in the 1992 book *Double Cross*. Giancana, Sr had expected JFK's allegiance because the mobster had once saved Joe Kennedy, Sr from a hit during Prohibition days. Instead, Robert Kennedy went gunning for organised crime. The theory goes that Giancana had Marilyn killed to embarrass RFK, but Bobby Kennedy foiled the plan by removing compromising evidence. Or could Robert Kennedy have done it, aided by agents of the Secret Service and CIA? This theory is put forth by the author Robert Slatzer in his book *The Marilyn Files*. According to Slatzer, Robert didn't apply the final touch, the fatal dose of Nembutal. But, like a general, he gave the command. Now on to organised crime again, but with a new twist in the mob and a mystery guest. The source of this theory is Milo Speriglio. In *Crypt 33* he claims that as a private eye he had investigated the death for nineteen years. Speriglio states that Monroe was murdered by the Mafia. He also claims that there is a connection to the Kennedys, but that John and Robert weren't involved in the death.

The 1962 Los Angeles County Coroner's report listed her cause of death as a suicide. At the time of her death Marilyn Monroe was surviving reasonably well, she was unhappy about the treatment she had received from the Kennedys but was probably more angry than depressed. Suicide does not appear to be an obvious first option, and an accidental overdose or murder do seem to be more likely. And of those murder may well be in prime position. Marilyn had threatened to expose rich and powerful figures and may have paid the price with her life. The suggestion that having been sedated she was then given a lethal overdose by an injection straight into the lining of the rectum leaving no marks or telltale evidence has been mooted as the method used by hired and highly professional killers. Sadly we may never know the exact circumstances of Marilyn Monroe's death, but certainly the world was a little more boring and darker for her passing.

1963 – THE WARD CONSPIRACY Though for ever known as the Profumo Affair, this was in reality the Ward Conspiracy. In fact it appears to have been a series of separate political intrigues and intelligence operations, not always well co-ordinated. These separate incidents were finally to become inextricably intertwined to make one dishonourable and unpleasant conspiracy to hide the embarrassment of the state, individual politicians, the intelligence services and probably members of the royal family. It also ensured that all the blame and public attention would eventually fall upon the shoulders of just one man, the eminently expendable Dr Stephen Ward. He had become well known as the society osteopath to the rich and famous, from Winston Churchill to Douglas Fairbanks, Jr. Confidant of Prince Philip and close friend of Viscount 'Bill' Astor, Ward was an immensely charming and gifted man. He lunched regularly at the select Thursday Club with Prince Philip; Baron, a photographer; David Milford Haven; Felixs Topolski; Lord Boothby – the lover of Prime Minister Harold MacMillan's wife – and many others. Ward was a guest at Sarah Churchill's wedding, a regular at Lord Astor's 'weekends', was friends with Maureen Swanson and Elizabeth Taylor, and was one of the guests at Douglas Fairbanks, Jr's daughter's 'coming-out party' along with Princess Margaret and half the royalty of Europe. His artistic ability was such that he had been allowed to draw numerous celebrities, including Stanley Spencer, A. P. Herbert, Churchill, Lord Shawcross and Professor Bernard Lovell. Many members of the British royal family would also sit for Ward, including the Duchess of Kent, Ward's close friends, Princess Margaret, and Lord Snowdon and Prince Philip. Indeed, his work would later be bought by a well-known art historian and disappear, avoiding further embarrassment to Buckingham Palace.

In the early 1960s Ward rented Spring Cottage on Lord Astor's estate. Although celebrities, politicians and statesmen of the time were more than happy to spend days or weekends as his guests there, nearly all of them abandoned him when he needed their support. Ward had entered a rather seedy world of promiscuity and private parties run by the likes of David, Marquis of Milford Haven and the cousin of Prince Philip. These often developed into full-blown orgies lasting over an extended weekend, with participants as varied as Baron and American superstar Bing Crosby.

By 1962, rumours had already been circulating for months about the private life of John Dennis Profumo, Secretary of State for War, and the 'object of his passion'. In the more deferential spirit of the 1950s, the rumours may have been dismissed. In the early 1960s, however, they flowered and the young woman was soon named, Christine Keeler. Keeler had left home at sixteen after an unhappy childhood and gravitated to London where she found work of a sort at Murray's Cabaret Club. There she met and befriended another showgirl, Marilyn 'Mandy' Rice-Davies. Soon, both young women had drifted into the cosmopolitan and exciting circle that surrounded Dr Stephen Ward. Both young women were to become celebrated players in Ward's celebrity sexual circus, which centred on his Wimpole Mews flat, equipped with two-way mirrors, Lord Astor's country mansion of Cliveden or weekends at Spring Cottage. Soon, Keeler, Rice-Davies and numerous other girls in Ward's 'harem' were sleeping around London and the home counties with publicly well-known figures, many of whom have successfully kept their anonymity.

It was at Cliveden that John Profumo was introduced to Keeler, a brief but passionate affair ensued, and tongues began to wag. Even then, it might have been brushed under the carpet in the time-honoured English way, but Profumo made a fundamental error: he lied to the House of Commons. In March 1963 he stated that there was 'no impropriety whatever' in his relationship with Keeler. Ten weeks later he appeared again before MPs to say 'with deep remorse' that he had misled the House and would resign. What brought Profumo down even more than his lies in the House of Commons was the startling revelation that Keeler was also having sex with Yevgeny 'Eugene' Ivanov, the naval attaché at the Soviet embassy and GRU intelligence officer. It was that detail which captured world attention, notably in the United States, where the FBI compiled a detailed report called Operation Bowtie. J. Edgar Hoover was fully aware that the Ward circle included many extremely well-known Americans, together with girls such as Mariella Novotny, one of Lord Astor's sado-masochistic lovers, who had been bedded by President John F. Kennedy. Novotny's lovers also included Malcolm X and the Rolling Stones guitarist, Brian Jones.

In Britain Profumo's disgrace naturally caused a huge sensation. Ward had been a friend to many in the highest ranks of society and knew of the well-established links with the security services and espionage. He also quite certainly knew far too many secrets, including those of certain members of the royal family. Lord Snowdon – Anthony Armstrong-Jones – husband of Princess Margaret, had known Ward since the early 1950s and had once worked for Ward's great friend and photographer Baron. The Snowdons often frequented clubs such as the Murray's Cabaret Club in Soho, and Peter Rachman's hideout, the El Condor Club. The Soviet GRU intelligence officer Ivanov was wined and dined around top London restaurants and at private parties as part of the 'honeytrap', and there was ample opportunity for arranged or accidental meetings with the Snowdons and other celebrities. The Snowdons and Ward's circle were certainly invited to many of the same social events and 'weekends'. Ivanov was, of course, the subject of a joint MI5-MI6 'honeytrap' operation designed to get him to defect, and though he was a fairly senior GRU Officer, he was considered to be vulnerable – incorrectly as it turned out. Ivanov very quickly spotted the trap, it is believed, but played along with the game as it suited the GRU to infiltrate such an officer into the upper echelons of British society. It is possible that at one time Ward was being used as a low-level, but extremely valuable, go-between at the height of the Cuban Missile Crisis – certainly by the Russians, as Ivanov was apparently sure that anything he told Ward would be quickly reported to British Intelligence and thence the CIA. When the bumbling Profumo's exposure compromised the operation, the Russians quickly withdrew Ivanov, the intelligence services dropped Ward, and society, his 'friends' and the media abandoned him to his fate.

The Snowdons, like so many others, were deeply involved in the amoral and decadent circles targeted and trawled by MI5, the

Russians and the CIA alike. It is interesting to note that Ward had a two-way mirror in his apartment and photographed celebrities in compromising activities, apparently for those with similar tastes, such as Milford Haven, and many others in the same circles, possibly including the Snowdons. Ward is also rumoured to have had three identical albums bound of the most 'interesting shots'. One album was reported to have been seized by the British police, another by a friend of Ward's, while the third disappeared. Ivanov is believed to have copied the most sensitive shots from this third album for the GRU headquarters in Moscow, and these pictures may or may not have been used thereafter to put pressure on leading politicians, business figures and celebrities, from the UK in particular.

The government and MI5 panicked at the thought that the Snowdons' odd lifestyle might leave them open to blackmail, and it is somewhat obvious that their behaviour would undoubtedly have attracted the attention of the Soviet intelligence services. Margaret would have been targeted as sister of the monarch and for having a lifestyle that made her an obvious subject as she successfully honed her reputation as a chain-smoking, party-loving night crawler. Both Armstrong-Jones, a serial bisexual, and Margaret were fond of cross-dressing and indeed had a taste for lurid pornography in common with both Milford Haven and Ward himself. Margaret, too, liked to play the field with a serious number of lovers who, in addition to the more well-known examples, reportedly included Mick Jagger, Robin Douglas-Home, Peter Sellers and Lord Patrick Lichfield, a relative – but as Princess Margaret remarked, 'We're kissing cousins, so it's OK.' Nor was Prince Philip considered immune, having been close to being exposed in a number of scandals in the late 1940s and 1950s. With friends such as Ward's circle and relatives such as Lord Mountbatten and Milford Haven, he had acquired a reputation for clubs and sex parties. His list of mistresses reportedly includes Helene Cordet (her son Max Boisot is supposedly Philip's), actress Merle Oberon, singer Pat Kirkwood and the model Mitzi Taylor.

As is usual in an attempt to cover up a possibly highly damaging scandal, official wrath was immediately turned on those least able to defend themselves. Stephen Ward was effectively set up in a totally disgraceful way by the British establishment and to the lasting dishonour of all those involved, abandoned by the rich and famous who had so often accepted his hospitality and his girls' favours. Ward was prosecuted on trumped up charges of living on 'immoral earnings'. On the last day of his trial, Ward supposedly killed himself with an overdose of sleeping tablets. However, there are grave doubts about this and the conspiracy theorists point to a number of suspicious circumstancdes that seem to suggest that Ward may have been murdered. Ward's death was timely as far as the establishment was concerned and, though distraught at being abandoned by all the society figures he had so long courted, was he really suicidal? There appears to be no concrete evidence of murder, but equally no compelling argument to accept suicide. A great friend of Ward's and a former RAF intelligence officer, as well as one of 'The Goons', Michael Bentine, refused to accept that Ward had died by his own hand. He claimed, 'A Special Branch friend of mine told me Ward was "assisted" in his dying. I think he was murdered.'

There is the suggestion that Ward's death was 'assisted' by a Polish émigré apparently working for MI6 or, more possibly, MI5 D Branch: one Stanley Rytter (1927–84), his cover was as a press photographer and journalist in London, and he was also at one time the manager of Peter Rachman's 150 Club on the Earls Court Road. An MI6 operative reportedly told the author Anthony Summers that 'Stanley Rytter is the one who killed Ward ... I know because he told me. I don't quite know how he managed it, I wasn't there. But Rytter was with Ward the night he died and Rytter told me he was paid to kill Ward. He was paid by our mob.' Rytter's fellow Pole Serge Paplinski has commented, 'Stanley was there with Ward on the last night . . . he always said that Ward was poisoned.' Paplinski also believed that Rytter was linked in some way to British intelligence. Ward told one of his closest friends not long before his death, 'I suppose they expect me to go along with this stupid public-school convention that good chaps don't tell. Well I didn't once.' (Referring to an incident during his school days at Canford in Dorset some forty years earlier.) 'But not this time. If I'm going down then they're going with me. I promise you that.' This statement takes on added significance taken with the disappearance of a letter written by Ward and believed to be 'naming names' to Henry Brooke, the Home Secretary, and photographed on the night before Ward's death by *Daily Express* photographer Bryan Wharton. Not only had the letter vanished when Ward was found next day, but the photographs developed overnight and the negatives had also disappeared from the newspaper's offices by the next morning as well.

Stephen Ward's downfall was highly convenient for the establishment as well as for the disgraced ex-minister for war John Profumo.

Focusing attention, as it did, on the sordid details of the lives of two pretty but extraordinarily silly girls, Ward's trial displaced the fact that Profumo had lied to Parliament about his private life from public awareness, and it prevented serious investigation of the real security aspects of the affair.

Less than two months after Ward's tragic and mysterious death, an official report was produced by the senior law officer, Lord Denning, master of the rolls. He criticised the government for failing to deal with the affair more quickly, but concluded that national security had not been compromised: privately both Denning and the government pushed the blame on to the shoulders of Sir Roger Hollis, Director General of MI5. He was responsible for not having warned his political masters of the possible security repercussions of the minister of war sharing a whore with a Soviet intelligence officer. The Denning report is considered by many to be nothing more than a disgraceful whitewash that successfully destroyed Ward's reputation for the sake of the establishment. Denning links Ward and Ivanov in so far as it supports his view that Ward was not to be trusted and a thoroughly 'bad lot'. Denning said, 'Ward admired the Soviet regime and sympathised with the Communists. He advocated their cause in conversation with his patients, so much so that several became suspicious of him. He became very friendly with a Russian, Captain Eugene Ivanov.' Since Denning didn't publish notes it would be interesting to know where those particular poisoned gems came from.

The Ward Conspiracy covered up a rather sordid era in Britain, and hid the possible involvement of important businessmen, politicians, aristocrats, royalty, celebrities and spies. MI5 reportedly ran a brothel in Church Street in Kensington throughout much of the 1950s and early 1960s for the use of visiting dignitaries, diplomats and intelligence officers. For those too important to visit such an establishment, certain discreet gentlemen were called upon to provide young female or male company directly to the VIP hotel bedroom; Dr Stephen Ward was probably one of those 'gentlemen'. He certainly had the right social connections, the girls and indeed he had an MI5 controller, Keith Wagstaffe (cover-name 'Woods'). John Profumo stumbled upon a joint MI5-SIS honey-trap operation designed to persuade Ivanov, the Soviet naval attaché and spy, to defect. Indeed, Sir Colin Coote, editor of the *Daily Telegraph* and a former officer in the Secret Intelligence Service was responsible for introducing Ward to Ivanov at the behest of his old service. A senior MI5 officer involved in the operation said that it was a pity that Ward's true role had not been revealed at the time of his trial. 'I think that everyone involved did feel sorry about Ward and the final outcome.' Ward, he added, was a patriot working for his country. 'Nowhere in the Denning Report does it say that Ward was acting under our [MI5] instructions. That is very unfortunate.' To cover up the risk of international humiliation, political and security embarrassment, someone had to be sacrificed. That someone was the unfortunate and very loyal Dr Stephen Ward. There can be little real doubt that a group of ministers, government officials, security and intelligence officers, with the reluctant help of the police, set out to deliberately destroy Stephen Ward.

1963 – DEATH OF A PRESIDENT Mention the word 'conspiracy' and to many millions of people around the world the first name that comes to mind is 'Kennedy'. Much has been written, broadcast, surmised, misunderstood and even invented about that dark day in Dallas forty years ago. However, there is a surprisingly large amount of information available that can be considered as undeniable fact, though it has been interpreted in different ways by serious observers of the Kennedy assassination, both pro-Lone Nut and pro-Conspiracy of one sort or another. Taken individually any of these items of information can mean very little, but sensibly put together, like a jigsaw, a whole picture emerges which seems to point unerringly towards a well-organised and very well-covered-up conspiracy. Wild conspiracy theories and suspected official misinformation smoke screens abound and either accidentally or deliberately obscure the whole view. This has interfered with a rational investigation and debate on one of the defining moments of the twentieth century. However, the interest in this and the related assassinations and political events of the 1960s have not waned with the passing years, and there are those, conspiracy theorists and serious researchers alike, who still want to know who pulled the trigger(s) and who, assuming a conspiracy, instigated the assassination of an American president.

The broadly acknowledged facts alone indicate the assassination resulted from a conspiracy, and that it was followed by an extensive cover-up. The most significant and largely unchallenged 'facts' include the following:

- J. Edgar Hoover informed Lyndon Johnson during a phone conversation the day after the assassination that someone had been impersonating Lee Harvey Oswald, the alleged single assassin, at the Soviet Embassy in Mexico City. The transcript of the conversation was among the documents released by the Assassination Records Review Board (ARRB). Also, in light of recent disclosures, there can be no credible doubt that the 'Oswald' who called the Soviet embassy from the Cuban embassy in Mexico City on 28 September 1963 was *not* the Oswald arrested in Dallas.

- Within days of the assassination, the Secret Service spoke to an informant about an anti-Castro Cuban activist in the Chicago area, Homer S. Echevarria. In a discussion about an illegal arms sale a short time before the President was killed, Echevarria said that his group had 'plenty of money' and that his backers would proceed with the deal 'As soon as we take care of Kennedy'. Bravado perhaps, but interesting in the light of future events. This information prompted the agent in charge of the Chicago field office to prepare a memorandum in which he said Echevarria's group 'may have a connection with the JFK assassination'. Echevarria belonged to the 30 November Group. Another member of this same group was Rolando Masferrer, who relayed money between Alpha 66 and Mafia kingpin Carlos Marcello. Former House Select Committee on Assassinations (HSCA) chief counsel G. Robert Blakey, along with many researchers, suspects Marcello to be one of the figures behind the assassination. Alpha 66 was a violent, radical anti-Castro group that had a safe house in Dallas at the time of the assassination.
- Dallas oil baron and extreme right-winger H. L. Hunt reportedly wanted President Kennedy assassinated too. According to German journalist Joachim Jösten, during a party held prior to the President's trip to Dallas several witnesses heard Hunt remark that there was 'no way left to get those traitors out of our government except by shooting them out,' apparently in reference to the President and his brother, Robert Kennedy. In a speech in Houston, Texas, given prior to the assassination, Hunt said the Kennedy Administration was a 'Communist government'. Hunt reportedly had ties to the US intelligence community, especially to the CIA.
- Joseph Milteer, a wealthy radical right-wing leader, told a Miami police informant named William Somersett, on tape, fourteen days before the assassination, that a hit on Kennedy was 'in the working'. He also reported that Milteer called him from Dallas two hours before the assassination and said President Kennedy would be in

Dallas that day and that Kennedy would not be visiting Miami again. In addition Somersett reported that soon after the assassination Milteer told him that Oswald had been framed and that there was no need to worry because Oswald didn't know anything.

- A retired El Paso policeman, Jim Bundren, has told researchers that in late September 1963 an army intelligence officer who had been arrested and taken into custody appeared to have foreknowledge of the assassination. The intelligence officer was Richard Case Nagell. Nagell reportedly also worked for the CIA at times, and a 1969 military intelligence 'Agent Report' states that Nagell 'conducted an inquiry into the activities of Lee Harvey Oswald' in August and September of 1963. Nagell was arrested for walking into an El Paso bank and firing some shots into the ceiling on 20 September 1963. Nagell claimed he was merely trying to get arrested for his own safety because he believed he was being followed. Jim Bundren is one of the police officers who escorted Nagell during one of his hearings. Here is what Bundren reported to a researcher during a taped interview: 'I was sitting next to Nagell at one of his preliminary hearings. I don't remember the exact date, but I know it was before the Kennedy assassination. Nagell looked over at me and said, "You're a pretty good cop, aren't you? You know, if I didn't want you to, you'd never have caught me." I said, "You didn't want to rob that bank, did you?" He just looked at me for a moment and he says, "What makes you say that?" I said, "I saw the shots you fired in the bank. With your army training and everything, I just felt like maybe it was some kind of a diversionary tactic." Nagell just smiled and said, "Well, I'm glad you caught me. I really don't want to be in Dallas." I said, "What do you mean by that?" "You'll see soon enough," he said.
- When asked to comment on Oswald's last rifle score as a marine, Lt. Col. A. G. Folsom said Oswald's score of 'Marksman' was indicative of someone who was 'a rather poor shot'. Nearly all of Oswald's fellow marines who were asked to comment on his shooting ability expressed the view that he was not a very good shot. Several of them, in fact, said he was a very poor shot, and apparently none of them described him as an excellent shot. Warren Commission staffer Wesley Liebeler stated in an internal Commission memo that critical persons would not take the Commission's claims about Oswald's marksmanship seriously.
- Monty Lutz, a former member of the HSCA's firearms panel and an

Above Watch your back: a conspirator in the assassination of Pompey, an increasingly vain and autocratic Julius Caesar (*right*) was himself killed at the base of Pompey's statue in the Roman Senate on 15 March 44BC. Historians are divided as to whether Brutus and Cassius, the main players in a plot known to at least sixty members of Rome's political class, were reluctant defenders of liberty or shamelessly treasonous opportunists. (Mary Evans)

Above The usual suspects: conspirators depicted in the accepted version of the Gunpowder Plot, as taught to schoolchildren for centuries. Evidence suggests this small group of Roman Catholic noblemen were themselves the victims of a state conspiracy to undermine once and for all the chances of Catholic succession to the English throne. (Mary Evans)

Right Hard to kill: the end meted out to Rasputin in 1916 was pointless as well as messy, since the October Revolution was soon to sweep away the Russian royal family, whose credibility it was intended to assist. (Mary Evans)

Below Germany's Reichstag Fire of 27 February 1933 was a classic act of misinformation, tragically successful in 'blackening' communist opposition to the rise of the Nazis. Less than a month later, Hitler was able to sell a fearful German parliament the measures contained in his Enabling Act, turning the country from a democracy into a totalitarian state and lighting a metaphorical fire that was not extinguished until 1945. (Mary Evans)

Left Egyptian president Anwar Sadat salutes army units during a parade in Cairo on 6 October 1981, minutes before he was killed. (Popperfoto)

Below Three other victims lie prostrate in the aftermath of the assassination of Anwar Sadat. Arrested by the British during World War Two for pro-Axis activities, it is sadly ironic that Sadat should be killed for trying to make peace with Israel. (Popperfoto)

Above Roberto Calvi, 'God's banker,' here pictured on trial for fraud in May 1981. His corpse was found hanging beneath Blackfriars Bridge in London in 1982, displaying forensic evidence inconsistent with asphyxiation. (Popperfoto)

Right Milk and Honey? An ambulance leaves the central Milan headquarters of the Ambrosiano Bank, carrying the body of Calvi's secretary, Teresa Graziella Corrocher, who jumped to her death from a fourth-floor window. Calvi's is only one of a handful of deaths surrounding the Vatican and Ambrosiano – including that of Pope John Paul I – which raise unanswered questions. (Popperfoto)

Indira Gandhi, pictured here in January 1966 as she was about to become India's prime minister, was killed by members of her own staff in 1984 in response to her hardline stance on Sikh militancy. Though not usually mentioned in the same breath, the Nehru family – with two political assassinations and one son killed in a plane crash – bears uncanny comparison to the Kennedys. (Popperfoto)

Above Coal not Dole! The police response to picketing at the Orgreave Colliery, Yorkshire, on 10 March 1984 during Britain's miners' strike was to produce scenes not dissimilar to those of the General Strike or Peterloo. Tabloid allegations that miners' leader Arthur Scargill took cash from Libya originated first with that scion of probity, Robert Maxwell. (Popperfoto)

Right Thousand-yard stare: National Union of Mineworkers President Arthur Scargill emerges from one of many meetings with Ian MacGregor in 1984. Evidence now suggests that Mrs Thatcher's government and MI5 personally targeted Scargill through extra-democratic means. (Popperfoto)

Above Up the Workers! Pickets at Thoresby Colliery relax between incidents, 20 March 1984. The placard refers to Sir Ian MacGregor, chairman of the National Coal Board, who was in fact Scottish by birth. (Popperfoto)

Below Striking miners demonstrate outside the Houses of Parliament, London, 6 July 1984. False allegations that Arthur Scargill accepted money from Libya were all the more powerful in undermining support for the strike among these NUM grass roots because they appeared in the *Daily Mirror*, at the time Britain's only left-of-centre daily paper. (Popperfoto)

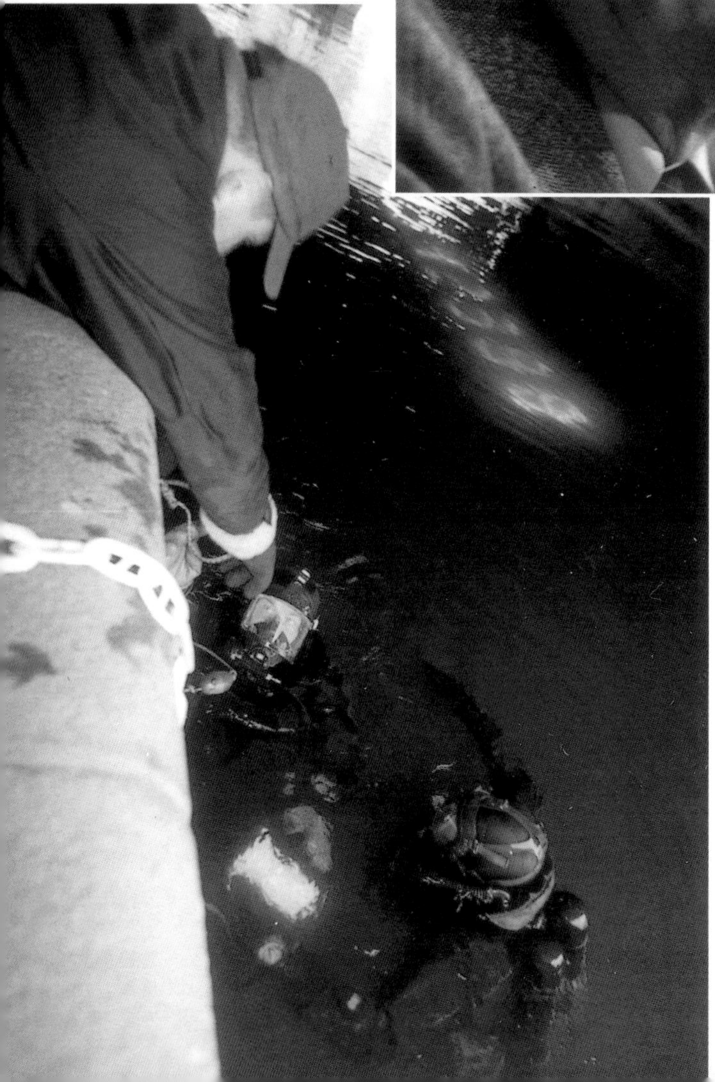

Above The assassination of Olaf Palme, Swedish prime minister, while out for a walk on 28 February 1986 deprived not just Sweden but the world of a compassionate and complex peacemaker. (Popperfoto)

Left Swedish police recover a weapon, believed to have been used in Palme's assassination, from a Stockholm canal in April 1998. (In the background is an underwater clock.) Initially blamed on Sweden's Kurdish community, the conspiracy has never been solved. The security services of Turkey, and apartheid-era South Africa, have also been implicated. (Popperfoto)

Above 'I promise to tell the truth ...' Marine Lt. Col. Oliver North is sworn in for his first day of public testimony before the House and Senate Iran-Contra committee, 7 July 1987. Iran-Contra remains a defining episode of US foreign policy, both as an example of the sponsoring of a group which spread terror within its own country – Nicaragua – and of a privately cavalier attitude to a collateral increase in drug use within the USA. (Popperfoto)

Above Lockerbie, Scotland, 22 December 1988: a policeman inspects the nose section of Pan Am flight 103. On impact it dug a hole thirty feet deep and over two hundred feet long. (Popperfoto)

Below Lockerbie, 22 December 1988: a rescue worker carries a rope through debris in the town. There were eleven fatal casualties on the ground, as well as 259 on board the plane. (Popperfoto)

Right Belfast solicitor Patrick Finucane, who was murdered on 12 February 1989 in front of his wife and three children. The Report of the International Human Rights Working Party of the Law Society of England and Wales in 1995 stated: 'There is credible evidence of both police and army involvement.' The trial of William Stobie for involvement in the killing collapsed at the Belfast High Court in November 2001. Stobie himself was murdered not long afterwards. (Popperfoto)

Below Wreckage from TWA Flight 800 is brought ashore in Hampton Bays, New York on 3 August 1996. The cause of this mid-air explosion is still unknown, although some witnesses and radar operators report the sighting of a missile, fired during nearby US naval exercises. (Popperfoto)

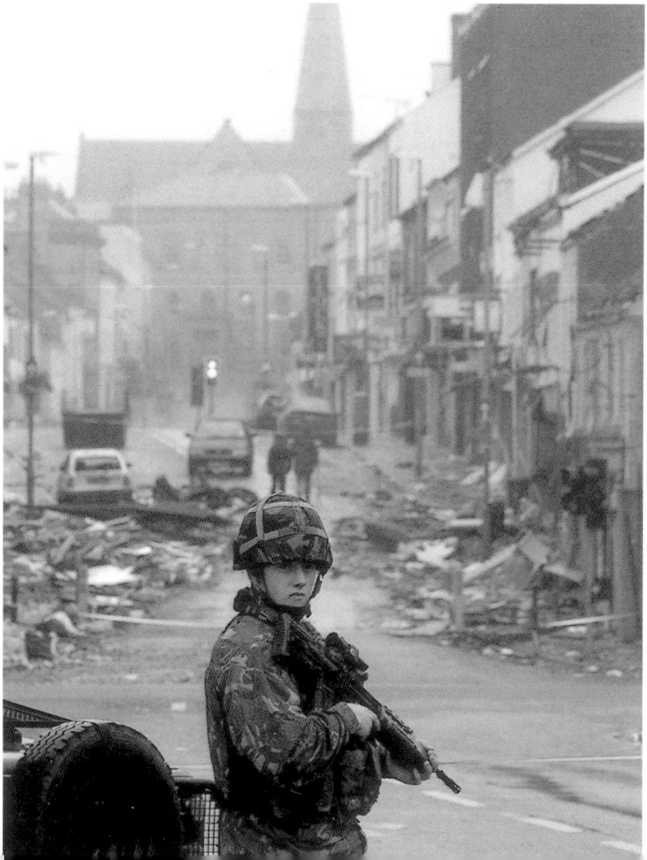

Above Omagh, Northern Ireland, 15 August 1998: police stand in the rubble from the car-bomb which ripped through the town, killing over twenty people. (Popperfoto)

Right Omagh, Northern Ireland, 16 August 1998: a soldier guards the aftermath. Was the bomb plot allowed to come to fruition because British intelligence officers were reluctant to compromise an informer within the Real IRA? (Popperfoto)

Above Abdel Basset Ali Al-Megrahi (*centre*) was found guilty in 2002 – at a special Scottish court convened at Camp Zeist in the Netherlands – of planting the bomb that blew up Pan Am Flight 103 over Lockerbie in 1998. His co-defendant, Al Amin Khalifa Fhima, was acquitted. Libya has benefited internationally since handing over the men, especially from the lifting of sanctions under UN resolution 1192, while there are other nations that, it is claimed, had a greater motive for the Lockerbie attack – most notably Iran, following the shooting down of an Iranian civilian flight by the USS Vincennes on 3 July 1988, with the loss of 290 lives. (Popperfoto)

Above Osama Bin Laden, pictured here at a news conference in Afghanistan on 26 May 1998, helped to create a worldwide terrorist conspiracy that year when Al-Queda was effectively merged with some ten or eleven other Islamic militant groups, and which reached its apotheosis on 11 September 2001. (Popperfoto)

The morning after: workers walk near the wreckage of New York's World Trade Center on 12 September 2001. (Popperfoto)

The Mother of all Conspiracies: in this aerial photograph taken on 26 September 2001, the ruins of the WTC still smoulder at Ground Zero. (Popperfoto)

expert rifleman in his own right, stated during the 1986 mock Oswald trial sponsored by a British television company that to his knowledge no one had ever duplicated Oswald's alleged shooting feat.

- The Warren Commission leaned towards the view that its alleged lone gunman did not fire until frame 210 of the Zapruder film. If the supposed single assassin didn't fire until Z210, then he would have had between 4.8 and 5.6 seconds to score two hits out of three shots at a moving target using a bolt-action rifle. The only way Warren Commission supporters can expand the alleged lone gunman's firing time from 5.6 to 8.2/8.4 seconds is to assume that he fired at around Z160 and that he completely missed, not only Kennedy, but the entire limousine. The limousine was less than 140 feet from the sixth-floor gunman at Z160. The Warren Commission expressed strong scepticism about the idea that its lone gunman would have missed the limousine with his first and closest shot.
- The world-class, Master-rated riflemen who took part in the Warren Commissions rifle tests expressed considerable criticism of the alleged murder weapon. They did not view it as a high-quality rifle, and they found its bolt to be difficult and its trigger pull to be rather odd.
- In the 1967 CBS rifle test, which was designed to test 'the Warren Commission's version of the shooting', not one of the eleven participating expert marksmen scored at least two hits out of three on his first attempt. Seven of them failed to do so on *any* of their attempts. Oswald would have had only one attempt.
- The HSCA concluded Ruby's killing of Oswald was not 'spontaneous', and that Ruby probably entered the basement with assistance. The HSCA found what it viewed as compelling evidence that Ruby had extensive ties with the Mafia. For the first few weeks after the shooting, Ruby was commonly characterised as a gangster, as a man who was involved with the Mafia. On 26 November 1963, four days after the assassination, the *Chicago Tribune* ran a story on Ruby's Mafia activity and connections in that city. Mafia man Johnny Roselli reportedly met with Ruby twice in the two months leading up to the assassination. Roselli was involved with Mafia kingpin Santos Trafficante and Sam Giancana in the CIA–Mafia assassination plots against Fidel Castro. Dallas police sergeant Patrick Dean, who was reportedly close to the city's mob boss, Joe Civello, failed a lie detector test with regard to his reassignment of

police guards away from the elevators and a door to a stairway just before Ruby shot Oswald.

Former Dallas police officer Billy Grammer has reported that on the night before Ruby killed Oswald, he received a call from Ruby at police headquarters warning that Oswald would be shot the following evening. Grammer says the caller did not identify himself, but that he is sure the voice was Jack Ruby's. Grammer claims he was well acquainted with Ruby. Grammer further reports that Ruby seemed to be aware of all the plans to transfer Oswald on Sunday from police headquarters to the Dallas County Jail, that he knew about the decoy vehicle assignment, and was aware of the approximate time the transfer would occur.

Two Warren Commission staff wrote the following in an internal Commission memo: 'In short, we believe that the possibility exists, based on evidence already available, that Ruby was involved in illegal dealings with Cuban elements who might have had contact with Oswald.' That is sufficient, according to many theorists, to assume at the least the possibility of collusion and therefore a conspiracy.

- According to a 25 November 1963 Associated Press report, William Crowe, an entertainer who had performed at Ruby's Carousel Club, told an AP reporter he was 'positive' he had seen Oswald in the club. *Dallas Morning News* reporter Kent Biffle said Crowe told him the same thing several days later. Karen Carlin, who had been a dancer at Ruby's club, told FBI agent Roger Warner on 24 November 1963 that 'she was under impression that Lee Oswald, Jack Ruby, and other individuals unknown to her, were involved in a plot to assassinate President Kennedy.' Another Ruby dancer, Janet Conforto, told Dallas newsmen shortly after the assassination that she had seen Oswald in Ruby's club. And yet another Ruby dancer, Kathy Kay, told the *Dallas Times Herald* the same thing in 1975. Four Dallas deputy constables told the *Dallas Morning News* in 1976 that shortly after the assassination they examined a box of handwritten notes and other papers in the Dallas County Courthouse that linked Ruby to Oswald.
- The Secret Service failed to employ a number of standard protection procedures for the Dallas motorcade. The HSCA found the Secret Service's protective measures for the motorcade were deficient. Among other things, the Committee said, 'Surprisingly, the security measures used in the prior motorcades during the same

Texas visit show that the deployment of motorcycles in Dallas by the Secret Service may have been uniquely insecure.' In film footage of other Presidential motorcades, it is seen that police motorcycle escorts rode on both sides and in front of the limousine during those events, forming a shield around the car and making it harder for a potential assassin or assassins to shoot the President. This was not done during the Dallas motorcade, and in fact security for the Dallas motorcade was reduced the day before the assassination.

- One or more senior military officers chose three poorly qualified, inexperienced military doctors to perform President Kennedy's autopsy, when much more capable and experienced doctors were readily available. Dr James Humes, the chief autopsy pathologist, burned the original autopsy report shortly after hearing Oswald was dead, and without making a photographic copy of it. The HSCA's medical panel concluded the autopsy on the President was inadequate. Private forensic experts have said the autopsy was a severely flawed postmortem examination.
- One of the autopsy pathologists said under oath in the Clay Shaw trial in 1969 that a senior military officer prevented him from performing a crucial autopsy procedure. A role of film taken during the autopsy by a medical corpsman was seized and destroyed by a Secret Service agent. Important photographs taken during the autopsy, some of which were apparently mentioned by one of the autopsy pathologists, are missing. The medical witness interviews conducted by the ARRB leave no doubt about this fact.
- Dr John Ebersole, the radiologist at the autopsy, told HSCA investigators that a sizeable fragment of occipital bone was missing from Kennedy's head and arrived late that night from Dallas. The occiput is located at the back of the skull. Yet the autopsy photographs of the back of the head, which were supposedly taken at or before the start of the autopsy, show the occipital region intact. Many researchers therefore believe the autopsy photos have been altered.

Over forty witnesses, many of them trained medical personnel, who saw President Kennedy's head wounds, said the large defect was in the right rear part of the head, in the right occipital-parietal region. A large wound in the back of the head indicates a shot from the front.

Two federal agents who attended the autopsy told the ARRB that the autopsy photos of the back of the head were not accurate, and that they recalled seeing a large defect in the right rear part of the skull. The agents suggested a flap of scalp was pulled over the right-rear defect before the photos were taken.

Dr J. Thornton Boswell, one of the autopsy pathologists, told HSCA investigators that the rear entry wound was right next to the external occipital protuberance and that part of that wound was contained in a fragment of bone that did not arrive from Dallas until late that night.

During an interview with HSCA investigators, Dr Finck questioned how one of the alleged autopsy photos of the back of the head had been established as having been taken at the autopsy.

- Dr George Burkley, the President's personal doctor, communicated through his attorney to the HSCA's chief counsel that he was aware of information that proved there must have been more than one person involved in the assassination. Dr Burkley volunteered to disclose this information to the Committee. Dr Burkley saw the President's body at Parkland Hospital in Dallas and during the autopsy. The letter that Dr Burkley's attorney sent to the HSCA at Dr Burkley's request was released by the ARRB. To date no record has been found that the HSCA sought to obtain the information Dr Burkley offered to provide.
- The Warren Commission said the wound in President Kennedy's back was at the base of the neck. Dr Humes placed the wound in this location, at the base of the neck, in the Rydberg Navy medical drawing. The HSCA, on the other hand, placed the wound nearly two inches lower than where it appears in the Rydberg drawing. The President's death certificate, which is marked 'verified', places the wound at the third thoracic vertebra (T3). On the night of the autopsy, Dr Boswell prepared an autopsy face sheet diagram in which he placed the wound at or near T3. The bullet holes in the back of the President's shirt and coat place the wound at or near T3. Several witnesses who saw the body said the back wound was well below the neck. One of those witnesses was Dr Ebersole, who said the wound was at T4. Three federal agents who saw the body drew wound diagrams for the HSCA. Those diagrams were recently released, and all three place the back wound near T3. The current single-bullet theory, which is the cornerstone of the lone-gunman scenario, is based on the assumption that the back wound was no lower than where the HSCA placed it, that is, no lower than T1, and that Kennedy was leaning 20–25 degrees forwards. If the

single-bullet theory is invalid, then there had to be more than one gunman, and therefore a conspiracy.

- The chief of the HSCA's forensic pathology panel, Dr Michael Baden, admitted the back wound was slightly *below* the throat wound.
- Dr David Mantik, a highly qualified radiation oncologist and physicist, studied the original autopsy x-rays and photographs at the National Archives, and concluded no bullet could have gone straight from the back wound to the throat wound without smashing right through the spine or without causing massive lung damage. The x-rays show no such damage to the spine or lungs.
- The two persons who claimed to have found CE 399, which is the so-called 'magic bullet' that allegedly went through Kennedy and Connally, both said the missile had a pointed tip, whereas CE 399 has a round tip.
- On the day of the assassination, Dr Malcolm Perry, the surgeon who performed the tracheostomy on the President's throat, said twice on national television that the throat wound was an entrance wound. When interviewed a short time later, he was asked about the report that the alleged sole assassin fired from a building which was to the rear of the limousine. Dr Perry suggested that the President must have been turned toward the building when the bullet struck his throat. Quite obviously, he was not.
- Dr Charles Carrico, who saw the throat wound before the tracheostomy was performed over it, described the wound as a 'penetrating wound' in his 22 November 1963 medical report.
- On the night of the autopsy, all three of the autopsy pathologists concluded, after extensive, prolonged probing, both with fingers and with a surgical probe, that the back wound had no point of exit. About half of the probing was done after the chest organs had been removed. James Jenkins, one of the medical technicians at the autopsy who witnessed the procedure, has reported he could see the surgical probe pushing against the lining of the chest cavity. Says Jenkins, 'I remember looking inside the chest cavity and I could see the probe . . . through the pleura or the lining of the chest cavity . . . You could actually see where it was making an indentation . . . where it was pushing the skin up . . . There was no entry into the chest cavity . . . No way that that [the bullet] could have exited in the front because it was then low in the chest cavity.'
- The *New York Times,* on 18 December 1963, quoted a source it

believed was familiar with the autopsy, who said that the bullet which struck the President in the back 'penetrated two to three inches'. Five weeks later, the *New York Times* said the bullet 'hit the President in the back of his right shoulder, several inches below the collar line, that the bullet lodged in his shoulder'. In accordance with this report, the *Washington Post* reported on 18 December 1963 that during the autopsy a bullet 'was found deep in his shoulder'.

- Two medical technicians at the autopsy have stated that a bullet rolled out from the area of the President's back when the body was removed from the casket prior to the autopsy. One of the med-techs said the bullet rolled out from the back, while the other says it rolled out from the sheets. A third med-tech from the autopsy has said he remembers personnel at the autopsy talking that night about a bullet that had fallen from the sheets.

  Admiral David P. Osborne, who was in attendance at the autopsy, reported that a bullet rolled out from the 'clothing' that was wrapped around the President's body, and that he actually handled the missile. The HSCA asserted that Osborne 'thought' he saw a bullet roll out, but that he later said he wasn't sure when told no one else at the autopsy recalled such an event. Admiral Osborne told researcher and author David Lifton that he and the HSCA had disagreed over the matter. Said Osborne, 'I told them, the HSCA investigators, that this was the way I remembered it, and they said: "Well, it must be wrong, because the Secret Service testified that the bullet was found in the hospital in Parkland, and brought back to Washington." And so I said: "Well, if that's true, then they brought it back to the morgue, because I had that bullet in my hand, and looked at it."' According to the official record of the chain of possession of the bullet that was found at Parkland Hospital, that missile was never taken to Bethesda Hospital, where the autopsy was performed. The HSCA's claim that no one else at the autopsy recalled seeing a missile fall from the sheets wrapped around the body is incorrect. As mentioned above, a medical technician who was at the autopsy has said he remembers seeing this happen, while another med-tech says he recalls discussion among personnel at the autopsy about a bullet having fallen from the sheets. Admiral Osborne has said that the bullet fell from the clothing wrapped around the body when the body was removed from the casket.
- The single-bullet theory is an abject impossibility. Dr Mantik found

by examining the photos and x-rays that no bullet could have exited the throat without doing extensive, massive damage to the bony structures of the neck or without causing significant trauma to the lungs. Furthermore, only a bullet exiting the President's throat at a markedly leftwards angle could have caused the nick that was allegedly made on the left edge of the knot of the President's tie. Allegedly, because a high-quality photo of the tie shows the nick to be visibly inwards from the knot's left edge, and the HSCA confirmed that the nick does not even come close to going all the way through the tie. But, assuming a bullet exited the throat and caused the nick in the tie, that missile could not possibly have struck Governor John Connally near the right armpit as required by the single-bullet theory. It appears virtually certain that the throat wound was actually an *entry* wound, not an exit wound.

- Numerous witnesses complained that the transcripts of their interviews with the FBI and/or with Warren Commission staffers were inaccurate, and in some cases that the transcripts significantly misreported important parts of their testimony.
- FBI and Secret Service experts who conducted the first two government re-enactments reached conclusions about the shots' trajectories and timing that were markedly at odds with the Warren Commission's claims. These findings were ignored and suppressed.
- Apparently only two shots were fired from the sixth-floor window of the Texas School Book Depository building. An original FBI evidence sheet and a Dallas police property clerk's invoice both record the receipt of two shells and one live missile from the sniper's nest. An FBI evidence envelope was later discovered that contained the two shells and the live round. The envelope also contained photos, and these photos show two shells and a live bullet. Also, a 22 November 1963 DPD Crime Scene Section document has surfaced that likewise says only two shells were found in the sixth-floor sniper's nest. This evidence strongly suggests that either the police initially were only going to admit to finding two shells or, somewhat less likely, that only two shells were found to begin with. The third shell, which only surfaced several days later, has a dent in it and could not have been used to fire a bullet during the assassination. It should be noted that originally Bonnie Ray Williams, who was standing next to the southeast fifth-floor window, directly beneath the sixth-floor sniper's nest with only thin

floor boarding separating the floors, said he only heard *two* shots. Howard Brennan, who was standing on the street below in a location that was almost directly beneath the sixth-floor window, likewise only heard two shots from that window. So if only two shots were fired from the sixth-floor window, someone else must have fired the other shot or shots.

- Most of the witnesses in Dealey Plaza who expressed an opinion on the subject did not believe all the shots came solely from the Book Depository. At least fifty Dealey Plaza witnesses believed shots were fired from in front of the President's limousine. A number of these witnesses said they were certain at least one shot came from in front of the limousine. Bystanders told four policemen that shots had come from the picket fence on the grassy knoll, which was to the right front of the limousine during the shooting.
- Deputy Sheriff Roger Craig and motorist Richard Robinson said they saw a man run down across the grassy incline in front of the Book Depository and get into a light-coloured Rambler station wagon after the President had been shot.
- Richard Randolph Carr, watching from a nearby building, said he saw a man in a tan jacket on the top floor of the TSBD shortly before the assassination, and that he saw the same man a few minutes afterwards walk 'very fast' down Houston Street, turn the corner on to Commerce Street and then get into a light-coloured Rambler station wagon.
- Three witnesses who saw a man in the southeast corner window of the sixth floor of the Book Depository said the man's hair was blond or light coloured. Oswald's hair was a definite brown.
- All five of the witnesses who reported seeing a gunman in the sixth-floor window of the TSBD said the man was wearing a light-coloured shirt. But Oswald wore a rust-brown shirt to work that day, and a policeman saw Oswald wearing that shirt less than ninety seconds after that shots were fired.

However, perhaps the most compelling evidence that Lee Harvey Oswald could not have shot the President, let alone been the sole assassin, comes from FBI agent and marksman Robert Frazier. On the morning of 27 November 1963 Agent Frazier took Oswald's Mannlicher-Carcano rifle to the local firing range and with the help of FBI agents Charles Killion and Courtland Cunningham, tested the weapon for accuracy. Each agent fired three rounds and all nine shots were high and to the right. Moreover, FBI agents had been firing at a stationary target just fifteen feet away. None of the agents was able to fire the shots in the same time that Oswald is said to have taken. That afternoon Frazier conducted another test to see how fast the gun could be fired. Frazier fired three rounds in 4.8 seconds, with a second set of three in 4.6 seconds, matching the time that Oswald is said to have taken – but with one ultra-important proviso: it could be done *only* if you didn't bother to aim at a target. The chances a moderate marksman such as Oswald hitting a moving target perhaps 160 feet or more away, even once, with this particular rifle is virtually nil; to hit the target twice in 4.6 seconds is absolutely impossible. It is almost certain therefore that Oswald was framed and that there was indeed a conspiracy. Over the next few months both the FBI and the US military were to test the weapon again and again for both speed and accuracy and not one single police officer or army sniper could be found who could reproduce the amazing marksmanship that Oswald would have needed in order to kill Kennedy.

Strangely there was one genuine professional assassin in Dallas on the day in question. He was known as Michael Mertz, a Corsican originally recruited by French intelligence to fight in Algeria, but who had later turned against President De Gaulle. Mertz was 'expelled' across the border into Mexico two days after the assassination. While talking to the US immigration official, he gave his name as Jean Rene Souetre. Now Souetre was an OAS assassin who had also tried to kill De Gaulle, but who appears to have been safely in Europe at the time. Souetre was to claim later that Mertz had tried to set him up to 'take a fall'. Michael Mertz was more than just a French gunman for hire as he was also understood to have been contracted as an assassin to the CIA on more than one occasion and is believed to have been given an agency code of QJ/WIN. Quite what this assassin was doing in Dallas on the day of Kennedy's death – or why he was 'helped' to leave the United States so quickly after such an important killing – is not known.

Public interest in the assassination of President John F. Kennedy has never died down and people around the world still want to know who killed the President and why. This instinct to discover the truth led in part to the formation of the HSCA, a congressional group which in 1978 came to a conclusion that many unofficial investigators had already reached, namely that the President's assassination *was* the result of a conspiracy. Surprisingly until that time the Warren

Commission report, originally released in September 1964, had been the only official investigation into the killing the American head of state. The report was to many impartial observers nothing more than a whitewash aimed at covering up, well, something! It had stated that a solitary gunman named Lee Harvey Oswald was responsible. Oswald killed the President, but was soon captured and held by the Dallas police for two days. Then Oswald himself was killed by Jack Ruby as he was being transferred from one jail to another. The Warren Commission decided that Ruby acted for twisted emotional reasons, that he was just a second lone nut, and that there was no conspiracy involved in either case.

The HSCA's declaration of conspiracy inspired a rash of books and at least two movies, as well as several TV programmes, but as yet none of these has been widely accepted as offering all the right answers. Perhaps, some theorists argue, this should be taken in itself as further proof of a successful and deeply hidden conspiracy?

The various theories on how the President was killed are as follows: the President was riding in his open limousine, his back to the Texas School Book Depository and its sixth floor where Oswald was supposed to be. Ahead and to the right of the President's motorcade was the grassy knoll. This area was fairly crowded with spectators. Behind them and hidden by a fence was perhaps another gunman who may have been waiting for his chance to fire. Some theorists argue, including the authors of *Six Seconds in Dallas*, that this was a classic triangulation killing with three gunmen: one positioned behind the stockade fence on the grassy knoll; one in the Tex School Book Depository and one in the Dallas Tex Building. Oswald was accused of firing several shots from his position in the Texas School Book Depository. Two of these struck the President in the back of the head. But a third shot is said to have entered the throat, just above his Adam's apple, and emerged through the back of his neck. Did this third shot actually go from the front of his neck to the back? Doctors at Parkland Hospital in Dallas, where the dying President was taken, and doctors at the Bethesda Naval Hospital, where the dead President was again examined, disagree. The Parkland group saw the President first, and they say there was an entry wound in his throat. The Bethesda group, on the other hand, says there was an exit wound in his throat. Many spectators standing on the grassy knoll at the time reported hearing at least one rifle shot fired from near by. They also reported seeing as many as four men hurrying away from the back of the knoll as soon as the shots were fired. The Warren investigators quizzed several of these witnesses but came to no conclusion.

In the light of so much evidence that casts doubt on the Commission's findings, it seems highly unlikely that Oswald killed Kennedy or was even directly involved, except as a 'patsy'. Nor was he even definitely linked with the sixth-floor window from where the shots were supposedly fired. Only minutes after the shooting, he was drinking a Coca-Cola several floors below. Could he have left the firing site and composed himself so quickly? Moreover, the inexpensive old rifle Oswald is supposed to have used should have left a powder burn on his cheek. After Oswald was arrested, his cheek was examined: no such powder burn was found. Additionally, if planning to shoot the President of the United States, why would a former US marine choose one of the least effective and inaccurate weapons available? Why didn't he purchase a sniper's rifle? They were available at a reasonable cost. Did he want to miss? After Oswald's death, his palm print was found on his rifle butt. Some investigators claim that a palm print could have been transferred from Oswald's hand to the rifle butt after his death. This could have been one of many illegal efforts to tie Oswald to the crime.

Why was President Kennedy assassinated? One set of theories says that it was the President's plans for Vietnam that prompted his murder. By 1963, the United States was becoming more and more involved in the Vietnam War. The US had already sent supplies, arms and several thousand 'advisors' and 'instructors' to aid South Vietnam, and Kennedy wanted to go no further. He was ready to stop sending aid, even though South Vietnam claimed to have a democratic government and an army eager to wage war against North Vietnam. The President said that Vietnam was not vital to US interests, that South Vietnam's government was actually a brutal dictatorship, and that the US should not become actively involved in what was really a local war. So, the theory goes, the President was killed by those who wanted the United States to become actively involved in the Vietnam War. In other words, he was killed by the military-industrial complex.

Another theory holds that Kennedy was killed because he failed to help the Cuban exiles in their 1961 attempt to invade Cuba and overthrow the Communist government of Fidel Castro, and therefore fell foul not only of the Cuban exiles but also of the CIA and organised crime, thwarted from recovering their highly lucrative casinos and brothels in Havana.

Another theory involves the President's relationship with his brother Robert, the attorney general. Robert had become a relentless enemy of organised crime and perhaps the only way to stop the attorney general was to kill the President. That's the view of a number of leading theorists, and they go on to accuse various Mafia leaders and Jimmy Hoffa, President of the Teamsters' Union. But why not kill Robert Kennedy instead?

The movie *JFK* made a considerable impact, though whether it advanced serious study is another matter. It follows the line of New Orleans District Attorney Jim Garrison's controversial view at least up to a point. The stunning conclusion abandons the cautious approach taken by Garrison. Instead, it puts a direct, sweeping accusation in the mouth of a fictitious character known only as 'X', who proclaims that the conspiracy to kill JFK extends right up to the highest levels of the US government, including the Pentagon, the joint chiefs of staff, the FBI and the CIA, and to the White House itself. Oliver Stone as the director, producer and writer is responsible for all these statements and more. He goes on to tie in the military and intelligence with corporate industry in a powerful alliance. It should be noted that Stone does not name names and only says that certain high-ranking men in these organisations were responsible for the death of the President. They wanted JFK killed because he was a threat to their plans. Stone further claims that American industry wanted the Vietnam War to continue for reasons of greed: the greater the level of conflict in Vietnam, the higher the industrial profits. X's charge of conspiracy reaches up into the White House. Although X does not directly accuse by name the President who followed JFK into office, there can be no doubt that he meant President Lyndon B. Johnson, in office from 1963 to 1969. Johnson was Kennedy's Vice President. Before that, he was the US Senate's Majority Leader. He ran the Senate with an iron hand. Kennedy had chosen Johnson as his running mate because Johnson could produce a winning number of votes. Johnson expected to take an active role in the Kennedy Government. After entering office in 1961, however, he was largely ignored. His duties were mostly confined to cutting the ribbon when a new bridge or park was dedicated. And Johnson was losing many of his once-loyal Texas followers. He sat silently biding his time and that time came, his accusers say, when the President rode in the open limousine down a Dallas street. Johnson, his enemies claim, engineered the whole assassination programme. However, as some theorists would argue, expanding the scenario into a mega-conspiracy, who would have been better placed to create the conspiracy, to pull the strings to make it work, to have the contacts in the military, the Dallas police, the FBI, the CIA and the Justice Department? Who was better placed to execute the cover-up than the man who stepped into the dead President's shoes? Who appointed the Warren Commission that so effectively whitewashed the killing and also opted for a lone-nut gunman, and conveniently a dead one? Who reversed Kennedy's policy on Vietnam? Who was threatened by Robert Kennedy becoming President and reopening the investigation, and who was still in a position to remove that threat in 1968? It makes for an interesting theory, and indeed some have argued that the killings of the Kennedy brothers were important parts of a coup that changed the face of American history. Of course, there is no proof that Johnson instigated the killing of his President, again there's no final proof of a conspiracy. There is, however, a mountain of circumstantial evidence that does point firmly at a well-organised conspiracy to kill Kennedy and provide for a cover-up afterwards.

1964 – THE GULF OF TONKIN INCIDENT The infamous incident in which a number of North Vietnamese torpedo boats apparently attacked two US navy destroyers in the international waters of the Gulf of Tonkin resulted in the first major military response by the United States directly against North Vietnam. It was from this point that US military involvement in its own right was assured. To many this incident marks the beginning of the Vietnam War, but did it actually happen in the way portrayed by the Pentagon at the time? The answer, yet again, appears to be no. In fact the US military contrived the incident with the obvious approval of President Johnson in order to remove any doubt that the US was engaging in a war of self-defence against an aggressive and well-armed Communist enemy.

The Gulf of Tonkin lies on the East Coast of North Vietnam and the West Coast of the Chinese island of Hainan. On 2 August 1964 the US Seventh Fleet, which included the American destroyers the *USS Maddox* and *USS C. Turner Joy*, and the aircraft carrier *USS Ticonderoga*, was involved in monitoring the communist coastline. The *Maddox* was conducting a 'DeSoto patrol' or covert intelligence mission and was actually engaged in aggressive intelligence-gathering manoeuvres in co-operation with co-ordinated attacks on North

Vietnam by the South Vietnamese navy and the Laotian air force. The North Vietnamese sent torpedo patrol boats to force the *Maddox* away from sensitive areas inshore. The US carrier *Ticonderoga* replied by sending strike aircraft to repel the North Vietnamese attackers and sank one boat while damaging other enemy vessels.

Two days later on 4 August in an attempt to provoke another engagement, both the *Maddox* and the *C. Turner Joy* were in the gulf and close to the North Vietnamese coast. The captain of the *Maddox* claimed that his ship's instruments showed that the ship was under attack or had been attacked and began an immediate retaliatory strike into the night. The two ships began firing rapidly on North Vietnamese with US warplanes in support.

However, the odd thing was that the captain had concluded hours later that there might not have been an actual attack. James B. Stockdale, who was a pilot of a Crusader jet, undertook a reconnaissance flight over the waters that evening and when asked if he witnessed any North Vietnamese attack vessels, Stockdale replied, 'Not a one. No boats, no wakes, no ricochets off boats, no boat impacts, no torpedo wakes – nothing but black sea and American firepower.' The entire event was purposely misconstrued when presented to Congress and the public by President Johnson and his administration, and on 7 August the 'Tonkin Gulf Resolution' passed, 416 to 0 by the House and 88 to 2 by the Senate. The resolution stipulated that the President of the United States could 'take all necessary measures to repel armed attack against the forces of the United States and to prevent further aggression.' In 1965 Lyndon Baines Johnson commented, 'For all I know, our Navy was shooting at whales out there.' But Johnson's deceitful speech of 4 August 1964 won accolades from editorial writers. The President, proclaimed the *New York Times*, 'went to the American people last night with the somber facts.' The *Los Angeles Times* urged Americans to 'face the fact that the Communists, by their attack on American vessels in international waters, have themselves escalated the hostilities.'

What was at first portrayed as an unprovoked attack on US warships in international waters turned out to be part of a US government conspiracy to find an excuse to go to war. After months of covert air raids on Communist positions, special forces and intelligence operations and a co-ordinated series of military provocations by the US, South Vietnamese and Laotian armed forces, the sole serious response by North Vietnam was a couple of ancient torpedo boats trying to hit back at a large and well-armed US destroyer supported by more warships, including an aircraft carrier. This, however, was sufficient for a US administration hell-bent on war. It was the culmination of the Johnson Administration's plans drawn up well in advance to increase military pressure on the Communists up to and beyond their breaking point.

Neither the news media nor the so-called expert defence correspondents spotted the anomalies and the faked actions because of two major weaknesses that are still painfully apparent in 2003. Firstly, most journalists and broadcasters show an almost exclusive reliance on government officials and handouts as their sources of information, and secondly, they demonstrate a marked reluctance to question official pronouncements on 'national security' issues. Nearly thirty years later during the Gulf War, columnist Sydney Schanberg warned journalists not to forget 'our unquestioning chorus of agreeability when Lyndon Johnson bamboozled us with his fabrication of the Gulf of Tonkin incident.' The same could be said in the virtual unanimity of information available in the press and on the nightly TV news and the unquestioning acceptance of the official line – even when it is palpable and obvious nonsense – during the Balkan conflicts, Afghanistan and the confrontation with Iraq in 2003. President Johnson's conspiracy to drag the US into a war that was to eventually ruin his chances of a second term and result in over 50,000 US and over 2 million Vietnamese dead, not to mention the damage done to East–West relations, to America's military image and to its self-belief. But he got away with the lies and the deceit at the crucial moment in August 1964. Has anyone learned the lesson of forty years ago, apart from the powers that be who, of course, will only try to ensure that the lid is kept on the secret for even longer next time?

1964 – JACK THE STRIPPER A belief that has gained credence among some conspiracy theorists is that a police investigation into a series of gruesome 'Thames nude' murders developed into a full-blown conspiracy to cover up missed clues and tragic mistakes in identifying the killer, which may have cost the lives of a number of London's prostitutes. Worse still is the chilling similarity to the Ripper murders, with a suggestion of the involvement of a famous personality. Seventy years after Jack the Ripper murdered and disembowelled prostitutes in London's East End, a new generation of girls earning a living on street corners had to cope with the ever-present fear of a lurking killer. The newspapers soon christened the killer

'Jack the Stripper' and, though he carried no knife, he was every bit as lethal. In fact he claimed at least seven victims to the Ripper's five, and operated over a period of nearly six years, compared to the Ripper's ten weeks. At the 'conclusion' of the case, both murderers shared a common attribute: despite a wealth of theories and a prolonged, but possibly flawed investigation, neither 'Jack' was ever captured or identified.

On 17 June 1959 a prostitute called Elizabeth Figg, aged just 21, was found floating in the Thames, clad only in a slip. Her death was later attributed to strangulation. Four and a half years passed before the discovery of the next murder, with the skeleton of 22-year-old Gwyneth Rees unearthed during clearance of a Thames-side rubbish dump on 8 November 1963. The cause of death was difficult to ascertain, and police investigators later tried to disconnect both murders from the later 'Stripper' series, but today a better understanding of the evidence suggests that these murders were committed by the same man. Thirty-year-old Hannah Tailford was the next to die, her naked corpse discovered in the Thames by boatman on 2 February 1964. Although her stockings were pulled down around her ankles, and her panties stuffed inside her mouth, she had drowned, and the inquest produced an open verdict, refusing to rule out suicide, however improbable it seemed. On 9 April 1964 twenty-year-old Irene Lockwood was found naked and dead in the Thames, floating just 300 yards from the spot where Tailford was found. Another drowning victim, she was four months pregnant when she died. A suspect named Kenneth Archibald confessed to the murder later that month, then recanted his statement, blaming depression, and he was subsequently cleared at his trial. Helen Barthelmy, age twenty, was the first victim found away from the river. On 24 April her naked body was discovered near a sports field in Brentwood, four front teeth missing, with sperm and part of one tooth found in the back of her throat. Traces of multicoloured spray paint on the body suggested that she had been kept for a while after death in a paint shop before she was dumped in the field. On 14 July 21-year-old Mary Fleming was discarded, nude and lifeless, on a dead-end London street. Witnesses glimpsed a van and its driver near the scene, but none could finally describe the man or vehicle with any certainty. Missing since 11 July Fleming had apparently been suffocated or choked to death, and her dentures were also missing from the scene. Margaret McGowan, 21, had been missing a month when her nude corpse was found in

Kensington on 25 November 1964. Police noted the familiar traces of paint on her skin, and that one of her front teeth had been forced from its socket in front by what investigators believed to have been extremely violent oral sex. The last known victim was 27-year-old Bridget O'Hara, last seen alive on 11 January 1965, her body only found on 16 February hidden in some shrubbery on the Heron Trading Estate in Acton. Her front teeth were also missing, and pathologists determined that she had died on her knees, almost certainly again due to violent oral sex. The corpse was partially mummified, as if from prolonged storage in a cool, dry place. Despite appeals to prostitutes for information on their 'kinky' customers, police were unable to come up with anything. Inspector John Du Rose suggested that in fact all of the last six victims had been literally choked to death during fellatio or oral sex by thrusting the perpetrator's penis deep inside their mouths and blocking his victim's airways whilst having an orgasm, loss or removal of the teeth in four cases lending more than a little support to the hypothesis.

Public hysteria swept across London and local police held a press conference stating they had narrowed down the number of suspects to three. Later that month one of the suspects, a lone bachelor in his forties, committed suicide, and here there appears to be more police confusion for one source claims it was by gassing himself in his kitchen, while another suggests that it was in an Acton industrial estate with the exhaust fumes from his car. However, he is said to have left a cryptic note, reported either as 'I cannot go on' or 'I cannot stand the strain any longer'. It might mean anything or, of course, nothing, but since the murders ended with the nameless suspect's death, the police seemed satisfied, although the case remains officially unsolved.

Who was the Stripper? One particularly high profile suspect was Freddie Mills, the former British, European, Empire and World light-heavyweight champion, who has been described as 'probably the greatest boxer Britain has ever produced'. He became one of the first sports personalities, a TV celebrity and a nightclub owner with criminal underworld connections. However, on the evening of 24 July 1965, Freddie Mills was found shot dead in his car parked in London's Soho district.The eventual verdict was suicide, though rumours persisted of a gangland killing with suggestions that he had in some way become a distinct liability to London's organised crime bosses. Another main suspect was a former police officer. However, Inspector John Du Rose reportedly favoured a private security guard on the Heron Trading Estate, his rounds including the paint shop where at least some of the victims were apparently stashed after death. The only evidence of guilt is the cessation of similar crimes after the latter suspect's suicide, but numerous serial killers, including possibly the Ripper and certainly the Zodiac killer in the United States, 'retired' once they achieved a certain body count. The best that that can be said for Scotland Yard's solution is that it is plausible but unconfirmed. While it would be unfair to saddle the police with an accusation of conspiracy for their failed investigation, the same could not be said of the murderer, for on the off-chance that there were two men involved as is the belief of a least one former Metropolitan police detective, then that would seem to rate as 'conspiracy to murder' at least.

1968 – RFK ASSASSINATION The number of people who have seriously investigated the RFK assassination is surprisingly small, given the time and energy expended by the countless numbers involved in researching JFK's murder. It is even more surprising if you believe that this killing is potentially of even greater interest. A second lone nut is even harder to accept than the first incarnation and the assassination occurred only five years after Dallas. Picture the scene: RFK is now running for President and what might he do if elected? End the Vietnam War? Crack down hard on organised crime? Reopen the investigation of his brother's assassination? Five years is a relatively short time, and if there had indeed been a conspiracy in 1963, wouldn't most of those involved still be alive and in positions of responsibility? Wouldn't they be gravely threatened by Robert F. Kennedy's election to the Presidency? If the answer is 'yes' in each case, then the next question is, wouldn't they do something to stop his election? If the answer were once again 'yes', then it would mean that both Kennedy killings were the result of a conspiracy and that the same conspirators probably instigated both assassinations. Therefore, the dedicated theorist will argue, if the lone-nut killing of RFK is disproved and a conspiracy is accepted, it must cast a very different light on the assassination in Dallas.

The assassination of Robert F. Kennedy could have been similarly designed to confuse and mislead. Robert Kennedy had obviously been shot. Sirhan fired a weapon: he must be the killer. Yet much of the physical evidence does not seem to support this conclusion. Some observers argue that Sirhan cannot have killed Kennedy, since it was not physically possible. Soon after midnight, on the morning of

5 June 1968, Senator Robert F. Kennedy has just finished his victory speech at the historic Ambassador Hotel on Wilshire Boulevard in Los Angeles after winning the California primary. Kennedy left the podium, walked down a ramp and entered a pair of swinging doors, heading east. Between the stage and the press area was the kitchen pantry; maître d' Karl Uecker gripped Kennedy's right wrist with his left hand. Ace Guard Service employee Thane Eugene Cesar joined Kennedy as he went through the double doors into the pantry, touching his right elbow. Bill Barry, an ex-FBI man who was ostensibly serving as Kennedy's bodyguard, had fallen behind Kennedy as he entered the pantry. As they headed east through the room, Kennedy stopped every few feet to shake the hands of hotel workers. The last hand he shook was that of busboy Juan Romero. Uecker pulled Kennedy as he moved forwards. The tiny kitchen held, by official count, 77 people, including Sirhan, who were all possible witnesses to what happened next. Uecker related that with Kennedy still in hand, he felt someone sliding in between himself and the steam table about two feet away from where he stood. Busboy Juan Romero and waiter Martin Patrusky saw Sirhan approach Kennedy, as did Lisa Urso, a San Diego high school student. Urso saw Sirhan push his way past her towards the Senator. She thought Sirhan was going to shake his hand, then saw a movement that made her freeze. Vincent DiPierro, a waiter who had seen Sirhan standing and talking to a pretty girl in a white, polka-dotted dress earlier that night, heard someone yell 'Grab him' a split second before the shots were fired. Somebody reported Sirhan saying, 'Kennedy, you son of a bitch', and then firing at Kennedy with his hand outstretched. Kennedy fell to the ground. Screams were heard as bystanders Paul Schrade, William Weisel, Ira Goldstein, Erwin Stroll and Elizabeth Evans were hit by flying bullets. Kennedy suffered gunshot wounds in three different places, with a fourth bullet passing through his coat without entering the skin. Uecker immediately grabbed Sirhan's hand and forced it down on to the steam table. A swarm of men descended upon Sirhan, surrounding him, holding the gun. Decathlon champion Rafer Johnson, LA Rams tackle Roosevelt Grier, George Plimpton and others formed a barricade around Sirhan, one holding his head, another with a finger in the trigger to prevent additional shots, another grabbing Sirhan in a crushing bear hug.

Uecker and DiPierro reported initially hearing two shots, followed by a flurry. DiPierro told the LAPD, 'I saw the first two go off. I saw them actually.' Several witnesses reported hearing one or two shots, and then a pause. Then all hell broke loose, and witnesses not within eyesight of what was happening thought they were hearing balloons popping or firecrackers. Los Angeles photographer Boris Yaro, in a phone interview with Robert Morrow, recounted his memory of the event: 'There was either one or two shots fired. OK. And then, boom, boom, boom, boom, boom. There was a pregnant pause between those two because my initial impression was some jackass has set off firecrackers in here; because I got hit in the face with debris . . . And then it hit me. Oh, my God, it's happened again.' Sirhan was eventually subdued, and taken into police custody.

The police created a unit, at first named 'Special Operations Senator', and renamed a week later 'Special Unit Senator' to investigate the circumstances surrounding the assassination. The unit put together the evidence that became the basis of the prosecution's case against Sirhan. The trial of Sirhan Bishara Sirhan seems to have been solely for the purpose of determining his sentence, not whether or not he was guilty of the crime. Sirhan claimed that he truly could not remember the incidents of that night. His defence only offered that he had not been in control of his senses at the time of the killing. Not surprisingly, given such a defence, Sirhan was sentenced to death, a sentence which was commuted by the abolishment of the death penalty in California.

Despite the seemingly open-and-shut case, some observers were already casting doubt on the handling of the investigation and the veracity of the evidence, while some conspiracy theorists were already suggesting that Sirhan's apparent loss of memory suggested something akin to brainwashing or MK-ULTRA-style activities. The circumstances of the killing, in a packed room with so many witnesses and a gunman who made no attempt to hide, led to confusion about the events. People tended to remember what they thought they saw, not what actually happened. Everybody was looking at Sirhan, but if the fatal shots came from behind Kennedy then nobody would notice the killer. Moreover, unlike the murder of JFK where the Warren Commission only required one magic bullet to create a lone-nut scenario, the Robert Kennedy assassination requires several magic bullets to reduce the bullet count to eight. Five people were shot besides Kennedy, one of whom was shot twice; Kennedy himself was shot four times. Making a grand total of ten bullets? But not if the LAPD could come up with some magic ones. The bullet that pierced

Kennedy's coat without entering him took a path of roughly 80 degrees upwards. The bullet was moving upwards in a back to front path, as were all of Kennedy's wound paths. But the LAPD argues that this was the bullet that hit Paul Schrade. Had Schrade been facing Kennedy, he would still not be tall enough to receive a bullet near the top of his head from that angle. But he was not standing in front of Kennedy. He was behind him by all eyewitness accounts and as shown by the relative positions where the two fell after being hit. For Sirhan alone to have fired all the shots, one of the bullets that entered Kennedy's coat just below the armpit would have had to exit up and out of the coat just below the seam on top of his shoulders, and then pulled a U-turn in midair to hit Schrade in the head. Schrade has been one of the most persistent in calling for a new investigation of this case for precisely this reason. He knows the report is incorrect, and if it is incorrect, there had to be at least one more gun firing in the pantry.

Ira Goldstein had been shot twice, although one shot merely entered and exited his trouser leg without entering his body. He was less fortunate on a separate shot, which entered his left rear buttock. But since there were no bullets to spare, according to the LAPD's strict adherence to the eight-bullet scenario, the trouser-leg bullet was made to do double duty. According to the LAPD, after passing through his trousers, the bullet struck the cement floor and ricocheted up into Erwin Stroll's left leg. The only bullet that seemed to take a plausible path was the one that hit Weisel in the left abdomen.

One of the big problems the LAPD had with the crime scene was the number of bullet holes in the ceiling tiles. Based on witnesses' recollections, there were too many holes to account for. There are photos of the LAPD running strings through bullet holes in the ceiling to establish trajectories. Somehow, these had to be accounted for. Elizabeth Evans had bent over to retrieve a shoe she had momentarily lost. Suddenly she felt something hit her forehead. Medical reports confirm that the bullet entered her forehead below the hairline and travelled 'upward', fitting the scenario she remembers. But because the LAPD needed to account for some of the bullet holes in the ceiling, they decided that a bullet from Sirhan's gun had been fired at the ceiling, entered a ceiling tile, bounced off something beyond the ceiling tile, re-entered the room through a different ceiling tile and struck Evans in the forehead. This bullet must have pulled more of a hairpin turn than a U-turn, if the LAPD's version and the medical reports are to be merged. This left still one unaccounted for hole in the ceiling. Or rather, at least one. It is not known how many holes there were because the tiles were destroyed. But the LAPD knew that there were more than two holes in the ceiling. One of the bullets that entered Kennedy passed straight through on a near-vertical path; parallel to the one that entered the coat, but not the body, of Kennedy, indeed the one that supposedly terminated its path in Schrade's head. This bullet supposedly passed through Kennedy and continued on upwards into the ceiling. Since Kennedy was facing Sirhan, the bullet would have had to implausibly enter back to front, to hit the ceiling nearly directly above Sirhan's head, according to witness placements of Kennedy and Sirhan. And indeed, there was a tile removed from that very spot. But Sirhan could not possibly have reached around Kennedy to shoot him from behind, while still standing several feet in front of the Senator. Yet another magic bullet it seems was involved in the assassination of a Kennedy brother.

The official police reports strove to present a plausible scenario for where each bullet went. And even if the accounts above are correct, the problem is bigger still. There is a substantial amount of evidence to show that more than eight bullets had been fired in the pantry that night. And if there were more than eight bullets, Sirhan was not a lone gunman, but somehow part of a conspiracy which has yet to be officially acknowledged. Evidence of additional bullets surfaced nearly immediately. On 5 June an Associated Press photo was published showing two police officers pointing at something in the centre frame of the swinging doors that led into the pantry. The caption read, 'Bullet found near Kennedy shooting scene'. In 1975 Vincent Bugliosi, who was then working with Schrade to get the case reopened, tracked down the two police officers depicted in the photograph. Bugliosi identified the two officers as Sgt. Charles Wright and Sgt. Robert Rozzi. Both Wright and Rozzi were sure that what they observed was not only a bullet hole, but also a hole containing a bullet. If the hole contained a bullet, then it would have been the ninth bullet, since seven bullets had been recovered from victim wounds and the eighth was to have disappeared into the ceiling, which was necessary to account for acknowledged holes in the ceiling tiles. So any additional bullet presented a serious problem for those wishing to state there was no conspiracy. In a declaration filed with the courts, Bugliosi stated, 'Sgt. Rozzi had told me and he told me unequivocally that it was a bullet in the hole and when I told him that Sgt. Rozzi had informed me that he was pretty sure that the bullet was removed from the hole,

Sgt. Wright replied, "There is no pretty sure about it. It definitely was removed from the hole, but I do not know who did it." ' Shortly after the assassination, the LAPD removed the doorjambs and ceiling panels in the Ambassador Hotel and booked them as evidence. What's more, theorists claim that FBI investigators found evidence from tiles and doorjambs destroyed by the LAPD shortly after the trial, proving that 12 or 13 bullets had been fired in the pantry.

According to a weapons expert for the LAPD, DeWayne Wolfer, the bullets that killed RFK were unquestionably fired from Sirhan's gun. However, some experts believe that Wolfer did his forensic testing not with Sirhan's gun but with a different .22-cal. weapon, which police also later destroyed.

Then there was the matter of the girl in the polka-dotted dress. Several people remembered seeing her with Sirhan and another man at the hotel before the shooting. *The RFK Tapes*, made by a National Public Radio programme in 1993 to re-examine the assassination, speculate that she was Sirhan's 'baby-sitter', or control. The LAPD, while purportedly trying to find the woman, tried harder to browbeat witnesses into changing their stories.

Further evidence contradicting the lone guilt of Sirhan came from the coroner's autopsy where Dr Thomas Noguchi testified that Kennedy had been killed by a bullet fired no more than three inches from the back of his head. Sirhan, according to many witnesses, was at least three feet in front of the Senator when he shot all eight bullets from his .22-cal. pistol. The conspiracy theory therefore rests on what would seem to be straightforward facts. There were simply more shots fired and bullets recovered than Sirhan's gun could hold, and a respected medical expert confidently stated that Kennedy had been fatally hit by a bullet fired no more than three inches from the back of his head; the nearest Sirhan got was three foot in front of the Senator. So unless the LAPD and FBI are unable to count, or Sirhan had a magic gun, or Dr Thomas Noguchi is lying or incompetent, then there must have been another gunman. Indeed, video footage, though not ideal, does suggest that someone in a guard's uniform appears to fire into the back of Kennedy's head. None of this potentially exonerating detail was fully explored in court. In what proved to be an astounding strategic misjudgement, Sirhan's chief attorney, Grant Cooper, did not challenge the prosecution's 'facts'. The defence relied entirely on a theory of impaired judgement, which the jury had no trouble rejecting. Sirhan's death sentence was subsequently reduced to life imprisonment, which he is serving at California State Prison in Corcoran.

1968 – PLUMBAT AFFAIR A German freighter is on the high seas en route to Italy via, surprisingly, Turkey, and with enough uranium in her hold to start a good few nuclear conflicts. Somewhere between Antwerp and Turkey on the first leg of her journey, the cargo disappears. The secret conspiracy to provide Israel with enough weapons-grade material for a veritable arsenal of nuclear bombs remained hidden very effectively for ten long years before the loss of this cargo was made public, by which point Israel was well on the way to becoming a significant nuclear power. Prime Minister Golda Meir went on record when she became Prime Minister in 1968 by saying that Israel had the right to 'act in such a way that the Jews who died in the gas chambers would be the last Jews to die without defending themselves'.

Israel had decided that it needed its own independent capabilities to complete its nuclear programme. Only five countries had facilities for uranium enrichment: the United States, the Soviet Union, the United Kingdom, France and China. The Nuclear Materials and Equipment Corporation (NUMEC), in Apollo, Pennsylvania, was a small fuel rod fabrication plant. In 1965 the US government accused Dr Zalman Shapiro, the corporation president, of 'losing' 200 pounds of highly enriched uranium. Although investigated by the Atomic Energy Commission, the CIA, the FBI, other government agencies and reporters, no answers were available in what was termed the Apollo Affair. Many remain convinced that the Israelis received 200 pounds of enriched uranium sometime before 1965. One source links Rafi Eitan, an Israeli Mossad agent and later the handler of US double-agent Jonathan Pollard, with NUMEC. However, in the 1990s when the NUMEC plant was disassembled, the Nuclear Regulatory Commission found over 100 kilograms of plutonium in the structural components of the contaminated plant, casting considerable doubt on 200 pounds going to Israel.

A joint venture with France gave Israel several ingredients for nuclear weapons construction: a production reactor, a factory to extract plutonium from the spent fuel, and the design. In 1962 Israel's Dimona reactor in the northern Negev desert went critical; the French resumed work on the underground plutonium reprocessing plant and completed it in 1964 or 1965. The acquisition of this reactor and related technologies was clearly intended for military purposes from the outset, but not for dual-use, as the reactor has no other function. The security at Dimona, officially the Negev Nuclear Research Centre, was particularly stringent. For straying into Dimona's airspace, the Israelis shot down one of their own Mirage fighters during the Six-Day War. The Israelis also shot down a Libyan airliner with 104 passengers in 1973, which had strayed over the Sinai with little reaction from outside the Middle East.

There is little doubt that some time in the late 1960s Israel became the sixth nation to manufacture nuclear weapons. However, they still desperately needed extra uranium and extra heavy water to run the reactor at a higher rate and allow them to greatly expand their nuclear weapons-building programme. Norway, France and the USA provided the heavy water and 'Operation Plumbat' provided the uranium. After the 1967 war, France stopped supplies of uranium to Israel. These supplies were from former French colonies of Gabon, Niger and the Central Africa Republic. Israel had small amounts of uranium from Negev phosphate mines and had bought some from Argentina and South Africa, but not in the large quantities supplied by the French. Through a complicated undercover operation, the Israelis obtained uranium oxide, known as yellow cake, held in a stockpile in Antwerp. Using a West German front company and a high seas transfer from one ship to another in the Mediterranean, they obtained 200 tons of yellow cake. The smugglers labelled the 560 sealed oil drums 'Plumbat', which means 'lead', hence 'Operation Plumbat'.

The Israeli operation was brilliantly conceived and carried out. A German freighter *Scheersberg A*, owned by an Israeli, was loaded with some 200 tons of uranium oxide or yellow cake in Antwerp and the new crew came on board. Most were apparently experienced Israeli naval personnel or commandos in disguise. The vessel sailed as normal and followed its expected route. The vessel could not be diverted directly to Israel without giving the game away, so on 28 November 1968 the *Scheersberg A* headed for a secret rendezvous with an Israeli merchant vessel guarded by two heavily armed gunboats in the waters between Cyprus and the coast of Turkey. The cargo of 560 metal drums of the vital uranium was offloaded one by one on to the Israeli vessel in complete silence. After four hours the Israeli flotilla turned south with its valuable cargo and the Israeli crew members for the long haul to Haifa, where the cargo was unloaded in the greatest secrecy on to military trucks. The convoy was able to safely deliver the uranium to the Dimona research site in the Negev desert by

3 December. The *Scheersberg A* sailed on to the Turkish port of Iskenderun.

The non-delivery to Italy of the cargo was not mentioned and the international network of government and Intelligence Service intrigue that had ensured the success of Operation Plumbat managed to keep the affair secret for another ten years. It is rumoured that the Israeli Intelligence Service, Mossad, used heavy methods, up to and including death, to silence anyone thought likely to expose the operation. Killings believed now to have been related to this operation were reported from various locations in Europe, including Norway, over the next five years. The West German government may have been directly involved and remained silent to avoid antagonising the Soviets or Arabs. Israeli intelligence information on the Nazi past of some West German officials may have provided the motivation for their assistance.

Norway sold 20 tons of heavy water to Israel in 1959 for use in an experimental power reactor, and while Norway and Israel concluded an agreement in 1990 for Israel to sell back 10.5 tons of the heavy water to Norway, recent calculations reveal that Israel has used just over 2 tons and still retains nearly 7 tons more. The first extraction of plutonium probably occurred in late 1965. By 1966 enough plutonium was on hand to develop a weapon in time for the Six-Day War in 1967. Some type of non-nuclear test, perhaps a zero yield or implosion test, occurred on 2 November 1966. Considerable collaboration between Israel and South Africa developed and continued through the 1970s and 1980, as South Africa became Israel's primary supplier of uranium for Dimona. A Center for Nonproliferation Studies report lists four separate Israel–South Africa 'clandestine nuclear deals'. Three concerned yellow cake and one tritium. Other sources of yellow cake may have included Portugal. It is confirmed that Moshe Dayan, the Minister of Defence, gave the go-ahead for starting weapon production in early 1968, putting the plutonium separation plant into full operation. Israel began producing three to five bombs a year. However, Israel is believed to have had two bombs in 1967, and that Prime Minister Eshkol ordered them armed in Israel's first nuclear alert during the Six-Day War. Munya Mardor, leader of Rafael, the Armament Development Authority, agreed that Israel 'cobbled together' two deliverable devices.

Having the bomb meant articulating, even if secretly, a use doctrine. In addition to the 'Samson Option' of last resort, other triggers for nuclear use may have included successful Arab penetration of populated areas, destruction of the Israeli air force, massive air strikes or chemical/biological strikes on Israeli cities and Arab use of nuclear weapons.

Statements made by Israeli whistle-blower Mordechai Vanunu to the London newspaper the *Sunday Times* in October 1986 imply that Israel had produced hollow-core boosted fission nuclear weapons using deuterium-tritium gas as a booster. Based on revelations by Vanunu, who was a junior technician at Israel's Dimona nuclear complex from 1977–85, Israel is believed to have the ability to produce thermonuclear weapons using lithium-deuteride. Israel could have produced 150–200 boosted warheads, using 3.5kg of plutonium and 4g of tritium each by the mid-1990s, and in 2003 her nuclear arsenal may include up to 250 deliverable weapons. A mixture of embarrassment and powerlessness to do anything positive has kept the European nations from criticising Israel publicly, and the US reaction, in stark contrast to the attitude towards North Korea, Iraq, Pakistan or even India, is one of admiration and private congratulation. The Israeli conspiracy to secure its nuclear future, carried out with the help of many international partners, was a triumph of nerve and steely determination.

1969 – SECRET ASSASSINS One ongoing conspiracy theory is that Britain possesses a paramilitary unit called Group 13. The sole purpose of this ultra-secretive unit is deniable assassination, and it operates in the world of shadows. So little is known about it that it is apparently exceptionally hard to document its activities with any certainty. Gary Murray, author of *Enemies of the State*, decided to research Group 13 in order to write a book on them, but he soon changed his mind as one day, during his research, he was forcibly dragged into the back of a Transit van and had a gun stuck to his head. A voice told him it would be unwise to continue his project. Sensibly, he decided to abandon the project and instead write a book on an altogether different subject. What has been gleaned about this secretive unit is that Group 13 is generally believed to have evolved from former SAS soldiers and Security and Intelligence operatives who were still active in Northern Ireland during the mid- to late-1970s when a Labour government was in power. Fred Holroyd, a captain in British Army Intelligence, served in Northern Ireland during this period. Holroyd was tasked with developing informers and other human intelligence sources connected to the IRA. It was inherently dangerous work, made a lot worse by a vicious turf battle between MI5 and MI6 for control of the Northern Ireland 'patch'. Matters grew increasingly nasty as 'assets' for each of the two contending groups were sacrificed to the IRA. Holroyd, when interviewed by *The X Factor* magazine, outlined some details of this dirty war, recalling incidents where bombs were placed by one of these factions and then roundly blamed on the IRA. Holroyd's story and later disgraceful treatment at the hands of the British army are recounted in his book *War without Dishonour*.

Holroyd's account sheds light on the so-called 'shoot to kill' policy in Northern Ireland that resulted in the dysfunctional investigation of former senior police officer John Stalker. By 1969, the SAS had been sent to Northern Ireland to perform covert operations against the IRA, which included assassination. To cover their deployment to this politically sensitive area they chose the guise of 'training teams'. A succession of cover names was used over the next few years; these included the Military Reconnaissance Force (MRF), the 14th Intelligence unit, and the Four Field Survey Troop, Royal Engineers. Fred Holroyd states that the latter was very definitely a SAS undercover unit stationed at the Royal Engineers' base at Castiledillon, Armagh.

1974 was a critical year in British politics. It saw the election victory of the Labour Party in February and was soon followed by rumours of an impending right-wing coup d'état as groups operating in the shadows of power began to form themselves. These groups viewed Prime Minister Harold Wilson and certain members of his Cabinet as no-holds-barred Communists taking orders from Moscow. One of these groups was named GB75 and was organised by David Sterling, founder of the SAS. Significantly, GB75 had close contacts with the British intelligence community, from which it probably received unofficial support. Another group, founded in 1970, called itself the Resistance and Psychological Operations Committee (RPOC). With tacit official approval the RPOC formed close ties with the British security and intelligence apparatus, and 'forged close links with the SAS's . . . own secret intelligence network'. RPOC was established in line with the Reserve Forces Association and was said to be a reflection of the Special Operations Executive (SOE). According to one former member, RPOC had a clandestine section, which formed an underground resistance movement in the event that Russia invaded the United Kingdom.

Ranulf Fiennes, the Arctic trekker, was a one-time member of the SAS. In his book *The Feather Men*, he reveals the existence of an unofficial group of former SAS officers and soldiers who, amongst other activities, are tasked with protecting members of the SAS whose lives are under threat as a result of their activities. According to his book, Fiennes learned that a contract had been put out on him, but only after this SAS secretive group had killed the members of a freelance assassination team sent to kill Fiennes.

Fiennes further alleged that this group had been founded by David Sterling. It is not possible to say with any certainty whether this evolved to become Group 13. However, the associations are clearly similar. Both are highly unofficial but desirable to certain factions within government. Both are said to be responsible for political assassinations in Northern Ireland and elsewhere. Both appear to lean towards right-wing agendas. Perhaps the best known incident that involved the SAS in a 'wet operation' was the assassination of an IRA unit in Gibraltar in 1988.

Because of the thick smoke screen about Group 13, speculation is rife about its alleged 'targets', and high on the list is the murder of defence journalist Jonathan Moyle in a hotel room in Santiago, Chile, in March 1990. Moyle had been gathering damning evidence of British involvement in equipping helicopters for Iraq. Although his killers were never found, US State Department and CIA documents reveal that, shortly before he was murdered, Moyle's hotel was regularly visited by two men with known British security and intelligence connections. Of some interest is the statement of a former CIA operative and former member of an American-based, international assassination team, Gene 'Chip' Tatum. The team, Tatum says, is called Pegasus and operates around the world. Targets are normally influential politicians and financiers. The British end of Pegasus was operated during the mid-80s by a high-ranking British government official.

According to some conspiracy theorists, another operation that carries SAS hallmarks is the murder of a young Metropolitan police officer Yvonne Fletcher outside the Libyan People's Bureau in London in 1984. This killing caused immense public outrage and quickly led to the removal of the Libyan diplomatic corp. In a contentious piece of television, Channel Four broadcast a *Dispatches* programme in 1996 that suggested WPC Fletcher was murdered by elements inside British and American intelligence. Among other startling facts, the programme makers stated that the shot that killed the police officer might have been a 'terminal velocity' round. This technique both reduces the sound of the gunshot as a result of its subsonic speed and creates the impression that the shot was fired from considerable distance. As the theorists gleefully point out, it is a known technique of SAS snipers.

There may also be other connections between Group 13 and the United States intelligence community. J. Orlin Grabbe, an American professor who runs his own financial advisory service, has earned a reputation within Internet conspiracy circles as being well informed about a number of illegal intelligence operations. One of these focuses on the alleged assassination of Vincent Foster, a close associate and legal advisor to President Clinton. Grabbe, a former professor at Wharton Business School, in one of his Internet posts alluded to the existence of a highly secret US assassination team that operates out of, rather oddly, the National Security Agency (NSA). The unit, Grabbe claims, is called I-3. In a recent communication he added that the information on this unit was provided by a 'former CIA agent with the CIA's highest security clearance'. It may just be a coincidence that this NSA unit shares a similar name to Group 13 and just happens to also be in the same line of business. However, in the closed world of the intelligence community such coincidences should be viewed carefully. Intelligence insiders allege that the Soviet Union, during the height of the Cold War, operated its own assassination squad under cover of the KGB's 'Department 13'. This has led some observers to muse that the British and US adoption of the number 13 for 'wet operations' may be an insider's joke.

Dr Gerald Bull, designer of the ill-fated supergun for Iraq, was shot from behind while outside his apartment in Brussels, in early 1990. Rumoured to be an Israeli hit, sources close to Israeli's Mossad have firmly denied this. A few months before his assassination, Bull, while writing to a colleague, had stated he was 'advised in a letter of an imminent accident'. Bull identified the threat as having come from Britain's Foreign Office, who, as David Guyatt, author of *Deep Black Lies* points out, responded by saying the 'action was by "a few irresponsible juniors".'

Despite the stiff secrecy and widespread smoke and mirrors that surround the activities of Group 13, some significant additional information came to light following the Scott Enquiry into the arms to Iraq affair. Gerald James, the former chairman of Astra Holdings Plc and a leading British munitions manufacturer, mentioned Group 13 in his explosive book *In the Public Interest*, which provided considerable insight into the British government's involvement in arming Saddam Hussein's armed forces. During a lengthy interview, James outlined how he had been ousted from the Board of Astra and that he believed his removal was orchestrated by non-executive director Stephan Kock, a self-acknowledged former security and intelligence officer in the employ of Midland Bank Plc. In written evidence presented to the House of Commons Trade and Industry Committee looking into exports to Iraq, on 5 February 1992 James stated that he was told, in an unguarded moment, that Kock was 'a former head of Group 13. This curious organisation is apparently a hit or contract squad for the Foreign Office and Security Services.' James adds, 'The Foreign Office is said to draw Group 13 operatives from the SAS as well as from private security firms,' and that 'Its duties involve "service to the nation".' James also makes clear that Kock had exceptionally high-level contacts inside the intelligence community and had boasted of his ready access to the highest levels of the British government, including 10 Downing Street. So the plot really thickens, according to the theorists, except of course that much of this information is safely in the public domain. The establishment prefers to simply ignore the material openly available, sure in the knowledge that the short attention span of the media will soon condemn the accusations to the 'interesting, but not that important' file.

1972 – WATERGATE CONSPIRACY An example of a half-baked political intrigue where, had the administration come clean quickly and apologised when found out, they might just have survived to fight another day. However, Nixon and his cronies simply conspired to dig a bigger hole for themselves. 'Watergate' is a now the general term used to describe a complex web of political scandals between 1972 and 1974, and is taken from the Watergate Hotel in Washington, DC. Richard Milhous Nixon is one of the most fascinating political figures of the twentieth century. His long political career began in 1947 when he was elected to the House of Representatives. By 1952 Nixon had been chosen as Dwight Eisenhower's vice-presidential running mate and was soon to become embroiled in a scandal that led to the infamous Checkers Speech in September of that year. Nixon served as Vice-President for eight years, then lost the 1960 election to John F. Kennedy. He recovered from political defeat to be chosen again as the

Republican Party's candidate at the 1968 election. Following a year of turmoil, including two political assassinations, Nixon became the nation's 37th President on 20 January 1969. Later that year, he delivered his 'Silent Majority' speech on the Vietnam War, articulating his belief that the bulk of the American people supported his policies and programmes. He was effectively vindicated by winning a landslide re-election and was sworn in for a second term in January 1973.

Watergate has entered the political lexicon as a term synonymous with corruption and scandal, yet the Watergate Hotel is one of Washington's plushest hotels. It has been home to former Senator Bob Dole and was once the place where Monica Lewinsky laid low. It was here that the Watergate Burglars broke into the Democratic Party's National Committee offices on 17 June 1972 in search of names, accounts and anything that could be used to undermine the Democratic campaign, its candidates and supporters. If it had not been for the alert actions of Frank Wills, a security guard, the scandal may never have erupted. By 1973, although Nixon had been re-elected, the storm clouds were building, and by early 1974 the nation was consumed by Watergate. Nixon made three major speeches on the Watergate scandal during 1973 and 1974. The first was on 30 April 1973, in which he announced the departure of John Dean, Nixon's former White House Legal Counsel, and H. R. Haldeman and John Ehrlichman, both senior White House staff. A more defiant speech was delivered on 15 August 1973. Undoubtedly the politically most difficult speech was the one on 29 April 1974, in which Nixon released partial transcripts of the White initial investigations of the Watergate affair and which was heavily influenced by the media, particularly the work of two reporters from the *Washington Post*, Bob Woodward and Carl Bernstein, along with their mysterious informant, Deep Throat. Political investigations began in February 1973 when the Senate established a Committee to investigate the Watergate scandal. The public hearings of the Committee were sensational, particularly the evidence of John Dean, Nixon's former White House Counsel. The Committee also uncovered the existence of the secret White House tape recordings of confidential and often controversial conversations involving the President, sparking a major political and legal battle between the Congress and the President. In 1974, the House of Representatives authorised the Judiciary Committee to consider impeachment proceedings against Nixon. The work of this Committee was again in the spotlight a quarter of a century later when

Bill Clinton was impeached. Nixon's last days in office came in late July and early August 1974. The House Judiciary Committee voted to accept three of four proposed Articles of Impeachment, with some Republicans voting with Democrats to recommend impeachment of the President. The final blow came with the decision by the Supreme Court to order Nixon to release more White House tapes. One of these became known as the 'smoking gun' tape when it revealed that Nixon had participated in the Watergate cover-up as far back as 23 June 1972. Around the country, there were calls for Nixon to resign. At 9 p.m. on the evening of 8 August 1974, Nixon delivered a nationally televised resignation speech. The next morning he made his final remarks to White House staff before sending his resignation letter to the Secretary of State, Dr Henry Kissinger.

Watergate had profound consequences in the United States. There was a long list of convictions and other casualties, including one presidential resignation, one vice-presidential resignation and forty government officials who were indicted or jailed. H. R. Haldeman and John Erlichman, both senior White House staff, resigned and were subsequently jailed. John Dean, White House Legal Counsel was sacked and subsequently jailed. John Mitchell, Attorney General and Chairman of the Committee to Re-elect the President (CREEP) was jailed. Howard Hunt and G. Gordon Liddy, ex-White House staff who planned the Watergate break-in, Charles Colson, Special Counsel to the President, and James McCord, Security Director of CREEP. The investigations into Watergate that led to the resignation of Richard Nixon are a case study in the operation of the American Constitution, political values and a courageous free press. Most of all, Watergate is now synonymous with the abuse of power and the fallout from this most foolish of conspiracies to burgle the democratic offices and the attempt to stage a massive cover-up.

1972 – LITTLEJOHN AFFAIR The British Secret Intelligence Service or MI6 got itself caught up in a messy little conspiracy to lay the blame for a series of bank robberies in the Republic of Ireland on the Provisional IRA. Using two rather inept brothers to stage the hold-ups hardly suggested that the spymasters in Century House, home to MI6 at the time, were exactly on top form. They deservedly got their fingers burned, but it is unlikely that such activities against the Republic would have been sanctioned without the approval of a government department or perhaps even a junior minister, so perhaps the blame goes even higher than the twentieth floor of the old SIS Headquarters at Century House.

In February 1972, when MI6 enlisted a pair of criminals, the Littlejohn brothers, Kenneth and Keith, the service seemed to have little idea of the problems they were taking on. When the Littlejohns were finally arrested for a Dublin bank robbery, they revealed that MI6 had provided them with arms and explosives to carry out the bank raids and attacks on police stations in the Irish Republic, knowing that these raids would be blamed on the IRA. British intelligence had also given them a hit list of leading Republicans they were to assassinate.

The Littlejohns were recruited to MI6 by 'Douglas Smythe'. His real name is John Wyman, and he handled a number of agents in the province, paid them substantial sums of money to infiltrate and inform on the IRA and, more importantly, to act as *agent provocateurs*, organising and conducting bank robberies and bomb attacks in the Republic of Ireland. Wyman told the Littlejohns that there was 'going to be a policy of political assassination' for which they were to make themselves available. Kenneth Littlejohn later revealed, 'If I was told about any illegal act before it happened, I would always discuss it with London. I was always told to go ahead. Smythe said, "If there is any shooting, do what you've got to do".' British intelligence hoped that these activities would force the Irish authorities to introduce stronger legislation against the IRA, many of whose members had fled to the south when internment began, and also would undermine the IRA's political support in the south. Between February and October 1972, Kenneth Littlejohn was involved in twelve bank robberies. Despite being arrested by RUC detectives in connection with one raid, no charges were brought. Individual officers have since stated that they were told to leave him alone by British intelligence. Wyman gave Littlejohn a list of IRA leaders to assassinate; these included Seamus Costello, Sean Qarland and Sean McStiofain. After passing on the name of Joe McCann, a leading Republican, to MI6, McCann was shot dead by British paratroopers a few days later as he walked unarmed through the Markets area of Belfast. Kenneth Littlejohn was also involved in two petrol bomb attacks on police stations at Louth and Castlebellingham, both in the Republic. Four other bank robberies which did not involve the Littlejohns were also cleared by British intelligence.

The career of the Littlejohns as British agents ended after a raid on the Allied Irish Bank in Dublin, which netted £67,000 and was then the biggest bank robbery in Irish history. They made no attempt to hide their faces, left their fingerprints all over the building and were subsequently identified by no less than fourteen members of the staff. A section of the Irish Gardai, disillusioned by having to take the blame for failing to curb 'IRA' activity which they knew was being caused by British intelligence, passed the Littlejohns' names on to Special Branch and the pair were arrested in England. The intelligence services were unaware of what had happened until Kenneth Littlejohn asked the arresting officer to phone an Inspector Sinclair at Special Branch, whose name Littlejohn had been given to clear the ground if he ran into trouble with the police. Upon being informed of their arrest, Sinclair's reply was 'So what?' However, MI6 were caught out. Prior to the Littlejohns' trial, Irish and British officials met to discuss the case, and the British fully admitted that the Littlejohns were their agents. The trial was held in camera (behind closed doors) and any witnesses who might testify that the brothers were acting on instructions from the British authorities were barred from taking the stand. The brothers were duly convicted; Kenneth received twenty years and Keith fifteen. However, despite the public embarrassment over the affair, the British government achieved its main objective: the passage of strong anti-terrorist legislation through the Dáil. Two car bombs almost certainly planted by British intelligence officers exploded in Dublin the night before the vote and produced an overnight switch of policy in the opposition Fine Gael and Labour parties, whose votes carried the measures through the Dáil.

When Kenneth Littlejohn escaped from Mountjoy Prison in 1974, MI6 sent another of its agents, Leslie Aspin, to find him and persuade him to give himself up, which he failed to do. Aspin had been an arms smuggler transporting weapons into Britain from the Middle East when he was recruited by MI6. He was sent back to the Middle East by MI6 to set up arms deals with the IRA, operating on behalf of a special unit composed of MI6, Customs and Special Branch officers at Tintagel House in London, which set up front companies for arms deals to see who used them. Aspin set up a shipment of rocket launchers and seven tons of automatic weapons from Malta via a Libyan diplomat. The Irish security forces failed to intercept the shipment and the arms fell into the hands of the IRA. Nonetheless, Aspin was paid both by MI6 and in a commission from the Libyan dealer. Aspin was later to become involved in the British end of the Iran-

Contra scandal, meeting secretly in London with Oliver North, who had placed $5 million in a Paris account of the BCCI Bank code-named Devon Island for the contract to ship TOW anti-tank missiles to Iran.

John Wyman was later arrested by Irish Special Branch in the act of receiving classified documents on the IRA from Detective Sergeant Patrick Crinion of Irish Special Branch. Both men were sentenced to six months' imprisonment by the Irish Special Criminal Court. Following a secret deal between the Irish and British governments, Wyman and Crinion were extradited to Britain to avoid embarrassing exposure of British operations in Ireland.

The Littlejohn Affair was a tawdry little conspiracy which was not only wrong in concept but unwise in choice of personnel, badly planned and executed. However, despite this level of failure, it was a positive success as far as the politicians were concerned and certainly helped to persuade the Irish government to reduce the public and private support the IRA could expect to get from the Republic.

1973 – KINCORA CONSPIRACY Did MI5, the Royal Ulster Constabulary, the British military and senior government officials deliberately cover up information that suggested a massive homosexual paedophile network was using a boys' home in Ulster? Was it because the young boys were being used to service the perverted tastes of well-known Ulster, British and perhaps foreign politicians, diplomats and others considered suitable targets for future blackmail operations? For years MI5 is believed to have been fully aware of a homosexual vice ring operating within the Kincora Boys' Home in East Belfast, which was run by William McGrath, a homosexual and leader of a strongly anti-Communist paramilitary organisation called Tara. McGrath was also a member of the Orange Order and of Ian Paisley's Free Presbyterian Church, and was employed by MI5 from the mid-1960s. Among various other Loyalist members of the homosexual ring was John McKeague, who ran the Loyalist paramilitary organisation the Red Hand Commandos, which was involved in many sectarian killings. When Loyalists threatened the Ulster Workers' Council strike as a means of bringing down the power-sharing executive which had been formed from an alliance of moderate Protestants and Catholics created by the Heath Government, Colin Wallace, an army press officer, was instructed to leak intelligence reports on Kincora to put pressure on key people who MI5 believed had influence over the Loyalists. This action was part of a project code-named 'Clockwork Orange 2'. However, after a short time Wallace was told to stop because London had a change of mind and wanted the Ulster Workers' Council strike to succeed. Wallace later discovered that this new strategy was part of the overall policy to discredit Harold Wilson because the Sunningdale Agreement had been a Conservative initiative and was now to be seen to fail under a Labour government. MI5 agent James Miller had infiltrated the UDA in the early 1970s, becoming one of its leading intelligence officers. He later revealed that senior MI5 officers had ordered him in early 1974 to 'get UDA men at grass-roots level to start pushing for a strike. So I did.' Therefore, according to the conspiracy theories, MI5 simply allowed the ill-treatment and sexual abuse of residents at the Kincora Boys' Home to continue. The fact that some of the Kincora children were also taken to Birr Castle in County Offaly in the Irish Republic, an area controlled by the Provisional IRA, was so secret that it took over twenty years to reach the public domain. It should be noted that Birr Castle is the home of the 7th Earl of Rosse, stepbrother to Lord Snowdon, Princess Margaret's estranged husband. The castle was built in the 1600s and the 1st Earl of Rosse, Richard Parsons, was one of the founder members of Ireland's aristocratic satanic cult the Hellfire Club.

There are many questions that have still not been properly answered. Were these abused youngsters flown to the mainland on occasions for the benefit of British politicians and foreign diplomats? There have certainly been rumours that boys as young as nine or ten were involved in operations to compromise intelligence targets at well-known hotels and country houses in and around London. Have any of the boys who attended Kincora gone missing? There are grounds for concern here, since some of those at the home may not have had any relatives, and the local social services seem to have paid little attention to the activities there.

While McGrath, Semple and Mains are widely known, it has become obvious that there are many other names of powerful and well-known people who have connections with Kincora and whose identities the British authorities have tried to keep secret since the scandal broke. Who are they? Some conspiracy theorists claim to have extensive lists of such VIPs and even (uncorroborated) reports of visits to Kincora by Ted Heath, the former Conservative MP and British Prime Minister. As mentioned above, John McKeague is also thought to be involved. In Paul Foot's book *Who framed Colin Wallace?* the author points to a connection between the murder of a ten-year-old boy called Brian McDermott in 1973 and John McKeague. It was believed that there were sexual and satanic overtones to the murder of the young boy whose body was dismembered and then burned before being thrown into the River Lagan. However, by Wallace's own admission, he and other members of the psyops group based in Lisburn were responsible for planting witchcraft and satanic paraphernalia in various locations around Ulster to give the impression that devil worshippers were active there. This was classic disinformation to discredit Republicans. When one considers the locations of the satanic sites where animals were discovered skinned and dismembered, one wonders if the Republican excuse was a valid one. The sites were located in Tower near Newtownards, Antrim, and in Coleraine – all Loyalist areas.

The Kincora Conspiracy was a sordid British cover-up of a paedophile ring for the very good reason that it was effectively run with the knowledge of the British security and police services. The information obtained, it is believed, promised just too useful to worry about the level of child abuse these young boys were made to suffer.

1973 – ALLENDE MUST GO 'I don't see why we need to stand by and watch a country go Communist due to the irresponsibility of its people.' So said Henry Kissinger, and this view obviously prevailed in Washington as it became involved in a conspiracy to put Chile firmly back in America's camp and do away with such 'nonsense' as free elections and the right of self-determination of an independent nation.

By the end of the 1960s, the polarisation of Chilean politics had overwhelmed the traditional civility of Chile's vaunted democratic institutions. The centrist agreements of the past, which had enabled presidents to navigate a difficult course of compromise and conciliation, became ever more difficult to attain. The CIA had certainly tried to influence elections in Chile dating back to 1958, but in 1970, despite the best efforts of the Americans, the socialist candidate, a physician named Salvador Allende, was elected President. In a reflection of Chile's increased ideological polarisation, Allende was elected with just 36.2 per cent of the vote and proved unable or unwilling to form coalitions. The left, centre, and right had all nominated their own candidates in the mistaken hope of obtaining a majority. After Allende's victory, Nixon, Kissinger, Jesse Helms and John Mitchell met on 15 September 1970. Helms came from that meeting with the impression that 'Nixon wanted a plan for action that would include a military coup and a broad-based destabilization effort that would "make the economy scream".' Helms' notes of the session read, 'Not concerned with risks involved. Full time job – best men we have.' An additional $6 million was spent over the next three years, including $1.5 million to rightist candidates in the March 1973 congressional election. The grand total of $8 to $11 million spend by the CIA since 1970 may have been worth $40 to $50 million after being funnelled through the black market.

After President Nixon had directed the CIA to prevent Allende's inauguration through a military coup, one of the opponents of an American-inspired coup, the Army Chief of Staff General Rene Schneider, was assassinated. At 2 a.m. on 22 October 1970, some Chilean army officers picked up three sub-machine guns and ammunition from the military attaché at the US Embassy in Santiago with the intention of kidnapping Schneider, who was 'one of the few strict constitutionalists in the upper ranks'. Six hours later the officers ambushed Schneider's car and killed him, apparently when he drew his own gun. However, Schneider's murder did not succeed in preventing Allende taking office as the legally elected President of Chile.

The Allende experiment enjoyed a triumphant first year, followed by two disastrous final years. According to the Popular Unity Coalition, Chile was being exploited by parasitic foreign and domestic capitalists. The government therefore moved quickly to socialise the economy, taking over the copper mines, other foreign firms, industries, banks and large estates. By a unanimous vote of Congress in 1971, the government totally nationalised the foreign copper firms, which were mainly owned by two US companies, Kennecott and Anaconda. The nationalisation measure was one of the few bills Allende ever got through the opposition-controlled legislature, where the Christian Democrats still constituted the largest single party. Socialisation of the means of production spread rapidly and widely and the government took over virtually all the great estates. It turned the lands over to the resident workers, who benefited far more than the owners of tiny plots or the numerous migrant labourers.

The most important opposition party was The Christian Democratic Party, and as it and the middle sections of society gradually shifted to the right, to form an anti-Allende bloc in combination with the National Party and the wealthy property and landowning class. Even further to the right were dedicated small paramilitary and neo-fascist groups like the Fatherland and Liberty (*Patria y Libertad*), who were openly prepared to sabotage Allende's regime. The Popular Unity Government tried to maintain cordial relations with the US, even while forging ahead with an independent position as a champion of developing nations and socialist causes. Much to the irritation of Washington it opened diplomatic relations with Cuba, China, the Democratic People's Republic of Korea (North Korea), the Democratic Republic of Vietnam (North Vietnam) and Albania. It befriended the Soviet Union, which sent aid to the Allende Administration, although far less than Cuba received or than Popular Unity had hoped for. Meanwhile, the US pursued a two-track policy toward Allende's Chile. At the overt level, Washington was frosty, especially after the nationalisation of the copper mines; official relations were unfriendly but not openly hostile. The government of President Richard M. Nixon launched an economic blockade in conjunction with US major multinationals such as ITT, Kennecott and Anaconda, and banks such as the Inter-American Development Bank and indeed even the supposedly neutral World Bank. The US squeezed the Chilean economy by terminating financial assistance and blocking loans from multilateral organisations. This, however, was not sufficient according to the prevailing view in Washington. As the conspiracy theorists probably rightly conclude, the US had by now determined that Allende must be removed and the Chilian socialist experiment terminated, and as soon as possible.

During 1972 and 1973 the USA increased aid to the Chilian military, a sector still deeply suspicious of the Allende Government. The USA also increased the training of Chilean military personnel in the United States and Panama. It was widely reported that at the covert level the USA worked to destabilise Allende's Chile by funding opposition political groups and media and by encouraging a military coup d'état. The CIA trained members of the fascist organisation Patria y Libertad (PyL) in guerrilla warfare and terrorist bombing, and indeed they were soon waging a campaign of arson and sabotage across Chile. Michael Townley, a former Peace Corp volunteer in Chile recruited by the CIA, directed groups of Patria y Libertad to paint 'Djakarta is approaching' slogans all over Santiago immediately before the coup in 1973. The CIA also sponsored demonstrations and strikes, funded by ITT and other US corporations with Chilean holdings. The CIA-linked media, including the country's largest newspaper, fanned the flames of dissent and distrust of Allende.

While these US actions contributed to the downfall of Allende, no one has established direct US participation in the coup d'état and few would accuse the USA of playing the prime role in the actual destruction of that government: that was to be left to America's supporters within the country, aided and abetted by the CIA. Political and economic problems increased under the constant barrage of right-wing opposition funded and encouraged by the US government and largely orchestrated by the CIA. The regular armed forces halted an attempted coup by dissident tank commanders in June 1973, but that incident warned the nation that the military was getting restless. Thereafter, the armed forces prepared for a massive coup by stepping up raids to search for arms among Popular Unity's supporters. Conditions worsened in June, July and August, as middle- and upper-class business proprietors and professionals launched another wave of industrial shutdowns and lockouts, as they had in late 1972. Their 1973 protests against the government coincided with strikes by the trucking industry. The CIA had helped finance truckers' strikes in 1972 and June 1973, probably through the International Transport Workers' Federation. CIA money also subsidised a strike of middle-class shopkeepers and a taxi strike in the summer of 1973 and by the left's erstwhile allies among the copper workers.

In early September, Allende was preparing to call for a rare national plebiscite to resolve the impasse between Popular Unity and the opposition. The military obviated that strategy by launching its attack on the government. Just prior to the assault, the commanders in chief, headed by the newly appointed army commander, General Augusto Pinochet Ugarte, had purged officers sympathetic to the President or the constitution. The CIA has been accused of 'blowing up bridges, railway lines, and killing people' shortly before the coup. The idea was to increase pressure on the military to act. There were forty terrorist attacks daily in the Santiago provinces alone, which gave the military an excuse to enforce the Weapons Act with massive searches for leftist arms in the weeks before the coup. No similar attempt was made to recover arms held by right-wing groups. Women demonstrated at army barracks to get some action, and threw corn and feathers at officers and called them chicken. The army was tense and exhausted by the time Plan Z was unveiled in August 1973. Plan Z was a leftist plan to liquidate the armed forces and their families (6,000 in

Valparaiso alone). 'The document was personalized, using a computer so that each officer found on the copy shown him his name among the list of intended victims as well as the names of all his children.' Writer Fred Landis and former CIA agent Philip Agee both feel that the CIA had something to do with concocting Plan Z. The CIA's presence in Chile was substantial before the coup. Almost one-third of the staff at the US Embassy in Santiago were on the CIA payroll. On 11 September 1973, amid the mounting chaos, Chile's military struck. In a classic coup d'etat, the army seized control of strategic sites throughout the country and cornered Allende in his presidential offices. He died in a firefight, apparently shooting himself in the head to avoid capture. Several cabinet ministers were also assassinated, the universities were put under military control, opposition parties were banned and thousands of Chileans were tortured and killed, many fingered as 'radicals' by lists provided by the CIA. Although sporadic resistance to the coup erupted, the military consolidated control much more quickly than it had believed possible. Many Chileans had predicted that a coup would unleash a civil war, but instead it ushered in a long period of repression. Nixon officials were ecstatic over the coup. 'Chile's coup d'état was close to perfect,' stated a 'SitRep', or situation report, from the US military group in Valparaiso. The report, written by Marine Lt Col. Patrick Ryan, characterised 11 September 1973 as Chile's 'day of destiny' and 'Our D-Day'.

CIA records detailing clandestine operations after the coup remain highly classified. But the 40 Committee, chaired by Kissinger, immediately authorised the CIA to 'assist the junta in gaining a more positive image, both at home and abroad', according to documents previously revealed by the Senate Intelligence Committee. As part of those efforts, the CIA helped the junta write a 'white book' justifying the coup. The CIA financed advisors who helped the military prepare a new economic plan for the country. The CIA paid for military spokesmen to travel around the world to promote the new regime. And the CIA used its own media assets to cast the junta in a positive light. The reality in Chile was far different, as the US government knew. Only nineteen days after the coup, a secret briefing paper prepared for Kissinger, entitled 'Chilean Executions', put the total dead from the coup at 1,500. The paper reported that the junta had summarily executed 320 individuals, some three times more than publicly acknowledged. Despite the carnage, US officials described the scene with soaring rhetoric. 'Now that they are in fact again a "country in liberty" no obstacle is too high, no problem too difficult to solve,' stated the Navy section of the US military group in a situation report on 1 October 1973. The CIA very rarely acted as a rogue elephant. When it plotted coups and shipped guns to murderous colonels, it did so on orders from whoever happened to be the United States President. The major media in the United States ignored the issue of CIA involvement until 1974, when Congressman Michael J. Harrington leaked details of secret Congressional testimony by William Colby. In late 1975 the Senate Committee, headed by Frank Church, released the report on 'Covert Action in Chile, 1963–1973'.

The Chilean coup leader, General Augusto Pinochet, held power for the next seventeen years, relinquishing control only in 1990 after arranging immunity for himself and his top generals. Pinochet had escaped all punishment for his actions, which left thousands dead and Chile a bitterly divided nation. The USA must bear responsibility for the consequences to the Chilean peoples of instigating a conspiracy that resulted in a coup by a group ultra right-wing generals to overthrow the democratically elected government of Chile and simply because it was presidential policy to do so.

In a quite extraordinary and rare admission of US guilt, the Secretary of State Colin Powell in response to a question from a student at a forum broadcast by Black Entertainment Television on 20 February 2003 said of the 1973 CIA covert action against Chile's President: 'With respect to . . . what happened with Mr Allende is not a part of American history that we're proud of.'

1974 – SHOOT TO KILL That the British government conspired with its own Security Service, Military Intelligence and the Royal Ulster Constabulary to pass intelligence on known or suspected Irish Republicans to the Ulster Protestant Death Squads run by the thugs in the Ulster Defence Association (UDA) and its many offshoots in the UVF, UFF and so-called Red Hand gangs is sadly almost certainly true. Successive British administrations have covered up this collusion with Protestant terrorists and killers, even though many of the victims were perfectly innocent working-class Catholics with no genuine connection with the Provisional IRA or any of the other Republican armed movements. Despite the best efforts of the government, military and certain compliant journalists, a surprising amount of information relating to a policy usually known as 'shoot to kill', but which in fact covered a much larger range of related killings, scandals and cover-ups, has surfaced. Quite sufficient in fact to convince many impartial observers that the British establishment regularly colluded with terrorists and sectarian killers in a province of the UK.

Many conspiracy theories and much factual information surround the allegations of collusion between the British army, the RUC and the Loyalist paramilitary groups, most notably after the murders of the only two lawyers to have been killed during the conflict, Pat Finucane and Rosemary Nelson. Moreover, since the signing of the Good Friday Agreement, Loyalist paramilitary groups have been responsible for the majority of people killed in the province in their attempt to undermine the Irish policies and peace settlement proposals of Tony Blair's government. As both MI5 and the Loyalist paramilitaries were involved in the undermining of the ceasefires in 1972 and 1975, many observers suspect that the ongoing violence in Ireland is a repeat of this, the long-term aim being the same as in 1974: the sabotaging of any peaceful resolution of the Irish question. In 1974 MI5 and the Loyalists succeeded in bringing down the Power-sharing Executive, and they appeared to colluded together in the attack on Dublin and Monaghan in May 1974, two days after the Ulster Workers' strike was declared, which killed 33 civilians. This act of state terrorism by Britain against the Irish Republic, largely ignored and uninvestigated by the media, remains the largest loss of life from any bombing in the last 35 years of conflict in Ireland, according to the theorists. In April 1999 it was reported that the Garda Special Branch were looking at fresh claims by a former member of the RUC that British military intelligence and the UDR were involved in the bombing. Apparently, it was long thought in the South that the UVF, who claimed responsibility for the attacks, were incapable of carrying out such a co-ordinated strike. Within a week of the bombings in 1974, the Gardai had drawn up a list of suspects, which included UVF members from Portadown as well as members of the British army and RUC Special Branch in the North. It is claimed that British intelligence agents supplied the explosives, and the home of an RUC officer was used to assemble the bombs. The destruction by MI5 and the Loyalist paramilitaries of the Power-sharing Executive and the 1975 ceasefire condemned Ireland to another 25 years or more of bloody conflict.

The collusion by elements of the British security forces with the Loyalist paramilitaries remains the biggest potential threat to a peaceful settlement of the war in Ireland. Special Military Intelligence Units were established by MI5 to provide support for the SAS in

Northern Ireland. At the forefront of these was the 14th Intelligence Company, which used the bases of regular army regiments as a cover, conducting covert operations under the title '4 Field Survey Troop, Royal Engineers'. It was also known as the Northern Ireland Training and Tactics Team. 14th Intelligence was equipped with unmarked civilian cars and non-standard weapons, including the Ingram silenced sub-machine gun. The team was commanded by Captain Julian Tony Ball, who later left to command the Sultan's Special Force in Oman. His second-in-command in the 14th Company was SAS officer Lieutenant Robert Nairac. Military intelligence officer Fred Holroyd described the work of 4 Field Survey Troop thus: 'In a cupboard in their armoury was a tray of 9mm Browning pistol barrels, extractors and firing pins which had been declared unfit for use and officially destroyed. These parts could be placed in normal issue Brownings, fired, destroyed and replaced with the original "official" parts. This would make it impossible to connect the weapon with any shooting – there would be no ballistic evidence.'

For the best part of three decades the counter-insurgency methods of the British government in Northern Ireland has, at times, involved a 'shoot-to-kill' policy – in direct ambushes when both innocent victims and suspects have been shot dead without warning, and in a sinister indirect campaign of murder which involved manipulation of Loyalist paramilitaries who were provided with security information and who then killed with the knowledge that they were free from prosecution. That appears to be the core of a large number of conspiracy theories put forwards not only by Irish Republican sources, but by a range of rather more independent, and hopefully impartial, observers. They state that this policy was pursued by small groups of RUC personnel, the British army and the secret intelligence network of M15 and M16. Moreover a section of the Northern Ireland administration is aware of this policy, and protects it by withholding information, conducting insincere cosmetic investigations, a non-prosecution policy and the curbing of inquests. FRU is still operating, running agents in Ireland, but since it became controversial it has adopted a new cover name. This is JCU (NI). It stands for the Joint Collection Unit (Northern Ireland). It works directly with the British Security Service or MI5, which also has offices and technical teams on the ground in Northern Ireland. To confuse the many British journalists who were investigating the activities of FRU, another intelligence unit was renamed FIU. This is the Force

Intelligence Unit. It has nothing to do with FRU, but runs more orthodox intelligence activities, such as the computer called CAISTER, which holds 'fine grain' intelligence files on most of the Northern Ireland population. It is controlled by the 12th Intelligence Company. A third group in the undercover world of Northern Ireland is the Joint Support Group (JSG). Closely linked to the 14th Intelligence Company or The Dets, it provides undercover teams for long-term surveillance activities. Its teams work closely with the SAS detachment based in Northern Ireland.

The whole shoot-to-kill conspiracy eventually encompasses the Wilson plot, Group 13 and the Colin Wallace affair, and features in numerous other entries including the Stalker affair and the Kincora scandal. It provides, according to many conspiracy theorists, a network of intrigue, scandal and murder, and to the interested observer it must quickly become apparent that if only 25 per cent is true then that would be disturbing enough and certainly worth far more investigation.

1974 – THE MURDER OF KAREN SILKWOOD Here is the quintessential nuclear conspiracy of all time, American style. This nuclear plant whistleblower was deliberately contaminated on several occasions by unknown persons from within the orbit of the Cimarron plant, owned and operated by the Kerr-McGee Corporation. The food in her home refrigerator was also found to be contaminated, showing that she had been the victim of a breaking and entering and that her food had been deliberately poisoned with radioactive materials by company thugs. When these scare tactics failed to dissuade Karen Silkwood from pursuing her safety agenda, she was fatally run off the road on 13 November 1974. That night she was carrying damning safety documents with her, which of course disappeared from the scene. The FBI and the Oklahoma Highway Patrol predictably said her death was an accident and closed the case.

During his farewell address to the nation, President Dwight Eisenhower spoke about a new industry in America, one of civilian businesses that provided war equipment to a standing army. He warned that we must never allow this multibillion-dollar partnership, which he called the military-industrial complex, become too powerful, lest it endanger our freedom. But the connections between government and big business in the US extend much further than the military. Take nuclear power plants, for example, which are owned and operated by power companies with the support and supervision of the Atomic Energy Commission (AEC). It costs a lot of money to build and operate a nuclear power facility, which is why the owners of such plants are very nervous about any potential threat to their investment. One such threat was a young woman named Karen Silkwood, who grew up in the heart of Texas oil country, Nederland. The black cloud of smoke that hung over her childhood motivated Silkwood's interest in cleaner energy forms. The propaganda of the late 1960s told high school students about the safe, clean aspects of nuclear power, and Silkwood was inspired to embark on a career in nuclear energy. After receiving a bachelor's degree in science, Silkwood applied to become a lab technician with Kerr-McGee, based in Oklahoma City. Founded by Robert Kerr, former governor of Oklahoma, Kerr-McGee had a reputation for ruthlessness and frugality, paying minimum wage and forbidding unions whenever possible. Enemies of Robert Kerr called him 'the last robber baron'.

Less than a month after Kerr-McGee's Crescent, OK, plant opened in 1970, a large amount of ammonia spilled into the nearby Cimarron River, killing 9,000 fish. Despite this dubious beginning, Kerr-McGee managed to convince the AEC that they could handle plutonium in their plant responsibly. Within the next two years, 24 workers were contaminated with radiation. Another died when a compressor exploded in his face. According to one former employee, 'Kerr-McGee didn't give a damn about the people they had working there. They didn't care whether the safety program worked or not, and they had enough cash to make sure the AEC was on their side.'

In the summer of 1972, Karen Silkwood arrived, fresh out of school and eager to begin her job testing plutonium fuel rods. Three months later she was on the picket line with the other members of the Oil, Chemical and Atomic Workers' Union (OCAW) Local 5-283, demanding safer conditions, better training and more pay. Ten weeks later, the strike broke. Those who had not been fired by Kerr-McGee for instigating the strike signed new contracts that stripped them of even more rights. Soon after, seven workers inhaled radioactive dust released by a fire. It wasn't until the next day that supervisors called in a doctor – and four days more before the workers' lungs were examined. Silkwood was appalled, and told her family that this was not the kind of career she had signed up for.

In July 1974 Silkwood herself was contaminated by radiation.

None of the plant safety respirators would fit her small face, so her supervisor sent her into the work area unprotected while a new respirator was ordered. Elected to the leadership council of OCAW Local 5-283, an increasingly militant Silkwood spoke out against the lack of safety regulations, the incompetence of untrained superiors, and the total lack of concern for workers well-being. After compiling a list of safety abuses, plant accidents and worker grievances, Silkwood flew to Washington, DC, on 26 September and spoke to the AEC, who promised an investigation. While in DC, Karen met union legislative assistant Steve Wodka, and told him she suspected that the results from fuel rod tests had been doctored, along with other plant records. Lacking sufficient proof to lodge accusations with the AEC, Wodka asked Silkwood to document everything she saw. Silkwood agreed. Two weeks later, on 10 October, leading plutonium expert Dr Dean Abrahamson stated that the 73 Kerr-McGee plant workers who had been contaminated in the past four years were in serious danger, and that the probability of contracting cancer was alarmingly high. Silkwood was one of those 73. The shock of this news almost destroyed Karen Silkwood. Her beloved nuclear power had failed, technically and morally. She began working at night and sleeping by day, immersing herself in work. Sleeping pills and a change of job were prescribed, but she vowed not to leave Kerr-McGee without the evidence needed to bring them down.

Silkwood spent the remainder of October searching through files after hours, compiling a dossier of what she told friends was compelling evidence against Kerr-McGee. What she didn't know was that plant security was aware of her spying, as were the board of directors at Kerr-McGee.Then, on 5 November Silkwood's body set off the radiation sensor at the plant entry. After it did so the next three days in a row, and with no accidents or leaks at the plant, she asked inspectors to check her home. The entire Silkwood apartment was contaminated with radiation levels 150 times above safety norms. The highest concentrations were found in tinfoil-wrapped cheese slices in the refrigerator, not a normal place for toxic radioactive energy to emanate from. Her apartment was sealed, and all her possessions were buried in concrete. The *New York Times* ran a front-page story on 10 November detailing the AEC's own documents – which stated that the AEC had 'repeatedly sought to suppress studies by its own scientists that nuclear reactors were more dangerous than previously acknowledged.' Silkwood was now convinced that she had proof that Kerr-

McGee had falsified records, proof that would combine with the *Times* scandal and force the AEC to act. She planned to deliver her bulging dossier on Kerr-McGee misdeeds to Steve Wodka and *New York Times* reporter David Burmingham in an Oklahoma City hotel on 13 November. She would never attend that meeting. Five minutes after that meeting was supposed to have begun, her white Honda Civic hatchback was found smashed headfirst into a concrete culvert wall off Highway 74, just over a mile from the power plant she had just left. Karen Silkwood was found dead on arrival. An autopsy revealed trace amounts of tranquilisers in her system, and the local police and FBI advisors happily leaped to the conclusion that an accidental overdose of sleeping pills had caused her to fall asleep at the wheel. The staggeringly fortuitous timing for Kerr-McGee had nothing to do with it. But Silkwood's doctor maintains that the pills were relatively mild, designed only to calm her hypertension and nerves, with chance of inducing sleep very minimal. Friends at the plant said she left for the meeting alert and determined. This was about fifteen minutes before she was found dead. Furthermore, given the curve and tilt of the roadway, an unconscious driver would drift to the right, whereas Silkwood's Honda was crumpled against the left side of the road. Independent investigators studied tyre tracks at the scene and determined that her car was braking hard when it swerved across the road to the left. Car-crash expert A. O. Pipkin found fresh scratches and dents on the rear bumper of the Honda. He concluded that Silkwood was rammed repeatedly from the rear by a late-model black Chevrolet, which accelerated within two feet of her vehicle and drove her car into the culvert as she attempted to stop.

Oklahoma State Trooper Rick Fagan was one of the first officers on the scene. He can be seen in the background of the crime scene photos, picking up dozens of pieces of paper scattered across the highway. He bundled all those papers into the manila envelopes found in the car. Lt Kenneth Vanhoy stated in his report that the papers were still in the car when it was towed away. Shortly after midnight of the same day, a group of Kerr-McGee and AEC representatives had the towing garage attendant unlock the gates, claiming that they had to check Karen Silkwood's car for 'plutonium contamination'. Then next morning when Wodka and *Times* reporter Burnham went to get Silkwood's report, they found her car stripped of every paper she had taken from the plant.

One former Kerr-McGee supervisor eventually admitted to

falsifying records, just as Silkwood had said her dossier would prove. 'I used a felt-tip marker to touch up photo negatives of fuel rods, to increase the number of rods in the photo,' he told an investigative committee in 1986, 'but I did it to make his job easier.' The AEC investigation sparked by Silkwood eventually conceded that there was truth to 20 of the OCAW's 39 grievances (which included plutonium stored in desk drawers and failure to report serious radiation leaks), but failed to penalise or even censure Kerr-McGee. Doing so would have damaged the already shaky reputation of the nuclear power industry.

How did that plutonium get into Silkwood's apartment? How can one of the rarest and most valuable substances on earth turn up in someone's fridge? Kerr-McGee suggested that she took the plutonium home to embarrass them. Silkwood family attorneys sued Kerr-McGee for wrongful death, with Steve Wodka acting as chief counsel. He alleged that Karen had been spied on at work and at home. Transcripts of conversations between Kerr-McGee, the FBI and an author with CIA links who wrote a disparaging book about Silkwood were used as evidence. The transcripts show a conspiracy to destroy Karen Silkwood's credibility, one that existed at the highest levels of Kerr-McGee. When Silkwood attorney Danny Sheehan tried to question the author/CIA mouthpiece in court, the FBI advisor to Kerr-McGee objected thirty times, on the grounds of national security. After conferring in chambers with FBI officials, the judge told Sheehan, 'The information you seek is secret and sinister, and should never see the light of day. Objections sustained.' Every attempt by Silkwood family attorneys to obtain information and documents was met with the indomitable wall of national security. The FBI even went so far as to try and get a gag order on Silkwood family attorneys to prevent them from publicly revealing the juicy details they were discovering on their own. Kerr-McGee company officials eventually admitted that some 40 pounds of plutonium were missing from the plant where Karen Silkwood worked, just as she had suspected. The British journal *New Statesman* was able to track the missing plutonium to places like Libya, Iran, South Africa and possibly Israel. Many of the companies used to mask and launder plutonium shipments can be directly connected to the CIA. Additionally, Silkwood attorney Danny Sheehan was warned by a source in the CIA that his investigators were in danger, and that he was risking his life by continuing to investigate. The Silkwood family, unable to penetrate the Kerr-McGee wall of silence, agreed to an out-of-court settlement of $1.3 million, with no guilt admitted.

Even those who would normally fight shy of conspiracy theories are pushed to accept this as a genuine conspiracy to cover up the dangers of a badly run nuclear facility and the embarrassment this would cause to major industries by a government which had much to lose, not least the many billions of dollars at risk in new investments and research.

1974 – THE LOSS OF THE *GAUL* The mystery surrounding the loss of the *Gaul* has still not been decisively solved, even after the finding of the wreck and more recently the discovery of what are believed to be human bones within the hull. In fact if anything the controversy around the sinking has grown as more information has become available on the employment of fishing vessels as spy ships by the Royal Navy with vessels such as the *Arctic Galliard*, *Lord Nelson* and the *Invincible* regularly being used for that purpose during the 1960s.

Take, for instance, the earlier history of the Grimsby trawler *Lancer* that gathered intelligence on Soviet naval operations in the Barents Sea northeast of Norway. Though lucrative for the time with a bonus of £10,000 per trip for the crew, it was also hard and hazardous work for the Grimsby fishermen. Between her launch in 1949 and 1954, the *Lancer* undertook no fewer than 45 spying missions against the Soviet Northern Fleet with the systematic recording of Soviet marine and aviation radio traffic and the photographing of Northern Fleet warships becoming commonplace. British naval intelligence officers regularly paddled ashore in kayaks from the edge of the three-mile territorial waters limit to conceal custom-built radio receivers and these were placed on the Russian mainland at key points all along the northern shore of the Kola Peninsula, from west of the Murmansk port and naval base complex as far east as Cape Svyatoy Nos at the mouth of the White Sea. Hazardous return missions were undertaken by the *Lancer* to recover the magnetic tapes and bring them back for detailed analysis by an intelligence team based at Pitreavie in Scotland. The *Lancer's* trawl net also proved useful. On her very first voyage, her crew managed to recover the fuselage of a crashed US reconnaissance aircraft. Its camera was intact and the processed film showed Soviet submarines on exercise. In June 1950 a live 24-foot Soviet torpedo was hauled up with the cod and haddock. 'Don't knock cargo,' Naval Intelligence HQ messaged them, rather tongue in cheek. On other occasions the *Lancer* carried Commander John G. Brookes, a senior officer in RN Intelligence who had been tasked to set up and co-ordinate Operation Hornbeam, the code name for the British fishing fleet's watch on the Soviet Northern Fleet. His intelligence controller was Rear Admiral Kyrle Pope RN, who ensured that the needs of MI6 were met. Such was the sensitivity of the activities of the Aberdeen, Peterhead, Hull and Grimsby-based intelligence gathering missions by trawlers that successive governments denied their existence for four decades.

The *Lancer*'s string of successful spy missions ended in 1954 with a dramatic escape through mountainous seas from a Soviet Border Guard's gunboat. The gunboat proved less seaworthy than the trawler and, as she rolled heavily, two of the Russian sailors were lost overboard. The Soviet government protested about the incident and the skipper of the *Lancer* had his licence suspended for three months. Naval Intelligence 'sweetened' this slap on the wrist by giving him a free pass to the local racecourses. Meanwhile, the sensitive spying equipment was removed from his ship before she was reassigned to routine fishing off Iceland. The skipper was rewarded with a brand-new German-built trawler which was capable of 18 knots, the *Coldstreamer*, and this vessel to be was specially fitted out for the Barents Sea and a return to the Cold War spy game.

There were at times as many as thirty commercially owned deep-sea trawlers operating as spy ships for the Royal Navy and GCHQ. The Soviet authorities suspected all UK fishing trawlers and RN Fisheries Protection vessels of involvement in intelligence gathering in the Barents Sea, and that many of them did exactly that remained a closely guarded secret to the British public until the mid-1990s. The fact, however, that certain selected vessels were used for highly sensitive 'close approach' operations has never been acknowledged.

Operation Hornbeam was clearly worth every penny to Royal Naval Intelligence and to US Naval Intelligence, with whom it shared the harvest and probably much of the costs. So when the *Gaul*, a well-built, well-maintained, steel-hulled modern trawler of some 1,106 tons disappeared without trace on or about 8 February 1974 without even being able to send a single distress call by its state-of-the-art communications setup, it caused consternation in its home port of Hull. Thirty-six competent and highly professional seamen had vanished without a sound. Then rumours began to circulate: had she been caught spying? Had she been boarded by Soviet commandos and were her crew in Soviet jails facing an uncertain future? The question of whether the *Gaul* had been spying was not that surprising – fishing communities are close and few matters remain secret for long. The Royal Navy had been outfitting Hull-based trawlers with high-tech surveillance and signals monitoring equipment, mounting batteries of additional aerials on the superstructure and providing groups of Naval Intelligence personnel to operate the electronics and sophisticated camera gear on board. These officers were often observed slipping aboard a soon-to-depart trawler late at night by the dock security staff, but like any community they closed ranks and nobody talked outside the fishing community. The *Gaul* fitted the above scenario perfectly. She was modern, large, fast, and photographs show her to have had far more aerials than a simple commercial fishing vessel would have. There were rumours that the *Gaul* had been in an area where considerable Soviet naval activity was expected, so had she got too close to sensitive operations and been captured or, worse still, sunk?

Surprisingly it took many years for her wreck to be found; yet there is a strong suspicion that the Royal Navy had a very good idea of where the vessel had been lost. The underwater photographs of the *Gaul* do not show any obvious signs of damage caused either by a Soviet attack or by a storm sufficiently violent to sink a trawler of over a thousand tons. Could she have been boarded and scuttled after the crew had been removed? The finding of human bones on board the vessel – if proved by DNA tests to be those of a known member of the crew – would complicate that theory, but not disprove it. The Soviets could have boarded the ship, seized intelligence equipment and code books and, to avoid the difficulties of prisoners, trials and diplomatic exchanges, simply shot the crew and sunk the ship. The Soviets, so the theory goes, could be pretty certain that the British government would be more interested in covering up the event than causing a diplomatic incident. An alternative theory suggests an accidental sinking by collision with a submarine. Despite denials, such incidents were quite commonplace and in the ten-year period from 1965 to 1975 US submarines on intelligence missions near the Soviet coast were involved in at least nine collisions, including the *USS Gato* on 14 or 17 November 1969 and the *USS Pintado* in May 1974.

Suspicions about the cause of the loss of the *Gaul* were increased by the ease with which a TV company was eventually able to locate the barnacled hulk, after years of government claims that a search would be impractical and too expensive. The later discovery of human bones was made a few days before the scheduled end of the £4 million robotic survey, carried out by a Sizeranger submersible based in Aberdeen. The survey was agreed earlier in the year by the Deputy Prime Minister, John Prescott, whose Hull constituency includes the docks where the *Gaul* was fitted out for her final voyage. Other mysteries surrounding the sinking were the fact that the sophisticated trawler sent out no distress call and that only a small buoy was found until the discovery of the wreck. A formal inquiry in 1974 concluded that the trawler capsized suddenly and sank in high seas, a theory supported by the discovery of a forced-open hatch on the wreck. Evidence from the current survey is likely to be put before a public inquiry next year.

The loss of the *Gaul* is another example of a conspiracy of silence that may not even be needed. If the vessel was lost with all hands because of a violent storm why didn't the government carry out a thorough search? If a TV company can find the wreck easily then the sophisticated equipment used by the Royal Navy would also have done so.

The *Gaul* was almost certainly used by the Royal Navy for intelligence missions, but was she involved in a mission on the day she disappeared and, if so, did it materially affect her loss? Until those questions are satisfactorily answered, the conspiracy theories will continue to feed on a maritime mystery.

1974 – A VERY ENGLISH COUP? A group of thirty or so renegade MI5 officers with a sprinkling of MI6 'spooks' conspire together with leading members of privately run paramilitary groups, leaders of business and industry, academics, newspapermen and Conservative politicians to undermine and eventually bring down the legally elected Labour government of Harold Wilson. The conspirators were prepared to use a combination of economic sabotage, political intrigue, disinformation, propaganda and, if necessary, direct action. A coup in fact. Well, that is what a lot of political and intelligence observers firmly believe to have happened in Britain between the general election of 1974 and Harold Wilson's 'surprise' resignation as Prime Minister in 1976.

Even before the Labour Party was returned to power in 1974, right-wing elements in the security services, the establishment, politics and fringe groups were conducting a low-level smear and disinformation campaign against the Labour Party and Harold Wilson, his closest colleagues and even his friends. Sir Michael Hanley became MI5 chief in 1972 and F2 was taken over by David Ransom. The agency saw a major change of policy, with much greater emphasis placed on dealing with 'internal enemies'. As extra resources were channelled into F2, an important section of MI5's 'F' Branch and responsible for monitoring political groups, MPs, trades unions and the media, Ransom increased the surveillance of a host of left-wing groups in Britain, such as the Socialist Workers Party (SWP), Workers Revolutionary Party (WRP), the Campaign for Nuclear Disarmament (CND) and the trade union movement. MI5 embarked on a massive campaign of telephone tapping, mail interception, disinformation, smear campaigns and psychological operations against trade union leaders. This was in contravention of the Security Service Act, which specified that MI5 could only target threats to national security; however, in regular breach of this was a GCHQ section called K24e, which dealt specifically with trade unionists. MI5 was to mislead Conservative Prime Minister Edward Heath into believing there was extensive Soviet infiltration of the Labour movement. Following the success of the 1972 miners' strike, the government set up the Civil Contingencies Unit (CCU), which worked closely with MI5's F2 section, providing ministers with detailed information during important strikes (based on phone taps and infiltrators) about the motivations and political allegiances of the strike leaders, internal divisions and prospects of industrial action. The train drivers' union leader Ray Buckton was the target of death threats, and the white-collar workers' leader Clive Jenkins had a bullet shot through his living-room window. Armed Special Branch guards were provided for several leading trade unionists, though Buckton was convinced that his death threats had been engineered to provide an excuse for round-the-clock surveillance. Forty volumes of material were collected by MI5 on the two most powerful trade union leaders of the 1970s, Jack Jones and Hugh Scanlon, in an attempt to link them with the Communist Party and East European intelligence agencies; the files were then used to bar them from government positions.

MI5 employed an extensive network of groups and individuals to carry out 'dirty jobs' felt to be too sensitive for the official intelligence agencies, which needed to be kept at arms' length from operations that would be politically embarrassing if they went wrong. It became common practice to hire private security companies for covert government operations. These companies were often in receipt of classified information from Special Branch files. At other times, MI5 used its own front companies for cover. One such company was the Institute of Professional Investigators (IPI), which included officials from the armed forces, Special Branch, the Foreign Office and the intelligence services. Members attended training sessions with the Army and Air Force Special Investigation and Counter-Intelligence branches. According to credible information provided to the media by conspiracy theorists, the anti-Wilson plotters contracted out some of their more dubious activities to private assets. One IPI operative, Gary Murray, who formed Euro-Tec (Private Investigators), revealed that his firm regularly employed operatives from MI5, the Army Special Investigation Branch, the Immigration Investigation Branch, the Royal Military Police, the SAS and the Parachute Regiment. Murray attended a seminar at the air force security school at RAF Newton, 'where we were given lessons in interviewing, interrogation and surveillance' and received firearms training at the Royal Military Police School at Chichester. Murray was recruited by MI5 as a freelance operative, paid a monthly retainer and expenses, and was required to take part in a variety of illegal acts, including the long-term infiltration of trade unions. Between June 1970 and July 1972, this top-secret operation, code-named 'Big Red', involved eleven private detectives, who successfully infiltrated the trade unions by obtaining manual or white-collar jobs in various firms. Once in place, they cultivated and recruited 110 informants over a period of two years. Shop stewards were monitored, as were numerous union officials, along with their families and friends.

As fears of another Labour government deepened with the forthcoming general election, George Kennedy Young (ex-Deputy Director of MI6) set up the Unison Committee for Action (aka Unison), a right-wing paramilitary 'strike-breaking' organisation, along with Ross McWhirter and General Sir Walter Walker, a former senior NATO commander. By the end of the year, an array of right-wing organisations had begun planning against the arrival of a Labour government. The CIA and British MI6 are believed to have set up the Institute for the Study of Conflict (ISC), led by Vice Admiral Sir Loius Le Bailley and other senior military and intelligence officers, which lectured the British army and police on 'subversion'. ICS's funding came from a variety of sources, including the CIA, the Ford Foundation and British companies such as Shell and BP. Information supplied by the CIA to the security services was used to find out if sufficient 'hard evidence' could be gathered to wreck the Labour Party's chances of gaining power. When the investigations failed to uncover anything of value, elements within the security services, supported by others in Whitehall, including former members of the intelligence and security services, embarked upon a disinformation campaign to achieve the same objective. These were times of extreme paranoia on the part of the intelligence services. John Biggs-Davidson, the extreme right-wing Tory MP and friend of George Kennedy Young, wrote,

> Today a 'thin blue line' contains the enemies of society. In the New Year, we must be prepared for new outbreaks of industrial intimidation, urban terrorism and political violence. I have called for a special anti-terrorist force and a mobile squad of motorised troops to counter the forces of red fascism which have turned picket lines into storm troops.

A leaked 1972 memo from the ICS revealed that John Whitehorn, Deputy Director of the Confederation of British Industry (CBI), was urging British companies to increase their funding to five anti-left-wing organisations. These were the Economic League and Common Cause (which ran their own intelligence operations and vetted employees for companies), Aims of Industry, Industrial Research and Information Services Ltd (IRIS) and the ISC. Distribution of these groups' anti-left propaganda was arranged by Tory MP Geoffrey Stewart-Smith, who was funded by MI5. Stewart-Smith planned to distribute between 1 and 3 million copies of the pamphlets 'The Hidden Face of the Labour Party' and 'The Hidden Face of the Liberal Party' in seats where those parties were thought likely to do well. A forged letter from the police to the Director of Public Prosecutions recommending charges against eight named Labour MPs for corruption was widely circulated to the press and TV. Other tactics included dissemination of intelligence files naming prominent Labour MPs as Communists and Aims of Industry's launch of a £500,000 propaganda campaign against the Labour Party.

In spite of this, Edward Heath's Conservative government drove headlong into confrontation with the miners during their 1974 strike and the Conservative Party narrowly lost the election that year. The Labour Party under Harold Wilson was returned to power, and alarm bells rang loudly behind the closed doors of the intelligence agencies.

Several more 'private armies' were formed by the secret services as a deterrent to any potential political strike, including General Sir Walter Walker's Civil Assistance and SAS-founder David Stirling's Greater Britain 1975 Organisation (GB75), whose members included the Jersey-based arms dealer Geoffrey Edwards. Field Marshall Lord Carver (head of the British armed forces) later confirmed that 'fairly senior' officers at the army's headquarters were talking about military intervention during the miners' strike in 1974. General Sir Walter Walker commented on the Labour government, 'There was a communist cell right there in the middle of Downing Street.' SAS-founder David Stirling, who plotted the military overthrow of the Labour government and was described by his biographer as 'well to the right of the Conservative Party', considered the left wing of the Labour Party to be 'a cancer'. His rabid right-wing ideology was summed up in one of his papers for GB75:

> Why are so many of us blind to an already far-advanced conspiracy by the broad Left to topple our democracy? It is now the broad Left which harbours the 'baddies' and which is devoted to creating a privileged class of rulers hell bent on demolishing our individual rights and on creating a totally socialistic and therefore totalitarian state. The near take-over of the Labour Party by its parliamentary left-wing activists in alliance with the trade union extremists poses the most menacing crisis our country has ever faced – more dangerous by far than the worst period of the last World War. This crisis cannot possibly be resolved within parliament alone.

In other words, fascism was a far preferable alternative to socialism, and Stirling was determined to use his contacts in political, business and intelligence circles to take covert action against the left. British intelligence provided covert assistance to Unison, GB75 and Civil Assistance. Thousands were recruited into Unison, ready to take over vital services in the event of a general strike in Britain. In Sir Walker's own words, he also had 'practical assistance' from Sir John Slessor, Marshall of the Royal Air Force and 'financial assistance' to the tune of £25,000 from Lord Cayzer, Chairman of British Commonwealth Shipping and member of the board of the Thatcherite think-tank Centre for Policy Studies. Sir John Slessor was also a member of Resistance and Psychological Operations Committee (RPOC), a clandestine anti-Communist guerrilla force with close links to the SAS.

Tory MP Airey Neave planned to set up an 'army of resistance' to the Labour Government to 'forestall a Communist takeover' and talked of assassinating Tony Benn should he become Prime Minister. A secret civil-military seminar on revolutionary warfare and the necessity for a 'third force', held at Lancaster University in 1974, was attended by a who's who of the army, police and the right-wing of the Tory Party; they included three chief constables, four assistant chief constables and Monday Club member William Deedes, editor of the *Daily Telegraph*. 'The undermining activities which Wilson complained of were far more menacing than he realized. Certain officers inside MI5, assisted by others who had retired from the service, were actively trying to bring down the Labour government.' The *Daily Mirror* newspaper tycoon Cecil King, a long-time MI5 agent, or asset, made it clear that he would publish 'anything MI5 might care to leak'.

Harold Wilson was in fact a social democrat of moderate political views, fully committed to continued membership of NATO and the retention of Britain's nuclear forces and a staunch anti-Communist. Nonetheless, many extreme right-wing intelligence officers viewed Wilson as a dangerous socialist. Wilson's predecessor, Hugh Gaitskell, had died of a rare tropical disease, lupus disseminate, following his return from a visit to Moscow. Certain paranoid MI5 officers were convinced that Gaitskell had been murdered by the KGB to get power for Wilson, who they believed to be a Soviet agent.

As soon as Labour won the February 1974 election, elements within MI5 began attempts to destabilise the Prime Minister Harold Wilson and disrupt his policies in Northern Ireland. A secret plot, code-named Clockwork Orange, was hatched to discredit Wilson and the Labour Party. In May 1974 the Power-sharing Executive was brought down by the Ulster Workers' Council strike, with the help of MI5 and the Loyalist paramilitaries. Two days into the strike, Loyalist paramilitaries exploded car bombs in Dublin and Monaghan, without warning, during the evening rush hour, killing 33 civilians – 26 in Dublin and 7 in Monaghan. As the MI5 campaign against Wilson intensified, so did the army's 'dirty tricks' operations in Ireland. In 1975, with Loyalist paramilitaries and the SAS unit at Castledillon, MI5 helped to undermine the ceasefire. Loyalist killings of civilians increased from 87 in 1974, to 96 in 1975, to a peak of 110 in 1976. The truce with the IRA had been secretly negotiated by MI6 in the aftermath of the Birmingham pub bombings. *Ambush: the War Between the SAS and the IRA*, a book attempting to detail the secret conflict in

Ulster and published in 1988, has scant details of this, although it confirms that the army was 'furious' with the secret talks with the IRA, believing that they had the IRA 'on the run'. Colin Wallace, a British army intelligence expert and senior officer of the Information Policy Unit, confirmed in 1980 that MI5 officers in Northern Ireland had not only objected to Wilson being Prime Minister, but to his Irish policies. According to Fred Holroyd, who had been working with MI6, MI5 were 'eager for a quick success and brought in a bunch of ruthless SAS blokes'. MI6 'lost control to MI5 and the SAS, who wanted a more aggressive policy, linked with the Protestant extremist groups. These groups sabotaged many of the operations which MI6 and the army had carefully built up.'

The evidence suggests that what has become known as the shoot-to-kill policy – a euphemism for routine SAS counter-insurgency activities and regular collusion between the security services and Loyalist paramilitaries, which has claimed almost fifty lives since 1975 – evolved out of the campaign of counter-terror that MI5 and the SAS used to try and destabilise the Wilson Government's policies in Ireland. Doyen of espionage writers Chapman Pincher confirms that a group of up to thirty MI5 officers hatched a plot to drive Wilson from office, while Colin Wallace revealed that the purposes of the MI5 plot were 'to prevent the election and re-election of a Labour government, to prevent any coalition between Labour and the Liberals, to collate and disseminate black information which could be used to discredit or control those politicians who were known to hold power behind the scenes in the three major parties, and to remove Heath as leader of the Tory Party and replace him with someone who held a harder view on how to cope with political and industrial unrest.' A 'secret' Swiss bank account for a senior member of the Labour Party, Edward Short, was forged by MI5 and distributed to MPs and journalists; the story was run by the *Daily Mail* in July 1974. The premises of the Labour Party, Wilson's solicitor and his former principal private secretary were all burgled, as were the contracts office of Yorkshire Television after it was announced that Wilson was doing some interviews with David Frost. MI5 distributed derogatory stories about Labour MPs to international news agencies such as Transworld News, Information Research Department and Forum World Features, which was in fact nothing more than a CIA front. In fact the overall conspiracy against Wilson in particular had more American involvement that is usually thought. James Jesus Angleton, the long time head of Counter-Intelligence operations for the CIA, worked closely with Peter Wright and his group of MI5 and MI6 renegades. Angleton deeply distrusted Wilson and anyone who wasn't a committed Conservative or a Republican. It was also planned to repeat the Zinoviev letter affair by leaking to sympathetic journalists details of false allegations against Labour Party members and trade union officials and to reveal suspicions that Wilson was a Soviet 'asset'.

Wilson resigned in 1976 and there can be little doubt that this was directly related to the political conspiracy that had been hatched against him. Wilson made several allegations that he was the victim of a plot, but was pressured by the new Prime Minister James Callaghan and others to drop the matter. Callaghan, however, is believed to have made significant changes within the security service to ensure that the plotters could not continue to damage the Labour government. In this the new Prime Minister at least partly failed, as the 'Winter of Discontent' and various other events suggest.

Under the heading 'Political Appreciations – General Notes', page 135 of the leaked Clockwork Orange papers states, 'The result of the general election indicates that unless there is a dramatic change in the future of the Conservative Party, it cannot win the next election under Edward Heath's leadership. The key issue therefore is whether there should be cosmetic treatment to help elect a weak government under Heath or major surgery to bring about a change of leadership BEFORE the next election. If Heath goes willingly before the next election, who will be his successor?' Emphasis should be placed on exactly what was meant by 'major surgery'. The replacement of Heath by Margaret Thatcher shortly afterwards fulfilled the secret services' desires, as Thatcher took the Conservative Party sharply to the right and changed the face of British politics. A very English coup: Wilson resigns and Thatcher replaces Heath. Some of the depths of the conspiracy can be gleaned from a 1975 internal planning paper from the Institute for the Study of Conflict, which stated the following: 'Specific aims within this framework are to affect a change of government in (a) the United Kingdom – accomplished. (b) In West Germany to defend freedom of trade and movement and oppose all forms of subversion including terrorism.'

Just after Thatcher – very much the creation of the conspiracy and its political supporters in the Conservative Party, according to the theorists – became leader of the Conservative Party, Civil Assistance was replaced by the National Association For Freedom (NAFF), later the Freedom Association. At one of meetings Chapman Pincher addressed thirty senior industrialists and businessmen on the 'grave dangers facing Britain from the left'. NAFF council members included ex-MI5 agent Stephen Hastings MP, Sir Robert Thompson, Britain's leading counter-insurgency expert, Paul Chambers (ex-head of ICI) and a group of right-wing Tory MPs: Jill Knight, Winston Churchill, David Mitchell, Rhodes Boyson and Nicholas Ridley. The last three were all made ministers in Mrs Thatcher's cabinet. In other words, NAFF's network of senior military and intelligence figures, senior industrialists, moneylenders and cabinet ministers had connections right to the top of the Conservative Party. NAFF founder member Robert Moss was a speech-writer for Mrs Thatcher; Airey Neave was Thatcher's mentor, election campaign manager and closest political colleague. Thatcher made Neave her Northern Ireland spokesman and he was due to become her intelligence 'supremo' overseeing the secret services. Neave was assassinated, supposedly by the INLA, a small Irish Republican group, shortly before he was due to take up this post. NAFF was at one time based at Kern House, headquarters of the CIA-run Forum World Features. Military intelligence officer Derek Jackson became campaign director in 1979 and the group was renamed the Freedom Association. David Stirling's GB75 was dissolved and incorporated into the Movement for True Industrial Democracy (TRUEMID), an organisation set up by the right-wing trade unionist Frank Nodes as 'an anti-extremist counter-force within the trade union movement'.

The above account provides only a small snapshot of the chaotic and dangerous period of the early and mid-1970s as put forwards by the conspiracy theorists. Despite denials from the media, the security services and politicians, the greatest part of it is probably true. We can only hope that successive governments have removed the sting from the intelligence community, but with a Labour government led by Tony Blair, which is in some ways more Conservative than Edward Heath's Tory administration, the danger of a right-wing coup is now non-existent. The right wing got their way, in effect, with the election of Mrs Thatcher and with the creation of New Labour.

1975 – WHITLAM DISMISSAL On Tuesday November 11th, 1975, the Governor-General of Australia, Sir John Kerr, dismissed Gough Whitlam as Prime Minister and appointed Malcolm Fraser as a caretaker Prime Minister. A Double Dissolution election was held on December 13th, 1975, at which the Whitlam Government was soundly defeated.

The government of a major British Commonwealth country dismissed by an official representing Queen Elizabeth II? Seems highly unlikely, but that in effect is exactly what happened in Australia. The reasons given were almost entirely spurious and the real reasons were both secret and scandalous. Edward Gough Whitlam's Labour government had been elected on 2 December 1972 and was the first Labour government in 23 years since the defeat of Ben Chifley in 1949. The new government was elected in a climate of great hope and optimism. Its demise a mere three years later at the hands of the Senate and the Governor-General is a fascinating political story that is still relevant to this day.

Whitlam's government was elected at a time of growing disillusionment with the Vietnam War, a concern about Australia's place in the world and great social change. Whitlam's 1972 election was the result of a programme of party reform, policy development and political salesmanship. The years 1972–75 were a whirlwind of activity, controversy and change, culminating in the dramatic events of October 1975 when the coalition parties in the Senate used their numbers to delay passage of the government's budgetary supply bills. A three-week constitutional impasse followed, culminating in Whitlam's dismissal by the Governor-General, Sir John Kerr, on 11 November. The dismissal raised a number of important constitutional, parliamentary and political issues, most of which remain unresolved to this day. Should the Senate have the right to block financial bills? How should a government respond when this happens? Should the Governor-General intervene in conflicts between the houses? When should the Governor-General intervene?

The man appointed by Whitlam to the position of Governor-General in 1974 is variously portrayed as a man of principle, a deceiver, an insecure man desperate to make his mark on history, a drunk.

The dismissal was the most traumatic and significant political event in the first 100 years of the Australian federation, but constitutionally little was changed by it. New Prime Minister Malcolm Fraser initiated a referendum in 1977 to ensure that the casual Senate vacancy rules could not be manipulated by State governments, but no other constitutional changes have occurred. The most significant change is probably political. It is difficult now to imagine the Senate being able to repeat its 1975 performance. The question of an Australian republic was rekindled by the dismissal, but this issue also remains unresolved.

It is now known that the real catalyst for the dismissal was Whitlam's lack of commitment to big power politics and the intelligence community. The USA in particular valued Australia's support in the Vietnam War and in Southeast Asia in general, but even more vital were the major US intelligence bases in Australia, and the NSA-CIA facilities at Pine Gap. Whitlam not only had been indiscreet in his public speeches and had exposed at least one spy base which was then closed down, but he was also threatening the closure of Pine Gap and the withdrawal of Australian facilities elsewhere. The USA was simply not prepared to see their vitally important intelligence and satellite surveillance network exposed and, even worse, closed down by the maverick Australian Premier. Enormous pressure was exerted on Australian opposition politicians and the Australian ASIS, ASIO and DSD intelligence services to do anything possible to undermine Whitlam's administration. The US President also appealed for the personal intervention of the British government and without much doubt, a conspiracy of the US and British governments working closely with opposition groups in Australia engineered the constitutional crisis that allowed the unusual dismissal of Whitlam by the Governor-General. Needless to say, Australia still houses not only major US intelligence facilities today but also the British Signals Intelligence base which moved from Hong Kong when the Chinese Communists finally took over the former British colony in 1997.

1977 – THE STRANGE DEATHS OF THE BAADER-MEINHOF GROUP Though few will mourn the passing into history of a particularly brutal group of terrorists, the nature of their deaths in a federal German prison suggests that a decision might have been taken to ignore the judicial process and simply remove a political problem once and for all.

On 5 September 1977 a chauffeur was driving a wealthy German businessman named Hanns-Martin Schleyer home from work. Schleyer was President of the Employers Association and a board member of Daimler Benz. Aware of the danger posed to people like himself by both ideological fanatics and kidnappers, Schleyer, as was his custom, had a car containing hired bodyguards tailing his vehicle. Suddenly a baby carriage was pushed into the middle of the road. Schleyer's driver slammed on the brakes. The car containing the bodyguards smashed into Schleyer's vehicle. A van drove up and gunmen jumped out, ran to the second car, immediately opened fire and killed the bodyguards in a burst of bullets. Then they shot Schleyer's chauffeur, pulled the businessman from the car, hustled the shocked and terrified man into the van and sped off. A letter was released the next day to the German media saying that Hanns Schleyer would be killed unless the RAF (Red Army Faction or Baader-Meinhof group) prisoners were freed, given 100,000 Deutschmarks each and flown to a country of their choosing. Accompanying this demand was a handwritten note from Schleyer saying, 'I have been told that if investigations continue my life is in danger. The same would apply if the demands are not met and the ultimatums observed. However, the decision is not mine.' Horst Herold, commissioner of the BKA, a West German agency that co-ordinates the law enforcement agencies of the various German states, asked that further proof be given that Schleyer was in fact still alive. The kidnappers complied by making a tape of the businessman answering several personal questions.

Denis Payot became the intermediary between the kidnappers and the West German governments. He travelled to Stammheim to hand out questionnaires to the prisoners to find out if they wanted to leave prison under these circumstances and to ask which countries they wished to journey to. The prisoners listed South Yemen, Vietnam, Algeria and Libya. On 25 September the BKA informed the kidnappers that both Libya and South Yemen had refused to accept the RAF terrorists. However, the BKA representative said that Vietnam had not yet answered. Two days later, Alfred Klaus of the BKA met with Jan-Carl Raspe, one of the RAF, at the latter's request. Raspe handed him a typewritten note listing other countries that he and his comrades would be willing to travel to: Angola, Mozambique, Guinea-Bissau and Ethiopia. Early in October, the terrorists holding Schleyer sent a recent photo of him, together with a letter written by the hostage, to Payot. Klaus again visited Andreas Baader and Gudrun Ensslin and found them extremely depressed. He believed they were contemplating suicide.

On 13 October 1977 a Lufthansa plane bound for Frankfurt was hijacked by Palestinians. The four hijackers, led by a man giving himself the odd name 'Captain Martyr Mohammed', demanded the release of the RAF leaders. Including passengers and crew members, the hijackers had 91 hostages. The terrorists forced the plane to land in South Yemen where they murdered the pilot, Jürgen Schumann, and unceremoniously shoved his corpse into a cloakroom. From there, they ordered the co-pilot to fly to Mogadishu, the capital of

Somalia. He complied with their demands. While this was going on, Schleyer's kidnappers issued another ultimatum: two Palestinian prisoners must be released and $15 million was to be paid for Schleyer's ransom. They wanted the ransom delivered by the businessman's son, Eberhard. Unknown to the four Palestinian hijackers of the plane on its way to Somalia, they were tailed by a plane carrying a German anti-terrorist unit. When the terrorists landed in Mogadishu, the second plane was right behind them and the GSG9 anti-terrorist unit, aided by a number of British SAS experts, stormed the hijacked plane. Three of the hijackers were killed and the fourth arrested. Luckily no passengers or crew members were physically injured except for a female flight attendant who suffered a leg wound.

Back at Stammheim prison, Raspe had been closely following this drama on a small radio that had been smuggled in to him. When the plane was retaken by West German authorities, Raspe communicated this dispiriting news to his comrades via a secret 'phone' system the group had rigged up using unused electrical wires between the cells. Apparently, they decided the only way out of prison for them was through death and they made a suicide pact. During the night of 18 October, which would become known as the 'Death Night' for the RAF leaders, Andreas Baader took a smuggled pistol out of its hiding place. He shot at the wall, then at a pillow; some observers would later speculate that he did this to simulate a fight. Then he put the gun behind his neck and pulled the trigger with his thumb, blowing a hole through the top of his forehead. Jan-Carl Raspe put a smuggled gun to his temple and pulled the trigger. Gudrun Ensslin chose a method of suicide similar to that of Ulrike Meinhof, who 'officially' had hanged herself back in May 1976. Ensslin took a piece of speaker wire and ran it through the narrow mesh grating covering her window. Then she made a noose, put her head through it, stood on a chair and kicked the chair out from under herself. Irmgard Möller stabbed herself four times in the chest with a stolen knife. She came within millimetres of her heart. In the morning, guards found Baader and Ensslin dead in their cells. Raspe was still alive but died soon after being rushed to the hospital. Möller was saved, and when she recovered, she vehemently denied stabbing herself but claimed that she and her deceased comrades had been attacked, giving rise to persistent rumours that this was an officially organised mass murder.

The kidnappers of Hans Schleyer apparently decided to take revenge for these deaths. Schleyer was driven to a wooded area and made to kneel. Three bullets were fired into his head at point-blank range. A leftist French newspaper received a letter telling of Schleyer's demise. 'After forty-three days, we have ended Hanns-Martin Schleyer's miserable and corrupt existence,' it read, and guided authorities to a green Audi with Bad Homburg plates in the rue Charles Peguy in Mulhouse, France.

The Red Army Faction had been severely disrupted, but was not yet extinct. Those who joined after its leaders were imprisoned or dead continued to commit atrocities in the name of the Communist revolution. Heinz Herbert Karry was the economics minister of the West German state of Hesse. Deeply concerned about the havoc caused by the RAF, he offered rewards for the arrest of its members. The gang assassinated him on 11 May 1981. However, by that time the RAF had dwindled considerably and its few remaining members were becoming worn out and disillusioned. The West German government offered leniency to those who surrendered and several took advantage of this offer, spending relatively small amounts of time behind bars for their crimes. An ailing Irmgard Möller was released in 1994 after serving 22 years in prison. In 1998 a rather tame communiqué was sent to Reuters declaring the RAF officially disbanded.

The above account is the official version of their deaths of the RAF's leaders and the events surrounding them; however, it is one which many were simply not prepared to accept. The Red Army Faction cell-block had been described over the previous five years as the most secure prison in the world. The press had been full of accounts of lawyers being searched for almost an hour before being allowed to visit their clients. So when it was announced that Baader and Raspe had shot themselves with two guns that they had smuggled into their cells, after listening to reports of the failed Mogadishu hijacking on smuggled radios and communicating with each other through a clever 'phone' system, many Germans were incredulous and remain so to this day. Indeed, it is an article of faith among German leftists that the RAF leaders were murdered by the state.

Despite conspiracy theorists' claims, there are suggestions that the RAF lawyers managed to make a mockery of the 'strict' searches and quite probably did smuggle in the guns and other contraband. The security within the prison may not have been as thorough as believed and the prisoners could have easily hidden the weapons. However, questions still exist about the exact circumstances of the deaths. This subject is still serious business in Germany. Some time ago the publisher of a semi-underground newsletter was fined over $1,000 for saying that Baader, Ensslin and Raspe were murdered. Leaving the final words to the conspiracy theorists, it is just conceivable that the German government simply, some might say reasonably, considered Baader, Meinhof, Ensslin and Raspe too dangerous to let out for any reason, so in the end all the hijackings and kidnapping efforts failed. They were all killed in their cells, and a clumsy attempt was made by the Germans to make it look like suicide.

1978 – THE MURDER OF POPE JOHN PAUL I The belief that Pope John Paul I was murdered by a conspiracy consisting of renegade members of the Vatican, corrupt bankers and organised crime bosses, while on the face of it pretty far-fetched, has, however, been accepted by increasing numbers of impartial observers. It seems that this peaceful and by all accounts delightful man had simply discovered too many of the Vatican's secrets and corrupt practices and, moreover, was determined to expose them. A reason for murder, say the conspiracy theorists.

The assassination by poisoning of Pope John Paul I occurred during the night of 28 September 1978, after a reign of only 33 days on the throne of Saint Peter. With his bright intelligence and naïve fearlessness, John Paul I penetrated to the heart of a maze of corruption within weeks of his coronation. On the evening of 28 September 1978, he called Cardinal Villot, the leader of the powerful *Curia*, to his private study to discuss certain changes that the Pope proposed to make public the next day. It has been reported that John Paul was also considering the release of the famous Third Secret of Fatima, which was supposed to have been given to the public in 1960. Among those whose forced 'resignations' would be 'accepted' by the Pontiff the following day were the head of the Vatican Bank, several members of the *Curia* and Villot himself. Moreover, Villot was told that John Paul I would also announce plans for a meeting on October 24 with an American delegation to discuss a reconsideration of the Church's position on birth control. When Pope John Paul I retired to his bedroom on the evening of 28 September clutching the paperwork that would expose the Vatican's financial dealings with the Mafia and purge the *Curia* of those responsible, a number of very ruthless individuals had a great interest in seeing to it that he would never awaken to issue these directives. Sister Vicenza found the Holy Father dead at approximately 4.45 a.m. on 29 September and was forced to keep silent by the Secretariat of State, Cardinal Villot, who imposed a vow of silence upon her to cover up the whole affair. When the Pope's housekeeper knocked at his door at 4.30 a.m. she heard no response. Leaving a cup of coffee, she returned fifteen minutes later to find the Pope still not stirring. She entered the bedchamber and gasped when she saw the Pope propped up in bed, still holding papers from the night before, his face contorted in a grimace. On the night table beside him lay an opened bottle of Effortil, a medication for his low blood pressure. The housekeeper immediately notified Cardinal Villot, whose first response to the news was to summon the papal morticians even before verifying the death himself or calling the Vatican physician to examine the body. Villot arrived in the Pope's room at 5 a.m. and gathered the crucial papers, the Effortil bottle and several personal items which were soiled with vomit. None of these articles were ever seen again. Although the Vatican claimed that its house physician had determined myocardial infarction as the cause of death, to this day no death certificate for Pope John Paul I has been made public. And although Italian law requires a waiting period of at least 24 hours before a body may be embalmed, Cardinal Villot had the body of Albino Luciani prepared for within 12 hours of his death. Moreover, the Vatican refused to allow an autopsy on the basis of an alleged prohibition against it in canon law, yet the Italian press verified that an autopsy had in fact been performed on one of the Pope's predecessors, Pius VIII. Furthermore, the conventional procedure for embalming a body requires that the blood first be drained and certain internal organs removed; however, neither blood nor tissue was removed from the corpse; hence none was available to assay for the presence of poison.

The spiritual leader of nearly one-fifth of the world's population wields immense power: but any uninformed observer of Albino Luciani at the beginning of his reign as Pope John Paul I would have found it difficult to believe that this man truly embodied such power. The diffidence and humility emanating from this small, quiet, 65-year-old Italian had led many to conclude that his Papacy would not be particularly noteworthy. The well-informed, however, knew differently: Albino Luciani had embarked on a revolution. It was by any standards a dramatic reshuffle. It would set the Church in new directions; directions which Villot, and the others on the list who were about to be replaced, considered highly dangerous. When these changes were announced there would be millions of words written and uttered by the world's media, analysing, dissecting, prophesying, explaining. The real explanation, however, would not be given a public airing – there was one common denominator; one fact that linked each of the men about to be replaced. Villot was aware of it. More importantly, so was the Pope. It had been one of the factors that had caused him to act: to strip these men of real power and put them into relatively harmless positions. The evidence the Pope had acquired indicated that within the Vatican City State there were over 100 Masons, ranging from cardinals to priests – despite the fact that Canon Law stated that to be a Freemason ensured automatic excommunication. Luciani was further preoccupied with an illegal Masonic lodge which had penetrated far beyond Italy in its search for wealth and power. It called itself P2 and the fact that it had penetrated the Vatican walls and formed links with priests, bishops and even cardinals made P2 anathema to Albino Luciani.

Karol Wojtyla was elected John Paul II and it is hard to believe that such an obviously intelligent man, well versed in the Vatican's establishment, should have been unaware of the problems his predecessor faced or the rumours that surrounded his unexpected death. However, he appears to have allowed a return to a normality willed by the assassins. The fact is that it was business as usual and all the racketeers kept their jobs. Pope John Paul II was in the unique position to bring all Luciani's plans to fruition. Not one of Luciani's proposed changes became a reality under the new Pope, however. Whoever had murdered the Pope had not murdered in vain. Villot was again appointed Secretary of State. Paul Cody remained in control of Chicago. Marcinkus, aided by Archbishop John Luigi Mennim, Pellgrino de Strobel and Monsignor de Bonis, continued to control the Vatican Bank and to ensure that its criminal activities with Banco Ambrosiano flourished. Roberto Calvi and his P2 bosses, Licio Gelli and Umberto Ortolani, were free to continue their massive thefts and frauds under the protection of the Vatican Bank. Michele Sindona was able, at least in the short term, to maintain his freedom in New York. Cardinal Sebastiano Baggio was not relegated from his powerful position in the Vatican to go to Venice as Pope John Paul I had apparently planned, and the corrupt Poletti remained Cardinal Vicar of Rome.

According to the theorists, liquidating Pope John Paul I provided a breathing space. Business could continue, but affairs were beginning to go badly wrong. Sidona was being pursued by the police, by the law courts, by the creditors and inspectors of the central banks, they had to kill in order to keep the wheels turning. Calvi, who had returned to Italy in 1978 following the election of John Paul II, was warned by Licio Gelli that inspectors Padolino and Sarcinelli of the Bank of Italy were closing in on him, so much so that Judge Alessandrini of Milan was about to issue a warrant for his arrest at any moment. Driving along the Via Muratori on 21 January 1979, the judge stopped at the red traffic lights and was assassinated by being riddled with bullets. With Alessandrini dead, Calvi was a new man. Meanwhile, a former member of the P2 imagined that he could defy Licio Gelli. It was the journalist Mino Pecorelli, who had arranged for the list of curial Freemasons to reach Pope John Paul I, the 'smiling Pope'. This time it would be his turn to suffer when, in Rome on 20 March 1979, he was shot twice in the mouth, *sasso in bocca*, to seal his lips for ever. Cardinal Villot died at about the same time still holding the vast array of official titles that had been his during Luciani's brief reign.

However, Chief Inspector Sarcinelli and the Governor of the Bank of Italy, Paolo Baffi, continued to demand the arrest of 'the Shark', the nickname by which Sindona was often known. Displaying the extent of their power, on 25 March 1979 P2 succeeded in having them arrested and imprisoned. When they were released, ill and disheartened, they decided sensibly on an early retirement.

For his part, Sindona saw his troubles grow. The New York Justice Department indicted Sindona and charged him with 99 counts of fraud, perjury and a major misappropriation of bank funds which had led directly to the collapse of the Franklin Bank. He issued a contract for the assassination of the District Attorney, John Kenney! Having failed to get the contract fulfilled, Sindona compensated for it by having Giorgio Ambrosoli, the liquidator of his Banca Privata Finanzaria, killed on 11 July 1979 by four bullets from a P38. Ambrosoli had been appointed by the Milan court and had made an important telephone call to the head of the security service in Rome, Lt Colonel Antonio Varisco. Two days later Varisco was killed along with his chauffeur by four shots from a sawn-off shotgun. Ambrosoli had also spoken to the head of the criminal section in Palermo, Boris Giuliano, and he too met the same fate as he was coming out of the Lux Bar in Palermo. Calvi was to be finally arrested on 20 May 1981 on charges of illegally importing $20 million (US) in Lire. He was found guilty later that year and sentenced to four years' imprisonment, but had been released pending an appeal at the time of his death. However, at the time of Calvi's trial the Vatican announced that Pope John Paul II had appointed a commission of fifteen cardinals to study the finances of the Roman Catholic Church. If he were not a member of the Commission, then it would be much easier for them to exonerate him. In the midst of the worst unrest, the Institute for the Works of Religion retained the confidence of 800 million faithful contributing their 'Peter's Pence'; of German Catholics paying their annual ecclesiastical tax; and of the '500', the 500 Roman or Italian fortunes reckoned to be Vatican Incorporated's biggest clients for laundering dirty money and transferring it abroad. Thus, it is alleged, on the one hand John Paul II covered his Freemasons, and on the other he covered his financiers, crooks, assassins or the accomplices of assassins.

If the new Pope was still unaware of the depth of the Vatican's problems and corruption then by 12 January 1982 he most certainly had been informed. It is known that he received a leetter, written in Polish, which revealed in some detail the full extent of the activities of the financial 'mafia'. It set out the links between Marcinkus, Calvi, Gelli and Ortolani and, through the latter, the Vatican's links with the international underworld of drug trafficking, racketeering and assassination. The authors of the letter, shareholders of the former Banco Ambrosiano from the time when it was still an honest bank, were not even graced with a formal acknowledgement. Little has seriously changed inside the Vatican under Pope John Paul II, though there have been half-hearted attempts at restructuring and modernising the financial framework. The Vatican still awaits a new Luciani.

1978 – THE JONESTOWN MASSACRE Twenty years after the world was shocked by the mass murder-suicide in the supposedly utopian community known as Jonestown, the questions linger: How and why did 913 people die? Some believe answers may lie in more than 5,000 pages of information the US government has kept secret. 'Twenty years later, it would be nice to know what went down,' said J. Gordon Melton, founder and director of the Institute for the Study of American Religion.

Over the years, there have been rumours of CIA involvement. Some people believe CIA agents were posing as members of the People's Temple cult to gather information; others suggest the agency was conducting a mind-control experiment. In 1980 the House Select Committee on Intelligence determined that the CIA had no advance knowledge of the mass murder-suicide. The year before, the House Foreign Affairs Committee had concluded that cult leader Jim Jones 'suffered extreme paranoia'. The committee, now known as the House International Relations Committee, released a 782-page report, but kept more than 5,000 other pages secret.

What is known about the end of Jonestown is that on 18 November 1978, Jim Jones ordered more than 900 of his followers to drink cyanide-poisoned punch. He told guards to shoot anyone who refused or tried to escape. More than 270 children were among the dead. Only two years before, Jones, the charismatic leader of the People's Temple, an interracial organisation that helped the desperate, was the toast of San Francisco's political circles. But after an August 1977 magazine article detailed ex-members' stories of beatings and forced donations, Jones abruptly moved his flock to Jonestown, a settlement in the jungle of Guyana, an Idaho-sized country on South America's northern coast. The plan was to create an egalitarian agricultural community. But People's Temple members who worked the fields and subsisted mostly on rice soon learned it was more like a prison. Dissent was apparently unthinkable and offenders sweltered in 'The Box', a 6- by 4-foot underground enclosure. Misbehaving children were dangled headfirst into the well late at night. Loudspeakers broadcast Jones's voice at all hours. In May 1978 Deborah Layton, a trusted financial lieutenant for Jones, slipped out of Guyana. She went to the US consulate and later to newspapers with a warning: Jones was conducting drills for a mass murder-suicide, but there was little official government action until November 1978 when US Representative Leo Ryan, who had been contacted by a number of people worried about their relatives in the People's Temple, decided to lead a delegation of reporters and relatives to Jonestown. Ryan's group arrived on 17 November. Their visit began happily enough, but the mood soured after some Jonestown residents indicated they wanted to defect. The group was ambushed the next day as they tried to leave at a nearby Port Kaituma airfield. Ryan and four others were killed. Later that night, Jones told his followers 'the time has come for us to meet in another place', and the mass suicide began. He was found shot through the head.

At the very least, the conspiracy theorist's maintain that the US government could have prevented the Jonestown massacre, but instead did nothing. At worst, the theorists maintain that Jonestown was a CIA-run concentration camp set up as a dry run for the secret government's attempt to reprogramme the American psyche. There are suggestions of parallel 'Jonestowns' and that the conspiracy did not end with the deaths in Guyana.

Jim Jones was born on 13 May 1931, son of a Ku Klux Klansman in Lynn, Indiana. His mother, he claimed, was a Cherokee Indian. That has never been verified. An unsupervised child, Jones became fascinated by church work at an early age. By 1963 he had his own congregation in Indianapolis: The People's Temple Full Gospel Church. It was an interracial congregation, something then unheard of in Indiana. Young Jim Jones crusaded tirelessly on behalf of blacks. He also suffered from mysterious fainting spells, heeded advice from extraterrestrials, practised faith healing and experienced visions of nuclear holocaust. Certain that Armageddon was imminent, that Indianapolis itself was to be the target of attack, Jones sought guidance. He found it in the January 1962 issue of *Esquire* magazine. An article in the occasionally ironic men's magazine named the nine safest places in the world to get away from the stresses and anxieties of nuclear confrontation. One of those retreats was Brazil. According to an article in the *San Jose Mercury News*, Jones's neighbours in Belo Horizonte, Brazil, remembered his claim to be a retired navy man who 'received a monthly payment from the U.S. government'. They also remembered that Jones, who would later claim that he was forced to sell his services as a gigolo to support his family, 'lived like a rich man'.

Some people, however, believed he was an agent for the American CIA. Before Jones arrived in Brazil, he had stopped in Georgetown, Guyana. Though his stop there was a quick one, he managed to garner some ink in the local media by publicly charging churches with spreading Communism. It appeared a calculated attempt to put himself on the record as a dedicated anti-Communist. Fifteen years later, he would tease his Jonestown flock with promises to move the People's Temple from Guyana to the Soviet Union. One former Jones devotee has raised the possibility of a Soviet conspiracy behind Jonestown. 'Jones was a Marxist,' Kerns wrote, 'who had numerous contacts with officials of both the Cuban and Soviet governments.' Among other suspicious facts, Kerns notes that shortly before the massacre two People's Temple members spirited $500,000 out of the cult's colony to the Soviet embassy. Jones's deputies did meet frequently with Soviet officials – so frequently, in fact, that they became a running joke in Guyana's diplomatic circles. Why exactly was Jones interested in the Soviets? He must have known that his professed dream of moving the temple to the USSR was only that, a dream. He dropped it quickly in favour of mass suicide. If the CIA had infiltrated the temple, or if the temple was, even in part, a CIA operation, then members' sojourns to the Soviet embassy would have had a more pragmatic purpose. The CIA had a considerable interest in Guyana and in the Jonestown colony, and to some Jonestown seemed to be more like a prison camp or penal colony where the inmates would be subjected to a range of mind control and drug-induced experimentation. Certainly it is believed that the CIA had planted a number of their agents in Jonestown, probably with the knowledge of Jones himself, who many observers believe was himself an agency asset. Whether this was all some form of extension of the MK-ULTRA programme or just a one-off experiment it certainly went horribly wrong. The real truth behind the setting up and running of the colony and probably the massacre itself almost certainly lies within the files retained in secret at the CIA's headquarters in Langley.

1979 – THE AFGHAN TRAP The USA effectively trapped the Soviet Union into a rash invasion of Afghanistan by arming and supporting the Mujhadeen in a conspiracy during 1979 against the pro-Russian regime in Kabul. Though Moscow's claims of US interference were widely dismissed by the Western media in the following years, a gloating Zbiegniew Brzezinski the former National Security Advisor to President Carter, confirmed in an interview in 1998 that it had been a very successful anti-Communist conspiracy all along. When asked whether he was aware of the former CIA director Robert Gates's admission that the USA had been active in Afghanistan six months prior to the Soviet invasion, Brzezinski answered, 'Yes. Now, according to the official version of history, CIA aid to the Mujhadeen began during 1980, that is to say, after the Soviet army invaded Afghanistan, 24 December 1979. But the reality, secretly guarded until now, is completely otherwise. Indeed, it was on 3 July 1979 that President Carter signed the first directive for secret aid to the opponents of the pro-Soviet regime in Kabul. And that very day, I wrote a note to the president in which I explained to him that in my opinion this aid was going to induce a Soviet military intervention.' Brzezinski added, 'We didn't push the Russians to intervene, but we knowingly increased the probability that they would.' Asked whether he regretted anything about America's secret activities, Brzezinski answered, 'Regret what? That secret operation was an excellent idea. It had the effect of drawing the Russians into the Afghan trap and you want me to regret it? The day that the Soviets officially crossed the border, I wrote to President Carter, in substance: "We now have the opportunity of giving to the USSR its Vietnam war."' Indeed, for almost ten years, Moscow had to carry on a war unsupportable by the government, a conflict that brought about the demoralisation and finally the breakup of the Soviet empire. When asked whether he regretted having supported the Islamic fundamentalists, having given arms and advice to future terrorists, Brzezinski's response was equally unforgiving and, in the light of future events, unfortunate: 'What is most important to the history of the world? The Taliban or the collapse of the Soviet empire? Some stirred-up Moslems or the liberation of Central Europe and the end of the Cold War?' The interviewer went on, 'But it has been said and repeated: Islamic fundamentalism represents a world menace today.' 'Nonsense!' said Brzezinski. 'It is said that the West had a global policy in regard to Islam. That is stupid. There isn't a global Islam. Look at Islam in a rational manner and without demagoguery or emotion. It is the leading religion of the world with 1.5 billion followers. But what is there in common among Saudi Arabian fundamentalism, moderate Morocco, Pakistan militarism, Egyptian pro-Western or Central Asian secularism? Nothing more than what unites the Christian countries.'

There perhaps in just a few short sentences delivered by one of the USA's most senior political advisors can be seen traces of what many conspiracy theorists would argue was the birth of the Reagan–Bush agenda that brought about the end of Communism as a world force, the demise of the Soviet Union as a superpower and the beginning of the path to the so-called New World Order, spiralling conflict in the Middle East, 9-11 and the war on terrorism. The Afghan trap was undoubtedly a political conspiracy of the greatest magnitude devised by Washington and an extraordinarily successful one. However, only time will tell whether it turns out to be part of a grand global conspiracy, as some would like us to believe, aimed at imposing a New World Order, Pax Americana and even greater dominance than America's position as the only superpower already gives it, or merely another example of traditional power politics.

Part Three
1980–Present

1980 – THE RENDLESHAM MYSTERY One of the few supposed encounters with an unidentified flying object that has created genuine interest outside the closed circles of Ufologists. This incident appears to have even seriously disturbed professional military personnel, not normally prone to fancy, panic or to having an overactive imagination. It has therefore entered the annals of 'close encounters' worthy of serious investigation. Information about the Rendelsham Forest UFO sightings, one of Britain's most famous UFO scares, was repeatedly suppressed by Government Defence chiefs, according to a Westminster watchdog. Parliamentary Ombudsman Ann Abraham reported that the Ministry of Defence (MoD) had broken open government rules over this case. Details of the alleged sighting at a Norfolk RAF base were only released after the Ombudsman ruled the MoD was wrongly suppressing them. The documents detailing this incident had only previously been made available to the very few people who used the American Freedom of Information Act to gain access to them. All of this has tended to stir the conspiracy theorists who believe that the obvious reluctance of the government and Ministry of Defence to either seriously discuss this case or make the vast amount of files they are believed to have amassed on the incident available for independent investigation strongly suggests a conspiracy to hide important evidence about some form of alien encounter.

The broad details of the alleged encounter are as follows. The UFO incidents began on 26 December 1980. Reports of a huge flying light plummeting down from the sky into the dense vegetation of Tangham Woods, which forms part of Rendlesham Forest in Suffolk, attracted the attention of three security guards on patrol at the twin RAF bases of Bentwaters and Woodbridge. It was also reported to have been tracked on radar crossing the coast off Lowestoft heading towards Rendlesham by several radar stations. In a report titled 'Unexplained Lights', USAF Lt. Col. Charles Halt, Deputy Base Commander at RAF Bentwaters, adjacent to Woodbridge, told how he witnessed an object emitting a 'red sunlike light' moving through the trees. In the early hours of 27 December 1980, a number of US Air Force men claimed to have witnessed an object hover in the darkness, transmitting blue pulsating lights and sending nearby farm animals into a 'frenzy'. As they approached even closer to the area where the object was hovering the guards were astounded to find what appeared to be a saucer-like craft – also described as aspirin-shaped, which may have resulted from viewing it from a ground-level perspective – with small, large-headed beings suspended beneath it by means of some kind of beam of light. The beings appeared to be effecting some repairs to the underside of the craft and initially did not acknowledge the guards. Keeping a healthy distance the men radioed for emergency assistance from the base. Assistance soon arrived in the form of a heavily equipped and armed unit including senior officers. Some later reports detailed amazing reality-bending effects, such as time displacement, experienced by the Air Force personnel that got closest to the craft. At some point, once the area had been secured, it is also alleged that the senior officers communicated with the beings in a manner that indicated prior experience. However, none of this latter detail has ever been, or perhaps is ever likely to be, substantiated.

In June 1983 a memo was sent to the British Ministry of Defence by the base commander, Colonel Charles Halt, who after promotion had continued to serve in the USAF. This, according to the conspiracy theorists, substantiates the story's authenticity, since the USAF is not usually known for promoting senior officers who report seeing little green men and therefore the Air Force Chiefs and Intelligence Officers must have accepted that this was in fact a genuine encounter. This memo is claimed to be one of the most important pieces of official evidence in UFO research history. Interestingly the halt memo refers to events that differ slightly from the other eyewitness reports. It states that two patrolmen encountered a saucer-like object in the forest adjacent to the bases. This object eventually manoeuvred through the trees, disappearing into the winter sky. The following day three marks were found at the spot, measuring 1½ inches deep and 7 inches in diameter, coupled with abnormal levels of radiation, which reached 0.1 milliroentgens of beta/gamma around the triangle of depressions. This, it is claimed, is some 25 times the normal background radiation levels for the countryside in the UK. That night, further lights were seen in the vicinity performing amazing movements, which defied the laws of physics before dividing into smaller lights and disappearing out of view. There was, however, no mention made of aliens, or communications between the US military and any craft occupants or indeed any occupants being witnessed. Nonetheless the disclosure in such detail by a high-ranking US officer of a supposed UFO encounter was unparalleled and is considered to be of extreme importance by Ufologists.

Some years later an audiocassette was released by Colonel Halt, which was purportedly recorded during the early hours of 27 December 1980. On it could be clearly heard various senior personnel, including Halt, communicating on walkie-talkies while moving through the woods towards the strange lights. The voices could be heard to reach a panic-stricken state as a beam of light projected from a craft and electrical devices faltered in the vicinity. What is more the tape, which seems to have been edited from a longer and perhaps more detailed recording, suggests that video and photographs were being taken at the same time. The theorists have naturally demanded that this evidence, presumed to be in existence somewhere, should be released without delay. Despite what appears to be overwhelming evidence that some extremely odd and unexplained event did actually take place, military and government officials still refuse to produce any further documentation or confirm the existence of any video or photographic material. The question of what really happened in Rendlesham Forest that night is still unanswered. There is no proof that an alien craft was involved, but former US Army Intelligence Officer Clifford Stone is reported in Nick Pope's book *Open Skies, Closed Minds* to believe that the US Intelligence Service thoroughly investigated the incident and indeed took away samples from the Forest. Stone believes that Washington has the answers, that a highly advanced technology appeared in those quiet Suffolk woods and that an advanced intelligence was involved. 'That Intelligence,' claimed Stone, 'did not originate on earth.'

1981 – ASSASSINATION OF ANWAR SADAT Anwar Sadat was once arrested by the British forces in Egypt during WW2 for pro-Nazi activities; it is a sad irony that he should die at the hands of an anti-Semitic Muslim conspiracy largely for trying to make peace with the Jewish state of Israel. The Camp David Accords between Israel and Egypt in 1978 led to a negotiated peace between those two nations in 1979, the first peace deal between Israel and any of its Arab neighbours. Egyptian President Anwar Sadat and Israeli Prime Minister Menachem Begin shared the 1978 Nobel Peace Prize for bringing their countries into those historic agreements. However, the initiative was far from universally popular in Egypt and the Arab world in general, particularly among Muslim fundamentalists. The Arabs believed that only a unified Arab stance and the threat of force would persuade Israel to negotiate a settlement of the Palestinian issue that would satisfy Palestinian demands for a homeland. Without Egypt's military power, the threat of force evaporated because no single Arab state was strong enough militarily to confront

Israel alone. Many Arabs felt betrayed and dismayed that the Palestinian issue, the core of the Arab–Israeli conflict, would remain an unresolved, destabilising force in the region.

The agreement with Israel brought peace to Egypt but not prosperity, and with no real improvement in the economy Sadat had become increasingly unpopular among his own people. His isolation in the Arab world was matched by his increasing remoteness from the mass of Egyptians and, while Sadat's critics in the Arab world remained beyond his reach, he increasingly reacted to criticism at home by further expanding censorship and jailing his opponents. In addition, Sadat subjected the Egyptians to a series of referenda on his actions and proposals that he invariably won by more than 99 per cent of the vote: in May 1979 the Egyptian people supposedly approved the Egyptian–Israeli peace treaty by 99.9 per cent. In May 1980, however, an impressive, non-partisan body of influential citizens charged Sadat with superseding his own constitution. Their manifesto declared, 'The style in which Egypt is governed today is not based on any specific form of government. While it is not dictatorship, Nazism, or fascism, neither is it democracy or pseudodemocracy.' In the months leading up to his assassination Sadat had lost much of his support at home and even in the West due to a brutal crackdown on fundamentalists. In June 1981 tensions between Muslims and Copts, a Christian sect in Egypt, exploded into a gruesome round of violence in the overcrowded Cairo slum of al-Zawiyya al-Hamra, precipitated by intense summer heat and coupled with frequent cutoffs in the water supply. Men, women and children were slaughtered. Egypt and the world were horrified by these events and tensions continued to mount as Muslims and Christians blamed one another in inflammatory press accounts. In September, Sadat cracked down on both sides with the use of brutal police tactics and mass arrests of at least 1,500 people according to the official figure but more according to unofficial reports. The powerful Islamic student associations were banned on 3 September and their leaders were arrested and subjected to tough treatment by the security forces. The head of the Coptic Church, Pope Shenuda III, was banished to a monastery.

On 6 October 1981, President Anwar al-Sadat, while watching a military parade commemorating the eighth anniversary of the October 1973 war, was assassinated by Lt. Col. Khalid al-Islambuli and members of the al-Jihad movement, Egyptian Islamic Jihad, a group of religious extremists. Sadat was saluting the passing columns of troops when the assassination team ran from one of the parade vehicles and began firing weapons and throwing grenades into the reviewing stand. Sadat was killed, and twenty others, including four American diplomats, were injured. Also in the reviewing stand with Sadat were the future UN Secretary-General Boutros Boutros-Ghali and Hosni Mubarek, the air force officer who was to succeed Sadat as President. Neither Mubarek nor Boutros-Ghali were injured. The killers were identified as Muslim radicals, members of the Egyptian Islamic Jihad. They opposed Sadat's landmark peace treaty with Israel and hoped to impose Islamic rule in Egypt. Hosni Mubarak and General Fouad Allam, head of Egypt's security service, launched a wide-ranging campaign against radical Islam that featured unlawful arrests, detention without trial, and torture to force confessions. Thousands of suspected terrorists were rounded up and jailed, among them Sheik Omar Abdel Rahman, who was later convicted of conspiring to blow up New York City landmarks, and Ayman al-Zawahiri, one of Osama bin Laden's two top lieutenants.

A number of Western leaders, including three former US Presidents, attended Sadat's funeral, yet only one member of the Arab League was represented by a head of state, Sudan, and only two others, Oman and Somalia, sent representatives. In Egypt 43 million people went on with the celebration of Id al-Adha, the Feast of Sacrifice, as if nothing had happened. There were no throngs in the streets, grieving and lamenting, as there was when Nasser died. In the Arab world, Sadat's death was greeted with jubilation, and in the subsequent trial in December it was revealed that the conspirators had obtained a fatwa from a blind sheikh at Asyut University, Dr Umar abd-al-Rahman, to the effect that killing Christians and stealing gold from Christian jewellery shops to finance the jihad was permissible since a technical state of war exists between Muslims and non-Muslims rendering the property 'spoils of war' rather than stolen goods. Two days later, 50 men attacked the police station in Asyut, 250 miles south of Cairo, where the conspirators were being held. The death toll from the subsequent gun battle was 87, 66 of whom were police. In April 1982 two of the conspirators were shot and three hanged. Another of Osama bin Laden's closest associates, Muhammad Atef, had strong ties to Egyptian Islamic Jihad (EIJ), the radical group behind the 1981 killing of Egyptian President Anwar el-Sadat.

In the West, where Sadat was often seen as a hero and a champion of peace, the Arab rejection of the Camp David Accords is often confused with the rejection of peace. The basis for Arab rejection was opposition to Egypt's separate peace with Israel. Although Sadat insisted that the treaty provided for a comprehensive settlement of the Arab–Israeli conflict, the Arab states and the PLO saw it as a separate peace, which Sadat had vowed he would not sign. Sadat's assassination at the hands of a Muslim extremist conspiracy therefore did not come as a great surprise to many Middle Eastern observers; however, it had little impact on Egypt's future foreign policy as Sadat had effectively moved his county out of the Soviet orbit and further confrontation with Israel and into a closer relationship with the United States and the West.

1981 – SILENCE THE POPE When Pope John Paul II was shot and very nearly killed in St Peter's Square on 13 May 1981, it was almost instantly hailed worldwide as the work of a lone fanatic, Mehmet Ali Agca, even though Italian authorities revealed ironclad evidence of a larger conspiracy. When it was finally and reluctantly conceded that Agca was himself part of a conspiracy, it was agreed that it was a right-wing, Turkish, Islamic fundamentalist conspiracy! Conspiracy theorists now argue that even after the terrorism expert Claire Sterling's detailed exposé *The Time of the Assassins* unequivocally demonstrated (and was later backed up by the Italian judiciary investigators) that Agca was a paid Soviet assassin, the US State Department, the White House, the CIA and the Western press still largely ignored the indisputable evidence. That evidence showed, argue the theorists, beyond a shadow of a doubt that the Soviet KGB had been operating through the DS Secret Service of the Communist regime in Bulgaria and the Turkish Mafia, whose headquarters were based in Bulgaria. This conspiracy had sprung Agca from a Turkish jail, trained him, provided him with weapons and false travel documents and fabricated a false 'right-wing' identity for him before the assassination attempt.

Although the plot to kill the Pope failed, the secondary objective, to provoke a widespread public reaction against right-wing terrorism and religious fundamentalism, worked marvellously as Western governments quietly and quickly worked to cover up any trace of Soviet involvement. Pope John Paul II bluntly rejected allegations that the former Communist government in Bulgaria was involved in the attempt his life. He said on a later visit to Bulgaria, 'I never believed in the so-called Bulgarian connection.' Three Bulgarians, however, had faced trial in Italy as alleged co-conspirators in Turkish gunman Mehmet Ali Agca's attempt to kill the Pope. They were later acquitted for lack of evidence, but allegations that Bulgaria's DS Secret Service and the Soviet KGB had played a role were never entirely put to rest. The Pope was considered to be a prime target for murder because of the important role he was playing in undermining the Communist government of his home country of Poland. Strangely, a counter-theory has it that the US CIA secretly manufactured the story about the Soviets' being behind the assassination attempt, and that this so angered the KGB that they then invented the story that biological warfare experiments by the CIA were responsible for the Aids epidemic. An interesting thought and possibly a double bluff: why would the Turkish Mafia wish to kill the Pope? The Russians certainly had cause to fear him. And Aids? According to the conspiracy theorists, the CIA are simply trying to further muddy the waters by suggesting that the story was Russian propaganda in order to make it easier to deny what is in fact the truth. This, like the death of John Paul I, is a conspiracy story that is simply not going to go away.

1981 – COLIN WALLACE CONSPIRACY The conspiracy to silence a former British military official and a whistleblower by framing him for manslaughter is about as dishonourable as it gets. But that is exactly what many conspiracy theorists believe a group of unnamed and unaccountable British Security Service and government officials have done to Colin Wallace. Thankfully for democracy it failed to silence him or to prevent his accusations from becoming public knowledge. Colin Wallace later revealed that the Information Policy Unit, a psychological warfare or psyops unit, had been established at the army's Lisburn headquarters in Ulster during 1971.

This unit was set up by Howard Smith, who was later to become the head of MI5, and he was believed to be using Northern Ireland as a theatre for 'black operations', popularly known as dirty tricks. The Information Policy Unit was responsible for the development of black propaganda, such as a 1972 ITN news bulletin alleging that the IRA used eight-year-old girls to plant a massive bomb in a pram outside Belfast's Victoria Hospital. The army later admitted that the story was untrue but ITN carried no denial. A similar fake story described how IRA men had raped several Belfast girls at gunpoint. Other fabricated stories planted in the British press by the Information Policy Unit included one that was released after British paratroopers had shot dead thirteen unarmed civilians in the 1972 Bloody Sunday massacre; it was about an IRA plan to dress up as soldiers and shoot civil rights marchers. Republican detainees were reported to be beating themselves up in police or army custody; the IRA was reported to be training in Libya, hiring Czech hitmen and Vietnam war veterans from America, smuggling Trotskyists to Ireland in Russian submarines, and plotting to kidnap English villagers; and unarmed victims of police and army shootings were falsely reported to have been armed or to have driven through non-existent roadblocks.

The propaganda war continued with a new committee chaired by Michael Cudlipp and staffed by representatives of the Northern Ireland Office, the RUC and the army, including Jeremy Railton, then head of the Information Policy Unit. Its main targets included both Republican and Loyalist extremist leaders. Lurid details of their personal lives, allegations of embezzlement and involvement in sectarian assassinations were fabricated and fed to selected journalists. These accusations were for the most part probably true, and to many serving in Ulster it must have seemed that Wallace was being difficult in complaining about the way such information was being used. The British establishment obviously decided, according to conspiracy theorists and perhaps a good few impartial observers, that Colin Wallace had to be silenced before these facts became public knowledge.

Wallace was framed for the manslaughter of Jonathan Lewis, a Brighton antiques dealer, found drowned and battered in the River Arun in August 1980. However, though Wallace was tried, convicted and jailed for a ten-year term, the verdict was eventually overturned by the Court of Appeal. Wallace claimed he had been the victim of injustice at his trial and called for a 'far-reaching' police investigation into the killing of Lewis. In a reserved judgement, Lord Bingham, the Lord Chief Justice, and two other judges ruled the conviction unsafe and cleared Wallace after new medical evidence led to the case being referred by the Home Secretary, Michael Howard, for review. Colin Wallace had spent six years in jail for a crime he hadn't committed.

Wallace appeared to have become mixed up in a parochial killing and the authorities took advantage of his predicament and manipulated the proceedings to ensure that his reputation was sullied, his truthfulness doubted and his presence temporarily removed to a prison cell. Wallace has continued to argue for an investigation into black operations by the military and MI5 both in Ulster and in Britain against the government of Harold Wilson in the mid-1970s. He has also received the continuing and unwanted attention of those still determined to cast doubt on his accusations of government wrongdoing.

1982 – LEBANON: COVERING UP MASS MURDER Accusations that have seriously scarred the international reputation of the State of Israel, and which raised a grave moral question mark over a future prime minister, revolve around the massacres in the Palestinian refugee camps of Sabra and Shatila in the suburbs of Beirut in 1982. These will for ever be remembered with horror by the Arab world and argued about in Israel. General Ariel 'Arik' Sharon, charismatic war leader and the Prime Minister of Israel since 2001, was the defence minister in Menachem Begin's government at the time and would later be held largely responsible for, if not instigating the massacres, then at least for complicity with the Christian Lebanese forces that carried out the killings. There is a deep and probably well-founded suspicion that General Sharon was involved in a widespread conspiracy between leading Israeli military and political figures and the Lebanese Christian Phalange to destroy the power of the Palestine Liberation Organisation encamped in Beirut. The United States was persuaded with little difficulty, it would seem, to turn a blind eye to the inevitable toll on civilian lives and the brutality not only of the massive Israeli artillery and aerial bombardments of the city, but also the intense hatred and cruelty of the Christian death squads. Some Israelis, such as the well-known Attorney Yosef Dar from Netanya, still argue that Sharon himself was a victim of a political witch-hunt by Aharon Barak, later the president of the Supreme Court and a member of the Kahan parliamentary investigation into the massacres. The intention of Barak's actions, it is claimed, was to cover up the part played by Prime Minister Begin, himself a former wanted terrorist, in allowing the mass killings of Palestinians to occur.

The tragedy that unfolded within the camps was denounced throughout the world and the United Nations Security Council was moved to condemn the massacre with Resolution 521 in September 1982. This would be followed by a 16 December 1982 General Assembly resolution qualifying the massacre as an 'act of genocide'. Sharon is intimately intertwined with the troubled relationship with both the Palestinians and Israel's Arab neighbours and his strong right-wing, militaristic and nationalist attitudes were the driving force behind Israel's original decision to invade the Lebanon and destroy the power of Yasser Arafat's PLO and Fatah once and for all. Sharon is also held by many to be indirectly responsible for the deaths of between 700 and 3,500 men, women and children in the atrocities and perhaps as many as a further 1,000 mainly young men who were taken away under the watchful gaze of the Israeli army by the Christian militiamen to be interrogated, tortured and murdered in the following few days. Indeed legal action has been attempted by relatives of the victims in Belgium in recent years to prosecute Sharon for war crimes.

On 6 June 1982, the Israeli army launched operation 'Peace in Galilee' and invaded the Lebanon with a large force of tanks and mechanised infantry backed up with immense bombardments by artillery and supported by large numbers of air strikes. After occupying the south of the country, the Israeli troops penetrated as far as Beirut, and by 18 June 1982 they had surrounded the Palestine Liberation Organisation's main positions in the west side of the city. The Israeli offensive, particularly the intensive shelling of Beirut, caused 18,000 deaths and 30,000 injuries, mostly to Lebanese and Palestinian civilians.

A cease-fire was negotiated through the intermediary of United States envoy Philip Habib. It was agreed that the PLO would evacuate Beirut, under the supervision of a multinational force deployed in the evacuated part of the town. The evacuation of the 14,000 or so PLO fighters, families and administration ended on 1 September 1982. On the 10 September 1982, the multinational forces left Beirut. The very next day Israeli Defence Minister Ariel Sharon announced that '2,000 terrorists' had remained inside the Palestinian refugee camps around Beirut. The controversial intention to send the Lebanese Christian Phalangist forces into west Beirut had already been announced by Sharon as early as the 9 July 1982 and he continued to ignore the warning signs including the increasingly desperate pleas for withdrawal of Israeli forces with the multinational peacekeeping force by Israel's director of intelligence, Major General Yehoshua Saguy, who argued that, 'There will still be terrorists in Beirut and the Phalange will find a way to get them and settle old scores,' and indeed, even more ominously, 'One day the murders will start and they will just go on and on without end . . . how can we operate without being tainted . . . ? they'll lay everything at our doorstep!'

Sharon remained committed to the 'meat-grinder' operations by his own forces and those of the regular Lebanese army to destroy the military capability of the Palestinians and their allies with the subjugation of such refugee camps as Burj el-Barajneh on the 23 August. Surrounded on three sides by Israeli troops, President-elect Bashir Gemayel ordered in a battalion of the Lebanese army to destroy the infrastructure of the camp, search for illegal arms and make mass arrests. Some of the Palestinian fighters undoubtedly escaped to the Sabra and Shatilla camps, further marking them out for eventual destruction. The Lebanese Christians certainly felt that the Israeli military command saw the problem, and the correct solution, in the same way as they did, and indeed Sharon and Bashir Gemayel had reached an understanding about sending Lebanese forces into west Beirut. The assassination of Gemayel lost Israel their supposedly most effective influence in the Lebanon, though suspicions exist that the President-elect had already angered leading Israeli hawks by his attempts to build bridges with the Lebanese allies of the Palestinians. At 9 a.m. on 14 September, the very day that Gemayel would be killed, Sharon ordered Chief of Staff Rafael Eitan to prepare his forces to launch 'Operation Iron Mind' to capture the vital road junctions and commanding areas overlooking the Palestinian refugee camps in west Beirut. Eitan's deputy, Lt. Col. Zeev Zachrin, would later testify to the Kahan inquiry, and in complete contradiction to Sharon's testimony, that at this meeting the defence minister had indeed confirmed his intention that the Lebanese Phalangist militia would enter the camps, and not the Israeli army. Significantly, no written orders detailing this damning evidence of prior Israeli knowledge of the use of Lebanese paramilitary units with a well-deserved brutal reputation for torture and murder were to be issued. An insight into the mind-set of the Christian militias can be gained from comments made by Jesse Sokar, a Phalangist liaison officer attached to the Israeli Paratroop Division deployed in the Beirut area, when he proudly told a visiting journalist that 'no rape of girls under the age of twelve is allowed'. Sadly, it is rumoured that girls, and boys, far younger would be raped, tortured and killed with impunity in the months that followed and with little serious attempt by Israel or its US and British allies to prevent the blood-soaked rampage by the militias through the streets and refugee camps of west Beirut.

From dawn on 15 September 1982 Israeli fighter-bombers were flying low over west Beirut and Israeli troops had secured the Phalangists' entry into the camps. From 9 a.m. General Sharon was present in the army's command bunker to personally direct the Israeli penetration. From midday, the camps of Sabra and Shatila were surrounded by Israeli tanks and soldiers and bombarded constantly with heavy self-propelled artillery. Shortly after 5 p.m. on 16 September, a unit of approximately 150 Phalangists entered Shatila camp from the south and southwest, apparently still thirsting for revenge following the assassination of President-elect Bashir Gemayel. At that point, General Drori telephoned Ariel Sharon and announced, 'Our friends are advancing into the camps. We have coordinated their entry.' For the next forty hours, the Phalangist militia raped, tortured, killed and wounded a large number of unarmed civilians, mostly children, women and old people. These actions were followed by systematic roundups of suspects, backed up by the Israeli army and resulted in many hundreds of disappearances. The Israeli army knew perfectly well what was going on in the camps, as they were in permanent contact with the militia leaders, had numerous observation posts overlooking the camps, signals intelligence monitoring sites and very probably liaison officers from the Mossad Intelligence Service and the Special Forces operating alongside the Christian militia units. Yet the Israelis made no attempt to intervene until the morning of Saturday 18 September 1982. Instead, they forcibly stopped civilians from leaving the camps to prevent the escape of any Palestinians on their wanted lists.

The death count of victims varies between the official Israeli figure of 700 and 3,500 quoted by Palestinian sources. The exact figure will never be determined because in addition to the approximately 1,000 people who were buried in communal graves by the International Committee of the Red Cross or in the cemeteries of Beirut by members of their families, a large number of corpses were buried under bulldozed buildings by the militia themselves, a tactic that Israel has since been accused of using within the occupied territories of the West Bank to hide the exact numbers of civilian casualties caused by Israeli military operations. In addition, and particularly on 17 and 18 September, many hundreds of Palestinians were moved in trucks to unknown destinations, none of whom have apparently ever been seen again. In the face of mounting world protests and growing unease even at home, the Israeli Knesset (parliament) formed a commission of inquiry presided over by Yitzhak Kahan in late September 1982. In spite of the limitations of the commission's mandate, it being political and not a true judicial investigation, and in the total absence of evidence from the families of the victims, the commission still found itself able to conclude that the minster of defence was to be held personally responsible for the massacres. Sharon resigned from his post of minister of defence but significantly remained in the government as minister without portfolio. In spite of evidence of what the UN Security Council described as a 'criminal massacre', and the sadly obvious fact that the Sabra and Shatila massacres rate among the great war crimes of the twentieth century, the man found 'personally responsible', his closest military and political associates and the Lebanese Christians who carried out the massacres have never been pursued or punished by the international community. In fact many have prospered politically in both Israel and the Lebanon and the notoriety surrounding Sharon did little to dent his burgeoning political career or inhibit his stance as Washington's staunchest ally in the Middle East. This despite the accusations of war crimes made against him being similar in nature, if not extent, to those levelled against the former Serbian leader Slobodan Milosevic and Iraq's dictator Saddam Hussein by the major Western nations.

In 1984, Israeli journalists Ze'ev Schiff and Ehud Yaari concluded their chapter on the massacres in their ground-breaking work *Israel's Lebanon War* with this reflection, 'If there is a moral to the painful episode of Sabra and Shatila, it has yet to be acknowledged.' As for Ariel Sharon, it can be left to some of his own words to hint at his real motives and attitudes. Transcripts of his conversations are known to include references to the Palestinian fighters in which he somewhat unambiguously states, 'I don't want a single one of them left!' At 10 a.m. on the fateful day when Rafael Eitan reported that the camps were surrounded by Israeli forces and that either the Lebanese regular units or the Christian militia were now free to enter, Sharon said, 'I'd send in the Phalangists.' This despite being later told by Eitan that 'They're thirsting for revenge' and 'there could be torrents of blood'. Later in the day Sharon would phone Prime Minister Begin and say, 'It's all over.' Though none of this can be taken as conclusive proof of guilt, the suspicion that Sharon may have conspired with the Lebanese Christians to destroy the Palestinian presence in Beirut by mass murder, torture and rape cannot be lightly dismissed.

1982 – THE DEATH OF GOD'S BANKER The death of Roberto Calvi has been called one of the great criminal mysteries of recent times. It is a strange story within a conspiratorial network stretching from corrupt Vatican figures to the Mafia and the Freemasons. Calvi was found dangling from a noose beneath Blackfriars Bridge in London in 1982 with his pockets and waistband stuffed with bricks. Ever since, questions have persisted about how this top Italian financier known throughout Italy as 'God's banker' really died. A London coroner concluded it was suicide, but Calvi's son and widow living in Montreal have doggedly tried to prove suspicions that Roberto Calvi was killed. In what appears to be a vindication of their beliefs, new forensic tests carried out on Calvi's exhumed body by an international panel for the Rome prosecutor's office have concluded the banker was the victim of murder, not suicide. The panel based its conclusion on evidence from Calvi's body that suggests very strongly that he was already dead when hung from scaffolding on the Blackfriars Bridge. The medical evidence suggested that his neck showed no signs of hanging, which has led experts to conclude he was strangled nearby and taken to the bridge by boat.

The Roberto Calvi story appears at first sight to be a far-fetched plot. But Calvi stood at the heart of one of the biggest scandals in modern banking history, one that implicated the Mafia, the Vatican and a secret Masonic lodge known as P2. As chairman of Banco Ambrosiano, he was an influential financier who was nicknamed God's banker because of his close ties to the Vatican. In June 1982, a year after being convicted of massive currency violations in Italy and with his bank teetering on collapse, he vanished. A week later, he was found hanging from beneath Blackfriars Bridge on the Thames. The London river police cut down his body from scaffolding under the bridge on the morning of 19 June. They found seven large bricks stuffed in the pockets and fly of the deceased. He was wearing a lightweight grey suit, had an expensive Patek Philippe watch on his wrist and about $14,000 (around £6,000 pounds at the time) in Swiss francs, British pounds and Italian lire in his wallet. The watch and money suggested he was not a victim of any common robbery. He also had in his pockets four pair of eyeglasses and a bogus Italian passport in the name of Gian Roberto Calvino, which was close enough to his name for him to be identified as Italy's fugitive banker.

Banco Ambrosiano collapsed with enormous debts in a $1.3 billion bankruptcy, and in the shock that followed evidence emerged of corrupt connections between Italian politicians, organised crime, the Vatican and the Masons. Calvi had made many enemies, both in the Vatican and the Mafia. Italian magistrates say he was overseeing money laundering for the Mafia and was killed in retaliation for mismanaging the plot and skimming off cash. Carlo Calvi believes his father died because he would have testified at his currency trial about the activities of offshore companies controlled by the Vatican. Near the end of his life, Roberto Calvi confided he was growing nervous about the people around him. 'He said his life was threatened but we didn't believe it until after his death,' his son said. Less publicised in the saga is the fact that Roberto Calvi had started to apply for landed-immigrant status in Canada a few months before his death. He had links with Alberta businessmen and hoped to retire in the province.

Italian investigators have since discovered a safety deposit box belonging to Roberto Calvi and held at a Milan branch of the Banco Ambrosiano. It reportedly contained a builder's brick, newspaper articles dating from the summer of 1981 and documents which police hope will help them to solve the puzzle of the banker's death. One mystery they will seek to clarify is how the bank safe remained unnoticed for all these years. It was registered in the names of Calvi and his mother and in recent years had been under the control of one of his brothers, Leone. Since the safe reportedly came to light, investigators have searched four properties belonging to Leone Calvi for further clues. Investigators said that the brick, wrapped in a copy of the newspaper *Corriere della Sera*, could constitute a cryptic reference to the Freemasons, as well as recalling the brick fragments that were found on Calvi's body. 'That brick could be a warning, a message in code,' an unnamed investigator told the Rome daily *Il Messaggero*. In 1997 Italian police charged several Mafiosi and a Sardinian businessman, Flavio Carboni, with complicity in Calvi's murder. Mafia turncoats have accused the self-confessed Mafia boss Francesco Di Carlo, who lived in the UK, of strangling Calvi to punish him for absconding with some of the *Cosa Nostra*'s money.

By 2002, however, a new inquiry came to the conclusion that Calvi was definitely murdered. A new autopsy concluded that Calvi was strangled near the bridge and then hung from it, and indeed that Calvi's neck bones did not show the kind of damage that would have been caused if he had hanged himself with a rope. It also found that his hands and fingernails were clean, and if he had stuffed bits of brick in his own pockets and climbed a rusty scaffolding to hang himself, there would have been traces under his fingernails or on his hands. Conspiracy theorists have long insisted that Calvi was murdered and they suspect Mafia involvement in his death. So who killed Roberto Calvi? He had certainly had enough enemies to pick from. Did he simply know too much about the vast financial scandals and money laundering schemes that involved banks, the Vatican, the Freemasons, organised crime and even the Italian Secret Service, many of whose senior officers were members of the P2 Masonic lodge, to be allowed to live?

1982 – ASSASSINATION OF BASHIR GEMAYEL They greet their leaders with a Hitlerian salute, sing their Arabic anthem 'Greetings to You, Syria' to the strains of 'Deutschland, Deutschland über alles' and march to the symbol of the red hurricane, a swastika in circular motion. These are the hallmarks of the Syrian Social Nationalist Party (SSNP), the oldest terrorist organisation in existence today and one of the most secret and deadly according to Middle Eastern conspiracy theorists. Western security organisations only really learned in the 1990s that a well-camouflaged arm of the SSNP had succeeded in setting up an underground terror network in Western Europe, complete with safe houses, weapons caches and forged passports. The USA has already suffered from the activities of the SSNP: the explosion aboard a TWA flight nearing Athens in April 1986, which cost the lives of four passengers, has been traced to May Mansard, a veteran member of the SSNP who left the aircraft at a previous stopover after placing a bomb under her seat.

Dedicated to the principle of establishing Greater Syria, which extends from the Euphrates to the Nile, an area that today includes Syria, Israel, Jordan, Lebanon and southeastern Turkey, the SSNP has little in common with the Shiite religious zealots of the Hizbollah, who operate from Iran to Lebanon. The SSNP secretly received money and, occasionally, small arms from the *Service de la Documentation Extérieure du Contre-Espionnage* (SDECE), who also persuaded the French authorities to turn a blind eye to the party's violent actions. The CIA also adopted this approach, viewing the SSNP as dubious but nonetheless deserving of support, because it adamantly opposed the vision of Arab unity being promoted by Nasser in the mid-1950s and it fought leftist movements. Moreover, the SSNP supported the programmes then being promoted by the West as a barrier against Soviet penetration.

The Lebanon has obviously been of paramount interest to the SSNP and by 1975 the party had been accepted into the coalition of Lebanese left-wing parties that formed around Yasser Arafat. After Arafat's forced removal by the Israelis from Beirut in 1982, the SSNP became a senior partner in the pro-Syrian camp in Lebanon. Radio Damascus even allowed one of the party's more prominent figures to broadcast a regular spot about the path to reaching Greater Syria. In May 1977 Menachem Begin's right-wing Likud Party came to power, ending nearly thirty years in which the Labour Party had dominated Israeli political life. Quite explicitly committed to a 'Greater Israel' policy, Begin expanded the Israeli relationship with the Maronites in the Lebanon, backing Pierre and Bashir Gamayel's Christian Phalangists against rival parties. Mossad, Israel's intelligence service, provided the Phalange with artillery, mortars, tanks, communications equipment, mines and explosives. Mossad officers were placed within the Christian command, ostensibly to provide help with Israeli weaponry but in reality to provide intelligence about the civil war and launch attacks against Palestinian strongholds in Lebanon. Later operations were to be extended against the Lebanese Shiites in southern Lebanon, who were then allied with the Palestinians. For the next five years, as the civil war waxed and waned in Lebanon with constantly shifting alliances, Israel continued to support the fascist Christian militia, to the tune of $100 million a year. In 1977 the Palestinians surrendered their heavy armaments under the first phase of the Shtaura agreement whereby the Lebanese government, Syria and the PLO imposed a freeze on cross-border raids by the Palestinians and attempted to resolve the civil war. The Israelis responded to this peace initiative by mounting a provocative and intensive bombing campaign in which seventy people, nearly all Lebanese, were killed. In addition, the Israeli-controlled Haddad militia in southern Lebanon launched an offensive with Israeli support aimed at disrupting the Lebanese government's plans to deploy its army in the south.

In March 1978 Israel invaded Lebanon in retaliation for a terrorist attack by Palestinian commandos, who had reached Israel by sea from Beirut and killed 34 Israelis. The bloody invasion led to the death of more than 2,000 people and drove more than 250,000 people from their homes in the south. Israeli bombardment continued in 1979. The Lebanese government compiled a list showing the scale of Lebanese casualties. Nearly 100 Lebanese were killed or wounded in just one day in April, while nearly 1,000 were killed and 224 wounded between April and August. According to Uri Avineri, the liberal Israeli journalist, Ariel Sharon had told him eight months before the invasion of Lebanon in June 1982 that he wanted to destroy the PLO in Lebanon, put the Phalangists in power – making Lebanon a kind of Christian protectorate – and get the Syrians out of Lebanon. He wanted to push the Palestinians into Syria in the hope that the Syrians would drive them down to Jordan, which would then be turned into a Palestinian state. The Israelis also imposed Phalangist Party presidential candidate Beshir Gamayel on Lebanon. To the dismay of the Israelis, Beshir tried to conduct himself as President of all Lebanon and not just a Christian militia leader, and this was to lead to a straining of relations with Israel, particularly while Sharon was still in Beirut.

When the Israel Defence Forces captured much of Beirut in 1982, Ariel Sharon neglected to order a search for SSNP activists who were believed could directly threaten the new Lebanese administration. The SSNP had been rearmed with Russian weapons by the Syrians, and its members underwent their baptism by fire in the battles waged by Syria against Arafat's forces in Tripoli in 1983 and against the Phalangist troops in the Shouf Mountains in 1984. The SSNP also played a role in instigating terrorist actions against the US marines in Beirut, although the Iranian-backed Hizbollah carried out the actual bombing.

The SSNP militia was not particularly numerous, according to Israeli intelligence. It boasts a total of only a few thousand fighters some of whom are reservists called up only in emergencies. But it has one great advantage over rivals and allies alike for, as Christians, its members enjoy greater freedom of movement than Muslims do in both the Lebanon and beyond. Moreover, in contrast to other terrorist forces, it is structured on a rigid hierarchy and exercises iron discipline. Because of its unparalleled control over its members, the SSNP has become Syria's most reliable instrument of terror, and it is employed for particularly sensitive and dangerous operations that are beyond the capabilities of the Palestinian terror groups whose headquarters are based in Damascus. Thus when President Assad let it be known that he wanted Bashir Gemayel killed before his inauguration as President of Lebanon, the SSNP were the chosen tool. An undercover SSNP agent, Habib Shartuni, planted a bomb in his own sister's apartment: Gemayel was scheduled to speak before a seminar on Phalangist ideology in the basement of the same building. A few days later Bashir Gamayel and dozens of friends, family members and other Phalangists were blown to pieces. Unusually it appears that Gemayel may have been the target of two assassination plots: one by the Syrians because he threatened their position in the Lebanon by his support for

Israel; and one by the Israelis because they believed he wasn't supportive enough and was trying to reach out to the rival Lebanese Muslim militias, who Sharon still wanted destroyed. However, it does appear that the SSNP got to him first. Either way the conspiracy to assassinate Gemayel certainly succeeded in prolonging Lebanon's nightmare of intercommunal fighting and the military occupation by Israeli and Syrian forces. Even in 2003 the legacy of that assassination can still be seen in the rival armed movements, Syrian garrisons and heavily armed Islamic terrorists in the Beka'a Valley and indeed in the ever-present threat of another Israeli invasion.

1983 – AIDS CONSPIRACY Some have argued that this is potentially the most explosive conspiracy of the century, with evidence pointing directly at the CIA, while there are those, including the CIA itself, who claim that it started off as a KGB disinformation operation to blacken the agency's reputation and, by default, that of the USA. Either way the story begins in 1983 with Dr Robert B. Strecker, who is a trained pathologist, holds a PhD in pharmacology and practised internal medicine and gastroenterology in Los Angeles. Dr Strecker and his brother, Ted, an attorney, were preparing a proposal for a health maintenance organisation for the Security Pacific Bank of California. The bank needed to know the long-term financial effects of insuring the treatment of Aids patients. This information was not readily available in 1983, so both brothers began researching the medical literature to learn what they could about this relatively new disease. The information they uncovered right from the beginning was so startling to them, so hard to believe, that it would dramatically alter both their lives and lead them on a five-year quest culminating with the creation of the Strecker Memorandum, the most controversial videotape of our time, and a remarkable set of documents called 'The Bio-Attack Alert'. Contained within the medical literature was, they believed, proof that the Aids virus and pandemic was actually predicted years ago by a world-famous virologist, among others. They found that top scientists writing in the *Bulletin of the World Health Organisation* were actually requesting that Aidslike viruses be created to study the effects on humans. In fact, the Streckers unearthed thousands of documents all supporting the man-made origin of Aids. The government was telling everyone that bites from green monkeys in Africa were responsible for the crossover into the human population but, as the Streckers' research continued, it became obvious from the documentation that the virus itself was not only created as requested, but actually deployed. Eventually, the Streckers came to realise that everything the government, the so-called Aids experts and media were telling the public was not only misleading but in some cases simply untrue.

The most dreaded fear that all oncologists (cancer doctors), virologists and immunologists live with is that some day cancer, in one form or another, will become a contagious disease, transferable from one person to another. Aids has now made that fear a reality, and if you think you are safe because you are not gay or promiscuous, or because you are not sexually active, then think again, warn the theorists. Over 100,000 Americans have already died because they didn't know the truth about Aids. Approximately 2–3 million Americans are already infected. It is claimed that as many as 1 in 60 babies born in New York City and three or four of every 100 college students in America are infected.

The most disquieting aspect of the conspiracy theory becomes apparent when the question is asked whether Aids is a biological experiment to rid the world of homosexuals, specific racial groups and other 'undesirables'. Ever since the Aids epidemic became 'official' in June 1981, there have been persistent underground rumours that Aids is a man-made epidemic with a genetically engineered (HIV) virus which was deliberately introduced into American gays and African blacks for 'elimination' purposes. The official story supplied by a top Aids expert, Robert Gallo, is that the Aids virus originated in African green monkeys and somehow 'jumped species' into humans. From there it supposedly spread to Manhattan via the Haitian connection. By repeating this story hundreds of times, government agencies and the media have turned the official monkey story into 'fact'. However, the experts and the media are silent about certain facts about Aids. For example, Aids in America can be traced back to hepatitis B experiments that were performed on thousands of gay volunteers between the years 1978–81. The experiment began in Manhattan in November 1978, when over 1,000 homosexuals and bisexuals were injected with the experimental vaccine. To be eligible for the experiment, the men had to be young, healthy, promiscuous and under the age of forty. Most of the men chosen were white. Three months after the experiment began at the New York City Blood Center, the first Aids case was discovered in a young white Manhattan gay. Beginning in March 1980, similar vaccine experiments took place in Los Angeles, San Francisco, St Louis, Denver and Chicago. In the autumn of 1980, the first Aids case was reported in a young, white, San Francisco gay man. A report from the Centers for Disease Control (CDC) in Atlanta, Georgia, in August 1981 covering the first 26 Aids cases showed that all were gay and previously healthy; 20 were from Manhattan; 6 were from Los Angeles and San Francisco; 25 were white; the average age was 39; and most were well educated. This is essentially the epidemiological profile of gays who were injected in the hepatitis B study.

The experiment was directed by Wolf Szmuness, MD, a Pole who was taken prisoner by the Russians in WW2 and sent to Siberia. After the war, he was trained as a medical doctor in the Soviet Union. He returned to Poland, defected from the communist state in 1969 and arrived penniless in New York City. He then got a job as a lab technician at the NYC Blood Center. Within a decade he was made Professor of Epidemiology at Columbia University and was placed in charge of the gay hepatitis study. Through State Department connections he was allowed to return to Moscow to speak as a hepatitis expert. Szmuness died in 1982 from cancer.

In the decade before HIV/Aids appeared, it is alleged virologists were busy learning how to transfer viruses from one animal species to another, in order to create a cancer-causing virus that could destroy the immune system. The purpose was to artificially create cancer in the laboratory. Thus the laboratory virologists discovered how to make animal viruses jump species. These genetically engineered animal viruses jumped species when researchers planted them into cancerous human cell cultures. Some of the people involved in deliberately infecting animals with cancer-causing and immunosuppressive viruses were later put in charge of the CDC-sponsored hepatitis B trials, which used gay men as guinea pigs. The virologists were aware of the possibility that one of these dangerous, altered cancer viruses might escape from their high-tech labs. Nevertheless, the researchers were determined to prove that animal cancer viruses could cause human cancer in what may now be considered to be a high-risk scientific experiment with little medical justification for the potential or actual dangers involved.

In 1973 a Biohazard Conference convened in Asilomar, California. The purpose was to set up government agencies to provide assistance in the event that one of these genetically engineered viruses escaped from the laboratory.

Aids cases in Africa and Haiti started to appear around the same time that gay cases were reported in Manhattan. Furthermore, a study group of elderly and now sexually inactive people in Kampala in Uganda, were tested. None showed HIV infection, suggesting that Aids has not been around 'for years' in central Africa.

On 11 May 1987, *The Times* newspaper in the UK carried a cover story connecting the World Health Organisation's African smallpox vaccine programs with the outbreak of Aids in central Africa. Even Robert Gallo agreed that the WHO vaccine program, which inoculated millions of blacks, could have awakened the 'dormant' Aids virus. This extremely important story was killed in the United States, and the story never appeared on TV or in any major newspaper.

The idea of Aids as a biological experiment is not without precedent. Over the past few decades, there is proof that government agencies have repeatedly exposed people to biological agents in secret experiments authorised by government agencies. The most well-known and notorious experiment was performed on 'poor Alabama blacks' infected with syphilis. In this Tuskagee experiment, the racist doctors wanted to determine what would happen to Afro-American men if they were not treated for syphilis. The physicians wanted to follow the progress of the infection until the men died and autopsies were performed. The doctors told the men they had 'bad blood'. The men were never told they had syphilis, and curative penicillin treatment was never offered. As a result, the men unknowingly spread syphilis to their wives, lovers and children. This experiment was conducted under the auspices of the US Public Health Service for forty years from 1932.

If it is the case that Aids is man-made, was the work carried out by the United States in secret laboratories at Camp Detrick and in other government facilities as part of a CIA project or is it, as the agency itself claims, all a fiendish KGB disinformation operation?

1983 – IRAN-CONTRA CONSPIRACY A conspiracy of far greater importance that the 'local unpleasantness' of Watergate and one that by rights should have bought down not just the President, but the whole administration as well. However, Reagan sailed though the political problems that arose when this conspiracy became public property, with little or no significant difficulty or lasting damage to the Republicans.

CIA Director William Casey and Ronald Reagan began putting this operation together in 1982. It involved building up a paramilitary group called the Contras to overthrow the left-wing government of

Nicaragua. The Contras were supposed to be seen as an indigenous fighting force, with the US role minimised or hidden. However, there were problems with this war at a very early stage – particularly because the Contras weren't very good at fighting. They would go into some of the small villages in Northern Nicaragua and commit atrocities, loot buildings and then disappear back into the jungle when the Nicaraguan army turned up. Congress began hearing about how the Contras lined up people in villages and killed them. The CIA prepared a plan written by the head of military operations, Rudy Enders. It was a blueprint for the overthrow of the regime, and not the interdiction of illegal arms to El Salvador that Congress believed they had sanctioned.

By early 1983 it became clear even to the CIA that the Contras weren't what they hoped for and because the whole operation was taking so long, it risked public exposure. CIA director Bill Casey was often misperceived by commentators; he was in fact a very smart man and he was extremely committed ideologically to what he was doing. He was a person who believed in making things happen, whatever the rules might be. He accepted in 1983 that plans had to be changed and quickly. The CIA needed more time to train the Contras and they had to create the impression the Contras were a fine fighting force. So it was decided that the CIA would start to send in its own paramilitaries and specially-trained 'Latino assets' to carry out the attacks which the Contras could then claim credit for. These included incidents such as blowing up the oil depot in the little town of Corinto on the coast and sabotaging the oil pipeline in Porto San Dino. Casey had some other interesting ideas. He began to put together what became known later as the Psychological Operations Manual or the Assassination Manual, and in the summer of 1983 he authorised another booklet on sabotage and homegrown terrorism. He also put together a remarkable operation called the Public Diplomacy Apparatus, which was to shape and finance the operation the American public would finally see. Inside the administration this was called 'perception management', and with US taxpayers' dollars they set up new facilities such as the 'Office of Public Diplomacy', which reported in theory to the State Department but reported in reality to National Security Council staff. It was organised by an officer named Walter Raymond, a thirty-year-old veteran of the CIA and who was effectively the top propaganda expert for the agency, and operated directly under Bill Casey. Psychological warfare experts were brought in from Fort Bragg to handle the cable traffic coming in from Central America. The main purpose of these specialists was to identify exploitable themes that could be used to encourage the American public to be even more angry about what was happening in Central America.

However, disclosure of the so-called Iran initiative in early November 1986 caused real problems. The President had authorised the first shipment of missiles to Iran through Israel without following proper procedure in 1985. He had not signed a finding and was therefore in violation of the Arms Export Control Act. The Iran-Contra scandal had now broken publicly. It consisted of three parts: the illegal shipments of weapons to the Contras in defiance of the law, the Boland Amendment; the violation of the Arms Export Control Act; and the use of money from illegal arms sales to Iran for the purpose of arming and supporting the Contras in their attempt to overthrow the Nicaraguan regime, the so-called 'diversion'. The White House stood its ground on 'diversion' and lied about the rest. Vice President Bush even went so far as to deny that he knew about the Contras; obviously he didn't read the *New York Times* or the *Washington Post* because they certainly knew about them. The White House put out false chronologies on Iran to show that the President did not know about the 1985 shipment.

The focus for the press and for Congress as the investigation geared up was whether the President was involved in a felony under the Arms Export Control Act. Was he involved in another type of crime by defying a law, a law he had passed, the Boland Amendment? Could the President unilaterally conduct war using third-country funding? All of these were very important questions, but the emphasis was on the element of diversion. And on that they felt they could contain the threat as long as John Poindexter, a senior White House aide, said the buck stopped here, which of course, as an ultra-loyal Reaganite, he did.

At this point the real Iran-Contra conspiracy got underway to contain the scandal. Obviously the White House and the Republicans had a very strong interest in a cover-up, but it actually seemed as if the Democrats and the media were prepared to let the President off the hook in order to contain the political fallout. Nobody, it seemed, wanted another Watergate. As long as someone got thrown to the wolves, someone was held responsible and could be found guilty, the administration was safe. Colonel Oliver North was duly lined up as the official scapegoat.

However, there was a potentially far more serious aspect to the whole Iran-Contra affair. The CIA's and later Oliver North's arrangements of extra-governmental financial support for the Contras had a deleterious impact on some US citizens. These arrangements led to well-documented US government involvement with, and support provided for, important drug traffickers in Mexico, Honduras, El Salvador, Costa Rica and Panama, as well as domestic drug smugglers in Florida, Arkansas, Louisiana, Kentucky, Michigan and California. This is the list of countries and US States which are fully documented; other areas are suspected but not proven. This recurring pattern of US government involvement with organised drug crime cannot be dismissed as accidental or coincidental. In some cases, Contras and their supporters became traffickers only *after* their contact with CIA field officers. It is believed that some Contra recruits were given to understand from their CIA handlers that funds should be raised for the Contras by *any means*, which was usually taken to include drug trafficking. Senior Contra officials claim to have heard the same indirect guidance from at least one senior CIA officer. It is also a matter of record that the CIA established contacts with those already known to US government officials as major criminals involved in drug trafficking. An example is Norwin Meneses, a highly publicised Contra supporter who had been listed as a trafficker in Drug Enforcement Agency records for some ten to fifteen years before the CIA enlisted his support. The CIA became, deliberately or not, a major partner in numerous drug crime syndicates and was involved in drugs pipelines to match the supply of illegal weapons.

The Iran-Contra affair hid a litany of plots, assassinations and, most shockingly of all, a network that provided for an intimate connection between the secret army and drug gangs. The same people were simultaneously shipping illegal arms, illegal drugs and receiving massive financial handouts of US taxpayers' money. Reagan survived intact and Bush succeeded him in the White House. North was found guilty of various sins and omissions in 1989 and the real political significance of the Iran-Contra affair was largely lost in the aftermath of the collapse of Communism and the Gulf War.

1984 – MURDER OF HILDA MURRELL Clear-cut examples of politically motivated murder are thankfully rare, at least on the mainland of the UK. However, on 21 March 1984 78-year-old Hilda Murrell was found murdered near her home in Shrewsbury. To this day nobody has been charged with the murder and it is almost certain that despite considerable advances in forensic science nobody ever will be. A trial would probably prove hugely embarrassing to both the police and the security services as well as initiating an unwanted political scandal and renewed media accusations of an official cover-up.

Hilda Murrell was no ordinary little old lady. She was a caring and concerned member of the public who was horrified at the levels of radiation that were reportedly being churned out by the Sellafield nuclear power station. The Irish Sea and the Cumbrian coastline are reported to be one of the most radioactively polluted environments in the world. Much of the sealife in the area is reportedly radioactive, as are the beaches, the sea spray, the air and even local dust. Hilda was so concerned that for many years she had been an active and articulate anti-nuclear supporter, and was, at the time of her death, preparing a paper to be submitted as evidence to the Sizewell nuclear power station inquiry. This is what, according to members of Special Branch and MI5, made her an obvious subversive, and this is why they put her under intense surveillance.

At around 12.45 p.m. on Wednesday 21 March, Hilda was abducted; it is believed by an MI5 contracted agent who had broken into her home. She was driven in her own car, allegedly by the agent who was now wearing a blonde wig and Hilda Murrell's hat, while being physically restrained in the passenger seat. Not surprisingly, Hilda put up as much of a fight as she could despite being a weak and frail old lady. Witnesses state that the car was being driven in a somewhat erratic manner at times, suggesting that Hilda must have resisted fiercely. Approximately twenty minutes later her car was abandoned. A local farmer reported the car to the police at 5.20 p.m. that day, and again on Friday, two days later. During this period, the local police made absolutely no attempt to find out if Hilda, the registered owner of the car, was all right, or how her car had come to be where it was found. On Saturday morning, 24 March, Hilda Murrell's body was found near where her car had been found. She had been systematically and ritualistically stabbed. A search of her home revealed that the telephone had been professionally disconnected, but that nothing obvious had been stolen. It is suspected that a thorough search had been made for sensitive papers or documents relating to her campaigning activities.

Murrell's nephew, Rob Green, a retired naval officer has suggested, however, that the real interest the secret state may have had in his aunt was her supposed possession of papers relating to the sinking of the Argentine cruiser *General Belgrano* during the Falklands Campaign.

Alternatively, a new contact that Hilda Murrell had recently made might have interested MI5 far more than either her Sizewell documents or any possible embarrassing material on the *Belgrano*. In the months before her death, Hilda had been meeting a retired nuclear scientist called Don Arnott. Arnott claims to have discovered a fundamental error in the design of the Sizewell reactor relating to a dangerous problem with a control rod system that if overheated might prove to be fundamentally unsound. In April 1983, about two weeks after he last saw Hilda Murrell, Arnott was speaking at an anti-nuclear conference at the Connaught Rooms in London, where he had a heart attack after the coffee break. Despite having had no previous reported heart trouble before or since, it put him in intensive care and out of the Sizewell inquiry in which no one else raised the control rod problem. Don Arnott remained convinced that corners were cut in the reactor's design, risking a Chernobyl-type catastrophe.

The freelance MI5 operative responsible for Hilda's surveillance, and the most plausible candidate for this particularly disgusting crime, is believed by many to be a Victor Norris, reportedly a fantasist with satanic and fascist beliefs, and certainly guilty of sex crimes, having previously served a six-year custodial sentence for pimping out his young daughter to his various paedophile friends. Norris was never charged with Hilda Murrell's murder. However, it is understood that the police did not pursue anyone else for the crime, and as Norris was working for MI5 at the time the establishment closed ranks and the case was quietly allowed to disappear from the headlines. Were agents working for the nuclear industry or MI5 to interrogate and murder Hilda Murrell? Perhaps they only meant to frighten an elderly lady half to death, but the contracted agent used was a criminal with a cruel and unstable nature. Either way, the suspicion remains that Miss Murrell was killed because of what she knew, or what someone thought she knew.

1984 – GET SCARGILL The Conservative government of Margaret Thatcher was determined to defeat the national strike by the powerful mineworkers' union and was prepared to use virtually any means to do so, at least according to conspiracy theorists – and a fair number of impartial observers as well. Having been on the receiving end of the miners' militancy both during Edward Heath's administration in the early 1970s and again in the early days of Thatcher's own government, ministers, security officials and industry leaders are firmly believed to have conspired together to produce a plan that included black propaganda, burglary, falsification of records and intimidation.

National Union of Mineworkers (NUM) president Arthur Scargill had first become a target for the security services after he masterminded the closure of the Saltley coke depot through mass picketing, during the 1972 miners' strike, but it wasn't until the 1984–85 miners' strike that MI5 was allegedly involved in a covert plot to discredit him. Scargill was one of the most prominent symbols of militant trade unionism in the country and was a feared and hated target of the right. At the start of the 1984–85 strike, Margaret Thatcher personally authorised MI5 to set up a 'Get Scargill' operation, aimed at destroying the NUM leader 'politically and personally'. The phone-tapping operation against the NUM during the strike was the most ambitious ever mounted by MI5, certainly in an industrial dispute. With the help of GCHQ, the NUM headquarters in Sheffield and the offices and homes of branch officials around the country were bugged. Transcripts from these taps were sent to the National Reporting Centre at New Scotland Yard, which was responsible for deploying police officers in the coalfields, and to MI5's F2 Branch transcription service then based in Curzon Street House in the heart of Mayfair. MI5 sent intelligence reports to the Civil Contingencies Unit in the Cabinet Office, while undercover Special Branch police and both MI5 officers and contracted private operatives masqueraded as miners during the strike, singling out miners for arrest or acting as *agents provocateurs* to provoke violent incidents.

In June 1984 two plain-clothes policemen were caught red-handed in disguise at the Creswell Strike Centre in Derbyshire. They were identified by a local reporter, Carmel O'Toole, whose newspaper, the *Worksop Guardian*, carried the story on its front page. However, the national media turned a blind eye to this important revelation and Scargill and other NUM national officials, such as the Scottish miners' leader Mick McGahey, remained under constant surveillance. McGahey's regular London hotel, the County, in Bloomsbury, was bugged by MI5 and so was the North Sea Fish Restaurant in Leigh Street, the fish-and-chip shop near the old NUM headquarters in Gower Street, London, where Scargill, McGahey and others used to meet to discuss tactics. Throughout the year-long dispute, the security services leased the building opposite the NUM's headquarters at St. James's House in Sheffield. Every single NUM branch and lodge secretary had their phones monitored, as well as sympathetic support group activists and trade unionists across the country. One former MI5 employee later described a training session where a woman lecturer told recruits, rather boastfully, that MI5 had 'long-term moles inside certain trade unions, so deep that even their families don't know their true purpose.'

Thatcher also ordered the mobilisation of British and US electronic surveillance networks throughout Europe to track down the movement of miners' funds invested abroad. This operation illegally breached the security of European bank transactions and, according to a parliamentary motion signed by five labour MPs in 1993, Stella Rimington, head of MI5's F2 Branch and later the first female director-general of the Security Service, sent an *agent provocateur*, rumoured to be Roger Windsor, into the NUM 'to destabilise and sabotage the union at its most critical juncture'. Windsor had previously been employed as finance officer of Public Services International (PSI), a global umbrella organisation for public-sector unions based in London, which had a history of involvement with British and US intelligence services. PSI was the front for a joint CIA/MI5 coup in the 1960s against Cheddi Jagan, the Prime Minister of British Guinea.

After joining the NUM staff as finance officer in 1983, Roger Windsor was quickly promoted to chief executive, no less than second in command to Scargill himself and a position which gave him privileged access to the most sensitive decisions and arrangements made by the union. Windsor was alleged to have created discontent between other senior members of the NUM and advocated the transfer of NUM funds into overseas trusts and accounts, in order to prevent possible sequestration. All of his recommendations were subsequently found to offer no protection to the union's assets and to involve tax disadvantages. Furthermore, Windsor's elaborate efforts to hide the NUM's funds overseas were the main basis for the courts' unprecedented imposition of receivership on the union. This was the worst thing that happened to the NUM; it paralysed much of the union's work during a decisive period of the strike; it cost millions of pounds; and it tied the union's leadership up in endless litigation. In spite of all the elaborate planning and financial manoeuvring arranged by Windsor, the sequestrators were tipped off about the whereabouts of the NUM's money and they traced the union's hidden cash very quickly. As Scargill later put it, 'They always seemed to be one step ahead of us.' Then, in the middle of the strike, and reportedly without the knowledge of the rest of the NUM executive,

Windsor visited Libya and was televised embracing Colonel Gaddafi. Coming barely six months after the murder of a policewoman outside the Libyan Embassy in London, when relations between Britain and Libya were at an all-time low, Windsor's trip was a public relations disaster for the NUM and led to widespread condemnation of the union in the British media.

MI5 was also involved in the production of a forged letter purportedly signed by David Prendergast, financial secretary of the Nottinghamshire Union of Democratic Mineworkers (UDM), which exposed the UDM as prepared to use undemocratic methods to link up with the electricians' union as part of an alternative right-wing TUC. The letter was circulated anonymously throughout the Nottinghamshire coalfield and the media in the immediate aftermath of the strike. As soon as it was shown to be a forgery, Prendergast began libel proceedings against Scargill, NUM general-secretary Peter Heathfield and the NUM itself. Although Scargill and Heathfield were dropped from the action, the forgery case still ended up costing the NUM more than £193,000 costs and damages in an out-of-court settlement.

The intelligence services even made an abortive attempt to deposit £500,000 in a Scargill-linked bank account in Dublin, with the aim of framing him as an embezzler: the transaction was set up to make it appear that Scargill had arranged for the 'disappearance' of large quantities of cash. Arrangements were made for the cash to be transferred from a Paris branch of the Bank of Credit and Commerce International (BCCI), which had intimate connections to American and British intelligence, but suspicions were aroused at the Dublin bank and the phoney deposit fiasco became the subject of a high-level official complaint to the British authorities by the Dublin government.

Windsor resigned from the NUM in 1989 and made a series of allegations against Scargill in the *Daily Mirror*, for which he was paid £80,000 by Robert Maxwell. Windsor claimed that the NUM had received money from Libya and that Scargill had hidden the money away and was guilty of financial irregularities and corruption. The *Mirror* conducted a lengthy front-page banner campaign against Scargill, branding him a liar and an embezzler of union funds. Windsor had allegedly arranged his Libyan contacts through a Doncaster-based Pakistani businessman, Altaf Abbasi, who worked for South Yorkshire Special Branch. Abbasi claimed that he had brought suitcases containing £150,000 worth of Libyan cash through

Heathrow Airport and that this money, which was intended for striking miners, was actually used to pay off the home mortgages of Scargill, Peter Heathfield and himself. The tabloid press campaign against Scargill grew more vociferous each day, with other papers regurgitating the *Mirror*'s fictitious claims, front-page headlines such as SCARGILL UNION IN £1 MILLION SCANDAL, GADDAFI: HOW I HANDED OVER THE LIBYAN CASH TO ARTHUR SCARGILL and Maxwell claiming that Scargill had not only demanded cash from Colonel Gaddafi, but guns as well. The affair was seized on by both Tory and Labour politicians, with calls for criminal prosecutions. Labour leader Neil Kinnock, who was fighting to turn the party drastically rightwards, and who loathed Arthur Scargill, joined in the calls for an inquiry and even presented the team of *Mirror* journalists responsible for the anti-Scargill smear campaign with the British Press Awards Reporter of the Year prize. The *Mirror* stories, and further damning publicity repeated in two episodes of Central TV's *Cook Report*, led to an inquiry by Gavin Lightman, QC.

For a time, speculation was rife that Scargill would be forced out of his job or even end up in jail. Gavin Lightman QC, now a High Court judge, led the inquiry into Scargill's financial affairs. However, despite Lightman's unjustified savaging of Scargill, all the allegations against Scargill were eventually found in court to be entirely untrue. Documents had proven that when Windsor and Abbasi claimed the Libyan cash was being brought into Britain in suitcases, it had still not been released; that the money was never delivered to Scargill and the NUM; that the money identified by Windsor as Libyan came from another unidentified source more than a month earlier; and that neither Scargill nor Heathfield had any mortgages to pay off, having already paid them fully several years earlier. In addition, the special investigating office of the Inland Revenue concluded in August 1992 that there was no corruption whatsoever in the NUM's finances and that the union's various accounts had been valid trusts which showed no signs of impropriety. Most major newspapers ignored this story. The damage in terms of publicity which had branded Scargill as corrupt in the minds of the British public, had already been done and the union had been drained of more than £750,000 in legal bills. Abbasi was later convicted of plotting to blow up mosques in Pakistan. At the time of Maxwell's campaign against Scargill, the *Daily Mirror* was the only mass-circulation paper which supported the Labour Party and, as surveys carried out at the time by the National

Coal Board showed, it was by far the most widely read daily paper among miners. There is no doubt that the attacks on Scargill and the NUM were effective because they appeared in the *Mirror*. Had the stories been run in a traditionally Tory paper like the *Daily Mail* or *Daily Telegraph*, they would have been easier to dismiss as typical attacks by the Tory press. Terry Pattinson, the main journalist behind the *Mirror*'s campaign against Scargill, later admitted that he had been approached by MI5 to work for them. This is in the main the view put forwards by those who accept that there was a widespread and determined political conspiracy between the government of Mrs Thatcher, the security services, the mining industry and certain elements of the news media to 'Get Scargill'. That it happened in a supposedly democratic country is disturbing; that it was not exposed by the free press is, to many independent observers, the most scandalous aspect.

1984 – ASSASSINATION OF MRS GANDHI An ill-starred dynasty with great similarities to the Kennedys: Mrs Gandhi came from a family steeped in politics, she was assassinated, one of her sons died in an aircraft accident and another was also assassinated after a term as Prime Minister. Indira Gandhi was the only child of Kamla and Jawaharlal Nehru. She spent part of her childhood in Allahabad, where the Nehrus had their family residence, and part in Switzerland, where her mother Kamla convalesced from her periodic illnesses. She received her college education at Somerville College, Oxford. A famous photograph from her childhood shows her sitting by the bedside of Mahatma Gandhi, as he recovered from one of his fasts; and though she was not actively involved in the freedom struggle, she came to know the entire Indian political leadership. After India's attainment of independence in 1947, and the ascendancy of Jawaharlal Nehru, then a widower, to the office of Prime Minister, Indira Gandhi managed the official residence of her father and accompanied him on his numerous foreign trips. She had been married in 1942 to Feroze Gandhi, who rose to some eminence as a parliamentarian and politician of integrity but found himself disliked by his more famous father-in-law. Feroze died in 1960 before he could consolidate his own political position. In 1964, the year of her father's death, Indira Gandhi was elected to Parliament for the first time and she was to become the Minister of Information and Broadcasting in the government of Lal Bahadur Shastri. When Shastri died unexpectedly of a heart attack less than two years after assuming office, the numerous contenders for the position of the Prime Minister, unable to agree among themselves, picked Indira Gandhi as a compromise candidate, each probably thinking that she would be easily to manipulate. Indira Gandhi, however, showed extraordinary political skills and ruthlessness and eventually forced her rivals out of power. She held the office of Prime Minister from 1966 to 1977.

Mrs Gandhi was riding the crest of popularity after India's triumph in the war of 1971 against Pakistan and the explosion of a nuclear device in 1974, which helped to further enhance her reputation among middle-class Indians as a tough and shrewd political leader. However, by 1973 Delhi and northern India were being rocked by demonstrations at high inflation, the poor state of the economy, rampant corruption and the poor standards of living among the working class. In June 1975 the High Court of Allahabad found Mrs Gandhi guilty of using illegal practices during her last election campaign and ordered her to vacate her seat. There were demands for her resignation. Mrs Gandhi's response was to declare a state of emergency, under which her political opponents were imprisoned, constitutional rights abrogated and the press placed under strict censorship. Meanwhile, the eldest of her two sons, Sanjay Gandhi, started to run the country as though it were his personal fiefdom, earning the fierce hatred of many who suffered from his actions. He ordered the removal of slum dwellings and, in an attempt to curb India's growing population, initiated a highly resented programme of forced sterilisation. In early 1977, confident that she had neutralised her main opposition, Mrs Gandhi called for fresh elections and found herself trounced by a newly formed coalition of several political parties. Her Congress Party lost badly at the polls. Many declared that she was a spent force; but, three years later, she was to return as Prime Minister of India. That same year, however, her son Sanjay was killed in an aircraft crash.

In her second period of holding the office of Prime Minister, Indira Gandhi was preoccupied by efforts to resolve the political problems in the state of Punjab. In her attempt to crush the Sikh militant secessionist movement led by Jarnail Singh Bindranwale, she ordered an assault upon the Golden Temple in Amritsar, the holiest of the Sikh shrines. It was here that Bindranwale and his armed supporters were based and it was from the Golden Temple that they waged their campaign of terrorism, not merely against the central government but against moderate Sikhs and Hindus. Operation Bluestar, launched by elite units of the Indian army in June 1984, led to the death of Bindranwale and many of the Sikh militants. However, the Golden Temple had been damaged, and Mrs Gandhi earned the undying hatred of Sikhs who bitterly resented the desecration of their sacred space. In November the same year, Mrs Gandhi was assassinated, at her residence, by two of her own Sikh bodyguards who claimed to be avenging the insult heaped upon the Sikh nation.

Mrs Gandhi acquired a formidable international reputation as a stateswoman, and there is no doubt that she was extraordinarily skilled in politics. However, the use of the army to resolve internal disputes greatly increased in her time, and she encouraged a culture of sycophancy and nepotism. At her death, her older son, Rajiv Gandhi, was elected party head and Prime Minister in her place. Rajiv Gandhi was eventually forced out of office in the 1989 general elections. He was assassinated while campaigning in southern India two years later in 1991.

The assassination of Mrs Gandhi does not usually rate highly on the conspiracy theorists' Richter scale, but she was a hugely important and influential figure throughout Asia and the developing world. She had made serious enemies of certain elements of the Sikhs, her own ruling party and the Hindu nationalists. It is inconceivable that at a time of open Sikh rebellion her bodyguards, both Sikhs, had not been properly vetted and monitored. A conspiracy to allow her assassination and organised by those close to her seems more than likely. Perhaps Indira Gandhi was after all a victim of her own unbending devotion to her beliefs and policies, and of her unwillingness to compromise to ensure vital support and protection in a crisis.

1986 – STALKER AFFAIR Following the accusations of a conspiracy against Harold Wilson and the controversy in Northern Ireland over a shoot-to-kill policy, and the collusion between the security forces and Protestant death squads, it was considered politically expedient to appoint a respected British police officer to lead an investigation into at least some of the allegations. However, it seems probable that he was not expected to be so conscientious or so effective in discovering politically sensitive material relating to events in the province. Never granted the full co-operation of the Royal Ulster Constabulary (RUC), Stalker persevered, despite being warned that he was making enemies. Eventually Stalker was considered to be getting too close for comfort, and a crude but effective series of false allegations of financial impropriety were made about his past conduct. He was immediately removed from the investigation and, though able to clear his name, the opportunity to find the real truth about events in Ulster had disappeared. The conspirators did their best to destroy a good man in order to hide the truth about murder and brutality in Northern Ireland.

The Stalker Affair began in Northern Ireland on 11 November 1982 when three unarmed men were shot dead by members of a special RUC anti-terrorist unit just outside Lurgan. Less than two weeks later, on 24 November, two youths were shot – one killed and the other seriously wounded – by the same unit in a hay shed also just outside Lurgan. The dead youth was Michael Tighe, who was seventeen years old, and the wounded one was Martin Macauley, who was nineteen. Three old pre-war rifles were recovered from the hay shed, but no ammunition found. Three weeks after that, on 12 December, two more unarmed men were shot dead, yet again by a member of the same special unit, this time in the city of Armagh. Initially the shootings were investigated by other members of the RUC and a file sent to the Director of Public Prosecutions for Northern Ireland. The first prosecution to come before the courts related to the last of the three incidents and was that of Constable John Robinson of the RUC's special unit. During the trial it emerged that many of the police's original accounts of the shootings were in fact lies. In a headline-making appearance in the witness box, Robinson said that he had been instructed by senior police officers to tell lies in his official statements. Robinson was eventually acquitted. His admissions caused uproar, fuelling accusations of a shoot-to-kill policy. Demands were made for an outside investigation.

In May 1984, the RUC's boss, Sir John Hermon, asked the Deputy Chief Constable of Greater Manchester, John Stalker, a highly regarded officer with a long track record as a detective, to conduct an inquiry. He appeared to be the establishment's man, recommended by his Chief Constable, James Anderton, and Sir Phillip Myers, Her Majesty's Inspector of Constabulary. Stalker set about the task with vigour. In September 1985 he gave a highly critical interim report, recommending the prosecution of eleven officers, to Hermon. He found that his relationship with the RUC was rapidly cooling. For example, one vital piece of evidence Stalker needed for the inquiry was a tape recording of the secret MI5 bug placed in the hay shed where the second shooting had occurred. Stalker asked Hermon for the tape; he promised to hand it over, and then refused. Stalker made it clear that he was unhappy with this decision. In May 1986, just before Stalker was about to confront the RUC with even more specific allegations against certain officers, he was removed from the case.

In 1986 Kevin Taylor was a successful businessman, the former chairman of the Manchester Conservative Association, and was living in a plush converted mill on the outskirts of the city. When John Stalker was removed from the inquiry into the Royal Ulster Constabulary's shoot-to-kill policy, it was his friendship with Taylor, who was suspected of criminal dealing, that was cited as the reason. Taylor suddenly became a national media figure and was to be subjected to a massive four-year police investigation that resulted in his bankruptcy but prosecution on a minor fraud charge only. Taylor subsequently sued the Manchester police for malicious prosecution and claims he was the victim of a high-level conspiracy to discredit Stalker.

What happened has long been the subject of controversy. Many journalists who investigated the Stalker affair believe him to have been the victim of either or both of two cabals of police officers who had turned against him. The first was a group of top level police officers, including Anderton, Hermon and Myers (perhaps under the orders of the government). The second was a group of senior detectives within the Greater Manchester police who wanted Stalker, a non-Freemason, removed as overall head of the CID. All those officers maintain they were only acting properly. Chief Constable Anderton had promoted Peter Topping to Detective Chief Superintendent in charge of CID operations. Topping was later to become famous for his extensive and highly publicised search for bodies on Saddleworth Moor in the Myra Hindley case in the late 1980s. In the Taylor court case, Stalker described Topping as a good administrator but an inexperienced detective promoted over the heads of several far more experienced officers. Quickly, Topping and his allies had made little secret of their disdain for many of the long-serving members of the CID who they portrayed either as corrupt or old-fashioned. Topping's allies saw John Stalker as the key proponent of the old-timers. Topping began placing his own men into key positions in the CID. Stalker said good officers were being moved out of specialist HQ departments to be replaced by Freemasons: 'I tackled DCS Topping about it. Topping was very proud to admit he was a Freemason. He said that he thought Freemasons were people he could trust and he would favour them in certain departments – but said ability came first and Freemasonry second.'

The schism was so bad that Topping set up a major secret inquiry team called the Drugs Intelligence Unit without informing a number of senior colleagues. Retired DCS John Thorburn, who was Stalker's number two in the shoot-to-kill inquiry and CID policy chief from 1985, said, giving evidence in Taylor's case, that Topping's secret unit caused a cancer through the force. The Drugs Intelligence Unit was not a drugs unit: the name was just a cover. However, one question that is still unresolved is whether it was set up to monitor organised crime or whether, from the start, it was aimed at the relationship between Taylor and Stalker. According to Topping's secret unit, Taylor was in social contact with members of the Quality Street Gang (QSG). The QSG was the name given to a loose-knit group of Manchester's leading villains who were involved in everything from serious crime to running arms to the IRA. Topping's secret unit became convinced that Taylor, while not a member of the QSG, was laundering money for them and had lent his yacht, moored in Spain, for drug running. However, real evidence was harder to come by. Topping's secret unit kept Taylor under constant surveillance for an incredible 114 days. He was also subject to telephone tapping and had his mail opened. Stalker's friendship with Taylor was open and well known to James Anderton.

The basis for Topping's investigation into the relationship came from two key conversations. In court, former DCS Bernard McGourlay said that he played golf in June 1984 with a Manchester businessman he had never met before called Gerry Waring, who mentioned a number of names of men associated with the QSG. McGourlay said, 'He went on in quite a joking manner about Mr Taylor and parties at his home in Summerset. He said one of my bosses went to the parties. Later I approached Mr Waring in the car park, told him I was curious to know who the officer was and he said it was Stalker. I was very concerned.' McGourlay said that he thought Stalker should have been warned about what was being said, and two days later he went to see Mr Topping in confidence. Around the same time two officers of Topping's secret unit interrogated a long-standing police informant called David Burton, a well-known conman and fraudster. He made allegations against Taylor of crimes for which he has never subsequently been charged. Burton also spoke of the Stalker/Taylor friendship. Anyone familiar with Burton would have known he was a less than credible witness. But Topping compiled a report of all the gossip and rumour on Stalker and passed it on to

James Anderton. It became the basis for Stalker's removal from duty. In court, Stalker described the report as 'histrionic and self-justifying'.

The timing of these events is interesting. Stalker had again asked the RUC for the MI5 tape. He was also due to interview Hermon on 30 April 1986; the RUC chief failed to keep the appointment. On 9 May 1986, Topping's officers raided Taylor's home. They took away, among other things, half a dozen photos of Stalker and his wife at a party given by Taylor some five years before. Those pictures were taken, along with Topping's report, to a secret meeting on 19 May in Scarborough of senior police officers, including Anderton and Myers. They decided Stalker would be investigated and taken off the shoot-to-kill inquiry. On 28 May 1986 Stalker received a phone call from Anderton removing him from all duties. He was suspended a month later. The Chief Constable of West Yorkshire, Colin Sampson, was asked to conduct an inquiry into all allegations concerning Stalker and also took over the shoot-to-kill inquiry. Anderton, when requesting Stalker's suspension, gave the local Police Authority chairman a report written by DCS Topping alleging that Stalker was 'an IRA sympathiser'. No evidence has ever been produced that even begins to support this remarkable accusation.

Some observers have argued Anderton and Topping did the right thing in tackling suspicions over Stalker's relationship with Taylor. However, Anderton had never given Stalker any indication that he was unhappy about his long-standing friendship with Taylor. The police intelligence implicating Stalker was little more than tittle-tattle that would have been treated with caution by experienced detectives. No one has found a shred of evidence that Stalker acted improperly in his friendship with Taylor.

Colin Sampson produced his report, alleging that Stalker had infringed some minor rules about using police staff cars. Stalker was reinstated to his post in the Greater Manchester police, but concluded that working with Anderton would be impossible. In March 1987 he retired to write his memoirs. Stalker himself said in his autobiography, 'I cannot impute mischief or malevolence to anyone, but nevertheless I believe, as do many members of the public, that I was hurriedly removed because I was on the threshold of causing a major police scandal and political row that would have resulted in several resignations and general mayhem.'

In early 1988 the British government acknowledged that the Stalker/Sampson inquiry in Northern Ireland had produced prima facie evidence of a conspiracy to pervert the course of justice by RUC men, but announced that no criminal proceedings would take place. They then appointed yet another senior British mainland police officer, Charles Kelly, the Chief Constable of Staffordshire, to investigate the RUC. Eventually, the only punishments handed out to any of the police officers were reprimands. The government had now successfully seen off attempts to find out why Michael Tighe, a seventeen-year-old youth with no paramilitary links, was shot dead by the RUC in May 1982, and much else has been swept under the carpet too. If nothing else, the Stalker affair proves beyond a shadow of doubt that in Britain, officials, even senior policeman, can be appointed to jobs that no one expects them to take seriously or do well. They are window-dressing for the media. John Stalker made the mistake of believing in justice and being a good policeman. For that he was made to pay a high price. And what has happened to all those senior officials who are believed to have been involved in the conspiracy to pervert justice? Well, as the cynics say, promotion and the honours list are the best silencers the British government could ever wish to have.

1986 – ROTHSCHILD CONSPIRACY Was one of Britain's most respected men and a member of one of its most distinguished banking families really a Soviet masterspy? As well as being one of Israel's most effective secret assets? Did he create a clever conspiracy to hide his secret life, using his wealth, his contacts and the media to deflect suspicion on to an entirely innocent and loyal MI5 officer? According to Roland Perry, author of *The Fifth Man*, the answer must be a resounding 'yes'. Indeed there is so much circumstantial evidence to back this theory up that it is strange that Rothschild has not been labelled more publicly as possibly Britain's biggest traitor. The accusation that Rothschild was the dominant member of the Cambridge Spy Ring, not Philby, Blunt, Burgess, Cairncross or Maclean, sits oddly with the fact that he was also a highly effective wartime MI5 officer and indeed decorated for his part in defusing a new type of German bomb. The Soviet intelligence officer Yuri Modin said, 'Just as the Three Musketeers were four, so the Cambridge five were six.' It can be argued that the number of Soviet agents in the so-called Cambridge spy ring actually numbered far more than six. However it can be argued that one of the most important, and perhaps number five chronologically, was Victor Rothschild. However, some would argue that at that point there was no problem with his loyalties, as Britain, the Soviet Union and the Jews all had a common enemy: Nazi Germany. It would only be after he officially left MI5 in 1945 that his double or treble life as a spy would have begun.

Rothschild was the British head of the famous banking dynasty, which, apart from prolific achievements in art, science, wine and charity, had shaped recent history by such acts as the financing of the British army at the Battle of Waterloo and the purchasing of the Suez Canal for Great Britain and Prime Minister Disraeli. Rothschild was to prove very useful to his Israeli friends and certainly played a part in the development of their nuclear programme. He had been given access in his scientific role to major atomic weapons secrets since the mid 1940s but he couldn't stay in Washington to monitor AEC-Manhattan Project progress. He much later hoped to persuade the Americans to ignore or avoid the McMahon Act and to return to the 'spirit of co-operation' engendered between the two nations during the war after the agreements between Churchill and Roosevelt. However, there was a new mood in Washington under President Harry Truman, who was against sharing, not the least because he was suspicious of the new Labour government under Clement Attlee. He was aware of some of the current cabinet members' efforts to improve relations with the British Communist Party.

Rothschild was on intimate terms with many of the most senior members of the intelligence and security services, such as Guy Liddell, Roger Hollis, Dick White, Stewart Menzies, Maurice Oldfield and Robert Vansittart, the Permanent Under-Secretary of State in the Foreign Office. It is largely accepted among MI5 officers that during the 1945–63 period, the Soviets were receiving vital information which enabled them to thwart British operations run against the Soviet embassy and the intelligence service. MI5 had apparently been penetrated by someone. The inference was always that it had to be an insider. He had left MI5 officially in 1945 yet unofficially still ran agents after the war in Israel, Iran, China and other nations from 1945 to at least 1969. He was the classic outsider-insider. His special place in the establishment as a power broker, with unsurpassed connections in every major institution in Britain, allowed him to bypass the usual restrictions on lesser-born citizens. He couldn't actually pull the files in M15 or M16, but he could always find someone who would do it for him if he needed access. Rothschild was a regular visitor to British intelligence offices. He lunched and dined constantly with its directors at his favourite pubs, Pratt's and White's, and always picked up the tab for expense-account-conscious spy chiefs. However, one of the leading Soviet double agents working for SIS (MI6), Oleg Gordievsky, who defected to Britain in 1985, denied that the Soviets had anyone of importance on the inside of M15 in the contentious years from around 1950 to 1963. Rothschild had been in MI5 during WW2. The argument is that he was recruited for the Soviet cause in pre-war years by playing on his undoubted commitment to a future homeland for the Jews and his anti-Nazi beliefs. Later, the fact that he had spied for the Soviets would have been used to blackmail him into continuing to do so, long after it became obvious that Jews were little-better treated in the USSR as in Nazi Germany. Fear of publicity was to be perhaps the driving force behind his supposed treachery and his later involvement in the Spycatcher affair.

In 1958 Rothschild's fostering of Peter Wright turned quickly to patronage on the basis that they were scientists who understood each other. Wright could have been an easy prey for the sophisticated peer. Although talented, Wright was not Oxbridge-educated and therefore an outsider in a service which was run by the old-school ties. For the first time in his professional life, Wright felt wanted, understood and appreciated. In this atmosphere, Wright may have spilled everything of importance in his section of MI5. Rothschild offered help. He was in the oil group Shell overseeing scientific development. He seconded staff to MI5. Wright told him about every piece of espionage technology under development. Rothschild offered ideas of his own and actually devised some new technology himself. He made introductions to heads of major British organisations like the AWRE (Atomic Weapons Research Establishment), which led to further expansion of MI5's research and development. Later, when Wright was deeply involved in 'mole' hunting, there were two Soviet code names which in particular interested him: DAVID and ROSA. The decoded messages indicated that they had worked together, most likely as a married couple. The Soviet defector Golitsyn asked for the files of all MI5 officers who had been working for British Intelligence at the time of the Venona traffic. He studied the files and after a week asked Wright to come and see him in Brighton. Golitsyn pointed to two files on the desk in the study. 'I've discovered DAVID and ROSA,' he said. 'My methodology has uncovered them.' Wright knew the names on the files well. They belonged to Victor and Tess Rothschild, both of whom had served in MI5. Wright told him not to be absurd; Rothschild, he informed the Russian, was one of the best friends the service ever had. Golitsyn, however, was emphatic. Fortunately for Rothschild, his close companion and confidant, Wright, had been the one informed and there was no further investigation. Golitsyn had earlier informed Wright about a file marked 'Technics' in a safe at the Moscow Centre. It was basically a file on all the MI5 technical operations which Wright and his team had initiated. This proved to Wright that a mole had indeed been spying directly upon him and his activities. Wright never discussed with Golitsyn what he had told Rothschild. If he had, the Russian would have realised that his 'methodology' had been accurate. According to an MI5 source, Rothschild was later fed information, probably in the late 1960s, which ended up 'in the wrong place'.

However, just as Philby had survived for so long because his colleagues and the establishment simply couldn't accept his treachery so, the argument goes, Rothschild's charmed life continued. Later, when Rothschild feared that journalists might link him to his close friend Anthony Blunt, he began to create a smoke screen, a highly effective conspiracy to deflect suspicion away from himself. He used his wealth and his myriad of contacts, particularly in the media. In particular he put in touch a by now retired Wright and *Daily Express* journalist Chapman Pincher, doyen of the specialist writers on intelligence matters. The resulting collaborative books, *Their Trade is Treachery* and *Too Secret Too Long*, neatly deflected suspicion away from Rothschild and on to Sir Roger Hollis. Wright's own book, *Spycatcher*, published in 1987, would reinforce the image that Hollis was the damaging mole. Rothschild, apparently still quite alarmed at the prospect of finally being exposed, begged Wright to 'write down every single point he could recall of the ways Rothschild had helped MI5', adding, 'Things are starting to get rough.' Rothschild also secretly channelled cash to Wright via a Swiss bank.

Rothschild was thought by many to be more loyal to his Jewish heritage than to the English. According to both CIA and Mossad sources, Rothschild was very useful to the Israelis in 'mending fences' with some neighbours in the Middle East after the disruption of the Six-Day War. For instance, he called on his old friend the Shah of Iran and suggested several crop breeding ventures which had been perfected in Israel and elsewhere. Some were adapted in Iran. To many observers Rothschild may have been an unwilling Soviet asset after the war until 1963, but there can be no doubt that he would have willingly spied for Israel. In fact, Philby claims that on leaving MI5 in 1947, Rothschild had seized or copied all the file cards listing known or supposed Soviet agents in Europe and elsewhere. These, according to Philby, were used by the new Israel intelligence service, Mossad.

Rothschild must have come under suspicion of being a spy either for the Soviet Union or Israel, for it is believed that he was investigated and interviewed no less than eleven times by MI5 and, when in 1986 he wrote a very public letter avowing his innocence, Mrs Thatcher's response was the famously terse 'we have no evidence he was ever a Soviet agent.' As a clearance it was less than fulsome. In defending himself, Rothschild instead chose the indirect but effective media route to keep the lid on accusations and deflect them away from himself. He wrote books and articles and made highly publicised speeches. These improved his image outside the secret world which had preoccupied him for fifty years of his life. He spoke and wrote only rarely and evasively about his links to those in the Cambridge ring of five. He could hardly dismiss his close friendships with Blunt and Burgess, but he tried to distance himself from them. When Rothschild died in 1990, Thatcher attended the memorial.

The Fifth Man's original motive was survival, for himself, his family, his peopls and his country. He was compelled to supply the Soviet Union with information that would smash Hitler. But after the war, the Fifth Man's ideological commitment caused him to go on spying for the KGB. In so doing, he became caught in a web of betrayal and tragedy, which lasted half a century. The publication of *The Fifth Man* was greeted in dignified silence by Rothschild's family. Rothschild's role in MI5 and within the scientific community is considerable; his role with Shell and later as head of Prime Minister Edward Heath's think-tank in the early 70s makes him an important player in post-war history. If sufficient information eventually became available to prove beyond doubt Roland Perry's belief in his treachery, then Rothschild will certainly have created a name for himself as the most important Soviet spy in history. That then, is the conspiracy theory, but the truth may well be remarkably similar. The conspiracy he designed to protect him from exposure as a major spy has not protected him for very long after his death.

1986 – ASSASSINATION OF OLAF PALME A political assassination in that most laid back and civilised country, Sweden, took the world by surprise. The fact that a Prime Minister could walk safely in the streets in Sweden without an army of bodyguards was highly prized, but it was an international conspiracy that took his life and, to many, the reasons for it have not been fully discovered. According to some reports, the former chief of the undercover police unit in South Africa, Eugene de Kock, has admitted that the white apartheid regime was responsible for the killing of Swedish Premier Olaf Palme. The Swedish Prime Minister had links with Nelson Mandela and the African National Congress. However, other conspiracy theorists have pointed towards the equally repressive regime in Turkey as being responsible for the assassination. Turkey had accused Olaf Palme of having links to the Kurdish rebels of the *Partiya Karkeren Kurdistan* (PKK) and it known that Palme wanted a general boycott of the Turkish state on the same level as South Africa. The question of whether there was collusion between the two regimes has also been raised, for although Turkey did publicly boycott South Africa, it was still a transit haven for the export of South African military equipment and at times for illegal advanced weaponry purchased on the black market by the white regime.

In the Middle East, there is an old policy: kill the friend of your number one enemy, tell others that he/she has been killed by your enemy and take care of the funeral. So it is not too surprising that the Swedish security services immediately launched a major investigation within the Kurdish community, taking many into temporary custody and searching their homes and businesses. There are numerous rumours that the Turkish intelligence service, the MIT, planted stories and perhaps even 'evidence' on the Swedish investigators to deliberately point them towards the Kurds.

The Palme Government gave asylum to many refugees from around the world, including those escaping from the Vietnam draft in the USA. Palme was also not afraid to take a more than courageous stance on the conduct of the USA in Vietnam, particularly when he controversially compared the bombing of Hanoi to the Nazi destruction of Guernica during the Spanish Civil War. In 1970 young Swedish members of left-wing political groups threw eggs at the US ambassador Jerome H. Holland, which was one among many anti-American incidents. All of these factors angered the United States and before long President Richard Nixon was to tell Sweden that their ambassador was no longer welcome in Washington – though relations were to markedly improve after the United States' withdrawal of troops from Vietnam. In 1976 the Social Democrats lost their position in the

Swedish government and were replaced by a centre-right party under Thorbjörn Fälldin.

However, it was during these years that Olof Palme became very active in the international arena when he joined the Brandt international commission on North–South problems, chaired his own commission on Common Security and became the United Nations mediator in the Iran–Iraq War. In 1977 he made a number of important speeches on African liberation, as well as leading the Socialist International mission to Southern Africa. In 1978 he was awarded a gold medal from the United Nations in recognition of his great contribution to the international campaign against apartheid. One of the major themes in Olof Palme's political career was solidarity with what he believed were oppressed ethnic groups. 'In order to live and survive a society must have a comprehensive solidarity, the ability to recognize the conditions of other people, a feeling of joint responsibility and participation. Otherwise, sooner or later, society will fall apart into petty, egotistical interests.' Palme's imagination and energy in no small measure helped to give Sweden an internationally respected status and in 1982 the Social Democrats were returned to power. 'We've won the victory for the welfare state,' Palme proclaimed. He continued to lead Sweden with fervour and even launched some highly controversial economic reforms.

Yet on 28 February 1986, during a cold evening walk with his wife, a dark-haired man wearing a blue ski jacket approached Palme and quickly fired two shots at a fatally close range. Olof Palme had been enjoying the freedom of being able to move around in the capital city without protection, unlike most other leaders who were constantly accompanied by large numbers of bodyguards. The murder came as a brutal shock to Swedish society. 'As numb and disbelieving Swedes gathered last week to stare at the small pool of blood in the snow where their leader had been gunned down, they wept not just in grief at the death of a shrewd and compassionate man, but at their unwelcome entry into the era of political terrorism,' commented one of Sweden's leading journalists. The murder of their Prime Minister sent Swedes into uncharted territory and it was a terrible blow to a nation that had long boasted of being a model society, thankfully lacking the political violence and terrorism of other countries. Swedes placed red roses and candles on the murder site, as well as a large banner reading, 'Why murder a true democrat?'. Condolences came to Sweden from all over the world – from

Vietnam to Nicaragua, from El Salvador to Palestine, from Sahara to South Africa.

To this day the Palme murder has not been solved, although there has been much speculation and investigation. A man named Christer Pettersson was arrested for the murder in 1988, but was later acquitted. Suspects range from Swedish right-wing party members to Kurds to a mass operation of over eighty South African secret police agents. It is claimed that there has been a lack of organisation on the Swedish investigation's part, and some believe a cover-up has taken place. Conspiracy theorists have openly speculated that Swedish political intelligence officers were involved. Hans Holmèr, originally in charge of the murder investigations, placed the blame on the Kurdish community in Sweden. However, there is a suggestion that Holmèr might even have been involved himself. He certainly lied about his whereabouts on the night of the assassination and produced a fake alibi that suggested he was in the town of Borlänge, which at the time was strangely confirmed by the state police. Further speculation on the Palme murder involved the undercover police of South Africa. An editorial in the Workers' World News Service observes, 'Eugene de Kock, head of a police hit squad, provided grisly details about how his agents deliberately massacred whole families of those opposing the apartheid system and they say that the 1986 assassination of Swedish Prime Minister Olof Palme was part of an operation called "Long Reach", carried out by a unit of the South African secret police'. In fact rumours inside the intelligence community have indeed tended to confirm the suspicion that the South African Intelligence service, BOSS, was directly involved in the murder, which took place just one week after Palme had spoken at an anti-apartheid rally. The Turkish and Kurdish elements may just have been a smoke screen. Olof Palme's very diverse associations in the international arena complicate the murder investigation and it also may have made him more at risk of assassination, especially with the outspoken stance he took on many controversial world issues.

Olof Palme was the foremost leader of Sweden in modern times. He was a controversial figure throughout his life, and remains so even after his death. His contribution to international peace was a lasting gift to the world, but that didn't prevent the conspiracy that killed him. The murder case may never be solved and indeed by a strange irony the regime that is thought most likely to have ordered his assassination now no longer exists.

1987 – THE KILLING OF PAT FINUCANE The death of a highly respected civil rights lawyer in Northern Ireland was shocking enough to bring a response from a United Nations Special Representative in October 1997, who called for a judicial inquiry into allegations that the British security forces had somehow been involved. Pat Finucane was shot dead by two masked men on 12 February 1989 in front of his wife and three children. His wife, Geraldine, was also injured in the attack. Responsibility for the killing was admitted by the paramilitaries of the Ulster Defence Association (UDA), who claimed that Finucane was nothing more than an IRA front man. This was denied by his family members, close friends and even in public statements by the RUC, not usually noted for having a high regard for troublesome Republican lawyers. One of the guns used in the attack was later identified as being part of a haul of thirteen weapons which had been stolen from a British army barracks in 1987 by a serving member of the British army's Ulster Defence Regiment.

The killing took place just a few weeks after the British minister Douglas Hogg had said to Parliament, 'I have to state as a fact but with great regret that there are in Northern Ireland a number of solicitors who are unduly sympathetic to the case of the IRA.' Later, when challenged, all Hogg was able or willing to add was, 'I state this on the basis of advice that I have received, guidance that I have been given by people who are dealing with these matters and I shall not expand on it further.' The brutal killing of Pat Finucane took place in an atmosphere poisoned by such political statements and the frequent allegations that RUC officers had made regular threats against, and highly abusive comments about, defence lawyers to detainees. Such allegations have been recorded by Amnesty International, the London-based British Irish Rights Watch, Helsinki Watch and the Lawyers Committee for Human Rights. Included in the allegations is a claim by Loyalist sources that UDA paramilitary members detained at the Castlereagh high security facilities prior to the murder were told by RUC Special Branch officers that Pat Finucane and a few other solicitors were helping to keep IRA gunmen out of prison. Further important corroboration comes from Brian Nelson – the British military intelligence undercover agent who also served as the chief intelligence officer of the UDA – following his conviction on other charges, alleged that he had directly assisted in the targeting of Pat Finucane. According to the journal written by Nelson, and quoted on the BBC *Panorama* programme in June 1992, Nelson was asked by his

UDA superiors to gather information about Finucane some weeks prior to Finucane's killing and informed a number of British intelligence officers of this request. He passed a photograph, apparently supplied by military intelligence sources, of Pat Finucane to UDA member Eric McKee just a few days before the killing. Loyalist sources claim that Nelson mounted surveillance on the Finucane home in co-operation with the killers in the days before the attack. Despite the warning to the security authorities, Pat Finucane was not warned of the imminent danger to his life. A similar threat at the time, against another prominent lawyer, Paddy McGrory, was not passed on to McGrory until two months after Pat Finucane's murder.

Nelson was never charged in connection with the killing and his claims have never been examined in an open court. No one to date has been prosecuted for the murder of Pat Finucane or even charged in connection with the murder. Three men were subsequently charged with possession of the murder weapon, however. According to Ed Maloney, a journalist for the *Sunday Tribune*, Eric McKee, who asked Nelson for the photograph of Finucane and who was subsequently taken to the Finucane home by Nelson, was the head of the UDA's paramilitary death squads. McKee served a sentence for possession of scores of leaked official security documents, along with four others, including a senior UDA leader, Tommy Lyttle. All were arrested by the Stevens inquiry team, but like the Nelson trial, a deal was struck which prevented the full details of collusion between British forces and Loyalist death squads coming out in open court.

The Stevens inquiry did not bother to interview Finucane's widow, his partner, Peter Madden, or any of his clients who knew of threats that had been made against Pat Finucane. The Report of the International Human Rights Working Party of the Law Society of England and Wales in 1995 states, 'There is credible evidence of both police and army involvement. We cite the most significant items below. There is further evidence in the hands of the police which we have not been given access.' The government's response to the UN Special Representative was that the DPP or Director of Public Prosecutions had stated that there should be no prosecution against any officer in connection with Finucane's death. Significantly the government did not deny that there had been collusion by the security forces and police in relation to this murder. It is understood that threats made against Pat Finucane by members of the RUC included death threats by Criminal Investigation Department (CID) officers, false allegations by CID officers that Finucane was a member of the IRA and threats by CID officers to pass his name and details to Loyalist paramilitaries. It is believed that none of these allegations was ever seriously investigated by the police. Detective Sergeant Simpson of the RUC told the inquest that some of the allegations were investigated by the Stevens inquiry, but John Stevens is reported to have claimed that as far as he could remember they were not. It is scandalous that in a democracy where the rule of law is supposedly paramount, such allegations should have remained unexamined.

Since the inquest two British army officers are strongly believed to have admitted to army participation in the UDA conspiracy to murder Pat Finucane. Brian Nelson was a British army intelligence officer who was placed in the UDA in 1987 and is currently serving a prison sentence arising out of his involvement in terrorist murders. The trial of Brian Nelson revealed that a very high level of information on both Loyalist paramilitaries and operations was held by both the British army and the RUC. The trial also highlights how little was done by the security forces to disrupt these Loyalist operations in order to save lives or to dismantle the Loyalist groups. Brian Nelson's military handlers who allegedly provided information that directly assisted in the targeting of some individuals for murder were not charged with any counts. The allegations of persistent collusion between British forces and Loyalist paramilitaries – including the 'smuggling' of a shipment of modern South African-produced infantry weapons in January 1988, which were used to re-arm the loyalist paramilitaries and give them firepower equal, if not superior, to that of the Provisional IRA – have never been properly investigated.

Conspiracy theorists point out that the full extent of the role of the British authorities in arming the Protestant Loyalists has to be finally exposed as part of the peace process, particularly in relation to the constant political demands made of the IRA to decommission its arsenal. The role of the British security and intelligence community – MI5 and Military Intelligence in particular – in the operations to supply sensitive intelligence information on prominent Republicans, to arm the UDA and UVF with modern weapons and the collusion with the paramilitary death squads who have probably claimed the lives of as many as 250 Catholics in Ulster, has, according to many observers, the tacit support of successive British governments. Significantly, confirmation that there had indeed been a widespread conspiracy of silence in Ulster over the level of collusion between

British Intelligence and military personnel and the Protestant 'death squads' was to come in April 2003 with the conclusion of the Stevens Enquiry. Sir John Stevens, the Commissioner of the Metropolitan Police Service, commented in his report that 'I have uncovered enough evidence to lead me to believe that the murder(s) of Patrick Finucane .... could have been prevented. I also believe that the RUC investigation of Patrick Finucane's murder should have resulted in the early arrest and detection of his killers.' However the most damning comment came when he added, 'I conclude there was collusion in both murders and the circumstances surrounding them. Collusion is evidenced in many ways. This ranges from the wilful failure to keep records, the absence of accountability, the withholding of intelligence and evidence, through to the extreme of agents being involved in murder.' Though Her Majesty's Government and its secret servants will undoubtedly do everything within their considerable power to limit the damage done, the truth has been at least partly exposed. MI5 and Military Intelligence officers did indeed target Catholics for killing by the Loyalist terror gangs, including those suspected of being Republican paramilitaries and others simply carrying out their professional responsibilities like Pat Finucane. How many other dark secrets about the long and terrible years of Northern Ireland's civil war still remain to be uncovered is a matter of conjecture. That there are a good few is now a certainty however.

1988 – LOCKERBIE CONSPIRACIES In the worst act of terrorism ever committed on or over the mainland of the UK, a modern passenger airliner is blown apart by a bomb and all those on board, along with further victims in a small Scottish town far below, are killed. But did the authorities really find the guilty men? Or was it a matter of expediency as the Gulf War approached? Did the real culprits belong to groups supported by Arab countries the USA and Britain would now need as allies in the coalition against Iraq? Was Libya a safe alternative to blame?

When Lord Sutherland was asked to throw out a conspiracy charge against Abdelbaset Ali Mohmed Al Megrahi and Al Amin Khalifa Fhimah, accused of murdering the 270 victims of the Lockerbie bombing, defence lawyers told the judge that a Scottish court should not be able to try the pair for conspiracy to murder because there was no plot on Scottish soil. The prosecution replied that the conspiracy had continued until the Pan Am airliner exploded over Lockerbie, therefore killing 270 people within the jurisdiction of the Scottish courts. 'Charge one is a charge of conspiracy used by the Crown as a device to introduce into evidence matters that would not be competent to introduce were the crime properly a crime of murder.' Scotland's Solicitor General responded that the conspiracy charge was valid and even hinted that there may be evidence of a possible Scottish link to the two accused men; on such a flimsy legal framework a second conspiracy was hatched, to lay the blame for Lockerbie on the maverick and unpopular regime in Libya. The counter allegations that it was Iran and not Libya that was behind the Lockerbie bombing came as no surprise to Middle East observers. But the assertion by a former Iranian intelligence official, Ahmad Behbahani, that he was responsible for all 'terrorist' operations carried out by the Iranian government beyond its borders and that included the Lockerbie bombing largely escaped the attention of the media and certainly did not influence the eventual trial of the Libyan suspects. The prosecution alleged that a bomb was planted on Pan Am Flight 103 by two members of the Libyan intelligence services. The accused, for their part, have consistently said they are innocent and pointed at Syrian-backed Palestinian extremists.

At the time of the bombing, however, it was Iran that was immediately the leading suspect and Iran's motive for carrying out the attack was assumed to be a desire for revenge for the shooting down of an Iranian civilian flight by the US warship, *USS Vincennes*, killing all 290 passengers and crew aboard on 3 July 1988. Iran's Ayatollah Khomeini vowed at the time that the skies would 'rain blood' in revenge. Conspiracy theorists maintain that Iran was behind the attack and say that Tehran sponsored one of a number of radical Palestinian groups to actually carry out the attack. Behbahani told the CBS *60 Minutes* programme that he had first suggested the plan to bomb the Pan Am flight to Ahmad Jibril, who heads a Syrian-backed armed group, the Popular Front for the Liberation of Palestine-General Command (PFLP-GC). This organisation was a prime suspect in the immediate aftermath of the Lockerbie attack, but has denied any involvement. However, Behbahani also and rather confusingly claimed that Iran had spent some ninety days training a group of Libyans for the operation; whether this was an official Libyan intelligence involvement was not made clear. German police raids on PFLP-GC hideouts in 1988 and 1989 yielded information that the group was targeting a US-bound flight from Frankfurt and turned up bombs that appeared to match the Lockerbie bomb. 'It's very difficult to believe there were two separate operations targeting the same flight,' said Vince Cannistraro, a former senior CIA official, who believes the PFLP-GC handed off the bombing to Libya after the raids compromised its operation.

The important conspiracy scenario laying the blame on the Palestinians, Iran and Syria is much better documented and makes a lot more sense, logistically and otherwise. Support for this scenario was, and remains, impressive to this day, as the following surely indicates. In April 1989, the FBI, in response to criticism that it was bungling the investigation, had leaked information to CBS that it had tentatively identified the person who unwittingly carried the bomb aboard. His name was Khalid Jaafar, a 21-year-old Lebanese-American. The report said that the bomb had been planted in Jaafar's suitcase by a member of the PFLP-GC, whose name was not revealed. In May the State Department stated that the CIA was 'confident' of the Iran-Syria-PFLP-GC account of events. On 20 September *The Times* reported that 'security officials from Britain, the United States and West Germany are "totally satisfied" that it was the PFLP-GC' behind the crime. In December 1989 Scottish investigators announced that they had 'hard evidence' of the involvement of the PFLP-GC in the bombing. A National Security Agency electronic intercept disclosed that Ali Akbar Mohtashemi, Iranian interior minister, had paid Palestinian terrorists $10 million dollars to gain revenge for the downed Iranian airplane. The intercept appears to have occurred in July 1988, shortly after the downing of the Iranian airliner. Israeli intelligence also intercepted a communication between Mohtashemi and the Iranian embassy in Beirut, 'indicating that Iran paid for the Lockerbie bombing'. Even after the Libyans had been indicted, Israeli officials declared that their intelligence analysts remained convinced that the PFLP-GC bore primary responsibility for the bombing.

In 1992 Abu Sharif, a political advisor to PLO chairman Yasser Arafat, stated that the PLO had compiled a secret report which concluded that the bombing of 103 was the work of a 'Middle Eastern country' other than Libya. Indeed, this was the original official version, delivered with the Olympian authority of the US government until the build-up to the Gulf War came along in 1990 and the support of Iran and Syria was urgently needed. Washington was anxious as well to achieve the release of American hostages held in Lebanon by groups close to Iran. Thus it was that the scurrying sound of backtracking became audible in the corridors of the White House and, as the conspiracy theorists point out, there was a new official version by October 1990. It was Libya, and strangely the Arab state least supportive of the US build-up to the Gulf War, that was behind the bombing after all, declared Washington. The two Libyans were formally indicted in the USA and Scotland on 14 November 1991. 'This was a Libyan government operation from start to finish,' declared the State Department spokesman. 'The Syrians took a bum rap on this,' said President George H.W. Bush. Within the next twenty days, the remaining four American hostages held in the Lebanon were released along with the most prominent British hostage, Terry Waite. In February 1995 former Scottish Office minister Alan Stewart wrote to the British Foreign Secretary and the Lord Advocate, questioning the reliability of evidence which had led to the accusations against the two Libyans. This move reflected the obvious concern of the Scottish legal profession, including elements within the Crown Office, Scotland's equivalent of the Attorney General's Office, that the bombing may not have been the work of Libya but of Syrians, Palestinians and Iranians. Theorists ask why former Prime Minister Margaret Thatcher, writing in her 1993 memoirs about the US bombing of Libya in 1986, stated, 'But the much vaunted Libyan counter-attack did not and could not take place. Gaddafi had not been destroyed but he had been humbled. There was a marked decline in Libyan-sponsored terrorism in succeeding years.'

According to leading conspiracy theorists, the key question in the PFLP-GC version has always been, how did the bomb get aboard the plane in, presumably, Frankfurt? One widely disseminated explanation was in a report completed during the summer of 1989 and leaked towards the end of the year, which had been prepared by a New York investigating firm called Interfor. Headed by a former Israeli intelligence agent, Juval Aviv, Interfor, whose other clients included Fortune 500 companies, the FBI, the IRS and the Secret Service, was hired by the law firm representing Pan Am's insurance carrier. The Interfor report said that in the mid-1980s, a drug and arms smuggling operation was set up in various European cities, with Frankfurt airport as the site of one of the drug routes. The Frankfurt operation was run by Manzer Al-Kassar, a Syrian and the same man from whom Oliver North's Iran-Contra network purchased large quantities of arms for the Nicaraguan rebels. At the airport, according to the report, a courier would board a flight with checked luggage containing innocent items; after the luggage had passed all security checks, one or another accomplice Turkish baggage handler for Pan Am would substitute an identical suitcase containing contraband; the passenger then picked up this suitcase upon arrival at the destination. The only courier named by Interfor was Khalid Jaafar, who had also been previously named by the FBI a few months earlier as the person who unwittingly carried the bomb aboard. It is claimed that the CIA in Germany discovered the airport drug operation and learned also that Kassar had the contacts to gain the release of American hostages in Lebanon. He had already done the same for French hostages. Thus it was that the CIA and the German Bundeskriminalamt (BKA) or Federal Criminal Office allowed the drug operation to continue in hopes of obtaining the release of American hostages. According to the report, this same smuggling ring's method of switching suitcases at the Frankfurt airport was used to smuggle the fatal bomb aboard flight 103, under the eyes of the CIA and the BKA. In January 1990 Interfor gave three of the baggage handlers polygraphs, and two of them were judged as being deceitful when denying any involvement in baggage switching. However, neither the US, UK nor German investigators showed any interest in the results, or in questioning the baggage handlers. Instead, the polygrapher, James Keefe, was hauled before a Washington grand jury and, as he puts it, 'They were bent on destroying my credibility, not theirs,' meaning the baggage handlers'.

To Interfor, the lack of interest in the polygraph results and the attempt at intimidation of Keefe was the strongest evidence of a cover-up by the various government authorities that did not want their permissive role in the baggage switching to be revealed. Critics claimed that the Interfor report had been inspired by Pan Am's interest in proving that it was impossible for normal airline security to have prevented the loading of the bomb, thus removing the basis for accusing the airline of negligence. The report was the principal reason Pan Am's attorneys subpoenaed the FBI, CIA, Drug Enforcement Agency, State Department, National Security Council and National Security Agency, as well as, reportedly, the Defense Intelligence Agency and the Federal Aviation Administration to turn over all documents relating to the crash of 103 that might provide further evidence of a drug operation preceding the crash. The government moved to quash the subpoenas on grounds of 'national security' and refused access to the documents. The two accused Libyans were eventually handed over by Colonel Gaddafi on the assumption that no significant evidence could be placed in front of the judges and that they would both be acquitted. The subsequent conviction and jailing of one of the Libyans may well be unsound and therefore a grave miscarriage of justice. The real culprits remain free, while the Arab nations that sponsored the terrorist outrage escaped punishment by the US. Syria, of course, was actually warmly welcomed as an ally of Washington in the Gulf War, just three short years after almost certainly helping to blow a Pan Am airliner out of the sky over Scotland.

1990 – CARLYLE GROUP Another of the favourites with modern 'mega-conspiracy' theorists is the undue influence super powerful groups of industrialists connected to the military and the intelligence services are supposed to have over the governments of the world – the White House in particular. When James Baker publicly offered advice to the Bush Administration on how they should proceed with their war on Iraq, what was not mentioned was that Baker was now employed by the highly influential Carlyle Group which, though the eleventh largest defence contractor in the USA appears to hit above its weight in political terms. In essence, then, we have a man trying to influence public policy while privately employed by a company that has a vested interest in activating America's war machine. The Carlyle Group has become a powerhouse in affecting the direction our foreign policy takes, especially in regard to war.

They now exert far too much influence to be healthy, say the theorists, and it all smacks of a conspiracy, based on an incestuous government–business partnership of musical chairs. The aim is power and influence for corporate America, retirement to cozy and well-paid directorships for the politicians and former government officials, and in the meantime, both get rich. They accomplish this by hiring former government officials, then investing in private companies that are subject to government change such as those contracted to the military, and telecommunications. Who do they take on to help secure their government contracts? Well, for starters the following are or have been employed: Frank Carlucci, Department of Health, Education and Welfare 1970s, Deputy Director, CIA 1978–81, Deputy Secretary of Defense 1981–82, National Security Director 1987–89; George Bush, CIA Director 1976–77, Vice President of the USA 1981–89, President of the USA 1989–93; James Baker, Whitehouse Chief of Staff 1981–85, Secretary of the Treasury 1985–89, Secretary of State 1989–93; John Major, former Prime Minister, UK; Fidel Ramos, former Philippine President; Afsaneh Beschloss, Treasurer & Chief

Investment Officer of the World Bank; Anand Panyarachum, former President, Thailand; Karl Otto Pohl, former President, Bundesbank; Louis Vuitton, French Aerobus Company; Park Tae Joon, former South Korean Prime Minister; Alwaleed Sin Talal bin Abdulaziz Alsaud, Saudi Arabian Prince; and George Soros, Bilderberg member and financier. Carlyle also employs the former chairman of BMW and Nestlé and once hired Colin Powell and AOL Time-Warner chairman Steve Case to speak at a meeting at Washington DC's Monarch House.

James Baker has also been on the board of Azerbaijan International Oil Company, in which two US oil companies hold 40 per cent of the shares. The first is Amoco, who has on its payroll none other than Zbigniew Brzezinski, Trilateral Commission founder, National Security Advisor for the Carter Administration and globalisation guru. The second is Pennzoil, who has on its payroll none other than Brent Scowcroft, former National Security Advisor under George Bush, Sr.

However, but the man that is really believed to have brought it all together is Frank Carlucci since he joined in 1989. He also holds directorships on such companies as General Dynamics, Westinghouse, the Rand Corporation and Ashland Oil, plus sits on the board of directors of twelve other companies. Carlucci was also the college classmate of someone very closely related to one of the most powerful men in the George W. Bush Administration, Defense Secretary Donald Rumsfeld. The influence for good or for blatant self-interest and corruption that these interlocking 'contacts' provide is immense. It is not difficult to see where the conspiracy theorists get their ideas of hidden agendas and secret business–political cabals, and their great distrust of the so-called New World Order, which is a form of the Carlyle Group on a grand, or should one say global, scale.

In February 2001 Carlucci and Vice President Dick Cheney met with Donald Rumsfeld when the Carlyle Group had several billion-dollar defence projects under consideration – successfully, too! It is claimed that the Carlyle Group has become the thread which indirectly links American military policy in Afghanistan to the personal financial fortunes of its celebrity employees, not least the current President's father.

The Carlyle Group is set to make huge amounts of money from the upcoming military conflicts and weapons expenditures. Dan K. Thomasson, former editor of the Scripps Howard News Service, summed it up best in March 2001: 'Nothing in recent history seems to approach the success this group has had in the wholesale conversion of former high government rank to gigantic profits.' Peter Eisner, Managing Director of the Center for Public Integrity, adds, 'It should be a deep cause for concern that a closely held company like Carlyle can simultaneously have directors and advisors that are doing business and making money and also advising the President of the United States', while the *Washington Business Journal* simply says, 'The Carlyle Group seems to play to a different set of rules.'

The Carlyle Group have their head office located only a few blocks from the White House and it was founded by three men: David Rubinstein, former aide in the Carter Administration, Bill Conway, Chief Financial Officer at MCI and Dan D'Aniello, a financial executive at Marriott. They named their group 'Carlyle' after a New York hotel favoured by one of their first investors, the Mellon family and now have a financial interest in well over 100 companies in over 50 countries, as well as billions of US dollars in capital. On 5 May 2001 the *New York Times* described the Carlyle Group as such: 'It owns so many companies that it is now in effect one of the nation's biggest defense contractors and a force in global communications. Its blue-chip investors include major banks and insurance companies, billion dollar pension funds and wealthy investors.'

The Carlyle Group is now deeply established as 'insiders', and the theorists argue, probably with some merit, that US taxpayers' best interests are definitely low on the group's agenda. But is there anything that the taxpayer, the voter, the concerned citizen can do? Very little in all probability. Should 'Joe public' be concerned? Without doubt. But as one Wall Street 'wag' said, 'It's the new world order folks, and you better believe it!'

1991 – MOSSAD KILLED MAXWELL? Was British media tycoon Robert Maxwell murdered by Israeli secret agents of Mossad? According to some conspiracy theorists, he was. Indeed, there are many within the media who suspect that his death may not have been a simple suicide. The allegations are that the flamboyant multimillionaire was an Israeli spy and probably had links to organised crime syndicates in Eastern Europe. Mossad apparently decided to get rid of Maxwell because he was threatening to expose his knowledge of Israeli secrets unless he received massive financial help in propping up his failing media businesses.

Maxwell's sudden death at sea in November 1991 off the Canary Islands precipitated the collapse of his worldwide publishing empire and led to theories ranging from suicide through murder to a tragic accident. Maxwell disappeared overboard just as the complex web of financial deals keeping his businesses afloat was beginning to unravel and a few weeks after US investigative journalist Seymour Hersh had published a book claiming Maxwell had close ties to Mossad. It is claimed that the Israeli agents, who had quietly boarded Maxwell's private yacht under cover of darkness, plunged a needle filled with a lethal nerve agent into Maxwell's neck. They then lowered his body into the sea. One conspiracy theory goes into considerable detail and claims that in September 1991 four Israelis met in a drab high-rise office on the King Saul Boulevard in Tel Aviv. They arrived separately and used only their first names: Zvi, Efraim, Uri and Nahum. Outside the shadowy world in which they moved, no one knew what they did and success depended on secrecy, for their work was assassination. The four men were agents of Israel's Central Institute for Intelligence and Special Duties, more commonly known as Mossad, and served in a special unit called the kidon or in Hebrew 'bayonet'. Its function was the efficient killing of Israel's enemies, and its success in that task had earned Mossad the unofficial title 'Executioner To The World'. The assassins were a close-knit elite, according to Rafi Eitan, a former deputy director of Mossad operations, who said, 'only a handful show the human requirements, a total coldness once committed to their mission, and afterwards, no regrets.' Yet when the four men reached Mossad's HQ at the Hadar Davna Building in King Saul Boulevard, and sat down in the kidon's sparsely furnished conference room on the fifth floor, they were apparently surprised to learn that their latest target was no terrorist, hijacker or crazed bomber. It was to be Robert Maxwell, something of an Israeli national hero, a hugely well-known global tycoon who had never forgotten his Jewish roots; a lavish supporter of Zionist causes, who had opened companies and factories across the land; a political powerbroker inside Israel. Just two months after that meeting in Tel Aviv Maxwell was dead. The mysterious circumstances of his final days and the aftermath that led to his exposure as one of history's greatest fraudsters have been a matter of conjecture ever since.

Mossad, it seems, is the most likely culprit, according to the theorists. Completely unknown to his wife and children, his closest business associates and, indeed, to anyone apart from a handful of men in Israel, and a number of British, US and probably Russian intelligence officers, was the startling fact that Maxwell was a Mossad spy, or perhaps less colourfully, an agent or even a major 'asset'. He had been recruited in the early 1980s at a meeting in the King David Hotel in Jerusalem, reportedly with Nahum Admoni, then director-general of Mossad, and Shimon Peres, the Israeli Labour Party politician. The two men wanted to exploit his unique contacts in Russia and Eastern Europe, where his business activities had made him the confidant of influential figures such as former KGB Chief Yuri Andropov and Markus Wolf of the East German Stasi secret police. The initial idea was that he could use his leverage to help bring Jews out of the Soviet bloc and 'home' to Israel. This he duly did and it is believed that he played a major part in acquiring around 300,000 exit visas in the following years. But Maxwell's activities ranged far wider. As an honoured guest in the East, it is claimed that he was shown secret briefing papers on economic and military affairs and senior Communist leaders gossiped with him as a trusted ally. Maxwell fed it all back to Mossad as well as whatever information he could glean from his equally assiduous courting of leaders in the West. Meanwhile, one of his many companies, Degem Computers in Tel Aviv, provided cover for Mossad spies and assassins posing as salesmen and technicians.

Maxwell was to become the single most important asset Mossad had ever employed, it is claimed. It was all fuel for his insatiable ego and Maxwell, who came from Jewish peasant stock in what became Czechoslovakia, was genuinely proud to serve the only state in the world to which he felt emotional allegiance. However, it seems that eventually Maxwell turned on his own masters and that was why the kidon assassins were leafing through his file on that September day in 1991. In his obsessive quest to extend his business empire, Maxwell had run up debts of £2.2 billion with no fewer than 44 banks, and now his creditors were closing in. He was plundering his workers' pension funds and using every crooked trick in the book to stave off the funds' managers, but his lies and frauds were at last catching up with him. Casting around for rescue, Maxwell put through numerous calls to senior figures at Mossad, imploring them to exert their influence over banks in Israel and, if possible, London and New York to provide him with the fresh funds he so urgently needed to fend off a financial collapse. He was told that his request was impossible and that it was simply beyond Mossad's remit. But he refused to heed the intelligence chiefs' implicit warnings not to involve them in his personal disaster and tried to extort money directly from Mossad by threatening to reveal all he had done for them. Maxwell wanted Mossad to reward his loyalty and the price of his silence was £400 million, the very least he needed to pay off his most pressing creditors. It was, of course, a threat that nobody could be allowed to get away with. The kidon killers were ordered to solve Maxwell's problems permanently.

It is claimed that the operation to trap him was sprung as he sat in his penthouse in Maxwell House, next to a bugging system relaying a conversation taking place in an office on the floor below. It was a meeting of the directors of Maxwell Communications Corporation, the umbrella group that sheltered his 400 private companies. From the tone of the conversation around the boardroom table, it was clear his closest associates felt bitter and disillusioned. Their talk was of giving up and of selling whatever was necessary of Maxwell's possessions to satisfy the bankers and brokers. Maxwell then received a mysterious private phone call from the Israeli embassy in Madrid. The caller asked him to identify himself and from this one simple call a web of Israeli conspiracy succeeded in drawing Maxwell away from London and to his luxurious yacht. Perhaps promises of financial aid and a way out of Maxwell's desperate situation were offered; whatever the truth, Maxwell headed for his beloved boat and an unexpected death. The kidon team monitored his every move from then on and contact was made with the *Lady Ghislaine* after it berthed at the fishing port of Darsena Pesquera, three miles to the north of Santa Cruz, capital of Tenerife. The kidon team tracked their prey from a distance, watching as the yacht moved to a quiet inlet for Maxwell to go swimming. Local fisherman Ernesto Krjus would later tell the authorities how he had watched the smaller boat, which bore no name and flew no flag, as it followed the *Lady Ghislaine* up the coast. Another fisherman noted how it tried to keep close, 'but not too close', to the larger vessel.

On the evening of 4 November Maxwell decided to have dinner ashore and a table was reserved for him at one of Tenerife's finest hotels, the Mencey in Santa Cruz. Sergio Rodriguez, the maître d', recalls Maxwell sitting with his back to the wall, mobile phone at the ready. 'He looked thoughtful, as if he was in another world,' Rodriguez remembered. 'His eyes kept going to the phone, then towards the door. I had the feeling he was either expecting a call or a visitor.' Maxwell's normal gargantuan appetite seemed to have deserted him: he toyed with his meal before saying his goodbyes with a flap of his hand. Next, he took a taxi to a café for cognac and a cigar. Staff noted that he stared at passers-by as if expecting someone, and repeatedly dialled a number on his phone without apparent success. Eventually, Maxwell returned to the *Lady Ghislaine* and told Captain Rankin they were to leave 'as soon as possible' and for a new destination, Los Cristianos on the far side of Tenerife. He had already announced that he would probably fly back to London the next day. But he had also warned the pilot of his Gulfstream jet, which had followed him to the island, that 'events might dictate' a trip to New York or Jerusalem instead. Maxwell retired to his cabin, but at 10.40 p.m. he was interrupted by a call from his son Ian. For once, the conversation was not about his business woes. Instead, it centred on a speech Ian had given to the Anglo–Israeli Association in London on his father's behalf. Ian was excited, as the speech had been well received. Ian said, 'See you tomorrow, Dad,' to which Maxwell is believed to have replied, 'You bet.'

At midnight, Captain Rankin was relieved on the bridge by his First Officer and the skipper gave one instruction before leaving his junior in charge: 'Call me if any craft shows up on radar within five miles.' Had Maxwell told Rankin he was expecting visitors? That question remains unanswered, because Rankin has never broken his silence about it. What is a matter of record is that at 4.25 a.m., Second Engineer Leo Leonard came up on to the aft deck to cool off from the heat of the engine room. He saw Maxwell standing a few feet away. 'He was in his blue-striped nightshirt, in his favourite place on the starboard side near his state-room door. 'With his left hand leaning on a stanchion and his back to the sea, he was looking towards the lights of Gran Canaria.' From where Maxwell stood, the security cameras, even if they had been switched on, would not have shown him on the closed-circuit monitors on the bridge. 'No one knew that better than Maxwell,' said Leonard. 'He had often used that spot to urinate over the side of the boat during the night, or simply to go on deck for fresh air. 'The bridge watch would not have been able to see him. Neither would they have known if an intruder boarded the boat.' Spotting Leonard, Maxwell said he wanted the air conditioning turned up in his cabin. The crewman left the deck and went to carry out Maxwell's order. It was now 4.30 a.m. Fifteen minutes later, the bridge received a call from Maxwell. He told Second Officer Mark Atkins his cabin was now too cold. 'Turn it up a degree or two,' he ordered. 'Straight away, Mr Maxwell.' The brief exchange was the last that Robert Maxwell would have with any crew member. His body would later be recovered from the sea and it was generally accepted that Maxwell had taken his own life in the face of an impending financial meltdown and public humiliation. A reasonable theory to many who did not know of his secret life and the attempts he was making to survive. It is claimed that only the four members of the Mossad kidon hit-team know the real truth about Maxwell's final minutes. The former Israeli intelligence officer and now a whistleblower Victor Ostrovsky has claimed that it was decided that 'Mossad's problem would be laid to rest in the salty waters of the Atlantic'. Maxwell was a fighter, and suicide seemed out of character, though under such enormous pressure even the strongest can crack. However, the theory that Israel's intelligence service murdered Maxwell must remain as one of the more likely conspiracies.

1994 – DEATH OF A ROCK STAR When a famous rock star dies, everyone seems to be interested; when someone like Kurt Cobain dies, who had rocketed to fame and worldwide adulation along with fellow band members Dave Grohl and Krist Novoselic in Nirvana, that interest risks becoming totally obsessive. According to the Seattle Police Department's report, Kurt first shot himself with something other than a shotgun; both arms were pierced by hypodermic syringes, although the toxicology report that would prove the use of drugs at the time of death has never been released to the public. He then placed the barrel of his shotgun, inverted for easier access to the trigger, in his mouth, and the rest is history. But the story of the shotgun doesn't begin and end there. The weapon, a powerful 20-gauge Remington M-11 semi-automatic shotgun, had actually been purchased by Kurt's best friend, Dylan Carlson, on 30 March 1994. Cobain told him he was concerned about intruders at his house, and bought the weapon under Carlson's name because he didn't want the police to confiscate it, as they had done with four of his guns after a domestic disturbance on 18 March that resulted from a violent quarrel with his wife Courtney Love, a rock star in her own right with the band Hole. Suicide or not, the shotgun Kurt purchased is ideal for home defence, packing a maximum punch, while reducing the chances of a shot penetrating a wall and wounding someone in another part of the house.

He may very well have had reason to fear for his own safety, suggests private investigator Tom Grant, who was originally hired by

Courtney Love to search for Kurt after he went missing from a Marina Del Ray rehabilitation centre some days before his death; also in the same period, Cobain walked out on a $9.5 million contract to headline the Lollapalooza touring rock festival. Courtney was apparently enraged when she found out about it in the *Los Angeles Times*, at least according to some sources, but then she wasn't the only one. 'Walking out on the Lollapalooza tour was a business decision that would cost others a great deal of money also,' Grant said. 'Kurt may have been intimidated into believing his life would be in danger if he failed to do the tour.' Conspiracy theorists go so far as to suggest that an organised crime syndicate may have 'hit' Cobain first because he had potentially just cost them a lot of money and perhaps also as a little reminder to all those other strutting, self-important rock stars to remember the old saying 'he who pays the piper, calls the tune'. Although this has not gained too much credence, it might be because a frightened music industry is staying sensibly silent about the whole issue.

Whatever the truth of a Mafia-style involvement, it is certainly true that Cobain had loaded that shotgun with three shells. Was there an unreported problem at the time? Was Cobain facing an intruder? Or even a deranged fan? Not an impossible scenario when the cases of John Lennon's murder, and George Harrison's near-killing by a so-called 'fan', are remembered. Or was this just part of some cruel conspiracy to make his suicide look like a murder? The police crime lab failed to lift any legible fingerprints from the shotgun, which is distinctly odd as it seems highly unlikely that Cobain would have taken the time and trouble to wipe the gun clean of fingerprints just before blowing out what little appeared to be left of his brains.

Then there's the small matter of the supposed suicide note. If you've got a suicide, you ought to have a suicide note. So, the theory goes, if you're going to kill someone and make it look like a suicide, you'll definitely need a letter of intent from the victim. The letter found with Kurt's body begins, 'To Boddah pronounced,' a reference to an imaginary childhood friend. What follows is an extremely odd and confusing suicide note that doesn't make a lot of sense – although in his probably drugged suicidal state, perhaps that's not too surprising. The note found with Kurt's body says nothing about suicide and was not written specifically to Courtney and daughter Frances Bean, who are only mentioned in a footnote. The tone of the note isn't particularly suicidal, with Kurt writing, 'I have it good, very good, and I'm grateful.' The entire note is written in the present tense, not the kind of finality you'd expect from a man who was supposedly preparing to kill himself. According to Grant, none of the psychologists who examined him at the rehab centre he had briefly visited shortly before his death found him to be suicidal and neither did his friend Dylan Carlson, who had seen him a few days before. Even more suspicious to some who believe that Courtney Love was somehow directly, or perhaps more likely indirectly, involved in Cobain's death, there's the second note that Courtney apparently kept in secret after Kurt's death which, it is claimed, she only let slip during a *Rolling Stone* magazine interview. In the second note, which it is reported she didn't share with the police in Seattle, Cobain is believed to have stated that he was leaving Courtney and leaving Seattle, providing more of a goodbye note to his fans rather than a death letter to his wife and child.

Then there was the Rome 'suicide attempt' in March 1994, which landed Kurt Cobain in the city's American hospital with a potentially lethal cocktail of Rohypnol and vintage champagne. He is believed to have written to Courtney after the incident and included one line which she said later was 'very definitely suicidal', adding, 'Dr. Baker says I would have to choose between life and death, I'm choosing death.' Which makes no sense at all as a suicide reference, according to Grant. No doctor in his right mind would ever offer suicide as an option to a patient; he was clearly referring to Cobain's heroin habit. Cobain was stating that he chose heroin or, in the doctor's view, death.

There's a tendency in conspiracy research to dig for holes in the story despite the human reality of a given situation. It's easy to replace flesh and blood with names, dates and facts, and worst still unfounded rumour and unprovable suspicions. Courtney Love does have an attitude problem and a fierce temper. As a couple they were dysfunctional and weren't getting along terribly well before his death. But conspiring with others to murder your husband is another matter entirely. If Kurt Cobain was murdered, then Courtney would obviously be a suspect and certainly had several possible motives, including the fact that in January 1994 Cobain told *Rolling Stone* that he might be divorcing Courtney in the near future. After his death, the magazine reported that divorce papers were already being drawn up at the time of his demise. However, as Courtney went on to later prove, as a successful musician and actress she didn't rely on or need Cobain.

The official police report, as well as police statements following the discovery of Kurt's body, contain a number of questionable discrepancies. As soon as Kurt's body was found, police apparently concluded that his death resulted from a suicide. It has been claimed that nowhere in the police handling of the scene will you find any indication that the detectives were there to do anything but write up a report on the death and get out of there. At first glance, it certainly must have looked like a suicide but, as officers of the law, the Seattle police had a duty to investigate thoroughly. The media dutifully reported police descriptions of finding Kurt's body 'blockaded' in the greenhouse; however, the only thing blockading any part of the greenhouse was a small wooden stool placed in front of a doorway leading to a balcony, not at the greenhouse entrance. The police report states that this tiny wooden stool impeded entrance to the greenhouse, which appears to be a ludicrous assertion. The police report also states that there were marks on Cobain's hands consistent with the firing of a shotgun. This is another highly unlikely claim: shotguns rarely leave visible residue on the hands of the shooter. Kurt's wallet was found closed near his body, but the media reported that it had been found lying open with the licence facing out, supposedly for the purposes of identifying his body upon discovery. In fact, one of the first officers on the scene had opened the wallet, putting the licence on display for the police forensic photographer. The media also planted horrific images of suicide in the minds of Cobain's fans, reporting that his head was 'blown off' by the shotgun blast and that his fingerprints were required for positive identification. However, Cobain's features were more or less intact and unlike most shotgun wounds, which leave a gaping exit wound, the barrel of Kurt's shotgun was placed against the hard palate of his mouth, which absorbed a great deal of the blast. The shot remained inside Cobain's skull.

Was it suicide or murder? The questionable police findings and inaccurate news reporting have complicated the issue, sadly. The theorists have had a field day in the years following Cobain's death, and Courtney Love in particular has come in for particular vilification from Cobain's obsessive fans. It has been suggested that she employed a hitman to rid herself of a turbulent relationship. But reality and common sense suggests that this was just another sad drug-induced episode in the ongoing rock and roll drama. Kurt Cobain wasn't the first, and certainly won't be the last, tragic victim of a highly public and personality-damaging lifestyle.

1995 – RABIN ASSASSINATION 'The last best chance of peace for a generation' was one moving description of Yitzhak Rabin. A fighting general who had proved his courage in numerous battles, as a politician and Prime Minister of his country Rabin tried to be a peacemaker. When he was assassinated it was not by Islamic terrorists or a Palestinian gunman but by ultra ring-wing Jewish religious fanatics with, at the very least, the connivance of Shabak, the General Security Service, and the very officers the Premier should have been able to rely on for protection. That Shabak appears to have been involved in a conspiracy to assassinate Rabin is slowly being exposed. There are rumours aplenty that the supposed assassin Yigal Amir did not murder Rabin, but that the Prime Minister was actually killed in his car after Amir fired three bullets, which either missed or, most surprisingly, were blanks. There is the suggestion that Amir was a government agent or that he had been the victim of a 'mind-control' operation. However, it is believed that the most convincing evidence that Amir did not kill Rabin comes from police forensics expert Baruch Glatstein, who testified at Amir's trial. After examining Rabin's suit and shirt, Glatstein concluded that two shots from point-blank range killed the Prime Mminister. Amir was filmed shooting from at least five feet away. According to Glatstein's testimony, one shot came from a distance of 25 centimetres, while the second was a contact shot. Glatstein rationally explained that Rabin's shirt was torn to shreds in a way that could only occur if the gasses from the cartridge exploded on his skin. Further, Glatstein tested the shirt of Yoram Rubin, Rabin's bodyguard, who was shot in the forearm. He found traces of copper and lead in the bullet hole while Amir's bullets were composed entirely of copper. In short, Amir didn't shoot Rubin either.

Glatstein's testimony agrees with that of Dr Skolnick, a surgeon who operated on Rabin. Dr. Skolnick concluded that Rabin's injuries were caused by contact shots. In July the Supreme Court heard testimony from a Tel Aviv taxi driver who picked up a passenger on the day Amir was convicted. After hearing a radio report on the conviction, the passenger said he was a pathologist at Ichilov Hospital who had examined Rabin. He insisted that Amir could not have shot Rabin because his wounds were from point-blank range. He then produced his Ichilov ID card, proving he was, in fact, a pathologist working at the hospital. Dozens of witnesses heard five shots fired, and in July a police officer assigned to the fateful rally where Rabin died, Yossi Smadja, told the press that he also heard five shots. But their testimony was not welcomed at the Shamgar Commission's cover-up of the killing. The 'amateur film' of the Rabin assassination has since been examined by numerous analysts in frame-by-frame sequence and found to have been sloppily cut and edited.

More sinister, according to this conspiracy, is Rabin's first reaction to being 'shot'. Instead of lurching forwards from the bullets, Rabin alertly turns back, seemingly aware of the events taking place. Most sinister of all, during the final seconds of the film while Rabin is supposedly being lain on the back seat of the car, followed by the wounded bodyguard, someone closes the opposite back passenger door of the car from inside. Clearly, that someone was awaiting Rabin from inside the car. Then there is the testimony of Shimon Peres, who saw Rabin's body in the hospital. He claimed in *Yediot Ahronot* that Rabin's forehead was swollen and bruised, he thought from being pushed on the pavement after he was shot. This is in direct contradiction to the eyewitness report of Miriam Oren, who was beside Rabin after Amir pulled the trigger. She told Israel Television news moments after the incident that Rabin walked into the car under his own power. Where, and how, did the bruises that Peres claims he saw occur? Finally, there is the indisputable proof offered unwittingly by Rabin's aide, Eitan Haber. While surgeons were operating on Rabin at Ichilov Hospital, for reasons unexplained to this day, Haber rifled through Rabin's suit and shirt pockets looking for something and pulled out the songsheet Rabin had held at the rally. Haber produced it for the cameras as he announced Rabin's death and it was deeply bloodstained. Unless Rabin put it in a non-existent back pocket of his suit, he was shot from the front. Support for that contention comes from a most unlikely source. On the night of the murder, a close Rabin compatriot, member of Knesset Ephraim Gur, left the Ichilov Hospital and told a Reuters reporter that he had seen Rabin and that he was shot through the chest and abdomen.

On 20 September two Israeli newspapers unexpectedly printed interviews with subtle advocates of the conspiracy thesis. After nine months of silence, Shlomo Levy gave an interview to *Yerushalayim*. Levy, an associate of Amir's at Bar Ilan University, was a soldier in the Intelligence Brigade of the Israel Defence Forces (IDF). After hearing Amir's threats to kill Rabin, he reported them to his commander who told him to go to the police. The police took his testimony very seriously and on 6 July 1995 passed it on to internal security or Shabak where it was apparently ignored until some three days after the assassination. The official internal inquiry concludes, 'Levy's was only one of a number of reports the Shabak ignored about Amir . . . The fact that the Shabak let the reports gather dust until Rabin was murdered lends credence to numerous conspiracy theories.' On the same day, Rabin's son Yuval was interviewed in *Yediot Ahronot* and when asked if he believed his father was killed by a conspiracy, he replied, 'I can't say yes or no. It's not hard to accept it.' By October the blatant inconsistencies between the official version of events surrounding the Rabin assassination and the rumours had become more noticeable. Early in the month, *Maariv*'s weekend magazine published a remarkable collection of testimonies from seven policemen and security agents on duty at the assassination scene, which fuelled suspicions of a conspiracy for many formerly sceptical readers.

Rabin's assassination came during a period of deep soul-searching within Israel, as the peace process with the Palestinians was not going well. The latest opinion poll in the daily newspaper *Maariv* showed that 78 per cent of the public wanted the process stopped until a national referendum was held to decide whether to continue or not. Only 18 per cent of Israelis trusted Rabin enough to have him carry on his diplomacy without a public referendum and Rabin couldn't step out in public without being heckled. His most humiliating moment came in August when he was introduced at a soccer game and 40,000 fans jeered him in unison. However, that evening a coalition of left-wing political parties and youth movements had organised a rally in his support and Rabin knew that, for a change, he would be surrounded by thousands of well-wishers. Which made his murder that evening doubly unexpected. At 9.15 p.m. Rabin ad-libbed a speech before 100,000 supporters gathered at a square outside Tel Aviv's city hall and a half hour later he was walking down the steps of the stage into the 'secure' area and on to where his car was waiting.

Supposedly he would be perfectly safe during this period as only authorised security personnel would be in the area. But something was very wrong in the parking lot below and the area, far from being secure, was crawling with unauthorised personnel. This is suspicious to many who are aware of Israel's paranoia over tight security. Basic measures were not in place; even the ambulance that should have been near his car at all public appearances was missing, as were most of the policemen. Dozens of policemen should have provided security, but only a few were in sight. The parking area was almost totally dark, whereas it was standard security procedure to illuminate his walking route. Rabin seemed buoyed by the success of his speech and uncharacteristically walked alone towards his car, unaccompanied by his wife, Leah. A few seconds before he reached his vehicle, a security agent of Shabak who was supposed to cover his rear stepped back, stopped and permitted an assassin, Yigal Amir, to get three clear shots at Rabin's back. As soon as the bullets were fired, a Shabak agent yelled, 'Srak, Srak,' or 'they're blanks, they're blanks', while another agent told Rabin's wife Leah a few moments later not to worry because 'the shots were blanks'. The agent next to Rabin pounced on the killer and cuffed him. His first words after being apprehended were, 'Why are you handcuffing me? I did my job. Now it is time to do yours.' The first question the Shabak agents asked the assassin was, 'Didn't you fire blanks?' Since there was no ambulance, Rabin was driven by car to a nearby hospital. The car was not equipped with a radio, an amazing omission in Israel of all places, so the policemen manning roadblocks did not clear the way in advance, and hospital staff were not awaiting the victim upon his arrival. A few minutes later, dozens of reporters received messages from a spokesman from an unknown group called Jewish Vengeance promising to get Rabin next time. After the announcement of his death, the spokesman called the reporters back, retracting the earlier announcement and taking responsibility for the murder. At 11.15 p.m. Rabin aide Eitan Haber, holding what he claimed was a bloody songsheet Rabin had sung from at the rally, announced the Prime Minister's death. That task done, Haber apparently rushed to Jerusalem and cleaned out the files of Rabin's Defence Ministry office. He apparently couldn't wait until the next morning and later told a reporter from the weekly magazine *Kol Ha'ir*, 'I wanted to be sure the files were donated to the archives of the Israel Defence Forces.'

The conspiracy story is in fact very likely to be the truth or very close to it. Either Shabak, one of the world's most respected security organisations, suddenly became totally incompetent for the evening or its agents on the scene allowed the assassination to take place. However, conspiracy theorists have also gone further, probably into the realms of fancy, for they conclude that it was all done with Rabin's knowledge and that the Shabak set up Amir. The theme of the gathering on the fateful night was 'No To Violence'. Amir was to have shot Rabin with blanks, Rabin was to have miraculously escaped an assassination attempt and then climbed back on the stage with a stirring speech, written by his close aide Eitan Haber. The public would react with revulsion against the attempted assassination by an extremist right winger and the government could justify a crackdown against opponents of the peace process. Well, that's the theory, but in both cases someone decided differently and when Rabin was pushed into his car someone was already in the back seat and murdered Rabin with two shots fired at virtually point-blank range. Whichever version you choose, if Amir was allowed that close in a secure area and whether he fired blanks or not, there appears to have been a successful conspiracy to murder the Prime Minister of Israel.

1996 – TWA 800 CONSPIRACY On the night of 17 July 1996 TWA Flight 800 exploded and crashed off the coast of Long Island, killing everyone on board. For months, investigators focused on three possible causes: a bomb, mechanical failure or a terrorist missile. While the National Transportation Safety Board eventually concluded that the jet had exploded due to mechanical failure, as far as many people are concerned what truly happened remains a mystery and to many conspiracy theorists it became a cover-up. According to the official investigators TWA Flight 800 crashed simply because its nearly empty centre fuel tank exploded. The centre tank lies at the heart of the 747's structure, embedded among the spars that support its wings and resting atop the keel beam that runs along its belly. When Flight 800's centre tank exploded, it broke two of the wings' three spars and led to the fracture of the keel beam. After that, the forward fuselage failed and was ripped from the aircraft, which then disintegrated, plunging into the Atlantic Ocean off Long Island, killing all 230 on board.

Just why the tank should explode has been open to some interpretation. The National Transportation and Safety Board (NTSB) suggests static electricity: sloshing or leaking fuel built up a static charge, causing a deadly spark; others suggest fuel-probe residue: mineral deposits on a fuel-level monitor reached dangerous temperatures, igniting the fuel. A large bomb has been ruled out, but small explosives planted on the centre fuel tank could have caused the blast. The Federal Aviation Administration (FAA) opts for chafing wires: rubbing wires near the wing tank started a fire that blew back through the vapour vent system to the centre tank. The rather fanciful meteors theory suggests that 'Space junk', possibly small meteors or missile fragments, hit the jet. Finally what is known as scavenge pump, a pump that bails fuel residue from the centre tank, overheated, touching off hot vapours.

However, it is the alternative theories that have proved most controversial and these include the friendly fire conspiracy. TWA Flight 800 was supposedly flying through the airspace near to where the navy was firing ship-based missiles at target drones. The missile hit the TWA aircraft by accident, resulting in an elaborate conspiracy/cover-up by the navy and the FBI. Then there's the theory that terrorists fired an anti-aircraft missile at Flight 800, blowing it up. More than thirty witnesses claim to have seen an object rising up towards and colliding with Flight 800 prior to the 747's explosion, the kind of visual a friendly fire or terrorist missile launch might have created. The FBI, the navy, the NTSB and others have vigorously denied the terrorist missile or friendly fire theories. Many Americans, including relatives of those killed in the Flight 800 explosion, support these theories, in particular the idea of friendly fire from a US warship. The US authorities from the NTSB, FAA, FBI to the Pentagon have poured scorn on the chances of a US missile being responsible for the aircraft's loss, and suggest that there couldn't be a conspiracy simply because you couldn't get the hundreds of people involved to keep quiet. Well, even if you only take the Manhattan project to develop the first nuclear bomb as an example, thousands of government and military personnel succeeded in keeping that out of the news for several years, but it is a serious point to counteract the theory.

However, it cannot be denied that over thirty witnesses saw a streak of light moving towards, or in the direction of, Flight 800 prior to its explosion. Two of the witnesses are military personnel who happened to be up in a helicopter in the area when the 'accident' took place. While there may not have a lot of evidence to back it up, the friendly fire scenario, as theorists claim, certainly appears to be worthy of further investigation. Indeed this is exactly what former newsman Pierre Salinger insisted on doing, and he has produced a 69-page document and a set of radar images to bolster his case. 'We have now reached the point where we are totally sure what we are saying is true,' Salinger, a former ABC News correspondent and press secretary to President Kennedy, told a Paris news conference. Salinger and Mike Sommer, an investigative reporter and former Salinger colleague at ABC News, showed radar images they said were taken from an air traffic control video from John F. Kennedy International Airport where the flight took off. The images, also released in the *Paris-Match* magazine, show a blip identified as Flight 800, and another blip heading towards it that Salinger claims is the missile that brought down the passenger jet. At the news conference, Salinger and Sommer claimed the 'missile was fired during a "super-secret" US navy exercise off Long Island and was meant to target a Tomahawk missile or drone, but hit Flight 800 instead when it 'lost its lock on its original target.' They claimed the missile was either a kinetic energy missile or a continuous rod missile. Sommer said the kinetic missile would explode near the target and a continuous rod missile would 'slice through' the plane. Salinger's first report says witnesses monitoring secret navy exercises reportedly heard a male voice say, 'Oh, my God, I just hit that plane.' But Salinger was to say later that there was, to his knowledge, no audiotape of a US sailor saying a missile from his ship had shot down TWA 800. Instead, Salinger said he spoke to the father of a sailor who said his son told him, 'Dad, we shot it down.' In an examination of an early draft of Salinger's report, it is claimed that it was found it to be littered with errors and misinformation. The report lacked legitimate attributions, beyond unnamed sources and unnamed experts. The FBI's lead investigator in the Flight 800 disaster, James Kallstrom, repeatedly has said investigators have reviewed every available radar picture and concluded there was no evidence of a missile being fired. The NTSB and the Pentagon have also dismissed Salinger's work. 'Our investigators have looked at all the radar tapes that exist from that evening and have not seen anything that indicates a missile track or missile hit.' 'We're going to continue this investigation. We'll be responsible and responsive to anything that's put out on the public airwaves,' said an official, 'but this just borders on irresponsible to say the Navy shot this down and that whole ships of people are involved in some massive government cover-up.'

The question of whether a terrorist group could be responsible is far easier to dismiss, for unless they hired a sizeable merchant vessel and equipped it secretly with a long-range, high-altitude surface-to-air missile system, the appropriate target tracking and fire control radar systems and had the well-trained personnel to operate all this advanced technology, then it's no go. Any of the available shoulder-launched or manportable missile systems would almost certainly not have the range, altitude or size of warhead to have knocked down TWA 800. There are some theorists, however, who believe that a terrorist bomb was responsible and that it had been planted by a group called the Islamic Change Movement. This is the group that had taken responsibility for the Riyadh bombing in 1995 that killed five Americans and two Indian nationals, and the Khobar Towers bombing in Saudi Arabia on 25 June 1996, which killed nineteen American servicemen. Early on 17 July 1996, the very day TWA Flight 800 was destroyed, this same group issued a communiqué that, according to Yossef Bodansky, 'laid the foundation for the downing of TWA 800'. As director of the Congressional Task Force on Terrorism and Unconventional Warfare, Bodansky knows the subject as well as any man alive. The communiqué was chilling: 'The mujahideen will deliver the ultimate response to the threats of the foolish American president. Everyone will be amazed at the size of that response,' it read in part. 'Their time is at the morning-dawn. Is not the morning-dawn near?' Dawn in Afghanistan corresponded almost exactly to dusk in New York, the moment of TWA Flight 800's demise. So powerful and public was the warning that, by the night of 18 July the State Department had already swung into denial mode. 'While it's up to those leading the investigation to make a judgement on what this means,' said spokesman Glyn Davies unconvincingly, 'we think that this is a common type of political tract circulated commonly in the Middle East, and that the only connection is a vague chronological one – that this thing surfaced at this dreadful time.' The State Department failed to note that on this same day, 18 July, the Islamic Change Movement released another communiqué through well-established Islamist terrorist channels in Beirut. It read in part, 'We carried out our promise with the plane attack of yesterday.' Bodansky was not impressed by the State Department denials. He raised the following chillingly prophetic alarm two years before 9-11: 'The case of TWA 800 served as a turning point because of Washington's determination, and to a great extent ability, to suppress terrorist explanations and "float" mechanical failure theories. To avoid such suppression after future strikes, terrorism-sponsoring states would raise the ante so that the West cannot ignore them. Less well understood is just which "terrorism-sponsoring state" was backing the Islamic Change Movement. To some this organisation is actually a cover name for overseas operations by the Iraqi intelligence services.'

So the jury remains out on TWA Flight 800. There is absolutely no evidence of either a mechanical failure, or of a bomb planted in the fuselage, or of a terrorist missile, or a friendly fire incident. It is somewhat unusual for there to be no definite pointers, but until an explanation can be found for the radar images and the reports of some thirty witnesses including military personnel airborne in a helicopter at the time, then the suspicion will remain that the US is conducting a cover-up to hide a tragic mistake by one of its warships.

1996 – SHAYLERGATE At a time when the Western world is supposedly involved in a life or death struggle against Islamic terrorism, it's mildly instructive that a former MI5 officer should be able to claim that Britain's overseas espionage organisation, MI6, should feel free to give £100,000 of British tax payers' money to an Islamic terrorist group linked to Osama bin Laden's al-Qa'ida for the express purpose of assassinating the leader of Libya. Even more interestingly a Labour government under Tony Blair reacted with all the old right-wing zeal of Mrs Thatcher in continually hounding David Shayler, preventing him having a chance to put his case in an open court, placing gagging orders on the free press and finally jailing Shayler. All this without once appearing to have seriously investigated something, which, if true, is almost certainly a criminal act both in Britain and internationally.

The ministerial gagging orders ensured that upon mention of Shayler's evidence, in court, of Britain's involvement in the attempted assassination of a foreign leader, all the news media would have to immediately leave the trial. This evidence is damning. The British government wanted to bury the story before it became too damaging. The government had been accused by lawyers of trying to interfere in the trial of David Shayler by insisting that part of the proceedings are held in private. Ministers demanded that trial judge Mr Justice Alan Moses agree in advance that the case go into private session without saying why and without hearing arguments to the contrary from the defence. In its efforts to contain Shayler's allegations to the privacy of the court, the government even went so far as stopping the media from reporting the government's successful attempt to win a gag order. The decision by an Old Bailey judge to stop the media from reporting parts of Mr Shayler's evidence came after two senior ministers, David Blunkett and Jack Straw, signed Public Interest Immunity certificates. Shayler's trial, on charges under the Official Secrets Act, was held at the Old Bailey, and Shayler defended himself during the trial, claiming that British secret service agents paid up to £100,000 to al-Qa'ida terrorists for an assassination attempt on Libyan leader Colonel Gaddafi in 1996. Startling revelations by French intelligence experts backed David Shayler's alleged 'fantasy' about the Gaddafi plot and indeed that

British intelligence officers actually thwarted early attempts to bring Osama bin Laden to justice.

The latest claims of MI6 involvement with Libya's fearsome Islamic Fighting Group, which is connected to one of bin Laden's trusted lieutenants, will be embarrassing to the government, which described similar claims by renegade MI5 officer David Shayler as 'pure fantasy'. The allegations have emerged in the book *Forbidden Truth*, published in the USA by two French intelligence experts who reveal that the first Interpol arrest warrant for bin Laden was issued by Libya in March 1998. According to journalist Guillaume Dasquié and Jean-Charles Brisard, an advisor to French President Jacques Chirac, British and US intelligence agencies buried the fact that the arrest warrant had come from Libya and played down the threat. Five months after the warrant was issued, al-Qa'ida killed more than 200 people in the truck bombings of US embassies in Kenya and Tanzania. The arrest warrant was issued in connection with the murder in March 1994 of two German anti-terrorism agents, Silvan and Vera Becker, who were in charge of missions in Africa. According to the book, the resistance of Western intelligence agencies to the Libyan concerns can be explained by MI6's involvement with the al-Qa'ida coup plot against Gaddafi. The Libyan al-Qa'ida cell included Anas al-Liby, who remains on the US government's most wanted list with a reward of $25 million for his capture. He is wanted for his involvement in the African embassy bombings. Al-Liby was with bin Laden in Sudan before the al-Qa'ida leader returned to Afghanistan in 1996. Astonishingly, despite suspicions that he was a high-level al-Qa'ida terrorist, al-Liby was given political asylum in Britain and lived in Manchester until May 2000 when he eluded a police raid on his house and fled abroad. The raid discovered a 180-page al-Qa'ida 'manual for jihad' containing instructions for terrorist attacks.

Shayler was eventually found guilty in 2002 and sentenced to six months in prison for disclosing documents obtained during his time as an MI5 officer. He was not allowed to argue that he made the revelations in the public interest. During his closing speech, Shayler repeated claims that he was gagged from talking about 'a crime so heinous' that he had no choice but to go to the press with his story. Shayler claims he was first briefed about the Gaddafi plot during formal meetings with colleagues from MI6 when he was working on MI5's Libya desk in the mid-1990s. It is now known that the MI6 officers involved in the alleged plot were Richard Bartlett, who has previously only been known under the code-name PT16 and had overall responsibility for the operation, and David Watson, code-name PT16B. As Shayler's opposite number in MI6, Watson was responsible for running a Libyan agent, 'Tunworth', who was providing information from within the cell. The assassination attempt on Gaddafi was planned for early 1996 in the Libyan coastal city of Sirte, and it is thought that an operation by the Islamic Fighting Group in the city was foiled in March 1996 and that in the gun battle that followed several militants were killed. In 1998 the Libyans released TV footage of a 1996 grenade attack on Gaddafi that they claimed had been carried out by a British agent. Shayler, who conducted his own defence in the trial, intended to call Bartlett and Watson as witnesses, but was prevented from doing so by the narrow focus of the court case.

David Shayler had joined MI5 as part of a recruitment drive in the early 90s to attract a new breed of non-public school, non-Oxbridge graduates who would shake up the moribund service. With the end of the Cold War, it was felt that MI5 had to shift the emphasis of its operations towards the very real threat from the IRA, Islamic fundamentalists and hostile regimes in the Middle East. According to Shayler, he and other officers of his generation soon became disillusioned with intelligence work. Most of it seemed to involve shuffling papers and getting official clearance for the endless MI5 phone taps on ordinary individuals. He became appalled by the level of surveillance of tiny extreme-left groups, while the intelligence service was unable to stop terrorist acts by the IRA such as the bombings at Bishopsgate and Canary Wharf. Most seriously he was convinced that MI5 and SIS (MI6) agents often acted outside the rule of law, knowing they were unlikely to be punished. After raising his concerns with senior officers he, like many of his colleagues, left around the time the Labour government came to power in 1997 pledging to make the intelligence services more accountable. He had worked for G Branch, dealing with international terrorism, C Branch, where government officials' backgrounds are checked and T Branch, targeting terrorism in Northern Ireland. Desk-bound and increasingly unhappy with his employer, Shayler quit his job in 1997. He took his concerns about the UK's secret services to *Mail on Sunday* journalist Nick Fielding. Shayler's revelations about MI5 and MI6 range from the general to the embarrassingly specific. In August 1997 the *Mail on Sunday* published his claims that MI5 was riven with incompetence and inefficiency. He also blew the whistle on alleged surveillance operations on such 'subversives' as Jack Straw, Peter Hain and Peter Mandelson, all of whom went on to hold senior government positions. Ex-Beatle John Lennon, UB40 and punk band the Sex Pistols were also investigated by MI5, said Shayler. Further allegations have followed, suggesting a bungling MI5 failed to stop the bomb attack on Israel's London embassy in 1994 and the IRA's 1993 Bishopsgate bombing, which killed one person.

In August 1998 Shayler renewed his attacks on the secret services, including details of a plot to assassinate Libyan leader Colonel Gaddafi. Robin Cook, then British Foreign Secretary, described Shayler's claims about the Gaddafi plot as 'pure fantasy'. However, the *Sunday Times* report of 13 February 2000 was titled intriguingly REVEALED: COOK MISLED PUBLIC OVER LIBYA PLOT. David Shayler's response was that he had been largely vindicated over the existence of a Gaddafi assassination plot. The report does confirm that MI6 had an agent who had prior information about the plans of a group of army plotters who had decided either to arrest or kill Gaddafi as part of a coup in February–March 1996. The report directly contradicts Foreign Secretary Robin Cook's assertion that the Gaddafi Plot was 'pure fantasy' and was sent to the Foreign Office's Permanent Under-Secretary's Department, which directly advises the Foreign Secretary. The Foreign Office therefore clearly knew that MI6 were at the very least aware of advanced plans to stage a coup in which Gaddafi would be arrested or killed. Robin Cook would indeed appear to have seriously misled parliament, the media and the general public.

The government's treatment of Shayler has been a shock to many who had believed Tony Blair's assertions on a free society and an end to cover-ups. When it came down to it, the government showed a lack of moral courage in not properly and openly investigating accusations of criminal activities carried on by MI6 and a self-serving cowardice in attempting to silence Shayler and avoid the truth from emerging in a court of law.

1997 – DEATH OF A PRINCESS At precisely 12.15 a.m. on Sunday 31 August 1997 the security staff of the Ritz Hotel were alerted. Dodi and Diana were ready to depart through the rear entrance of the hotel. A green Range Rover and the decoy black Mercedes (the latter driven by the hotel's senior limousine driver) pulled out into the Place Vendome, circled the square and returned to their parking spots. The photographers there were stymied.

Meantime, a second black 1994 Mercedes S-280, with Henri Paul at the wheel and Trevor Rees-Jones in the passenger seat, sped away from the rear of the Ritz; Dodi was behind Paul, Diana on his right, behind Rees-Jones. In the excitement, only Rees-Jones fastened his seat belt. It was 12.20 a.m. when the car sped south on Rue Cambon, then went along Rue de Rivoli and past the splashing, illuminated fountain and Egyptian obelisk of the Place de la Concorde. By the time the Mercedes was hugging the Seine and heading toward the underpass, the few paparazzi on motorbikes had dropped behind. Photographs of speeding cars (more to the point, of their occupants) are notoriously difficult to obtain at night; besides, the windows of the Mercedes were heavily tinted and none of the photographers wish to risk their lives by edging their bikes close to a speeding vehicle. Of course, the 'Paparazzi killed Diana' theory turns out to be total nonsense as everyone should have realised, except that is for certain major television news stations and newspapers who tried to suggest otherwise. The distinctly unpleasant small of cant and hypocrisy was in the air. The news media who had willing used the paparazzi for years now found a new moral stance and condemned the practice of car chases and door-stepping. By the time Henri Paul and his passengers entered the Alma tunnel, the photographers were almost a quarter of a mile behind, keeping the car in sight but not endangering themselves by approaching the speeding Mercedes. It would be enough to arrive at Dodi's apartment, where several other colleagues of the pursuing paparazzi had already been alerted.

The official French investigation begins at 12.23 a.m. in the Place de l'Alma Tunnel. It notes that the paparazzi who had been stalking Diana and Dodi since their arrival earlier that day in Paris appeared on the scene two minutes after the collision. But another limousine driver entered the tunnel not far behind Paul, and this driver made a sworn statement of what happened, events that occurred within a few seconds and which changed the course of countless lives, to some extent the course of late-twentieth-century history and certainly the perception of many observers. The driver's account, it must be said, was in every way supported by police and by later forensic investigations of the site.

Police believe that driver Henri Paul braked suddenly when he came upon a slow-moving car in the Alma tunnel, then sped up and tried to pass the car on the left. Tyre tracks a few feet further into the tunnel suggest that in trying to regain control of the car, Paul stepped on the gas and fatally lost control. The French police have solved some of the mystery by reconstructing the accident in the Alma tunnel and consulting photographs taken at the scene. The pictures showed that, contrary to what was at first thought, six cars passed the wreck before traffic was stopped. During the reconstruction, everyone noticed that the tunnel's yellowish lighting greatly distorted colour. It had been assumed that all of the photographers were some 200 metres behind the Mercedes when it entered the tunnel from the Place de la Concorde. But there is significant evidence, *Newsweek* learned, that at least one was on a motorcycle in front of the Mercedes. Mark Butt, a friend of Dr Mailliez's who arrived on the scene with him, said that as they approached the tunnel from the west, they saw a motorcycle with a single rider emerge from the east, therefore travelling in the same direction as the Mercedes. Butt says it stopped, made a U-turn and drove against the direction of traffic back into the tunnel.

If Diana had died in the USA, someone could ultimately be held financially responsible for her demise. But, the Princess of Wales died in France, where massive punitive awards are neither the custom nor the law. And it is important to add that all police and official investigations discounted the proximity of paparazzi with blinding flashbulbs, on motorcycles. Paul entered the tunnel on the left of two lanes, speeding at 60 to perhaps 80 miles an hour, which is not at all unusual in European cities, and then he found his car was behind a slower vehicle. Careful though this driver might otherwise have been, it is easy to imagine Dodi urging him on: 'Faster! Lose them! Go on!'; as friends and colleagues recalled, he usually did. Life was apparently a game Dodi wanted always to win, a game in which he wanted both to be in the limelight and to retain his privacy. Henri Paul, in a healthier condition, may well have been more cautious, but as Claude Luc said, Fayed employees usually did what they were told. Paul apparently veered the Mercedes to the right, to pass the car ahead of him in the left lane. But then everything went out of control, the right rear of the Mercedes swerved and hit the right wall of the tunnel with a loud crash. Attempting to correct the situation, Paul turned sharply left and within seconds the Mercedes crashed into one of the reinforced concrete dividing pillars that separated the lanes from oncoming traffic and also supported the roof. The sound, like an explosion, was nearly deafening. The car ricocheted again, hurtling across the road and spinning around before coming to a full stop. It had been immediately reduced to a barely recognisable mound of steel: the front end telescoped into the engine, which was forced almost through the driver's seat. Inside the pile of rubble, Henri Paul and Dodi al-Fayed were dead, their bodies hideously mangled. Trevor Rees-Jones was seriously injured, but Diana, Princess of Wales, was near death.

It was 12.24 a.m. and one minute before the arrival of the photographers, approaching in his car from the opposite direction was Frederic Mailliez, an emergency doctor employed by SOS Medecins, a private firm, who stopped and ran to the spot. He saw at once that two of the passengers were dead, but that two others, including a blonde woman, were perhaps still alive. In an interview with *Newsweek* he described what happened next. 'I held her hand and spoke to her, took her pulse, put the resuscitation mask on her, assured her that she was safe.' He also called for help. Within five minutes of the accident, two ambulances arrived, each with a doctor. Within seconds, the pursuing photographers had caught up. Nestled among sheets of police reports, carefully sketched diagrams and statements from witnesses are photographs of Diana in the wreckage of the Mercedes. Taken by a paparazzo, Diana, eyes open, appears conscious and unhurt; there is no sign of blood. Appearances aside, Diana was badly hurt and less than four hours later, she was dead. At the same time, police and firemen arrived, alerted by cars exiting the tunnel ahead of the Mercedes, and very soon they identified the woman passenger. By 1.15 a.m. the bodies of Henri Paul and Dodi al-Fayed had been removed from the wreck.

Later, after repeated toxicological tests, it was determined that Paul's blood contained four times the legal amount of alcohol permitted for drivers. There was also evidence in his system of two prescription medications for psychological and emotional stress: fluoxetine, which is the generic name for the American drug Prozac, and Tiapride, a European compound often used to calm aggressive patients being treated for alcoholism. Diana and Rees-Jones, both of them barely alive, took longer to be extricated. Jean-Pierre Chevenement, the Interior Minister, was contacted by senior police officials and sped to the Hospital de la Pitie-Salpetriere, where Diana and Rees-Jones were taken. They arrived at two that morning. A team of surgeons and nurses set to work on Rees-Jones, who underwent the first of many operations to reset and restructure his shattered jaw and broken arm. Subsequently, he was in a coma for weeks and had little memory of anything after the car left the hotel. It took the emergency workers a full 52 minutes to place Diana in the ambulance. It proceeded slowly along the Seine, led by a motorcycle escort. At the Point d'Austerlitz, a short distance from the hospital, the motorcade pulled off the road; Diana's heart had stopped beating. She was injected with a strong dose of adrenaline, and the ambulance continued on. Finally, at 2.05 a.m., 43 minutes after leaving the scene, Diana arrived at the Pitie-Salpetriere Hospital, a 3.7-mile trip. After trying for two hours to save her, doctors officially pronounced Diana dead at 4.05 a.m.

To many, the elapsed time from the arrival of the ambulance at the accident scene to the hospital, a total of 1 hour and 45 minutes, seemed inordinately long. Diana, after all, didn't have to be cut out of the car (though both Rees-Jones and Paul did). In addition, the ambulance bypassed at least two major hospitals. To Parisians, the pace of the trip was entirely understandable. French ambulances are always staffed with a fully qualified doctor and are considered an extension of the hospital; driving slowly is standard. 'It's worse to go fast,' says Mailliez. 'Braking and accelerating can literally kill your patient, because the blood races to head and feet alternately.' And the Pitie-Salpetriere has the best-equipped emergency room in Paris. In the end, Diana's internal injuries were so massive (most important, a severe lesion to her pulmonary vein) that even if the accident had happened in front of an emergency room, she couldn't have been saved. In lay terms, 'her heart had been ripped out of its place in her chest,' said Mailliez. 'There was no chance for her.'

No chance even for her to speak? News reports said the Fayed family had been given a message containing Diana's final requests, but a spokesman at the Pitie-Salpetriere said that 'during her hours at the hospital, Diana, Princess of Wales, was unconscious and could therefore make no statements or remarks.' If Diana had any last words, Mailliez probably heard them. The paparazzi at the scene have been quoted as saying that Diana told rescue workers, 'Leave me alone' and 'My God'. Mailliez would not tell *Newsweek* what Diana said. 'I must respect the privacy of the patient.' Could she have left any message to pass on to family? 'When you're in that kind of pain, you don't about giving testaments to the next generation. The only thing you think of expressing is the pain.' Diana's condition was terminal and she was undoubtedly fading fast. A surgical team laboured over her for almost two hours. She had sustained massive chest injuries and had bled profusely, then a vein split and her blood pressure dropped to a dangerous level. At first it seemed that her age and fitness might save her, but then it became clear that, despite the successful repair of the torn vein, all her internal organs were gravely damaged. She suffered cardiac arrest, and her heart failed to respond to open massage. Electric shocks were unavailing.

Much of the world still wonders what, exactly, happened that night. 31 August 2003 will be the sixth anniversary of Diana's tragic death and, weird theories of satanism, cabals and the like apart, the only conspiracy theory that has attracted serious attention is the suggestion that MI6 murdered the Princess of Wales either on the orders of the royal family or on those of the military-industrial complex because her international charity work included campaigning against such controversial subjects as landmines. Details of small groups of MI6 officers flying to Paris a few days before her death and mysteriously leaving hours afterwards are supposed to be proof of their involvement, but that is clutching at straws. The fact that these visitors included quite senior MI6 officers such as Richard Spearman, Chief of Staff to David Spedding, the head of the intelligence service at the time, Nicholas Langman, principle assistant to Spearman and Richard Dearlove, a future head of MI6, does not in itself constitute grounds for a conspiracy to murder Princess Diana. Not only could there be a dozen valid reasons for their behaviour, but if they had really been involved in such a high-profile killing they may indeed have been rather more discreet in their movements. What did, however, raise a few eyebrows was the rather alarming similarity in one of the methods MI6 was prepared to use to assassinate President Milosevic of Yugoslavia – an ambush involving an ultra-bright flash of light directly into the eyes of the driver of the President's vehicle while travelling through an underpass in Belgrade. Conspiracy theorists had their collective spirits raised by this seemingly damning information; however, it must be said that unless more concrete evidence of a conspiracy comes to light, then it would appear that the Princess, Dodi Fayed and Henri Paul died as the result of a tragic accident caused by carelessness and speeding.

1998 – OMAGH COVER-UP The British security forces didn't intercept the Real IRA's Omagh bombing team because one of the terrorists was a British double-agent whose cover would have been blown as an informer if the operation was uncovered. This the basis for a conspiracy that suggested security officers were responsible for one the worst terrorist outrages in the history of the Northern Ireland 'Troubles'. According to one observer, 'The only reason the RUC would not act on a tip-off which stated a bomb was in the offing is if a member of the bombing team was a highly placed agent and they needed to keep him in place. If the operation was allowed to go ahead then the agent would be seen as a good guy by the Real IRA; but if it failed, he could have come under suspicion of being an informer and been killed.'

The security forces were forced to hope that their agent would provide them with intelligence in time to ensure that the bomb would go off without casualties. In the event, however, due to blundering handling of telephone warnings, 29 people died on 15 August 1998. The claims follow a statement by another British double-agent in the IRA, 'Kevin Fulton', who said that he had phoned a warning to his Royal Ulster Constabulary handlers some 48 hours before the Omagh bombing in which he told them clearly that the Real IRA was planning an attack and gave details of one of the bombing team and the man's car registration. The RUC chief constable Sir Ronnie Flanagan claims no such information was received, despite Fulton claiming to have a tape of a conversation with his handler in which the officer appears to admit the tip-off was received. Both Republican and British intelligence sources say the RUC did not act on the information as one of the Omagh bombing team was a British informer. It is not known whether he was operating for the RUC E4 anti-terrorist unit, military intelligence or MI5. There is speculation he could also have been working for the Garda Special Branch in the Irish Republic. Republican sources indicated that the Real IRA had launched an internal inquiry to find the 'spy' in their midst. The man believed to be the agent was thought to be a senior member of the organisation, but that was later claimed to be a 'black propaganda operation' by MI5 to further sow distrust within the ranks of the breakaway Irish Republican terrorists.

Could the British have deliberately allowed the Real IRA to explode such a deadly bomb simply to protect an important double-agent? Not likely it would seem: the British security forces have regularly 'fingered' or exposed their own informers or 'snouts' to the IRA when it suited them. Few informers, even deep-cover double-agents would have been considered important enough to sacrifice the lives of civilians. Some conspiracy theorists will beg to differ of course.

1998 – NEW WORLD ORDER Is there really is a sinister plot to set up a one-world government? The conspiracy theory about the New World Order is not new, but it was the one that everyone was talking about as we drew closer to the year 2000. A growing number of Americans are still so convinced that the NWO is about to take over that they are making plans to fight back, stockpiling foods, weapons and ammunition. Major Boyd is a trooper in the New Mexico Militia, an armed unit of volunteers – farmers, salesmen, former police officers – who are preparing to take the New World Order on. He confidently claimed, 'There are 19 million armed American patriots ready to take their country back.'

What is the New World Order? Simply put, it is a shadowy collection of elite bankers, politicians, intelligence and military leaders who want to control the whole world with a single dictatorial government usually described as the One World Government or the New World Order. This is a shadowy collection of people who want to control the whole world. It has been linked with theories of Jewish plans for world domination, the Illuminati, Bilderberg, Bohemian Grove, Reagan Agenda, Freemasons and perhaps even with a plot by extraterrestrials to take over control of planet Earth by the use of proxies, willing dupes who will be the worlds 'quislings' or jailers for an alien race. Heady stuff some of these conspiracy theories, but believed by hundreds of thousands, if not millions of people. Mind control, men in black and these mysterious unidentified flying helicopters, also usually black, are all believed to be outward signs of the global conspiracy. Some believe that preparations for the takeover are already underway. They claim that gigantic detention facilities, many underground, have been built across the country where anyone who disagrees with the government will be locked up. 'Their soldiers will come to get us in their black helicopters,' said one survivalist. These helicopters with no visible unit markings and charcoal black paint are a common theme for the theorists, but the US government says that they don't exist. BBC producer Richard Vadon claimed to have seen two of them landing at an air force base in New Mexico, and others say they were seen hovering over David Koresh's homestead on the day that the federal authorities ended the 51-day siege at Waco, killing 82 Branch Davidians and 4 agents. Whatever the rather shaky foundations these New World Order conspiracy theories may have, while they are firmly believed by so many, otherwise seemingly perfectly rational, people, then they will continue to have an importance uniquely their own.

1999 – CONSPIRACY OF ILLUSIONS With the approach of the millennium a veritable explosion of conspiracy theories from the interesting to the whacky, outlandish and seriously disturbed flooded the Internet and the mass media. Helicopters and men in black, secret underground bases, shape-shifting lizards, alien nations and imminent extraterrestrial takeover were all piled upon the conspiracies to fake the moon landings in 1969, Roswell and a thousand other 'explanations' of government clandestine operations, plans by groups of Jewish bankers or any of the other favourite groups that are supposedly trying to take over and impose a New World Order and a One World Government. Thankfully sanity still largely prevails, though the willingness of hundreds of thousands of seemingly rational people to believe what is usually quite obviously lacking logic or rationality suggests not only a collapse in trust of the 'official version' of worrying or tragic events, but a fear of a world that is ever-harder to understand and cope with. The plethora of loony conspiracy theories does, however, also have a more serious side effect. It lessens the interest of the media and the thinking citizen in the real conspiracies that are illuminated throughout this book and throughout history. These are the genuine conspiracies and cover-ups that can affect every aspect of our lives and sometimes lead to countless deaths in conflicts that could have been avoided. Perhaps the biggest beneficiary from the unhealthy fascination with the 'X-File' mentality and the latest mega-conspiracy theory are those governments with so much to hide.

The notion of secret bases is linked firmly to the idea of hidden worlds and underground civilisations, whether of alien or terrestrial origin. It is not a new idea as both Jules Verne and Edgar Rice Burroughs successfully wrote about subterranean nations. However, the modern theorist suggests that new 'giant underground facilities' are really concentration camps and part of a fiendish plot to cage the survivors of an impending invasion by aliens, or one of many variations on this theme. There are of course vast numbers of genuine underground control and command bunkers and deep-shaft nuclear facilities dating from the end of WW2 and the long years of the Cold War. They exist in the USA, Russia, China, Britain, France, Germany and probably many other countries, but the true fascination the theorists seem to have with such bunkers is based largely on the fear of what can't be seen: if it is hidden it must be something bad. It gets really strange when underground bases are believed to be cities full of extraterrestrials. Somewhere near Dulce in New Mexico there is supposed to be a sprawling multilevel facility tunnelled deep beneath the desert floor and some theorists suggest that this has been provided 'super secretly' by the US government to house a population of some 18,000 aliens from a variety of planetary systems scattered across the Galaxy, including Greys from Orion and Zeta Reticulli and earth humans or Terrans in the terminology of the soon-to-be-created 'Galactic Federation'. Work started in 1948 soon after the Roswell incident as a direct result of a so-far-unannounced human–alien non-aggression pact! This of course melds very nicely into all the alien nation theories that range from hostiles to friendlies to 'just looking, Officer'. But whatever else the aliens may be – shape-shifters or hybrids resulting from all those alien abductions and experimentation incidents – or whatever they may be doing, there's one thing that's certain, according to the theorists, 'they're doing it here!'

One of the most disturbing aspects of the growth in conspiracy theories has been the large number of neo-fascist, right-wing and anti-Jewish quasi-religious groups blaming the Jews for everything from the murder of JFK and planning world domination to being shape-shifting lizards. That this is a popular theme running through the world of the feckless, dysfunctional and prejudiced who seek scapegoats for their own inability to prosper is quite clear; that it may be used as a propaganda weapon and a smoke screen for the re-emergence of widespread anti-Semitism and Nazi-style politics must be of far greater concern. Despite the fact that most of the way-out conspiracy theories demand little intellect and are really entertainment based, these and many others still to be invented will no doubt continue to puzzle, amuse and irritate for the foreseeable future. You have been warned!

2001 – A CLASSIC CONSPIRACY TO CONVICT On 31 January 2001 Abdelbaset Ali Mohmed al Megrahi was found guilty of placing a bomb on board Pan Am Flight 103, destroying the aircraft over the small Scottish town of Lockerbie just before Christmas 1988. The special Scottish court in The Hague found his co-defendant, Al Amin Khalifa Fhimah, not guilty on basically the same evidence. To many it seemed that though the evidence was thin, almost to laughable at times, at least one of the accused had to be found guilty if only to spare the British government's blushes. Coming the month after the election of George W. Bush, The Hague verdict could have been dubbed Supreme Court II, another instance of non-judicial factors fatally clouding judicial reasoning. The three Scottish judges could not have relished returning to the UK after finding both defendants innocent of the murder of 270 people largely from the UK and the USA. Not to mention having to face dozens of hysterical victims' family members in the courtroom. The three judges also well knew that the White House and Downing Street fervently wished for a conviction in this case: it was politically imperative. If both men had been acquitted, the US and Great Britain would have had to answer for a decade of sanctions and aggressive tactics towards Libya.

Some expert observers who have waded through the entire 26,000-word 'Opinion of the Court', as well as being very familiar with the history of the case going back to 1988, are claimed to strongly question the judges' verdict. The key charge against Megrahi was that he placed explosives in a suitcase and tagged it so it would lead the following charmed life: first loaded aboard an Air Malta flight to Frankfurt without an accompanying passenger, then transferred in Frankfurt to the Pan Am 103A flight to London without an accompanying passenger and finally transferred in London to the Pan Am 103 flight to New York, again without an accompanying passenger. This scenario by itself would have been a major feat and so unlikely to succeed that any terrorist with any common sense would have found a better way. But, aside from anything else, there is the first step, loading the suitcase at Malta where there was no witness, no video, no document, no fingerprints, nothing to tie Megrahi to the particular brown Samsonite suitcase, no past history of terrorism, no forensic evidence of any kind linking him or Fhimah to such an act. And the court admitted it: 'The absence of any explanation of the method by which the primary suitcase might have been placed on board KM180, Air Malta, is a major difficulty for the Crown case.' Moreover, under security requirements in 1988, unaccompanied baggage was subjected to special x-ray examinations, and because of recent arrests in Germany it is known that the security personnel in Frankfurt were on the lookout specifically for a bomb secreted in a radio, which turned out indeed to be the method used with the Pan Am 103 bomb.

Requiring some sort of direct and credible testimony linking Megrahi to the bombing, The Hague court placed unusually great weight upon the supposed identification of the Libyan by a shopkeeper in Malta as the purchaser of the clothing found in the bomb suitcase. But it must not be forgotten that this shopkeeper had earlier identified several other people as the culprit, including one who turned out to be a CIA agent. When he finally identified Megrahi from a photo, it was after Megrahi's photo had been in the world news for years. The court acknowledged the possible danger inherent in such a verification: 'These identifications were criticized *inter alia* on the ground that photographs of the accused have featured many times over the years in the media and accordingly purported identifications more than ten years after the event are of little if any value.' Yet still found him guilty! There were also major discrepancies between the shopkeeper's original description of the clothes-buyer and Megrahi's actual appearance. The shopkeeper told police that the customer was 'six feet or more in height' and 'was about fifty years of age'. Megrahi was 5′8″ tall and was 36 in 1988. The judges again acknowledged the weakness of their argument by conceding that the initial description 'would not in a number of respects fit the first accused' and that 'it has to be accepted that there was a substantial discrepancy.' Nevertheless, the judges went ahead and accepted the identification as accurate.

Before the indictment of the two Libyans in Washington in November 1991, the press had reported police findings that the clothing had been purchased on 23 November 1988. But in the indictment of Megrahi it clearly states that he made the purchase on 7 December. Is this because the investigators were able to document Megrahi being in Malta, where he worked for Libya Airlines, on that date but cannot do so for 23 November? If the bomber needed some clothing to wrap up an ultra-secret bomb in a suitcase, would he go to a clothing store in the city where he planned to carry this out, where he knew he would likely be remembered as an obvious foreigner, and buy brand-new, easily traceable items? Would an intelligence officer, which of course Megrahi was alleged to be, do anything so amateurish and so likely to provide a trail of evidence? Wouldn't it make more sense to use any old clothing, from anywhere, or even rags? Furthermore, after the world was repeatedly assured that these items of clothing were sold only in Malta, it was learned that at least one of the items was actually 'sold at dozens of outlets throughout Europe, and it was impossible to trace the purchaser'.

The 'Opinion of the Court' placed considerable weight on the suspicious behaviour of Megrahi prior to the fatal day, making much of his comings and goings abroad, phone calls to unknown parties for unknown reasons, the use of a pseudonym and so on. The three judges tried to squeeze as much mileage out of these events as they could, as if they had no better case to make. But if Megrahi was indeed a member of Libyan intelligence, then intelligence agents have been known to act in mysterious ways. The court, however, had no idea what assignment Megrahi might have been working on.

There is much more about this case that makes the verdict highly questionable, although some credit can be given to the court for stating frankly what it was doing: 'We are aware that in relation to certain aspects of the case there are a number of uncertainties and qualifications,' the judges wrote. 'We are also aware that there is a danger that by selecting parts of the evidence which seem to fit together and ignoring parts which might not fit, it is possible to read into a mass of conflicting evidence a pattern or conclusion which is not really justified.' It is remarkable, given all that the judges conceded was questionable or uncertain in the trial and not to mention all that was questionable or uncertain that they didn't concede, that at the end of the day they could still declare to the world, 'There is nothing in the evidence which leaves us with any reasonable doubt as to the guilt of [Megrahi].' The *Guardian* later wrote that two days before the verdict, 'senior Foreign Office officials briefed a group of journalists in London. They painted a picture of a bright new chapter in Britain's relations with Colonel Gaddafi's regime. They made it quite clear they assumed both the Libyans in the dock would be acquitted and in this the Foreign Office officials were not alone. Most independent observers believed it was impossible for the court to find the prosecution had proved its case against Megrahi beyond reasonable doubt.' It is true to say that the judges nearly agreed with the defence. In their verdict, they tossed out much of the prosecution witnesses' evidence as false or questionable and said the prosecution had failed to prove crucial elements, including the route that the bomb suitcase took. Michael Scharf, professor at the New England School of Law, said, 'I thought this was a very, very weak circumstantial case. I am absolutely astounded, astonished. I was extremely reluctant to believe that any Scottish judge would convict anyone, even a Libyan, on the basis of such evidence,' while Robert Black, Scottish law professor who was the architect of The Hague trial added, 'A general pattern of the trial consisted in the fact that virtually all people presented by the prosecution as key witnesses were proven to lack credibility to a very high extent, in certain cases even having openly lied to the court,' and 'While the first accused was found "guilty", the second accused was found "not guilty". This is totally incomprehensible for any rational observer when one considers that the indictment in its very essence was based on the joint action of the two accused in Malta.'

This, according to the conspiracy theorists, was a conspiracy that was instigated at the highest levels in the White House and in Downing Street, for after a decade of diverting blame away from the real culprits, Syria, Iran and their Palestinian allies, towards Libya, it would be a political nightmare and diplomatic humiliation if both of the accused had been found not guilty, as they almost certainly should have been. The last word can be safely left to Hans Köchler, appointed as an international observer of the Lockerbie Trial by UN Secretary-General Kofi Annan, 'Regrettably, through the conduct of the Court, disservice has been done to the important cause of international criminal justice.'

2001 – 911: A CAUSE FOR CONSPIRACY The tragic events of 9-11 have already spawned more crackpot conspiracy theories than any other event. It would seem that the so-called collective consciousness cannot accept truly earth-shattering events at face value: there simply has to be an answer when the fast moving and complex reality simply doesn't provide one. Enter the conspiracy theorist with the answers to all the questions demanding a response. No matter if they are convoluted, ultra-complex, irrational or totally absurd, to many it appears to be safer and more acceptable to have an answer, any answer. This trait can get in the way of a serious and sensible investigation of events, often much to the relief of governments concerned. However, the establishment both on the right and left of politics has largely accepted the official version of what happened on 11 September 2001, both the facts and the cover-ups of mistakes and gross inefficiency.

Numerous respected commentators across the spectrum have ardently criticised widespread public speculation that the Bush Administration had advance warning of the 11 September terrorist attacks, sufficient to prevent them from occurring. The Central Intelligence Agency, as the name suggests, was founded to centralise the intelligence function of the United States. It was a good idea then and it is a good idea now. Unfortunately, it is an idea that has never been truly implemented and from which, over time, the government has moved away. A centralised intelligence capability is essential if the USA is to have a single, integrated, coherent picture of what is happening in the world, but the present bureaucratically fragmented intelligence community in the USA has generated a dangerously fragmented picture of the world. Given that a proper analysis of the structure, capabilities, recent co-ordination and record of success of the US intelligence community provides little support for the total 'incompetence theory' of a counter-terrorist intelligence failure, it is likely that the 9-11 intelligence failure was a consequence of the higher political bureaucracy refraining from acting on intelligence provided by the CIA, NSA, DIA and its allies in the global intelligence community. As always, analysis, interpretation and distribution of intelligence has proved more difficult than the collection and interception of the raw intelligence 'take'. In this context, it is perfectly legitimate to investigate the 9-11 intelligence failure with due consideration given to both the admittedly unlikely 'incompetence theory', as well as what might be termed the 'political inaction' theory, of which the 'foreknowledge hypothesis' is one variation. Either way, the likelihood of political inaction being behind the administration's failure to foil the al-Qa'ida plot in itself implicates the existence of a web of strategic and economic influences acting upon the political establishment, creating a form of political inertia in peace that can verge on paralysis in times of crisis.

Conspiracy theorists have had, of course, a veritable feast at the table of doubt and suspicion over 9-11 and indeed there are numerous scenarios to choose from, including: the World Trade Center was destroyed not by planes but by explosives; the planes were not hijacked at all, but commandeered by remote control by NORAD (the North American Aerospace Defense Command); the planes were hijacked, but the hijackers were double-crossed and the planes were taken over by remote control by NORAD; the hijackers were actually working for the US government; US intelligence knew about the plot, but intentionally did nothing so as to cause massive deaths that would mobilise public support for a war on terrorism that would benefit the government; the plot was actually organised by Mossad; Mossad knew about the plot, but did nothing, hoping that the massive deaths would mobilise public support for Israel's war on the Palestinians; Tower Two of the World Trade Center was hit by a missile; there was a joint plot by rogue elements in the CIA, the Mossad, other US government agencies and Mobil who were being investigated in a criminal case and all of the evidence against them was in the FBI offices in the World Trade Center; and lastly Russian organised crime gangs were involved.

Without a shadow of doubt, and despite the most extraordinary interest, the giant conspiracy that suggests that President Bush and his most senior advisors planned this appalling attack on their own nation to provide an excuse to bomb mountain goats in Afghanistan or, more seriously, to open the nation up to a war on Iraq so that the 'oil interests' in the White House could steal Iraq's oil reserves, are nonsensical. Is the present administration really capable of such a conspiracy, either morally or intellectually? Conspiracy theorists will point to Operation Northwoods when US generals reminiscent of *Dr Strangelove* planned to blow up John Glenn, among other crackpot schemes, and blame it on Castro to provide an excuse to invade Cuba; or perhaps remember Pearl Harbor and the suggestion that Roosevelt deliberately sent thousands of young American servicemen to their graves for political expediency. This is certainly not to say that the US government and its various arms of state do not have matters they wish to hide or that they be called to answer for. But in most cases, and in the absence of a genuine 'smoking gun', the answer will probably be found in mess, mania and malpractice, inefficiency rather than cunning, inattention rather than foreknowledge and cock-up rather than cover-up.

2002 – GLOBAL TERRORIST CONSPIRACY Osama bin Laden helped to create a new worldwide terrorist network in 1998 when al-Qa'ida was effectively merged with some ten or eleven other Islamic militant groups. Few realised that this represented the tip of a massive international Islamic terrorist conspiracy that would be seen to threaten the world in the aftermath of 9-11. It has spread in the last few years to include additional organisations in Muslim countries and indeed to new links forged with right-wing and anti-Semitic groups in Eastern and Central Europe, and by 2003 in Western Europe and the USA. What is also only slowly becoming apparent is that much of this was avoidable and that to some extent the USA unwittingly funded and encouraged the birth of this new wave of internationalised terrorism, much as Britain's SOE and America's OSS unwittingly taught the tricks of sabotage and subversion to the first generation of post-war nationalist independence movements between 1941 and 1945.

Osama bin Laden was at least in part a CIA creation. His organisation, al-Qa'ida, was funded, trained and equipped along with other local resistance groups to kill and maim Russian troops during their occupation of Afghanistan. During the Balkan wars that raged for much of the 1990s the USA was prepared to help the Albanian and Kosovan Muslim terrorists to attack the Serbians, and the Americans were believed to have worked, knowingly or unknowingly, closely alongside al-Qa'ida personnel. Britain is rumoured to have paid a terrorist group linked to al-Qa'ida to try to assassinate Libya's Colonel Gaddafi and indeed both Washington and London have been accused of having deliberately blocked a Libyan attempt to have bin Laden arrested. It would appear to many outside the West that neither Britain nor the USA were particularly bothered about Kashmiri Muslim attacks on Indian civilians or Chechen Muslims bombing apartment blocks in Moscow until, that is, the USA suddenly realised that it needed India and Russia as allies in the war on terrorism declared in the wake of the Islamic attacks of 9-11.

In this new world order the sheer scale of the terrorism struck a fear of the future into many ordinary people. The staggering thing about the attacks of 11 September was just how enormously destructive they were. It was certainly the first time since Pearl Harbor that the USA would suffer a surprise attack where the casualties were numbered in thousands, and this time it was largely civilians and in a major city in the USA itself. Pearl Harbor was a military disaster and the bombs still fell thousands of miles from continental USA. The two other terrorist attacks with high numbers of casualties would be the bombing of the Marine barracks in Lebanon in 1983, which killed over 200 US Marines, and then the mid-air bombing of Pan Am Flight 103 in 1998, when close to 300 people were killed, including residents of Lockerbie in Scotland. It had been feared that terrorists might try to cause mass casualties at some time, but of course few outside of Hollywood could have anticipated the form that this would take. This type of attack was inventive and it combined two methods of terrorism in a way that was largely unexpected. There had been aircraft hijackings going back over the last 35 years. The Popular Front for the Liberation of Palestine hijacked an El Al plane to Algeria in the late 1960s and bargained with the Israeli government for the release of political prisoners, and on that occasion Israel did give in, though the government quickly concluded that it was unwise to do so and has refrained from playing the terrorists' game ever since. Indeed, Israel now refuses even to negotiate with hijackers.

In 1970 three aircraft, including one Pan Am plane, were flown to Dawson's Field in Jordan by the Popular Front for the Liberation of

Palestine and at the same time another aircraft was hijacked to Cairo. Fortunately the passengers were released, but the passenger aircraft were blown up. Until 11 September, that was the most spectacular multiple hijacking carried out by terrorists. Though it was a hijacking it was carried out to make a political point, to draw attention to a cause, but it was not an open declaration of war designed to inflict maximum casualties. The first major hijacking that involved the USA was in 1985 with the seizure of a TWA jet to Beirut. On this occasion one of the passengers, Robert Stethem, was killed. The hijackers were associated with the Shiite movement in Lebanon and were undoubtedly assisted by Iran, which was becoming ever more involved in the Lebanese civil war. The incident received a great deal of publicity in part because of the demand by the hijackers for the release of some 400 Arab prisoners in Israel. After the aircraft had been held in Beirut for about two weeks, the passengers were taken off the aircraft and distributed throughout Beirut so that the USA could not mount some sort of rescue mission. The event made a big impression on Washington and the loss of life was thankfully small. The idea of gesture politics began to lose its attraction and the largely casualty-free hijacking of aircraft seemed to fade away as a preferred tactic of terrorists. They were no longer useful as devices for bargaining with governments and the terrorists took a different path, at least temporarily.

This path was suicide bombing, which began in the early 1980s; one of the areas to suffer this new tactic most was Lebanon. There were attacks on US military targets, including the US marine barracks in Lebanon and another against the US embassy in Beirut, which was bombed twice in one year and once the following year. Suicide bombings were considered a highly effective means of undermining morale and were hard to defend against. They usually involved cars or trucks carrying large amounts of often homemade explosives and booby-trapped vehicles designed to cause the maximum casualties; rarely did an individual become a human bomb with the explosives wrapped around his body, that particular variation was to follow later. Of course security forces everywhere found the development of new techniques to guard sensitive buildings, strategic targets or important individuals to be a new nightmare, but to try and defend a city centre or a small village from the devastation of a large vehicle-mounted bomb was virtually impossible. The only thing that could stop massive casualties from being inflicted was an adequate period of warning from the terrorists; this was usually delivered by phone and authenticated by the use of a code word agreed in a macabre, but necessary, deal between the terrorist and the security authorities. Suicide bombings were later carried out in Israel by two different Islamic groups: Hamas and the Islamic Jihad. These would develop into a campaign that continues to the present day, often using very young men and occasionally girls who are prepared to walk on to buses, into markets or cafés with bombs strapped to their bodies to blow themselves up along with as many innocent victims as possible.

What made the attacks of 9-11 so unique was not only the level of casualties but the fact that it was carried out inside the USA, that the hijacked aircraft were used as weapons and lastly because it was in effect a mass suicide by the hijackers. Not since the Japanese wartime kamikaze attacks had so many young men willingly committed suicide in a single attack. And what has changed dramatically is that the terrorist is no longer part of some small organisation or ethnic group. In the past there has often been a loose co-operation between separate national terrorist groups. In the 1970s several different Latin American extremist groups co-operated with each other and even felt confident enough to hold transcontinental conferences, but it was really far more talk than operational action. During the 1970s through the 1980s Western intelligence and security forces were becoming more concerned about the terrorist groups in the Middle East and the groups in Western Europe who had formed alliances. In 1972 the Black September attack on the Munich Olympics was carried out with the assistance of certain left-wing groups in West Germany; the 1976 attack on the OPEC oil ministries meeting in Vienna was also a combined operation. The 1976 hijacking to Entebbe, Uganda, was a combined Palestinian–West German operation and this resulted in the brilliantly conceived and executed rescue by an Israeli military force. The following year saw the spectacular aircraft hijacking to Mogadishu, capital of Somalia, where the West German GSG9 with SAS assistance managed to rescue the passengers; this, too, was a combined Palestinian–West German terrorist operation.

What was not present, however, was a true transnational conspiracy in which extremists from many different countries were involved in multinational groups, such as al-Qa'ida, and also where the group had cells in many different countries. So the scope, the elaborateness, the complexity of the conspiracy that has become apparent in the last few years caught even the most experienced security services off guard. It is fair to say that some observers sounded a warning, but these were all too often ignored. The USA has been monitoring al-Qa'ida from the mid-1990s and has been more than aware of their capabilities since they helped in its formation. When investigations into the first World Trade Center bombing in 1993 led the CIA and the FBI to discover the trademark of Osama bin Laden in anti-American terrorist operations, such as the bombings of the US embassies in Kenya and Tanzania, the US was finally convinced the al-Qa'ida group were responsible. Indictments were handed down against bin Laden and his associates and a trial eventually took place in which four people were convicted of the bombings, but they were only low-level members of al-Qa'ida.

It has also become apparent in the aftermath of 11 September that the extent of Egyptian involvement in al-Qa'ida is larger than was previously thought. The implications of this particular merger, involving a very active and determined extremist group in Egypt that had been associated with the assassination of Anwar Sadat, and a group that considered Sheik Omar Abdel Rahman as a spiritual mentor, are huge. The West has been rocked by the sheer size of this conspiracy, by its real transnational dimension and the almost daily revelations of its different aspects. This is truly the start of a new way of war, according to the theorists and many terrorist experts. Call it alternative, call it unconventional or asymmetrical; none satisfactorily describes the new global terrorism. Again, it builds on past precedents, but it is very different. There is a new level of destructiveness and sacrifice that stuns the West.

India, too, has been on the receiving end of fundamentalist fanatics and is at a loss to know how to cope with it or to know how to defend adequately towns and cities, strategic targets and important persons. It is a war of shadows and rarely will the US military have significant terrorist targets to hit. Even in Afghanistan the al-Qa'ida training camps were empty by the time the first cruise missiles exploded. In 1998 President Clinton retaliated for the bombings of US embassies in Kenya and Tanzania by attacking a pharmaceuticals plant in Sudan. The plant was suspected of supplying the chemical precursors that Osama bin Laden would require to make some sort of weapons for chemical terrorism. The USA also bombed al-Qa'ida's training camps in Afghanistan because bin Laden had been expelled from the Sudan to Afghanistan in 1996 and had set up headquarters there. Those bombings, in retrospect, accomplished little other than to demonstrate that the USA took terrorism seriously and would act as a way of demonstrating resolve. The retaliatory attacks of 1998 were explained by US officials as an effort to pre-empt bin Laden as al-Qa'ida was thought to be planning further attacks. That assumption was very quickly proved wrong, however, when the *USS Cole* was damaged in Aden and several other plots by the bin Laden organisation were uncovered, including the famous millennium plan of 1999. This plan was revealed when an Algerian was caught coming across the border from Canada with highly volatile explosives in the trunk of his car. Planned attacks to kill American and other tourists in Israel and in Jordan were also discovered. The retaliatory nature of the air raids in 1998 did not pre-empt bin Laden's plans in any way. 11 September is, tragically, the best possible evidence of that. Despite the assault on Afghanistan and the overthrow of the Taliban regime, al-Qa'ida escaped and moved into preplanned positions around the world. They continue to carry out devastating terrorist attacks, such as the Bali bombing in 2002, but far worse is the growing evidence that they are not alone.

Al-Qa'ida, the conspiracy theorists confidently argue, is just a highly visible part of a genuine worldwide Islamic terrorist conspiracy with but one aim: the destruction of the US and its allies. This then, the theorists would argue, is a broad outline of the immense problems now faced by the West. A war with Iraq may rid the Middle East of yet another dictator, it may secure access to vast oil reserves, but in a conflict with an Islamic conspiracy Iraq provides a unique strategic position that may one day prove its weight in gold or, of course, a giant American version of Dien Bien Phu.

2002 – DEATH OF A SENATOR Was Paul Wellstone the victim of a political assassination? It is possible that there will emerge a credible explanation of the 25 October plane crash that killed Wellstone, his wife Sheila, daughter Marcia and five others near Eveleth, Minnesota. Initial reports, however, are disturbing and none of the typical causes of a small plane accident – engine failure, collision, icing or pilot error – appear to be involved.

The plane, a twin-engine Beechcraft King Air A100, was apparently in good condition when it hit the ground and exploded into flames about two miles from the Eveleth-Virginia airport in the Minnesota iron range. The Beechcraft model has an excellent safety record, with only two fatal crashes in the past six or seven years. Debris recovered from the crash site includes both the plane's engines, which suffered blade damage, suggesting that the engines were running when the plane crashed. While weather conditions were less than ideal, with some ice and freezing rain, two smaller Beech Queen planes had landed at Eveleth without incident two hours before the crash, when temperatures were colder. Wellstone's plane was reportedly equipped with two separate de-icing mechanisms. Visibility was limited but well above the minimum required – between two and two and a half miles. Although the approach to the airport was being made using instruments, the airport would have been in clear view of the pilot once he descended below the lowest cloud layer at about 700 feet. The plane's two pilots were both experienced; the senior man, Captain Richard Conry, had an airline transport pilot certification, which is the top industry qualification, while co-pilot Michael Guess was also a fully certified commercial pilot.

Wellstone was by all accounts a cautious flier, and there is no suggestion that the decision to fly that day was a reckless one. The acting chairwoman of the National Transportation Safety Board, Carol Carmody, said there was a slight irregularity in the Eveleth airport's radio beacon, but it is not yet possible to say whether this contributed to the accident. The plane's altimeter and 'possibly one other gauge' have been recovered and sent to the NTSB lab in Washington for analysis, Carmody said. The plane was not required to have a cockpit voice recorder and was not equipped with one.

According to air traffic control records, the flight had proceeded without incident until its last moments. Wellstone's plane took off at 9.37 a.m. from Minneapolis, St Paul, received permission to climb to 13,000 feet at 9.48 a.m. and received clearance to descend towards Eveleth at 10.01 a.m., at which time the pilot was told there was icing at the 9,000–11,000-foot level. The plane began its descent at 10.10 a.m., passed through the icing altitude without apparent difficulty and at 10.18 a.m. was cleared for approach to the airport. A minute later, at 3,500 feet, the plane began to drift away from the runway. It was last sighted at 10.21 a.m. flying at 1,800 feet. Carmody said that the impact area was 300 feet by 190 feet, with evidence of 'extreme post-crash fire'. The plane apparently was headed south, away from the Eveleth runway, when it hit the ground. 'The angle was steeper than would be expected in a normal stabilized standardized approach,' she said. Some press reports cited eyewitness accounts of a near-vertical plunge.

Under different political circumstances it might be possible to dismiss the Eveleth crash as a tragic accident whose causes, even if they cannot be precisely determined, lie in the sphere of aircraft engineering and weather phenomena. But the death of Paul Wellstone takes place under conditions in which far too many strange things are happening in America, according to many conspiracy theorists. Wellstone's death comes almost two years to the day after a similar plane crash killed another Democratic Senate hopeful locked in a tight election contest, Missouri Governor Mel Carnahan, on 16 October 2000. The American media duly noted the 'eerie coincidence', as though it was a statistical oddity, rather than suggesting a pattern. One might say that to lose one senator is a misfortune, but to lose two senators, the same way, is positively suspicious. Last year two leading Senate Democrats, Majority Leader Tom Daschle and Judiciary Committee Chairman Patrick Leahy, were targeted for assassination with letters laced with anthrax. The federal Justice Department, headed by John Ashcroft, who lost to the deceased Mel Carnahan in the Missouri contest, has significantly failed to apprehend the anthrax mailer. Wellstone was in a hotly contested re-election campaign, but polls showed he was beginning to pull ahead of Republican nominee Norm Coleman, the former mayor of St Paul, in the wake of the vote in the Senate to authorise President Bush to wage war against Iraq. The liberal Democrat was a well-publicised opponent of the war resolution, the only senator in a tight race to vote against it. More broadly, with the Senate controlled by the Democrats by a margin of 50–49, the loss of even a single seat could shift control to the Republicans. The immediate effect of Wellstone's death is to deprive the Democrats of a majority in the lame-duck session scheduled for late November. Without exaggerating Wellstone's personal significance, as he was in many ways a typical and conventional bourgeois politician and certainly no threat to the capitalist system, there are enormous financial stakes involved in control of the Senate, and Republican control would make it possible to push through new tax cuts for the wealthy and other perks for corporate America worth billions of dollars – more than enough of an incentive to commit murder. The supposed ultra right-wing elements within and around the Republican Party, it is claimed by certain theorists, have already demonstrated their contempt for democracy, first in the protracted campaign of political destabilisation against the Clinton Administration, then with the theft of the 2000 presidential election. They are also prepared to slaughter tens of thousands of Iraqis in order to grab control of the second largest oil reserves in the world, or so we are told. To imagine that they would suffer moral qualms over a conveniently timed plane crash would be naïve in the extreme. Furthermore, there is another curious and suspicious factor. Virtually every day the Bush Administration issues warnings of terrorist attacks on trains, nuclear reactors, airports or government buildings to keep the American people off balance and bulldoze the public into supporting the war on terrorism and action against Iraq. Government officials are prepared to attribute virtually any act of violence, such as the Washington sniper shootings, to al-Qa'ida if they can. Yet there has been no suggestion that the destruction of Wellstone's plane was the result of terrorism. Perhaps in this case they prefer not to inquire too closely into the causes. In the current climate of war, repression and right-wing provocation, it is perfectly reasonable to ask whether Wellstone was the victim of a political killing. No investigation deserving of the name can exclude sabotage as a possible cause of the plane crash. And yet, given the present state of American democracy, the official investigation will in all probability conclude that Wellstone's death was the result of an unfortunate but unexplainable mechanical malfunction and not part of a conspiracy to remove another of the few remaining independent and troublesome politicians.

2003 – REAGAN–BUSH AGENDA Is Washington plotting to take over the world? Is a cross between Dr No and Napoleon Bonaparte stalking the corridors of the Pentagon? According to many conspiracy theorists and a good few seasoned and highly experienced observers, it would indeed appear to be America's intention to form a new world government, but one not even pretending to be comprised of representatives of all its nation states through the United Nations. The USA will rule, not according to painstakingly developed international law and norms, but by what is solely in America's best interests. In declaring its intention of being the world's policeman or, according to another view, defender of the world, the USA will have no accountability to non-US citizens. It will bomb who it likes when it likes, change regimes when and as it sees fit and it will have no intention of allowing itself to be subject to investigations for war crimes, torture, or breaches of fundamental human rights, according to the new breed of mega-conspiracy theorists. When it asked the United Nations to sanction an attack on Iraq, it was not demanding agreement to a strong case for action. There appeared to be no concrete evidence at the time of Washington's first approach to the UN that Iraq was preparing to use weapons of mass destruction against any other country and certainly not the USA, Britain or Israel. Even Saddam Hussein was probably not that suicidal. The Americans had simply stopped pretending and demanded outright capitulation to its view and its wishes. The world will be policed in American interests with its closest allies picking up the scraps. Washington, or so the conspiracy theory goes, and despite any promises of a benevolent dictatorship, does not aim to build, stabilise and promote democracies. It aims to impose puppet regimes that are to look after America's best interests before those of their own people. It is only concerned with the disastrous results of such dictatorships when imposed in the past, in so far as they proved less than satisfactory in protecting US interests. From now on American forces, with or without allies, will do the job themselves if no suitable local proxy is available. The great struggles of the twentieth century between democracy and totalitarianism ended with a decisive victory for the forces of freedom.

US official statements have made it clear that 'The United States enjoys a position of unparalleled military strength and great economic and political influence'. Referring to the Islamic challenge, the USA has stated, 'To defeat this threat the USA will make use of every tool in its extensive arsenal – from better homeland defenses and law enforcement to intelligence and cutting off terrorist financing. The war against terrorists of global reach is a global enterprise of uncertain duration. America will help nations that need our assistance in combating terror. And America will hold to account nations that are compromised by terror, because the allies of terror are the enemies of civilization,' and, 'Finally, the United States will use this moment of opportunity to extend the benefits of freedom across the globe.' Further excerpts argue, 'For most of the twentieth century, the world was divided by a great struggle over ideas: destructive totalitarian visions versus freedom and equality. That great struggle is over. The militant visions of class, nation, and race, which promised utopia and delivered misery have been defeated and discredited. Today, these ideals are a lifeline to lonely defenders of liberty. And when openings arrive, we can encourage change – as we did in Central and Eastern Europe between 1989 and 1991, or in Belgrade in 2000.'

Washington now appears to see itself surrounded on all sides by spitting snakes, ungrateful nations that survive on US generosity and those actively planning the destruction of US interests. In the 1990s Washington witnessed the emergence of a small number of rogue states that, while different in important ways, share a number of attributes. These states brutalise their own people and squander their national resources for the personal gain of their rulers; display little or no regard for international law, threaten their neighbours, and violate international treaties to which they are party; and show a determination to acquire weapons of mass destruction along with other advanced missile technology. The very nature and motivations of these new adversaries, their determination to obtain destructive powers hitherto available only to the world's strongest states, and the greater likelihood that they will use weapons of mass destruction against us, make today's security environment more complex and dangerous. In just a decade or two, the world has changed: different dynamics, different rules and different challenges.

At the outset of the Cold War, and for the following three decades, the condition known as MAD, or mutual assured destruction, resulted in a rather stable form of deterrence, referred to as counter-value deterrence. However, with the introduction of precision-guided, multiple warhead missiles in the mid-1970s, another form of deterrence emerged, known as counter-force deterrence. In the former, high-value targets such as cities would bear the brunt of a nuclear attack; in the latter version, missiles targeted missiles. This newer form of counter-force deterrence was less stable because there was potentially more rationale for a pre-emptive nuclear strike. By the late 1970s it became obvious that the Soviet Union was exploiting this potential instability with a nuclear force structure designed for pre-emption. In 1981, and as result of a massive Soviet build-up of offensive-capable nuclear capability, the USA responded with the Reagan Administration's strategic modernisation programme. An effective cover for a major clandestine plan and a very effective political conspiracy to finally undermine Communism and bring about the financial collapse of the Soviet Union. The first public sign of this new policy of secret confrontation with Moscow came in the now-famous speech President Reagan delivered on 23 March 1983 when he launched what would become the Strategic Defense Initiative (SDI) or Star Wars to its critics. This was combined with a decision to attack the Soviet Union on all fronts: economic, diplomatic and militarily in Afghanistan. The propaganda war was markedly stepped up, as was subversion within Moscow's satellite nations. Many of the same team that brought about the outstanding success of the Reagan agenda to outspend the Soviet Union on defence, ranging from conventional weapons, to advance nuclear programmes to Star Wars, and to confront Moscow on every front in order to further strain its ailing economy, were responsible for eventually undermining the Communist system. They played a major part in bringing an end to the Berlin Wall and destabilising the Warsaw Pact, followed by the collapse of the Soviet Union itself, all within a period of only a couple of years, and they went on to mastermind George Bush, Sr's liberation of Kuwait.

The unexpected election of Bill Clinton caused an eight-year hiatus in the implementation of the 'agenda'; however, the period in the political wilderness was not wasted. When George W. Bush was elected, the Reagan–Bush agenda had been refined and expanded to cover the problems of overcoming future energy shortages, Islamic terrorism and the unfinished business of Saddam Hussein. It is now perfectly apparent that initial planning for a war on Iraq was underway well before the unrelated tragedy of 9-11. Rumsfeld, Cheney, Poindexter, Pearl and others have been joined by a younger generation of modern crusaders determined to ensure that Pax Americana will be imposed on a reluctant world by any and all means available to the world's only superpower. George W. Bush has been enthroned in near-absolute power by just 21 per cent of the American electorate and may indeed be the first President to 'win' an election by methods used in Florida which would not be unknown to the average tinpot Third World dictator, according to some commentators. It seems strange that any democratic government unsupported by a full 79 per cent of the voters should claim a 'mandate' for its programme of permanent war against terrorism and the destruction of any nation not playing by Washington's rules.

There appears to be little doubt in the minds of many observers that George W. Bush has inherited a secret agenda that is already responsible for fundamentally changing the future history of the world by defeating the Communist enemy – but where his administration intends to take the agenda, and America, is another matter. Only time will tell whether this modern grand conspiracy will produce a US empire or plunge the world into a genocidal nightmare, at least according to many of the more apocalyptic conspiracy theorists. Certainly the determination of the US administration and its British allies to attack Iraq, with or without 'smoking gun' evidence and with or without United Nations and world approval, to many conspiracy theorists and observers smacks of an arrogance and intolerance of any opposition to their plans for future defence, economic development or for the security of natural resources worthy of the most megalomaniac members of the supposed New World Order. Few will deny that it promises to be a very interesting twenty-first century indeed!

BIBLIOGRAPHY

Of the eight hundred or so publications consulted during the writing of *Conspiracy*, the following were probably the most interesting:

The Lincoln Conspiracy, D. Balsiger & C. Sellier, Schick Sunn, 1977
The Paperclip Conspiracy, Tom Bower, Michael Joseph, 1987
Courtney Love, Poppy Z. Brite, Orion, 1997
Out of Control, Leslie Cockburn, Bloomsbury, 1988
The Plumbat Affair, E. Davenport & D. Gillman, 1978
Westminster Babylon, Alan Doig, Allison & Busby, 1990
MI6, Stephen Dorril, Fourth Estate, 2000
The Silent Conspiracy, Stephen Dorril, Heineman, 1993
Smear, S. Dorril & R. Ramsay, HarperCollins, 1992
The Fall of Pan Am 103, S. Emerson & B. Duffy, Putnam, 1990
The Irish War, Tony Geraghty, HarperCollins, 1998
Above Top Secret, Timothy Good, Sidgwick & Jackson, 1987
A Higher Form of Killing, R. Harris & J. Paxman, Hill & Wang, 1982
The Target is Destroyed, Seymour Hersh, Random House, 1986
Defending the Realm, M. Hollingsworth & N. Fielding, André Deutsch, 1999
Haunting America, Jim Houghton, Morrow, 1978
Secret Agenda, Jim Houghton, Random House, 1984
Lockerbie, David Johnson, St Martins Press, 1989
RFK Must Die!, Robert Kaiser, Dutton, 1970
The Royals, Kitty Kelly, Warner, 1997
Who in Hell, S. Kelly & R. Rogers, Robson, 1996
Jack the Ripper, Stephen Knight, Granada, 1977
Plausible Denial, Mark Lane, Thunder's Mouth, 1999
Encyclopaedia of World History, William Langer, Harrap, 1987
The Wilson Plot, David Leigh, Heinemann, 1988
The Belarus Secret, John Loftus, Penguin Books, 1982
Murkin Conspiracy, Philip Melanson, Praeger,1989
Enemies of the State, Gary Murray, Simon & Schuster, 1993
Conspiracy of Silence, Anthony Pearson, Quartet, 1978
Open Skies-Closed Minds, Nick Pope, Simon & Schuster, 1996
AIDS Inc, Jon Rappaport, Human Energy Press, 1988

Shadow Warrior, F. Rodriguez & J. Weisman, Simon & Schuster, 1989
Betrayal at Pearl Harbor, J. Rusbridger & E. Nave, Michael O'Mara, 1991
Blowback, Christopher Simpson, Weidenfeld & Nicolson, 1988
The Marilyn Conspiracy, Milo Speriglio, Pocket Books, 1986
Operation Splinter Factor, Stewart Steven, Hodder, 1974
Honeytrap, A. Summers & S. Dorril, Weidenfeld & Nicolson, 1987
The Kennedy Conspiracy, Anthony Summers, Warner, 1980
Goddess, Anthony Summers, Onyx, 1986
Gideon's Spies, Gordon Thomas, Macmillan, 1999
The Big Breach, Richard Tomlinson, Cutting Edge, 2001
The Assassination of Robert F. Kennedy, W. Turner & J. Christian, Thunder's Mouth, 1993
Big Boys' Rules, Mark Urban, Faber & Faber, 1992
UK Eyes Alpha, Mark Urban, Faber & Faber, 1996
Conspiracies, Cover-ups & Crimes, Jonathan Vankin, Dell, 1992
The Intimate Sex Lives of Famous People, Irving Wallace, Hutchinson, 1981
Gehlen, Charles Whiting, Ballantine, 1972
The Illuminoids, Neil Wilgus, Sun Books, 1978
In God's Name, David Yallop, Jonathan Cape, 1984

INDEX